CW01276510

Willie Llewellyn
The Road to Victory
over the 1905 All Blacks

Willie Llewellyn

The Road to Victory
over the 1905 All Blacks

Philip J Grant

Printed in 2018

ISBN 978-0-9567271-1-4

© Philip J Grant, 2018

Philip Grant has asserted his right under the Copyright, Designs
and Patent Act, 1988, to be identified as Author of this Work.

All rights reserved. No part of this book may be reproduced, stored in a
retrieval system, or transmitted in any form or by any means, electronic,
electrostatic, magnetic tape, mechanical, photocopying, recording
or otherwise without permission in writing from the publisher.

Printed in Wales
at Gomer Press, Llandysul, Ceredigion SA44 4JL

CERTIFICATE

This is to certify that only
500 copies of the book

Willie Llewellyn
The Road to Victory over the 1905 All Blacks

have been printed

Courtesy of the New Zealand Rugby Museum

This book is copy number __351__ of 500

Philip J Grant – Author

Contents

	Acknowledgements	ix
	Foreword	xiii
	Introduction	xv
1	The Christ College Years	1
2	Llwynypia Football Club Invincible Season 1896–97	41
3	Llwynypia Football Club 1897–98 Season	69
4	Willie Llewellyn's First Welsh Cap – 1898/1899 Season	93
5	Willie Llewelyn moves to London – 1899/1900 Season	139
6	The London Welsh Years 1900–1903	179
7	Newport Rugby Football Club 1903–04	265
8	The Anglo-Australian Rugby Football Team 1904	291
9	Willie Captains Wales to a Fourth Triple Crown	323
10	1905 and the Greatest Game Ever Played	353
11	Life Beyond Rugby	397
	An Appreciation	439
	Website Bibliography	441
	Source Material and Further Reading	443

Acknowledgements

WRITING THIS BOOK has been a most enjoyable experience and the hours of research rewarding and satisfying. So many people have contributed and I hope to acknowledge them all but firstly I must thank some very special people. I first met Dr Michael Jones (Willie Llewellyn's grandson) back in 2005 when I wrote my first book and we have been friends ever since. Over the years whenever I came across any information relating to Willie I would make a copy and send it off to Dr Mike for the family archive. Eventually there was such a wealth of information that I approached Dr Mike to explore the possibility of writing the biography of Willie Llewellyn. His response was very positive and immediate and over the past three years we have worked together to produce what we believe to be a fairly comprehensive record of Willie's life. Throughout the project the support of Dr Mike, his wife Mary and their family and the support of my wife Rose and our family has culminated in this wonderful story of a true legend of Welsh rugby.

Six other people who have been pivotal in the production of this book are Felicity Kilpatrick, John Griffiths, Howard Evans, Peter Owens, Stephen Berg and Dave Dow. I first met Felicity Kilpatrick at Christ College, Brecon in December 2016. Felicity, teacher and College archivist, had anticipated my every question with regard to Willie and within two hours I had been furnished with all the information relating to Willie during his time at Christ College. Felicity has continued to be a constant source of information with regard to the mass of information relating to Christ College and I am so grateful for all her help and support, and grateful for permission to include photographs from the Christ College archive.

John Griffiths has been my rugby history mentor throughout the project. He has read every line and examined every photograph and made all the necessary corrections which has improved the quality of the information immeasurably. Again I am so grateful for all the help John has given me throughout the duration of this venture.

With regard to Howard Evans his book *Welsh International Matches 1881–2011* has been my constant companion for the past three years. During that time I would get regular e-mails from Howard, day and night, with all sorts of information relating to Willie. Since my very first book Howard has been a constant source of help and inspiration and I value greatly his help and friendship.

Peter Owens in his capacity as friend and heritage manager for the Welsh Rugby Union has been a wonderful source of photographs and information. My every request for information was quickly responded to and you will appreciate from the sheer quantity of photographs from the Welsh Rugby Union what a significant contribution he has made to the book.

Similarly Stephen Berg and the New Zealand Rugby Museum responded positively to every request I made. Again I am very grateful for the help and support Stephen has given me throughout this project.

One man who has improved the quality of the book immensely is Dave Dow. His ability to take poor quality photographs and transform them into something spectacular never ceased to amaze me. Without Dave's help many of the photographs used in the book would have been of such poor quality it would have been debatable whether they should have been used at all. Dave has also been the link to Swansea Rugby Football Club and I am very grateful for all their help and willingness to supply information and photographs.

In addition to those mentioned above I have always believed that history is better illustrated by the photographs of that time and several people have been instrumental in providing many of the original images that appear in the book, notably: Frederic Humbert, Timothy Auty, Stephen Bennett and Newport RFC, Chris Clews and Sir Bryan Williams of Ponsonby Rugby Club, Peter Douglas-Davies, Elspeth Orwin and Auckland Libraries, David Maddox, Ken Baguley and the Auckland Rugby Union, Dai Richards of Rugby Relics, Dylan Jones and St Fagans National Museum of History and Dick Williams at Gloucester RFC.

I would also like to sincerely thank Dennis Gethin, President of the Welsh Rugby Union, for so willingly agreeing to write the foreword.

At Neath Grammar School Dennis was Head Prefect and was encouraged to pursue his twin passions of history and rugby and won a place at Selwyn College, Cambridge where he achieved both a Master of Arts Degree, and a Master of Laws Degree. After leaving college in 1967 Dennis went on to train as a solicitor and qualified in 1971. Following a brief period in private practice he joined Glamorgan County Council as their assistant solicitor and after two years moved to Taff Ely Borough Council where he became the Council's Chief Executive. In 1998 Dennis left local government and became Secretary of the Welsh Rugby Union; a post he held for 5 years. After retirement from the WRU he joined the BBC Broadcasting Council in Wales and was a member from 2004 until 2009. Dennis was elected President of the Welsh Rugby Union in 2007 an office he holds to the present time. In addition Dennis is also President of Wales Deaf Rugby, Chairman of the Welsh Rugby Charitable Trust, a patron of Glamorgan County Rugby, a life member of Welsh Academicals RFC and Seven Sisters RFC, President of Cor Meibion Pontypridd and Vice-President of Cor Meibion De Cymru.

Rugby has always played a major part in Dennis's life. He became a Welsh Secondary Schools International in 1963, obtained two Rugby Blues at Cambridge (1965 & 1966), played fullback for his home village of Seven Sisters before playing for Swansea, Neath, Cardiff (1966–1971), and finally Glamorgan Wanderers. Whilst playing for Cambridge he played against the 1963 New Zealand All Blacks and the 1966 Australian Wallabies. During his playing career with Cardiff he became their record points scorer and played against the South African Springboks in 1969.

In 2009 Dennis was awarded the Chancellor's Medal by the University of South Wales for his services to rugby, and in 2014 he was made an Honorary Doctor of Laws by Swansea University in recognition of his outstanding contribution to Welsh cultural life. In recognition of the major contribution Dennis has made to Welsh rugby he was awarded an OBE in the Queen's 90th Birthday Honours list in 2016. I am truly delighted that a man who has contributed so much to Welsh rugby has taken the time and effort to write the superb foreword for my book.

The help of the following people is also very much appreciated, their contribution has added greatly to the quality of the book: Pam Adams and Phil Adrian of Ponsonby Rugby Club, Phil Atkinson, Paul Beken,

Ken Bogle, Clare Brittain of the Fusiliers Museum of Northumberland, Hilary and Stan Casson, Damian Dolan, Eric Edwards, Ian Ellis and Rhondda Golf Club, Emyr Evans and Elan Owen of the National Library of Wales, Dave Fox, Rhys and Ralitsa Grant, Rhiannon Griffiths and Tony Hopkins of Gwent Archives, Mark Hoskins, Kevin Jarvis, John Jenkins, Matthew Johnston and Julie Wakefield of the Royal Pharmaceutical Society Museum, Geraint Jones, Robert (Joe) Jones and London Welsh RFC, Nicola Kearton and Gonville and Caius College, Cambridge, Derrick King and Bridgend Ravens RFC, Mrs Gillian Lawrence, Owain Lewis, Bob Luxford; Gemma, Ian, Jack, and Sophie Mabbett; Deborah Mason and the World Rugby Museum, Twickenham, Hywel Matthews of Treorchy Library, Graham Morris, Mrs Judy Moss, Michael Partridge and Eastbourne College, Eleanor Phillips, Mike Price and Neath RFC, Bill Richards, Ian Richards, Dudley Roberts, Ray Ruddick, David Smith, Norman Spain, Graham Sully, Jane Taylor at the WRU, Miss Mary Vile, Noel Williams, and Tony Woolway of Media Wales.

The acknowledgements would not be complete without mentioning the tremendous support and help I have received from the printers, Gomer Press, Llandysul through John B Lewis and Louise Jones.

While every effort has been made to trace and acknowledge the owners of copyright material used in this book, in a few cases this has proved to be impossible and I take this opportunity to offer my apologies to any copyright holders whose rights may have been unwittingly infringed.

Foreword

DURING THE second half of the Nineteenth Century the economy and population of South Wales expanded more quickly than at any other time in history. Coal was king and people from all over Europe migrated in great numbers to the valleys of South Wales to work in the mines. In the middle of that period and close to the geographic centre of this dynamic area Willie Llewellyn was born in 1878 in Tonypandy. His parents were hoteliers/publicans with a little more money available from that trade than miners had in their pockets. That money was important in that it allowed his family to send young Willie to Christ College, Brecon. Willie was a receptive student, sound enough academically to later qualify as a pharmacist and talented enough as a sportsman to star as an athlete, cricketer and most of all as a rugby footballer.

It was as a rugby player that Willie quickly made a name for himself. He was a wing three-quarter of great quality. His speed was alloyed with fine footballing ability honed to the highest degree in the red hot temperature of tough matches for his clubs: Llwynypia, Newport and London Welsh. In his late teens Willie was a regular try scorer in club rugby and by the time he was 21 years old the Welsh selectors had noted his talent and called him into the Welsh team to play England in 1899. Willie went on to become one of the great players of the First Golden Age of Welsh Rugby at the beginning of the Twentieth Century. He scored 16 tries in his 20 matches for Wales, toured Australia and New Zealand with the British Lions in 1904 and in 1905 played for Wales in their famous victory over New Zealand in Cardiff. That was Willie's last international match, he retired at the top of his fame. He is still remembered as one of Wales's greatest players.

As a man Willie was held in high esteem in the communities in which he lived. During the Tonypandy riots of 1910 many shops in the town were damaged but Willie's chemist shop was left without harm as a mark of his standing in the community. He served on the Committee of Bridgend RFC and became the Club's Chairman and later he became the first life member of Pontyclun RFC. When Willie died in 1973 he was the last of the great team of 1905 to pass on, a grand man who lived to a grand age.

Willie's story has been meticulously researched by Phil Grant. Phil tells that story of this rugby great with style and I would commend it to all who have an interest in the history of the game of rugby.

Dennis Gethin
President of the Welsh Rugby Union
June 2018

Introduction

WILLIE LLEWELLYN was one of the first super stars of Welsh rugby. Just six days after his twenty-first birthday he gained his first Welsh cap against England in January 1899. He celebrated the occasion by scoring a record four tries. This achievement has been equalled by eight other Welsh international rugby players, but never bettered. Willie Llewellyn is the only Welsh rugby international to score four tries on his debut. He went on to gain another nineteen caps for Wales and scored another twelve tries. Willie won three Triple Crowns with Wales and captained the Welsh Triple Crown team of 1905. He played for the British Isles on their tour of Australia and New Zealand in 1904 and featured in all four test matches. Willie Llewellyn's Welsh rugby career culminated with the game against New Zealand at Cardiff Arms Park in December 1905. Probably the most famous Welsh victory ever, Wales won the match by just 3 points to nil with Teddy Morgan scoring the winning try. New Zealand came to Wales having played twenty-seven games and had won them all, including internationals against Scotland, Ireland and England. Wales' victory was New Zealand's only defeat in a tour of 36 matches in which they won 35 and scored over a thousand points with only 72 points conceded.

Willie Llewellyn played his first and last games of rugby on the playing fields of Christ College, Brecon where he developed under the tutorship of Welsh rugby international William Llewellyn Thomas, who was a past pupil of Christ College. After studying at Oxford, where he won two rugby Blues, Thomas returned to his old school as an assistant master and rugby coach to the first XV.

Another great influence on Willie Llewellyn's rugby career was Tom Williams of Llwynypia. Willie Llewellyn played for Llwynypia whilst he was still at Christ College and when he left school in 1896, he went straight into the club's senior team. He played outside Tom Williams and in their first season together Llwynypia won the Glamorgan League Challenge Cup; Willie Llewellyn was top try scorer that season with 38 tries. Tom Williams was second top try scorer with 24 tries. Tom Williams played in several Welsh rugby trials and was a certainty for a Welsh international cap had he not gone North. He joined Salford Northern Union Club in September 1897 and captained them from 1898 until 1902.

The first chapter of the book is about Willie's early life and time at Christ College, Brecon. The next chapters chart Willie's rugby career while playing for Llwynypia and getting his first Welsh cap. Chapter six focuses on the three years Willie was captain of London Welsh. This chapter also covers in detail the game against England 1902 when probably the best three-quarter line that has ever played for Wales played together for the first time. Teddy Morgan joined the already capped Willie Llewellyn, Gwyn Nicholls and Rhys Gabe in the three-quarters to narrowly defeat England at the Rectory Field, Blackheath. Wales had played England at the Rectory Field on four previous occasions and had lost them all, but a try apiece for Rhys Gabe and Will Osborne, and a penalty goal by John Strand-Jones gave Wales victory by 9 points to eight. This exceptional three-quarter line played together on a further six occasions and they were never on the losing side. After defeating England at Blackheath, Wales overcame Scotland and Ireland to gain their third Triple Crown. Injuries to Willie Llewellyn and Gwyn Nicholls prevented the formidable foursome playing together until Wales demolished Ireland at Cardiff Arms Park in 1903. The quartette came together for the fifth time when they drew with England at Welford Road, Leicester in 1904. The following year Wales won their fourth Triple Crown when Willie Llewellyn, Gwyn Nicholls, Rhys Gabe and Teddy Morgan reunited to defeat Ireland in the Triple Crown decider at St Helen's, Swansea. They appeared together on the seventh and final occasion when Wales defeated New Zealand in 1905. Individually they were brilliant (gaining collectively eighty-four caps for Wales), but when they played together it was with overwhelming effect. In seven outings as Wales' three-quarter line they contributed sixteen tries between them.

Chapter seven develops the story during Willie's playing career with Newport and chapter eight is devoted to the British Isles tour of Australia and New Zealand 1904. Chapter nine concentrates on the year Willie captained Wales to their fourth Triple Crown and the penultimate chapter is predominantly about Wales' victory over New Zealand in 1905. The final chapter is concerned with Willie's other achievements, family life and interests beyond rugby. He had two children, a boy and a girl. His son, Flying Officer William Glyn Llewellyn DFC, died during the Second World War at the age of 35. Willie's daughter, Mary (Mollie) Llewellyn, was the mother of Dr Michael Jones of Pontyclun who has been the real inspiration for this book.

During the Tonypandy Riots of 1910 it is said that Willie's Llewellyn's Chemist shop was the only business premises in the area left undamaged. The rioters apparently said it was because Willie was a member of that famous Welsh side that defeated New Zealand in 1905.

He became the last surviving player of that famous match and when the All Blacks toured the UK in 1972 they visited Willie at Pontyclun not long before his death, aged 95, in 1973.

Although the book is predominantly the biography of Willie Llewellyn, it does track the progress of the other fourteen Welsh players who played alongside Willie in his last international against New Zealand in 1905. The book is fully illustrated in colour with many rare and previously unpublished images. Consisting of eleven chapters, it is the complete history of Willie Llewellyn's rugby career at school, club and international level.

Philip J Grant

Chapter One

The Christ College Years

WILLIE LLEWELLYN was born on Tuesday 1st January 1878. Willie was one of ten children born to Howell and Catherine Llewellyn of The Bridgend Inn, Tonypandy. They later moved to the Clydach Vale Hotel, Ystradyfodwg, Rhondda. Willie's elder brother John (Johnnie) Howell Llewellyn was born two years earlier in 1876. Evan followed Willie in 1880 and Mary Jennett in 1882. Albert, who was born in 1883, sadly died in his first year. Annie was born in 1885 followed by George in 1887. Catherine, who was born in 1888, sadly died as a toddler. Ivor was born in 1890 and finally, Katie, the youngest child, was born in 1892.

In September 1888, at the age of twelve, John Llewellyn went to study at Christ College, Brecon. John, who attended Morton's House, studied at Christ College from 1888 until 1894 and played both cricket for the First XI and rugby for the First XV. John played in the forwards for the First XV from the 1891–92 season until the 1893–94 season when he was captain. Willie, at the age of eleven, went up to Christ College the year following John in 1889. He too attended Morton's House and having played rugby for the junior teams Willie played his first game for the senior team during the 1893–94 season when his brother John was captain. Willie studied at Christ College from 1889 until 1896.

George Llewellyn was the third brother to attend Christ College, Brecon. As with his two elder brothers before him he also attended Morton's House. George was at Christ College from 1899 until 1905.

Another talented sportsman, George played cricket for the First XI and rugby for the First XV. George was captain of the First XV in 1904–05 and 1905–06.

A major feature of sport at Christ College was the annual athletics sports held over two days in the summer term. At the 1892 athletic sports John Llewellyn won the 220 yards flat race, handicap (open) and Willie Llewellyn came second in the consolation race for those under fifteen years old. Arthur Harding also featured greatly in the same sports giving an early indication to his athletic ability. On the first day of the sports he won the 150 yards flat race for boys under fourteen years old. On the second day he came second in the 220 yards handicap for those under fifteen and

Christ College Brecon, Rugby First XV 1891–1892

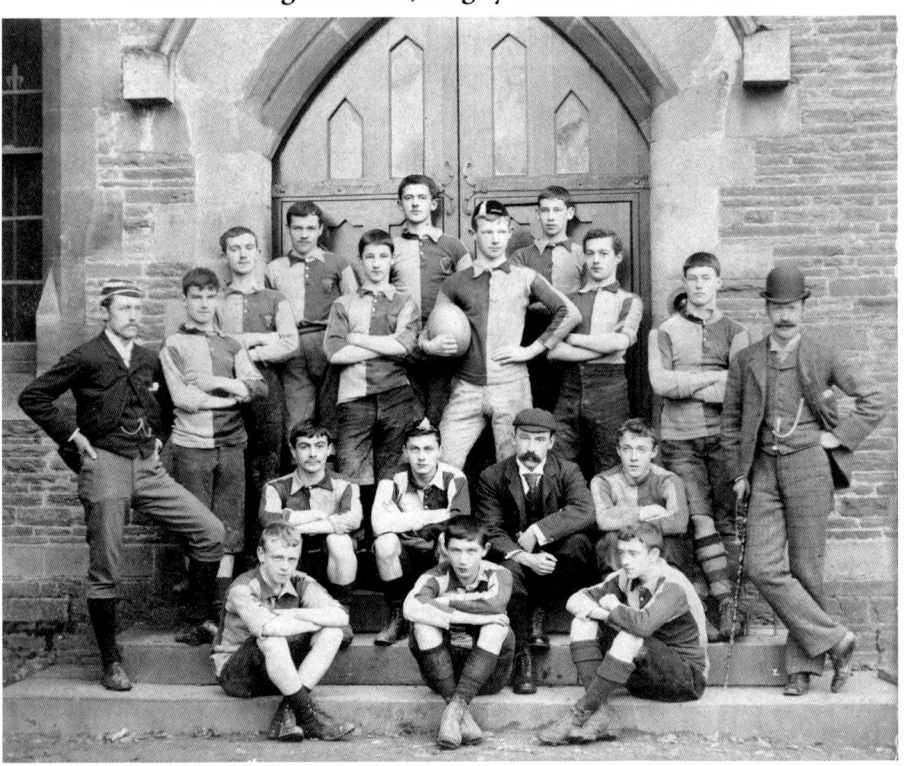

Back Row: Mr Allen, D L Davies, W M Walters, J Thomas, J H Llewellyn, W C R Johns, T P Thomas (Captain), W T Ritchie, H P Williams, E H Phillips, Mr Harding. *Middle Row*: H T Evans, W L Harris, Mr Peacock, L Pierce. *Front Row*: R F Williams, T J Thomas, R P Thomas.

won the three-legged race with J R Powell. *The Breconian* reported, 'The Three-legged Race was well patronised. No fewer than twenty-one pairs started but A F Harding and J R Powell soon left the rest behind and reached the goal easy winners.' Arthur Flowers Harding attended Christ College between 1890 and 1897. He went on to play rugby for Wales on twenty occasions and captained the British Lions (Anglo-Welsh) on their tour to Australia and New Zealand in 1908. Both he and Willie Llewellyn toured with the British team (Anglo-Australian Rugby Football Team) to Australia and New Zealand in 1904.

The first report of Willie Llewellyn playing rugby for Christ College was in the 1893 March edition of *The Breconian. The Breconian* was the Christ College magazine which was published three times a year. The report relates to the game between Christ College 2nd XV and Merthyr 2nd XV. The game, which was played on Thursday 16th February, was the first second team fixture of the season. The weather was atrocious with rain pouring down unceasingly throughout the game. With the weather so bad scrummaging was the order of the day and Merthyr, with their superior weight, held the advantage. Although the College backs tackled well on many occasions and prevented several scores, the Merthyr forwards eventually got the advantage and Jones scored their first try. The try went unconverted. Owing to the greasy state of the ball the College backs were unable to demonstrate their passing skills and there were no further scores when half-time was called.

In the second half the superior weight of the Merthyr forwards took its toll on the College team and Merthyr scored another three unconverted tries through Beddoe, Jones and Powell. The final score was Merthyr 12 points Christ College nil. The report in *The Breconian* stated, 'The form shown by our second XV was good under the circumstances; they would undoubtedly have done better on a dry ground. Our back kicked well and stopped some dangerous rushes. Our three-quarters did not get a chance of showing their offensive powers, but played a good defensive game. Our half-backs certainly had an advantage over our opponents' halves, dribbled well and saved on several occasions. The forwards were not able to hold their own in the tight scrums but did fairly well in the open.'

The Christ College team was as follows: Back, H M Hughes; three-quarter backs, C D Phillips (Captain), J B Powell, J Edwards,

W M Llewellyn; half-backs, P O Ward and W D Perrott; forwards, A L Phillips, C L Williams, W R Twyning, Macfarlane, M John, D Fitzwilliams, C F Thomas and H A Thomas.

In the same edition of *The Breconian* is the report of the return game with Merthyr 2nd XV played at Merthyr on Thursday 2nd March. Again the weather was not good and the pitch was really muddy, another match having been played there immediately before the Christ College fixture. The College pressed early in the game but were unable to score. On one occasion J Edwards intercepted a pass and ran well into the opponents twenty-five but was collared before he could cross the line. It was then Merthyr who took control and put the College on the defensive. Their forwards, who were very heavy, worked their way to the College line and here one of them got over for an unconverted try. Although the College responded well, it was Merthyr who scored again when one of their three-quarters gathered the ball near the half-way and ran through to score in the corner. Again the try went unconverted. With no further scores Merthyr led at half-time by 6 points to nil.

Early in the second half the College forwards attacked vigorously for some time and had hard lines in not scoring, getting within a few yards of the line on several occasions. Merthyr responded with a rush up the field which resulted in them scoring a converted try to take their advantage to 11 points. Despite some pretty passing by the College three-quarters, some weak tackling let Merthyr in again for another unconverted try by Beddoe. After the drop out the Merthyr forwards continued to attack and were rewarded with another unconverted try. With it now getting dark and the ground enveloped in mist, time was called leaving Merthyr victors by 17 points to nil.

The Breconian reported, 'The team as a whole displayed a marked inability to tackle low and it is on this account that several tries were scored. Hughes was fairly good at full-back, kicking and tackling well. Edwards was the best of the three-quarters, Llewellyn and Powell also played fairly well. Perrott was the best of the halves, both however played a capital game. Of the forwards G J C Thomas played a sterling game, his tackling at times being brilliant. C F Thomas, Twyning and H A Thomas were also conspicuous.'

The Christ College team was as follows: Back, H M Hughes; three-quarter backs, J B Powell, J Edwards, W M Llewellyn, T Walters; half-backs, P O Ward and W D Perrott; forwards, A L Phillips (Captain), C L Williams, W R Twyning, Macfarlane, M John, C F Thomas, H A Thomas and G J C Thomas.

The 1893 annual athletic sports, having been postponed the previous term, took place on 13th and 14th May. Both John and Willie Llewellyn featured heavily in the 1893 event. On the first day John came third in the 100 yards flat race and second in the 220 yards flat race (handicap). Willie came second in the under sixteen long jump and first in the under sixteen high jump with a jump of four feet two inches. On the second day John came third in the 100 yards hurdle race (open) and won the high jump with a jump of four feet ten inches. He came third in the long jump and third in the three-legged race with Harding.

Arthur Flowers Harding also performed well in the sports. On the first day he won the under sixteen long jump with a distance of fifteen feet and half an inch and on the second day came second in the 220 yards flat race (handicap) under 15 and third in the three-legged race with John Llewellyn.

The usual pattern was rugby in the winter and cricket in the summer and it was the summer of 1892 when John Llewellyn played his first game of cricket for the First XI. He also played the following year and in 1894, his final year at Christ College, he was elected the rugby First XV captain and also captain of the cricket First XI. Willie, who was also an accomplished cricketer, joined John in the First XI in 1893 and also played rugby under his captaincy during the 1893–94 rugby season.

John Llewellyn played in all eight fixtures for the First XI during the 1893 cricket season. Of the eight matches played they won 4, drew 2 and lost two. The second eleven played four matches and Willie Llewellyn played in them all. Of the four matches played the second eleven won 2 and lost 2. In the First XI game against the Next XVI John played for the First XI and Willie played for the Next XVI. John scored nine runs while Willie was bowled out for a duck. The First XI were all out having scored 174 runs. When time was called the Next XVI had scored 34 runs with nine wickets down and with seven men left to bat, the game was declared a draw.

With all the second eleven fixtures completed for the season Willie joined his brother John in the first eleven. Willie featured in all three

Christ College Brecon, Cricket First XI 1893

Back Row: J B Stratton, H R Thomson Esq, R F Williams, E C Green, W R D Twyning, Rev O W Horsburgh, H Williams, G H Peacock Esq, D H M Thomas. *Middle Row*: T P Thomas, W M Walters, H T Evans (Captain), W M Llewellyn, J H Llewellyn. *Front Row*: H M Hughes and L Pierce.

remaining fixtures against Clydach Cricket Club, Brecon Cricket Club and the final game of the season against Llandovery School. Willie played well in his first game against Clydach scoring 25 runs and taking one catch. He didn't do so well in the game against Brecon for although the College won by 117 runs, Willie was bowled out for a duck. In the annual match against Llandovery School, the match of the season, Willie made a patient 7 runs in a first innings that netted the College a total of 81 runs. John made 7 runs, not out. Although the College batted again and scored 131 runs for eight wickets, the result was decided on the first innings which gave the College a great victory by 16 runs.

Christ College Rugby Season 1893–1894

The annual exodus of pupils at the end of the previous academic year probably hit the 1893–94 First XV rugby team the hardest. Only the half-backs and three forwards remained from the previous season, one of whom was John Llewellyn. In December 1893 the College magazine *The Breconian* reported that up until the end of November results had not been great with the College only winning one of six games played, drawing two and losing the remaining three. Their only victory so far had been against Monmouth Grammar School. Probably the forwards were the strongest point of the team, and considering their weight they really did fairly well, packing tightly and wheeling with tolerable accuracy. The scoring power of the three-quarters was thus far absolutely nil, notwithstanding the fact that the Christ College team were vastly superior up front. Nevertheless the three-quarters had shown no lack of courage and it was anticipated that there would be a vast improvement before the end of the season.

By Christmas there were eleven Christ College rugby games recorded, not all of which were by the first fifteen. The first fifteen had played nine games and the second fifteen had played two. The record of the first fifteen was not good having won only one of their nine games, drawing one and losing the remaining seven. The second fifteen had drawn their game against Merthyr seconds but had an absolute pasting against the Llandovery College second fifteen. They lost by 58 points to nil with the opposition scoring fourteen tries, eight of which were converted.

Christ College Brecon Rugby Games 1893-1894 Season			
Willie Llewellyn Rugby Games Played 1893-1894 Season			
Willie Llewellyn Rugby Games Possibly Played 1893-1894 Season			
Date	Home Team	Away Team	Result/Score
07.10.1893	Christ College	The Garrison	Lost 3-11
11.10.1893	Monmouth Grammar School	Christ College	Won 14-13
18.10.1893	Christ College	R Mullock Esq's Team	Drawn 8-8
21.10.1893	Christ College	Brecon Town	Lost 0-6
26.10.1893	Christ College 2nd XV	Merthyr 2nd XV	Drawn 3-3
28.10.1893	Christ College	Swansea 'A'	Lost 0-17
16.11.1893	Christ College 'A'	Merthyr 2nd XV	Lost 0-17
25.11.1893	Christ College	Newport Reserves	Lost 0-6
02.12.1893	Llandovery College	Christ College	Lost 0-9
06.12.1893	Bromsgrove	Christ College	Lost 3-10
06.12.1893	Christ College 2nd XV	Llandovery School 2nd XV	Lost 0-58
Unknown	Christ College Past	Christ College Present	Won 6-0
16.12.1893	Christ College	Dr Parham's XV	Lost 3-6
03.02.1894	Swansea 'A'	Christ College	Lost 0-12
10.02.1894	The Town (Brecon)	Christ College	Lost 0-3
14.02.1894	Christ College	Mr E B Reece's XV	Won 14-12
15.02.1894	Merthyr Thursday	Christ College	Lost 0-6
22.02.1894	Christ College	Aberystwyth College	Won 3-0
17.03.1894	Christ College XV	Mr T P Thomas' XV	Won 31-0

Christ College Brecon, Rugby Games Played and Results 1893–1894 Season

CHAPTER ONE

Willie's first recorded game for the senior rugby team was against the Brecon Garrison. Played at home on Saturday 7th October, this was the first game of the 1893–94 season. The heavy forwards of the visiting team gave them the advantage and they won comfortably by 11 points to three. In the first half Kerr opened the scoring for the visitors with an unconverted try. Eventually the College three-quarters had a lovely round of passing from which M T Williams secured and scored the first try of the season for the home side. Just before half-time the Garrison secured possession of the ball and scored a try which was converted. At half-time the visitors were leading by 8 points to three.

In the second half the Garrison forwards took advantage of their superior strength and after a good kick by one of the Garrison three-quarters Morgan was able to score another unconverted try for the visitors. Despite some good play by the home side there was no more scoring and the game finished with the visitors winning by 11 points to three.

Willie also played in the second game of the season against Monmouth Grammar School away at Abergavenny. A last minute converted try by M T Williams turned defeat into victory and the College won by 14 points to thirteen. *The Breconian* reported, 'When the two teams lined up in the centre of the ground it was clear that size and weight were this season decidedly against us. This was particularly noticeable in comparing our three-quarters with theirs who appeared to be older and more experienced in the game.' This was very noticeable when within two minutes of the start of play the Monmouth captain, George Harman, raced past the College men to score a try behind the post. With the try converted the College were very quickly five points behind. In a game where both John Llewellyn and M T Williams got a special mention for their good play, M T Williams scored a try for the College but this was not converted and the visitors led at half-time by 5 points to three.

In the second half J B Powell retired hurt and the College were down to fourteen men. Despite the disadvantage in numbers the College played a very hard game and spent long periods in their opponents half. Then, against the run of play George Harman picked up the ball within a few yards of his own line and easily outpaced the College backs to score another try which was converted into a goal. Almost immediately after the restart the College were awarded a penalty which resulted in a goal. George Harman then scored his third try of the afternoon and, although it was not converted, the visitors had increased their lead to seven points before the College fought back. Firstly an unconverted try by E C Green brought the College within four points of their opponents. Then a brilliant try by M T Williams which he converted himself turned defeat into a victory for the College by 14 points to thirteen. George R A Harman later played twice for Ireland and faced Willie when Ireland beat Wales at Cardiff in 1899.

Willie and John had played in the first two games of the season and this partnership continued for the next two games. They drew the game against R Mullock Esq's Team played on the School grounds on Wednesday 18th October at 8 points all, J Edwards and Willie Llewellyn getting a special mention for their good play. The visitors scored eight unanswered points in the first half to lead at the interval. In the second half M T Williams scored a try for the College which he failed to convert. Hardly had the game recommenced when Harding executed a brilliant dribble right up to the visitors line which enabled Macfarlane to score close to the touch line. A brilliant kick by M T Williams scored the goal and made the game level. With no further scores the game was drawn at 8 points all.

Three days later Christ College played Brecon Town on the school ground. The College lost by the small margin of 6 points to nil. Despite playing well in the second half a try in each half by the visiting team sealed the fate of the College.

Having played in all four games together so far this season the partnership of the two brothers, Willie and John, was broken with the second fifteen game against Merthyr Seconds. Although Willie played, John, who was captain of the first fifteen, was not in the team and the role of captain was taken by Arthur Harding. With no scoring by either side in the first half it was left to Harold Williams to open the scoring for the College with a fine try which went unconverted. An unconverted try by Beddoes for Merthyr brought the scores level and with no further scores the game ended in a draw.

John and Willie resumed their playing partnership for the next game against Swansea Seconds played on the school ground on Saturday 28th October. There was an Owen playing for Swansea in this game but

CHAPTER ONE

Dickie Owen of Swansea gained thirty-five caps for Wales between 1901 and 1912.

it is unlikely it was Dickie Owen. It is more probable that this was Sid Owen who played for Swansea Seconds around this time. Dickie Owen did not really appear in the Swansea Seconds until around the 1898–99 season. Dickie Owen and Willie Llewellyn played together for Wales on twelve occasions. On the final occasion they were both in the Wales team that defeated New Zealand in 1905. Although this was Willie's last game for Wales, Dickie Owen went on to win another twenty-one caps for Wales in a twelve year international career that gained him thirty-five caps. On this day it was Swansea who were the victors winning the game by 17 points to nil.

The Christ College v Mr Henshaw's XV game which was due to be played on the school ground on Friday 10th November was cancelled owing to the fact that it was impossible to get the visiting team up from Newport.

Willie played again for the College when the 'A' team travelled over the Brecon Beacons to play Merthyr Seconds on Thursday 16th November. The final score was Merthyr Seconds 17 points Christ College nil. John Llewellyn didn't play in this game and Arthur Harding again captained the side.

Although not recorded in *The Breconian*, there was a report of a game between Christ College Brecon and Newport Reserves in *The South Wales Daily News* on Monday 27th November 1893. The game, which was played on Saturday 25th November on the Christ College ground in windy weather, resulted in a win for the visitors by 6 points to nil. The *Evening Express* reported on the same day that 'The fixture between the Brecon Second and Dowlais Second, for some unexplained reason, did not come off.' It can therefore be assumed that the game between Christ College and Newport Reserves was a First XV fixture.

Another game not reported in the March edition of *The Breconian* in 1894 was the game between Llandovery College and Christ College Brecon played at Llandovery on Saturday 2nd December. Apart from a small mention in the Editorial there was no mention of the details of the game. For such an important game as the 'Welsh Varsity Match' it would be expected that both teams would field their strongest sides, this was certainly the case with Christ College. The Christ College team was as follows: Back, C D Phillips; three-quarter backs, W M Llewellyn, J Edwards, D F H Williams, H M Hughes; half-backs, R F Williams, D H M Thomas; forwards, J H Llewellyn (Captain), M T Williams, E C Green, G E Williams, W R D Twyning, A F Harding, J B Powell, H A Thomas.

The only mention of the game, which Llandovery College won by 9 points to nil, was in the Editorial of *The Breconian* and stated, 'The conditions under which we met Llandovery contributed in no small degree to the result of the match. To hear one's feet clattering on the ground as hard as a pavement, is, to put it mildly, not calculated to make a somewhat inexperienced team show its best form. Had it been football weather, the result must have been much closer.'

On Wednesday 6th December the first fifteen travelled to Hereford where they played Bromsgrove School. Although the full teams are not mentioned in the match report there are several references to Willie Llewellyn. After an exciting game Bromsgrove were the victors by 10 points to three with M T Williams scoring an unconverted try for the College.

On the same day the second fifteen played Llandovery College seconds at Brecon. The College team were absolutely hammered losing by 58 points to nil. They had fourteen tries scored against them, eight of which were converted into goals. The report in *The Carmarthen Journal and South Wales Daily Advertiser* on Friday 15th December commented on a 'hollow victory for Llandovery by 8 goals and 6 tries to nil. Both forward and behind the Llandovery team showed greater superiority. In the first ten minutes a goal and two tries were scored and this rate was maintained throughout the match. With the wind in their favour the Breconians did somewhat better, but were unable to check the scoring for any length of time.' The hero of the match was Evan Williams who ran in for no less than seven tries. On the other wing Lewis Lewis scored another three. At half-back J L Jones scored two tries and T Jenkins and W S Probert one apiece. T Jenkins also proved very accurate at place-kicking.

The final rugby game before the Christmas break was played on the school grounds when a Christ College XV played Dr Parham's XV. The final score was in favour of Dr Parham's XV who won by 6 points to three. Hugh Morgan and J H R Powell scored unconverted tries for the visitors while Arthur Harding scored an unconverted try for the College.

With all the rugby completed for the term the boys of Christ College commenced their Christmas holidays on Wednesday 20th December. The previous evening, as usual, the annual end of term entertainment took place at the College after which the boys could look forward to the

Christ College Brecon, Rugby First XV 1893–1894

Back Row: A F Harding, J B Powell, H A Thomas, G E Williams.
Middle Row: R F Williams, J M Macfarlane, W R Twyning, E C Green, J H Llewellyn (Captain), M T Williams, D H M Thomas, C D Phillips.
Front Row: H M Hughes, W M Llewellyn, J Edwards, D F H Williams.

Christmas break. They would return on Tuesday 16th January 1894 for the start of the new term.

Sometime between the match against Bromsgrove School on Saturday 6th December 1893 and the game against Swansea 'A' on Saturday 3rd February 1894 a game took place between Christ College past and present students. In the first half M T Williams scored for the College Present. Just before half-time the College Present scored again when Twyning crossed for a try. Neither tries being converted the College Present led by 6 points to nil at the interval. With nothing much of interest happening in the second half the game ended in a victory for the Present team by 6 points to nil. Both Willie and John Llewellyn played in this game.

The game against Swansea 'A' on Saturday 3rd February was played at St Helen's, Swansea. As had been the case earlier in the season Swansea had a strong side which included many first team players. John Llewellyn again captained the College side and Willie played in the three-quarters. Swansea kicked off and very quickly they worked their way into the College half of the field. Here a scrum was formed and Tucker, one of the Swansea three-quarters received a splendid pass which resulted in him scoring an unconverted try. After the kick out some loose play saw the College make headway right up to their opponent's goal line but they were driven back to their half of the field. A scrum took place in front of the College goal posts but the College managed to clear. However, sustained Swansea pressure and some good passing again saw the visitors cross the College goal line for a try. The try was not converted and at half-time Swansea led by 6 points to nil.

Early in the second half a scrum was formed in the Swansea half of the field but a free kick enabled the visitors to invade the College twenty-five. Here the Swansea captain got away but he was collared by M T Williams who had been brought out of the forwards to help the three-quarters. Shortly afterwards Swansea crossed for another unconverted try. After the drop out J B Powell got away and made a very good run, and when pressed, passed to M T Williams who got within a foot of the Swansea line. Although the College pressed hard they could not score and just before the final whistle Swansea scored again when Oldham gathered and crossed for another unconverted try. The final result: Swansea 'A' 12 points, Christ College nil.

The next game against Brecon Town was very controversial. With regard to the game *The Breconian* wrote: 'As a matter of a fact the game was totally spoiled by the inefficiency of the referee, who was not only ignorant of the most elementary rules of the game, but was obviously partial to the Town side.' The Town were awarded a dubious try which was not converted. After this there was a change of referee and the game was of a more even nature. With no further scores the Town won by 3 points to nil. John Llewellyn is mentioned in the match report but there is no mention of Willie. As this was a first team fixture and many of the regular first team players are mentioned it is assumed that Willie Llewellyn also played.

Selwyn Biggs, the Cardiff outside half, and J Alexander, the Penarth wing, played for Mr E B Reece's XV against the College in their next game on Wednesday 14th February 1894. Selwyn Biggs was the youngest of six Biggs brothers who played for Cardiff between 1886 and 1907. He scored forty-six tries for Cardiff in 176 appearances. This was probably the first meeting between Selwyn Biggs and Willie Llewellyn but they would go on to play together for Wales on three occasions; against Scotland and Ireland in 1899 and again against Ireland in 1900. Selwyn Biggs was the younger brother of Norman Biggs who represented Wales on eight occasions between 1888 and 1894.

The game against Mr E B Reece's XV, played on the school ground in ideal football weather, was a fast and open one. The College opened the scoring with an unconverted try by M T Williams and soon afterwards another unconverted try by D H M Thomas gave the College a six point lead. Alexander, who was always dangerous, scored two tries in quick succession for the visitors and as neither were converted the scores were equal. Just before half-time

Selwyn Biggs represented Wales at stand-off on nine occasions between 1895 and 1900.

Courtesy of the Welsh Rugby Union

M T Williams scored again but failed to convert his own try leaving the score at Christ College 9 points to the visitors six. In the second half Alexander scored another two unconverted tries to give the visitors the lead by 12 points to nine. Shortly before time was called D H M Thomas got over for his second try and M T Williams was successful with the conversion from a difficult angle. The College won by 14 points to twelve.

The College played Merthyr Thursday away on Thursday 15th February on a wet ground which made three-quarter play almost impossible and as a result the game was a battle between the forwards. Despite the forwards playing very well against a bigger and stronger pack and holding their own for much of the game the College lost by two unconverted tries to nil.

On Thursday 22nd February the College won a very tight game against Aberystwyth College. A single unconverted try by M T Williams was enough to give the College victory by 3 points to nil. Once again John Llewellyn was captain of the side and Willie was playing in the three-quarters. The College won the toss and played towards the orphanage with the sun at their backs. The College held the advantage in the early stages of the game where scrums in the opposition's half of the field were the order of the day. This monotony was relieved by the College half-backs getting the ball and passing to the three-quarters. The ball after being handled by the four three-quarters was kicked into touch by Willie Llewellyn. Here the College were awarded three free kicks, none of which were successful. M T Williams was unlucky not to score from any of them with one striking the posts. Later in the half D H M Thomas charged a penalty kick down and following up smartly together with Twyning made a good dribble to near the goal line. Here R F Williams broke away and passed to one of the forwards who passed to M T Williams who dropped over the line for a try which was not converted.

The College pressed hard in the second half but despite getting close to their opponents line they were unable to score. Late in the game C D Phillips saved a dangerous rush by the Aberystwyth forwards and a little later collared one of their three-quarters who got away from the touch line. Time was called shortly afterwards leaving the College victorious by one try to nil.

In the final game of the season against Mr T P Thomas' XV the College had a fine win by 31 points to nil. The College scored seven tries, two of which were scored by Willie Llewellyn, his first tries of the season. The team brought by Mr T P Thomas, captain of the Christ College first fifteen the previous year, was much weaker than originally intended. After a very pleasant game the College were left victors by 5 goals and 2 tries to nil. The following scored tries for the College: R F Williams 1, M T Williams 2, A F Harding 1, R F Rynd 1 and Willie Llewellyn 2.

This had not been a great season for the College first fifteen and of the seventeen games played they had won just five, drawn one and lost eleven. They had scored 82 points for with 138 points against. The College scored 21 tries, 8 conversions and 1 penalty. Of the twenty-one tries scored M T Williams scored eleven and probably kicked all the goals. The other tries were scored by Willie Llewellyn (2), D H M Thomas (2), E C Green, M Macfarlane, W R Twyning, A F Harding, R F Williams and R F Rynd all with one try each. Nevertheless a lot of the games they lost were not by a big score with the heaviest defeats coming against Swansea 'A' and Merthyr 2nd XV, both by 17 points to nil. Willie definitely played in thirteen of these first team fixtures and probably in the remaining four other games where there is no team detail. Willie also played in the drawn game between the Christ College Second XV and Merthyr Seconds on 26th October 1893.

The Breconian in describing the rugby First XV said of Willie Llewellyn, 'For a light-weight plays a very good game. Kicks well, is plucky and has the makings of a good behind.' Of his brother John H Llewellyn, who captained the side throughout the season, *The Breconian* said, 'A thoroughly good forward; captained his men well and made of the forwards as good an all-round eight as we have had of late years; a hard and unselfish player, with good scoring power and a keen tackler.'

Another First XV player who played with distinction during the 1893–94 season was Arthur Flowers Harding. He played in the majority of the games during the 1893–94 season and was described by *The Breconian* as, 'A good forward in the open, who also pushes well; has great scoring power; a good tackler and shot at goal.' This was the first of four seasons Arthur Harding played for the Christ College First XV. In his final season, 1896–97, he captained the side.

Arthur Harding represented Wales as a forward on twenty occasions. Willie Llewellyn and Arthur Harding played together for Wales on eleven occasions including Willie's final game for Wales in their famous victory over New Zealand in 1905.

After being chosen to represent Wales against England in 1902 while playing for Cardiff he moved to England in the early part of the 1902–03 season to play for London Welsh. During the 1903–04 season Harding was chosen to captain London Welsh, a position he held for four seasons.

In 1904 Harding was one of eight Welsh players chosen for the British team to tour Australia and New Zealand under the captaincy of D R Bedell-Sivright. He played in every game including all three internationals against Australia and the international against New Zealand.

Arthur Flowers 'Boxer' Harding gained twenty caps for Wales between 1902 and 1908.

In 1908 Harding himself was chosen to captain a British Isles team on a 26 match tour of Australia and New Zealand. Scotland and Ireland had declined to nominate players for this tour and the team has gone down in Lions annals as an "Anglo-Welsh" combination. Although the Australia leg of the tour was successful, the Anglo-Welsh team were outclassed by a very strong All Black's team, drawing the second test but losing heavily in the first and third tests.

Annual Athletic Sports 1894

In 1894 the annual athletic sports took place on Friday 30th and Saturday 31st March. The weather was fine on both days and as a result a large number of spectators were present to witness the event. John Llewellyn was again very successful. On the first day he came second in the 100 yards flat race (open), throwing the cricket ball and the 220 yards race open (handicap). On the second day he came second in the 100 yards hurdle race (open) and the quarter-mile (open). Willie Llewellyn on the other hand had a very quiet sports only winning the three-legged race with Arthur Harding on the second day. Arthur Harding also won the long jump (under 16) event and came second in the high jump (under 16). Before the prizes were given out by Mrs William de Winton, the headmaster, Mr Bayfield, expressed his pleasure that so many had taken part in the games and he hoped that it would remain a tradition that everyone would enter for the annual sports.

Christ College First XI Cricket Season 1894

John Llewellyn was the captain of the Christ College First XI for the 1894 season. Of the 15 matches they played during the 1894 season they won 8, drew 3 and lost four. They scored 1444 runs with 1414 conceded. The 1894 July edition of *The Breconian* made the following comments with regard to the 1894 cricket season: 'Our doings on the cricket field this term afford a striking illustration of the truth of the old maxim that "nothing succeeds like success." We began well by winning our first five matches, and have throughout the term maintained a high standard of excellence. Up to the moment of writing, out of thirteen matches we have won seven, lost three, and drawn three. Unquestionably our strongest point has been the batting, which is decidedly above the average. Griffith, Rynd,

CRICKET—1894. RÉSUMÉ. FIRST XI.

DATE.	CHRIST COLLEGE v.	CHRIST COLLEGE 1st ins. 2nd ins.	OPPONENTS 1st ins. 2nd ins.	RESULT.
Sat., May 19..	W. T. Harding's XI.	114	46 34	Won
Sat., May 26..	Brecon C.C.	102 (8 wks.)	57 —	Won
Sat., June 2 ..	Hereford County Coll.	68	33 —	Won
Thurs., June 7.	University Coll., Cardiff..	123 (5 wks.)	25 —	Won
Sat., June 9 ..	Crickhowell C.C.	114	87 —	Won
Tues., June 12.	Crickhowell C.C.	73	118 51 (3 wks)	Lost
Thurs., June 14	Clydach C.C.	80	90 —	Lost
Sat., June 16 ..	University Coll., Cardiff..	49	60 —	Lost
Sat., June 23..	Brecon C.C.	77	65 —	Won
Wed., June 27.	Monmouth G.S.	241 (8 wks.)	156 —	Won
Thurs., June 28	F. H. Hurman, Esq's. XI.	71 (5 wks.)	138 —	Drawn
Sat., June 30..	Swansea C.C.	58 (4 wks.)	152 —	Drawn
Sat., July 7 ..	Llandovery College	116 (8 wks.)	205 —	Drawn
Sat., July 14..	Brecon C.C.	100	153 — (3 wks)	Lost
Sat., July 28..	Old Breconians	58	29 —	Won

Christ College Cricket Games Played and Results 1894

W M Llewellyn, D H M Thomas, R F Williams and Twyning, have been scoring well and consistently throughout the season; and to Twyning belongs the proud distinction of making our record score (122) against Monmouth.'

Both John and Willie Llewellyn played in all the thirteen matches recorded in the 1894 July edition of *The Breconian*. In those thirteen games Willie scored 143 runs and John 57 runs, notwithstanding the fact that of the thirteen matches played by John there were three occasions when he was not required to bat. Both Willie and John probably played in the final two matches against Brecon Cricket Club and the Old Breconians but no information is available for these games. In a critique of the 1894 Christ College first eleven *The Breconian* said, 'W M Llewellyn (1893–4). – A sound and pretty bat, good cut, and excellent hitter to leg; rather too fond of trying to drive a rising ball, hits hard and clean, good field, fair change bowler.' Of the captain, John Llewellyn, *The Breconian* said, 'J H Llewellyn (1892–3–4). – Captained the team very well. A safe bat, with good forward strokes, was unlucky; very fair field.'

Having played cricket for the first eleven for three seasons this was John's final season and he left Christ College at the end of the 1894 summer term.

Christ College Rugby Season 1894–1895
Looking ahead to the coming football season the July 1894 edition of *The Breconian* made the following observation: 'As to football next term, it is perhaps too early to form any conjecture. We fear that we shall be losing the greater number of last year's men. Of course it will be difficult to replace them. At the same time there is no reason to be despondent. There is undoubtedly some good material in the school, and with sound and careful instruction, a very respectable fifteen should be turned out.'

The 1894–95 season was always going to be a difficult one for the Christ College rugby first fifteen. Only five players from the previous season remained: H M Hughes, Willie Llewellyn and D F H Williams in the backs and Arthur Harding and E C Green in the forwards. The captain for the 1894–95 season was E C Green.

It appears that Christ College, Brecon played only nine first fifteen matches during the 1894–95 season but for some reason *The Breconian*

Christ College Brecon Rugby Games 1894-1895 Season			
Willie Llewellyn Rugby Games Played 1894-1895 Season			
Date	Home Team	Away Team	Result/Score
Unknown	Christ College	T P Thomas, Esq.'s XV	Lost 3-16
Unknown	Christ College	W T Davies, Esq.'s XV	Lost 8-15
Unknown	Merthyr	Christ College	Lost 3-23
Unknown	Christ College	E B Ll. Reece, Esq.'s XV	Lost 3-22
24.10.1894	Christ College	Mr S Rooney's Team	Lost 3-12
20.11.1894	Christ College	Col.-Sergt. Clarke's XV	Won 4-0
01.12.1894	Christ College	Llandovery School	Won 5-3
05.12.1894	Monmouth Grammar School	Christ College	Lost 0-11
13.03.1895	Christ College	Swansea Reserves	Lost 3-9

Christ College Brecon, Rugby Games Played and Results 1894–1895 Season

only had reports of six games, those against: T P Thomas Esq.'s XV, W T Davies Esq.'s XV, Merthyr, E B Ll. Reece Esq.'s XV, Col.-Sergt. Clarke's XV and Llandovery College. Further research revealed that another three games were definitely played, against: Mr S Rooney's Team, Monmouth Grammar School and Swansea Reserves.

Eight of the games were played before Christmas then an outbreak of measles and scarlet fever in Brecon resulted in all the elementary schools, attended by between 700 and 800 children, being closed until January. Although no case had occurred at Christ College, the headmaster the Rev. M A Bayfield took the precautionary step of closing the College until the beginning of the following term. In a letter to the parents of the boys, a copy of which was posted in the *Evening Express* on Friday 7th December, the headmaster said, 'Dear Sir, An outbreak of scarlet fever in the town of Brecon, which has been causing me anxiety, has now assumed serious proportions. I have, therefore, thought it my duty to dismiss the school and your son will return home tomorrow (Thursday). The school is at present absolutely free from the epidemic; but it seems wiser to anticipate its possible arrival than to await it, especially as we are not far from the end of the term. You will receive notice of the date of the re-opening of the school, which I hope will be in five weeks' time. Trusting I shall have your approval in the course I am taking. I am yours very truly, M A Bayfield.' The letter was dated Wednesday 5th December, the same day the First XV played Monmouth Grammar School. As a consequence of the closure, the fixture, scheduled to take place on Saturday 8th December, against Swansea 2nd XV was cancelled.

THE CHRIST COLLEGE YEARS

The first game of the season was against T P Thomas, Esq.'s XV. The game was played on the College ground in fair weather and resulted in a victory for the visitors by 16 points to three, Harold Williams getting the first try of the season for the College. John Llewellyn, who was playing for the visitors, ran the whole length of the field to score their third try. Willie Llewellyn did not play in this game but returned for the second game of the season against W T Davies, Esq.'s XV. As with the first game, John Llewellyn, Willie's elder brother, played for the opposition and scored their opening try which was converted to give them a five point lead. After this the College responded with some good play which resulted in an unconverted try for R C Menneer. With no further scores in the first half the visitors led at the interval by 5 points to three. Another converted try early in the second half gave the visitors a seven point lead. Again the College responded and H M Hughes scored behind the posts and Harold Williams added the extra points. Towards the end of the game Howell scored a try for the visitors which he converted himself and with no further scoring the College were defeated 15 points to eight.

Willie played again in the first away match of the season against Merthyr. The College were well beaten going down by 23 points to three. The Merthyr team were much heavier than the College team and as they were playing without Mr Borrow the forwards were a lot lighter than usual. This disadvantage resulted in Merthyr scoring two unanswered tries in the first half both of which were converted. Early in the second half Merthyr scored two tries in quick succession, only one of which was converted. After this the College started playing really well and they were rewarded when Seaton crossed for an unconverted try. But it was Merthyr who had the final word and before the final whistle they scored another converted try to take their total to 23 points thus winning by 23 points to three.

Progress was disappointing for the College team and matters did not improve in the next game against E B Ll Reece Esq.'s XV. The opposition were very strongly represented, the team mainly drawn from the Penarth club. Although Willie scored a try the College were well beaten going down by 22 points to three.

On Wednesday 24th October the College played against Mr S Rooney's Team at home. Willie was again in the side that went down by 12 points to three. The College played well in the first half and held their own quite well and up until half-time neither side had scored. In the later stages of the second half however, the visitors had matters much their own way and scored four unconverted tries in quick succession. The College did manage to score a consolation try but it was not enough and in the end they were well beaten.

At last, on Saturday 20th November, after five consecutive defeats, the College won their first game of the season against Col.-Sergt. Clarke's XV. A second half drop goal by Arthur Harding was the only score of the game and the College won by the narrow margin of 4 points to nil.

With only one victory to their credit the College next faced the old enemy, Llandovery College, at home on Saturday 1st December. The 'Welsh Varsity Match' was always well contested and this game was no different. In the first half Harold Williams scored a try which he converted himself. In a hard fought second half O L Evans kicked a penalty goal for the visitors. Very little time remained and Llandovery made strenuous efforts to score, but a fine kick by Llewellyn, a run by Seaton and a combined rush by all the College forwards took and kept the ball in the visitors' twenty-five until the whistle sounded for the end of the game and Christ College were victorious by 5 points to three. *The Breconian* reported, 'The game throughout was interesting and exciting; play was fast as well as loose. The victory was a well-deserved one. Our game was a defensive one, and a fine run by Harold Williams early in the game gave confidence to the team, who acquitted themselves admirably.' Willie Llewellyn was again in the side and *The Breconian* reported that 'Llewellyn made no single mistake and was the pick of both third lines.'

The final game before Christmas, played on Wednesday 5th December, was against Monmouth Grammar School at Abergavenny. Fresh from their victory over Llandovery College, Christ College were expected to defeat Monmouth, who had only once in a long series of previous battles gained victory over their Welsh opponents. But in a game where the College never seemed likely to score, they were defeated by one goal and two tries (11 Points) to nil. The first try was scored by Bennett followed by tries from Reg Skrimshire and F Nicholas. This was the second time Willie Llewellyn had faced Reg Skrimshire, they having faced each other in the same fixture at Brecon the previous season when the College won by 14 points to thirteen. In January 1899 Willie Llewellyn and Reg Skrimshire were two of seven debutants in a Wales team that defeated England at St Helen's by 26 points to three. Willie Llewellyn scored four tries and Viv Huzzey, on the other wing, scored the other two. Billy Bancroft of Swansea converted four of the tries.

Reginald Truscott Skrimshire played three times for Wales. He was centre in three internationals against England, Scotland and Ireland in 1899. Reg Skrimshire was the only Welshman on the 1903 British Isles tour of South Africa. He played in all twenty-two games including all three internationals. Of the twenty-two games played they won eleven, drew three and lost eight. They lost the series one nil having drawn the first two tests before losing the third. Reg Skrimshire was top points and try scorer with 59 points.

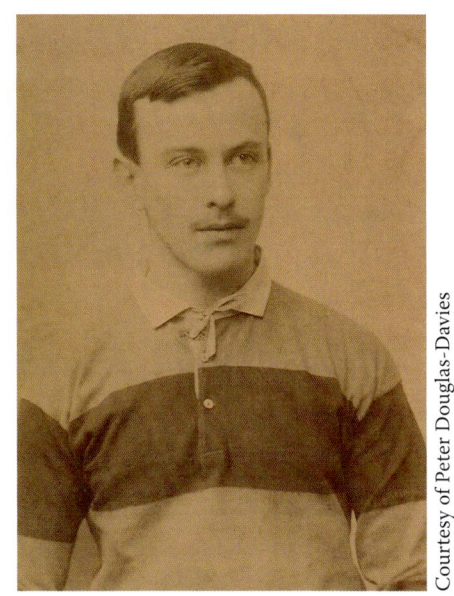

Reginald Truscott Skrimshire played in the centre for Wales on three occasions. Against England, Scotland and Ireland 1899.

The only other game recorded for the Christ College First XV during the 1894–95 season was against Swansea 2nd XV. Originally scheduled for Saturday 8th December 1894, the fixture was cancelled because of the outbreak of scarlet fever in Brecon. The game was then scheduled for Friday 8th February but did not take place, probably because of frost. Finally the game was played on Wednesday 13th March. There are no team details for this game but records show that Swansea won the game by 3 tries to a penalty goal (9 points to three).

With the season over the Christ College First XV had played nine games, won two and lost seven. It is likely that Willie Llewellyn played in eight of these games. This was a disappointing season for the First XV, but considering that only five players had played the previous season and their victory over old rivals Llandovery College, they could look forward to the 1895–96 season with optimism.

Christ College Brecon, Rugby First XV 1894–1895

Back Row: M C Menneer, E C Green (Captain), D Fitzwilliams, C P Turner.
Third Row: C B Mansfield, A F Harding, E G Droiser. Second Row: R F Rynd,
E Yorath, W M Llewellyn, H M Hughes, D F H Williams, Mr Borrow.
Front Row: G S Seaton, W H Griffiths, W B T Rees.

Annual Athletic Sports 1895

Willie Llewellyn was dominant in the annual Christ College Easter Sports which were held at the College on Friday 5th and Saturday 6th April 1895. The sports began in splendid weather and the large number of spectators witnessed Willie Llewellyn in impressive form. On the first day he won the 100 yards flat race (open) and the 220 yards (open handicap) race. The weather for the second day was not so good and a strong wind and heavy rain had left the ground very heavy. Willie won the quarter mile (open) and with a jump of 16ft 11.5ins won the long jump (open). He also came second in the 100 yards hurdle race (open).

Willie Llewellyn's outstanding performance in the sports was well rewarded; he won the silver medal (given by the games committee) and the silver Challenge Cup (presented by the governors and masters of the

College). John Llewellyn returned to Christ College for the Easter Sports and won the Old Breconians' 150 yards handicap race. The prizes were presented by Mrs Bayfield, the headmaster's wife.

Despite being only fourteen years old Teddy Morgan gave an indication of his future potential by winning the under 16 long jump and coming second in the 100 yards flat race for boys under 15.

Christ College Cricket Season 1895

With regard to the cricket season, the July 1895 edition of *The Breconian* reported, 'the season had been fairly successful up to the time of the Llandovery Match, but this, unfortunately, resulted in a victory for our opponents by 70 runs, a thing which has not happened for four years. We had, however, the misfortune to lose the toss, and this fact alone contributed in no small measure to the disaster which befell the XI, and it may safely be said that, had we been successful there, our display of batting would have been much more creditable. Only one of the XI figured favourably in this respect in the first innings, F Stratton putting together the substantial total of 44 runs. In the second innings a much better stand was made, over a hundred runs being obtained for the loss of six wickets. Notwithstanding this defect, we consider that the greatest praise is due to our Captain, H M Hughes, for his untiring efforts to turn out a good team. He has certainly succeeded, for the XI is well up to, if not above, the average, and that it should have lost the School Match (the two others having been won) is in no way due to him, but to the unkindness of fortune. Many spectators admitted that we were not the worse team, and the opinion was expressed by a competent judge that we had on our side the best bat who has played in this match for most years.'

The loss obviously hurt, it was considered the most important match of the cricket year and having not lost the match for four consecutive years the defeat was a particularly painful one. Llandovery batted first and were all out for 145 runs. In reply the Christ College XI could only amass a first innings score of 75 and thus lost by 70 runs. Only one player managed double figures and that was F Stratton with 44. Willie Llewellyn only managed to score one run in the first innings but scored a respectable 22 in the second innings. As was often the case, if time allowed, the teams would bat again and in the second innings Christ College played much better scoring a respectable 113 for six, but to no avail with the result being decided on the first innings score.

Christ College played eight games during the 1895 cricket season, winning four and losing four. Willie Llewellyn did not play in the first match of the season against J H Stratton Esq.s' Old Boys Team. The College batted first and were all out for 70 runs. In reply the opposition scored 92 all out and thus won the match by 22 runs.

Willie played his first match of the season in the second game against G H Peacock Esq.'s XI. The College were well beaten losing by 96 runs. Only one player managed to get to double figures; E S Jones with 13 runs. Willie was second top scorer with just 6 runs.

The first victory of the season came in the next match against Brecon Town with both sides playing twelve men. Played on the Brecon Town ground, the College batted first and were all out for 85 runs. In reply Brecon were all out for 50 runs giving the College the victory by 35 runs. Willie scored a respectable 10 runs with F Stratton top scorer with 21 runs.

The College were also successful in their next match against Crickhowell. The College batted first and scored 131 runs all out. Mr Borrow was top scorer with 25 runs and others with good scores were H M Hughes with 24 runs and Mr Peacock and W H Griffiths with 23 runs apiece. Willie was bowled out for 5 runs.

Christ College continued their winning ways in their next match against Hereford County College played at Hereford. Both sides batted twice with Christ College scoring 68 runs in their first innings. Hereford replied with a poor score of just 26 runs. Christ College scored 127 runs in their second innings thus setting the County College 168 runs to win the match. The task was too much for them and they were all out for 67 runs leaving Christ College victors by 102 runs. W H Griffiths had a brilliant day with the ball, he took seven wickets for 9 runs in Hereford's first innings and then followed that up with another four wickets in their second innings. Willie was out for a duck in the first innings and scored 9 runs in the second.

The College were well beaten in their next match against Mr T P Thomas Esq.'s Team. The College could do nothing against the strong

Christ College Brecon, Cricket First XI 1895

Back Row: Mr W S Borrow, Mr G H Peacock, J S Bookless, Mr H R Thomson, Rev. C W Horsburgh. *Third Row*: C P Turner (Umpire), E S Jones, P J Menneer, E C Green, D F H Williams, W B Thomas, W B T Rees (Scorer). *Second Row*: W H Griffiths, H M Hughes (Captain), W M Llewellyn. *Front Row*: F Stratton and A Griffiths.

bowling of A W Samuels who took five first innings wickets, reducing the College to all out for just 48 runs. In reply the visitors scored 125 runs giving them victory by 77 runs. W H Griffiths again bowled well for the College taking six wickets for 45 runs. Although to no avail, the College batted well in their second innings scoring 108 runs for 6 wickets with H M Hughes 69 runs not out. Willie scored 7 runs in the first innings and 3 runs in the second.

The next match was against Llandovery College which resulted in defeat by 70 runs as previously described. The final match of the season was played at Newport against Monmouth Grammar School. Willie Llewellyn did not play in this game but the College were victors by 89 runs. The College batting first, were all out for 183 runs; D F H Williams scoring a magnificent 86 runs. In reply, Monmouth Grammar School were all out for 94 runs. H M Hughes bowled exceptionally well taking 8 wickets for just 35 runs.

With regard to Willie Llewellyn, *The Breconian*, in a critique of the First XI, said the following: 'W. M. LLEWELLYN (1893–4–5). Has not come on as well as was expected; the chief reason of his comparative failure lies in his anxiety to get runs at any cost. Strong on the leg-side, but developed a curious "half-cock" stroke on the off from a half-volley; fair change bowler, and good field.' Willie played in six of the eight matches played during the 1895 season. He scored 63 runs, took 1 wicket and made 4 catches.

The Christ College annual Speech Day took place on Saturday 25th July 1895 and when the headmaster, Mr Bayfield, read the honours list it was announced that Willie Llewellyn had won the science prize. This would be one of the last duties performed by the headmaster, who, after five years at the helm, was moving to Eastbourne College to take up the post of headmaster.

Christ College Rugby Season 1895–1896
With regard to Rugby, Willie Llewellyn was elected captain of the first fifteen for the 1895–96 season. A report in the *South Wales Echo* on Saturday 19th October 1895 gave the following report: 'Christ College, Brecon, this season is led by Mr W M Llewellyn. Mr Llewellyn has for the past three years represented his school both in football (rugby) and cricket, and his merits were fully recognised by the boys at a meeting of the whole school some three weeks ago when he was elected their captain for the season. Though now only seventeen and a half years old he won the College Championship in athletics in April of this year, and has on very many occasions, since he was a small boy, done good services for his school. He is a brother of Mr J H Llewellyn, the Brecon captain of two seasons ago, who is now playing for Pontypridd. If the example he sets his team is followed up, Christ College has reason to hope that last year's victory may be repeated in its annual encounter with its old rival, Llandovery, which takes place early in December. Mr Llewellyn has much cause to welcome back to Christ College as a master that well-known Oxford Blue and Welsh International, Mr W Ll. Thomas, who will be of great assistance to him in getting his team into proper form.'

William Llewellyn Thomas played on the wing for Wales in three internationals, against Scotland in 1894 and England and Ireland in 1895. Thomas won two Blues in 1893 and 1894. He made the winning try for R H B Cattell in the 1893 Varsity match and scored the try when Oxford drew five points all with Cambridge in the 1894 Varsity match. After leaving Oxford he returned to Christ College where he was an Assistant Master from 1896 until 1898. Following his ordination into the Church in 1899 he became a curate in Rushall, West Midlands until 1903. From then until 1907 he was at All Saints, Oystermouth and from 1907 until 1912 he was at Cefnllys, Llandrindod Wells. In 1910 he was captain of Llandrindod Wells Golf Club. From 1912 to 1924 he was vicar of Irton, in the Lake District. From 1924 until his death in 1943 he was the vicar of Bootle in Cumberland. He was the cousin of R T D Budworth, the English rugby international, who won three caps for England between 1890 and 1891. Budworth also attended Christ College, Brecon.

William Llewellyn Thomas who gained three caps for Wales between 1894 and 1895.

During the 1895–96 season the College played fourteen games of which they won five and lost nine. Willie Llewellyn was captain in all of them. The College scored 103 points and conceded 161. Willie Llewellyn scored twenty-eight points from eight tries and one dropped goal. In addition to the games Willie Llewellyn played for Christ College during the 1895–96 season he also played rugby for Llwynypia. During the Christmas holidays he played seven games for Llwynypia and between the end of March and the end of April he played another five games. Centre Charlie Williams had left Llwynypia early in March 1896 to play for Ebbw Vale and with Isaac Edmunds moving to the centre this enabled Willie Llewellyn to fill the spot on the wing. Still only seventeen at the start of the season Willie

Llewellyn had a promising future before him. He had an excellent turn of speed, could give and take passes with equal facility and was a ferocious tackler.

Willie Llewellyn played in all fourteen games played by the Christ College first fifteen during the 1895–96 season. The season did not start too well with the College losing their first two games. In the first game of the season against Mr J Thomas' team they went down by 9 points to three. The visitors were the first to score with an unconverted try which was quickly followed by another. In reply Willie Llewellyn scored an unconverted try for the College. Eventually the visitors scored another try under the posts but astonishingly the kick at goal failed. Nevertheless this was the last score of the game and as stated previously the game ended in a win for the scratch fifteen.

In the previous two years of playing for the first fifteen Willie Llewellyn had not been a try scoring machine but this try in the first game was the start of a good season of scoring for Willie. He scored a total of eight tries and a drop goal for Christ College and eight tries for Llwynpia during the season.

The College also lost their second game against a Newport Third XV. In the first half the visitors scored an unconverted try and a converted try and led by eight points to nil at the interval. Early in the second half Harding scored a try for the College which Harold Williams converted but this was the College's only score and late in the game Newport scored another two unconverted tries and won the game by 14 points to five.

The first victory of the season for the College came in the next game against Mr V H T Thomas' Swansea team. Willie Llewellyn opened the scoring with a try which Harding just failed to convert. Rees scored again for the College before half-time and Harold Williams was successful with the conversion so the teams crossed over with the College ahead by eight points to nil. In the second half Griffiths scored another try for the College which Harold Williams again converted. With no further scoring the College were victors by 13 points to nil.

Willie Llewellyn was now getting into his stride and although the College lost their next game to Mr Percy Morton's XV by 7 points to three, Willie scored the College try. Willie also scored in the next two games. He scored two tries in the 29 points to eight victory over Merthyr

Thursday and another in the defeat to Llandovery College. In the game which took place at Llandovery, the College lost by a dropped goal and three tries to a goal; 13 points to five.

The College played three further games before the Christmas break. They lost to Swansea Reserves by 19 points to five, beat Monmouth Grammar School by 3 points to nil and then lost to Christ College Past by 11 points to ten.

During the Christmas break Willie Llewellyn played seven games for Llwynypia. His first game for the club, with which he would be associated for the greater part of his rugby career, was against Roath at Llwynypia. Playing with only fourteen men throughout the game, Llwynypia were victorious by 26 points to nil. Willie had an outstanding debut scoring two of the six tries.

The next game was not so good as Llwynypia went down to Ferndale by 5 points to nil. This was a really interesting game as play only lasted ten minutes before the Llwynypia players walked off the field without consulting the referee. The apparent reason was the state of the ground. After Llwynypia had left the field Ferndale scored a try which was converted by Edwards and the referee, Mr A H Williams, awarded the game to Ferndale.

Willie crossed again in the next game when Llwynypia defeated Treherbert by 8 points to seven, and scored the winning try in the 3 points to nil defeat of Penygraig. Tries for Willie were coming thick and fast and he scored again in the drawn game with Morriston. Although he did not score Willie is mentioned in the match report for the next game against Treorky on Saturday 18th January 1896, a game Llwynypia won by 14 points to three. In his final game for Llwynypia (during the Christmas holidays) Willie played against Mountain Ash. Willie did not score and Llwynypia lost by 11 points to eight.

Willie returned to Christ College and played in the first fifteen game against Merthyr Thursdays. The interesting feature of this game was that Willie Llewellyn opened the scoring with a drop goal. *The Breconian* commented how, 'From a loose rush by the Merthyr forwards Llewellyn picked up and took a shot, landing a goal from close to the touch line.' As far as the Christ College rugby records go this is the only drop goal Willie ever kicked for the first fifteen. This was the only exciting feature

Courtesy of Christ College, Brecon

Willie Llewellyn's Christ College first fifteen rugby cap.

of the game as far as the College were concerned. Despite being ahead at the interval by 4 points to three Merthyr came back and scored three second half goals which gave them victory by 18 points to four.

The College returned to winning ways in their next game against E B Reece Esq. XV. Willie opened the scoring with a try which Harold Williams converted. Griffiths scored again for the College and Harold Williams again converted. In the second half Mr Thomas scored an unconverted try for the College before Willie Llewellyn scored his second try of the game. Harold Williams again converted leaving the College victorious by 18 points to nil.

The College won their next game against Aberystwyth College by the narrow margin of 3 points to nil but were then defeated by Swansea 'A' by 14 points to nil. In their final game of the season the Christ College first fifteen were heavily defeated by Newport Extras by 48 points to nil. Played at Newport, the College were unlucky to have three or four of their regular players on the injured list. The Newport team was far too good and with at least three first team players in the side they scored twelve tries, six of which were converted.

This was the last game Willie Llewellyn played for the Christ College first fifteen. He would leave the College at the end of the summer term but not before he took part in the annual athletics sports and played his last season of cricket for the College First XI. Willie played approximately forty games for the Christ College first fifteen over three seasons. An interesting note in the 1896 April edition of *The Breconian* made reference to the weight of the first fifteen players, it read as follows: 'The following are the weights of several members of the team as taken last term: Full-back: Dawson, 9st. 6lbs.; Three-quarters: W M Llewellyn (capt.), 10–1; D F H

Willie Llewellyn Rugby Games Played 1895-1896 Season						
Willie Llewellyn Rugby Games Probably Played 1895-1896 Season						
Date	Team	Opposition	Venue	Score	W Llewellyn Tries
23/10/1895	Christ College	Mr J Thomas' Team	Home	Lost 3-9	1
26/10/1895	Christ College	Newport Extras (3rd)	Home	Lost 5-14	0
06/11/1895	Christ College	Mr V H T Thomas' Team	Home	Won 13-0	1
09/11/1895	Christ College	Mr Percy Morton's XV	Home	Lost 3-7	1
20/11/1895	Christ College	Merthyr Thursday	Home	Won 29-8	2
30/11/1895	Christ College	Llandovery College	Away	Lost 5-13	1
07/12/1895	Christ College	Swansea Reserves	Away	Lost 5-19	0
11/12/1895	Christ College	Monmouth Grammar School	Away	Won 3-0	0
13/12/1895	Christ College	Christ College Past	Home	Lost 10-11	0
25/12/1895	Llwynypia	Roath	Home	Won 26-0	2
28/12/1895	Llwynypia	Ferndale	Away	Lost 0-5	0
04/01/1896	Llwynypia	Treherbert	Away	Won 8-7	1
06/01/1896	Llwynypia	Penygraig	Home	Won 3-0	1
11/01/1896	Llwynypia	Morriston	Away	Drawn 3-3	1
18/01/1896	Llwynypia	Treorky	Home	Won 14-3	0
01/02/1896	Llwynypia	Mountain Ash	Away	Lost 8-11	0
06/02/1896	Christ College	Merthyr Thursdays	Away	Lost 4-18	1DG
Unknown	Christ College	E B Reece Esq. XV	Home	Won 18-0	2
27/02/1896	Christ College	Aberystwyth College	Home	Won 3-0	0
14/03/1896	Christ College	Swansea A	Home	Lost 0-14	0
19/03/1896	Christ College	Newport Extras	Away	Lost 0-48	0
28/03/1896	Llwynypia	Blaina	Home	Won 41-3	2
04/04/1896	Llwynypia	Northampton	Away	Won 7-6	0
06/04/1896	Llwynypia	Bedford	Away	Drawn 3-3	0
11/04/1896	Llwynypia	Pontnewydd	Home	Won 20-0	0
18/04/1896	Llwynypia	Neath	Home	Won 26-5	1

Willie Llewellyn Rugby Games Played and Results 1895–96 Season

Williams, 10–8; H M Hughes, 10–8; F Stratton, 8–0; W H Griffith, 10–2; Half-backs: W B T Rees, 10–3; W B Thomas, 9–8; Forwards: A F Harding, 12–0; T R Williams, 9–13; A J Harding, 10–8; M H Williams, 10–7; Ll. David, 8–6; J Buer, 10–0; J H Scott, 8–2; H H Hopkins, 8–4.'

With the Christ College rugby season over for another year Willie Llewellyn played rugby for Llwynypia for the remainder of the season. Of the five games he played Llwynypia were undefeated. In the game against Blaina Willie scored two of the eleven tries recorded in a 41 points to three victory. Llwynypia then defeated Northampton away and drew with Bedford. In the final two games of the season Llwynypia beat Pontnewydd by 20 points to nil before thumping Neath by 26 points to five at home. This was a great victory against a strong Neath side that included Joe Davies, Fred Hutchinson and Bill Jones. Joe Davies was reserve to the great Welsh full-back W J Bancroft on no fewer than seventeen occasions. Fred Hutchinson was capped by Wales in 1894 and Bill Jones was a Neath legend. He captained Neath for nine seasons and in recognition of his outstanding service was elected the club's first life member after Neath won their first championship in 1909–10. Willie scored another try in the game against Neath which brought his total for the season to sixteen tries in twenty-six games.

This was a very good season for Llwynypia. Under the captaincy of W H Mills they played thirty-nine games, won twenty-six, lost ten and drew three. They scored 435 points with only 135 against. Tom Williams was top try scorer with twenty-two followed by Charlie Williams with twelve. Willie Llewellyn, who only played in twelve games, scored eight tries in what was his first season with Llwynypia. At the end of the season the *Evening Express* said of Willie Llewellyn, 'a Brecon College boy, returned home and was given a place in the team and proved himself to be a player of exceptional quality.'

Bill Jones, Neath RFC 1890–1910. Joined Neath as a wing but eventually landed up playing in the forwards. He gave Neath RFC outstanding service and was their first life member.

Courtesy of Mike Price and Neath RFC

Annual Athletic Sports 1896

The annual sports were held on Wednesday 1st April 1896. The sports were held earlier than usual because of an outbreak of smallpox in Brecon. *The South Wales Daily News* reported on Saturday 4th April: 'The Brecon Board of Guardians on Thursday had under consideration the further outbreak of smallpox at Brecon, there being four cases in the town, two of which were in the Workhouse. It was agreed to rent a cottage, the property of Lord Tredegar, for the purposes of isolation.' As a result of this outbreak the boys at Christ College finished a week earlier for their Easter holidays.

This was another successful sports for Mr Percy Morton's House in general and Willie Llewellyn in particular. The report in the July edition of *The Breconian* made the following comments: 'The weather has been very favourable to cricket, and better still, we had a fine day for last term's sports. Those were very satisfactory, though owing to the scare they had to be rather hastily run off. The company, considering the circumstances, was as large as could be expected. Some of the events were run in very good time, and the open long jump deserves special mention. The main feature of the sports was the continued success of Mr. Morton's house, by whom 21 prizes were carried off; a feat probably unparalleled in the history of the house, though it has been for long *facile princeps* in the playing fields.'

Having won the Christ College Athletics Sports Challenge Cup the previous year, Willie Llewellyn retained the cup in 1896. He came first in the 100 yards open, the 440 yards open, the high jump open, the 100 yards hurdles open and the long jump open.

Back Row: J T Williams, Willie Llewellyn and J H Scott.
Front Row: Edward Morgan, Arthur Harding, Harold Williams and Miss Gwendoline Morton.

It was also another good sports for Arthur Harding. He came first in putting the shot and second in throwing the cricket ball, the quarter mile open and the 100 yards hurdles open. He also came third in the mile open.

Another Morton's House boy, D F H (Harold) Williams, took four prizes. He came second in putting the shot and the 220 yards open (handicap) race. He was also third in the high jump open and the long jump open. Harold Williams also took the shooting prize for the best aggregate score.

Edward (Teddy) Morgan, again at Morton's House, came first in the under 16 long jump and the 440 yards (handicap) under 16 race. He came second in the under 16 high jump and also won a prize in the under 16 throwing the cricket ball. Teddy Morgan also took the open fives prize and the golf prize.

Although Willie Llewellyn and Teddy Morgan played cricket in the same team for the Christ College first eleven they never played rugby in the same team. By the time Teddy Morgan had progressed to the first fifteen Willie Llewellyn had left Christ College. Nevertheless they did play senior rugby together. They played club rugby together for London Welsh and County rugby for Surrey. In addition they both played for the Anglo-Australian Rugby Football Team (British Isles) on their tour to Australia and New Zealand in 1904 and played together for Wales in eleven internationals. It was Teddy Morgan who scored the winning try in Willie Llewellyn's final international match for Wales against New Zealand in 1905.

Two further Morton's House boys to win prizes in the 1896 athletic sports were J H Scott who won the throwing the cricket ball competition and J T Williams who came second in the 150 yards under 14 race. Other honours bestowed upon these Morton's House boys were football colours for Willie Llewellyn, Harold Williams, Arthur Harding and J H Scott. Cricket colours were also gained by Willie Llewellyn, Harold Williams and Teddy Morgan in 1896. Willie Llewellyn and Harold Williams were also school prefects in 1895 and 1896. Willie Llewellyn, who was the football captain in 1895–96, was succeeded in the post by Arthur Harding in 1896–97.

Christ College Cricket Season 1896

There are eight recorded first eleven cricket matches in the 1896 July edition of *The Breconian*. The team, which was captained by H M Hughes, won seven of these games and drew the other one. There may have been other games played but these eight are the only ones recorded. Willie Llewellyn played in all eight games and scored 72 runs. Unfortunately he also had four ducks. Of the 1896 first eleven *The Breconian* said of Willie Llewellyn: 'A good bat, with the fault of playing across a ball on the leg stump, as if it were off the wicket on the leg side; otherwise plays well all round the wicket. Does not invariably try to get over the ball. An excellent catch and field, with a quick return. A fair change bowler with a puzzling low delivery.' During the 1896 season Willie also made two catches and took two wickets.

In the first game of the season Christ College beat Percy Morton Esq.'s eleven by 11 runs. The College were all out for 144 runs with Harold Williams top scorer with 37 runs. Willie scored a duck in this game. Percy Morton's XI could only score 133 runs in reply and thus were defeated.

Willie Llewellyn's batting didn't improve in the next game against Crickhowell when he was again out for a duck. The College batted first and were all out for 141 runs. The masters contributed the lion's share of the runs with Mr Borrow gaining 20 runs, Mr Thomas 42 and Mr Lattimer not out for 56. In reply Crickhowell were all out for 109 runs and thus the College were the victors by 32 runs. There was some conciliation for Willie in as much as he fielded well and took a catch early in the game. At last in the next game Willie Llewellyn managed to get some runs on the board scoring 8 in a game which saw the College defeat Brecon Town by 20 runs.

In the match against Dr Reid's Swansea XI the game ended in a draw. The visitors batted first on a fine wicket and scored 183 runs for five wickets declared. W H Griffiths took all five wickets. In reply the College managed to score just 73 runs for six wickets but with time running out the game was declared a draw. Regrettably Willie had his third duck in four games.

At last, in the next game against 3rd Batt. South Wales Borderers, Willie put together a really good inning scoring 29 runs not out. The Borderers batted first and were all out for 128 runs. In reply the College scored

136 runs for six wickets and won by four wickets. Again there were some good scores on the College side. In addition to Willie Llewellyn's 29 runs Mr Lattimer scored 21 runs, W H Griffiths 47 runs and H M Hughes 27 runs.

The next game against Llandovery College was described as 'the most exciting match ever played on the College ground.' With regard to this game the editorial of the July 1896 edition of *The Breconian* stated, 'This term opened prosperously with the news of M H Ll Williams' Scholarship at Jesus College, Oxford: and the promise which it showed thus early in the class room has been continued in the playing fields by a succession of brilliant victories for the XI. First and foremost, after the most exciting contest ever witnessed since the two schools first met in the cricket field, we beat our ancient rivals by three runs. It is certainly a day that will be held in remembrance; indeed a game in which the fortunes of the two sides were so varied, would be remarkable in any cricket annals, and, while congratulating ourselves that the fortune of the game, always *variuvi atque mutabile*, had the grace eventually to decide in our favour, still, the last few minutes of the game must have been decidedly trying to the partisans of both sides. We beg to offer our sincerest congratulations to the captain and the team in general on their victory, the crowning point of a season exceptionally successful.'

It certainly was an exciting game with the result in doubt until the very last seconds of the match. Christ College batted first and were all out for 94 runs. There were some good scores with W H Griffiths knocking 26 runs, W B Thomas with 17 runs and B K Stratton with 12 runs. No one else managed to get into double figures with Harold Williams on 9 runs and Willie Llewellyn and W R Williams on 7 runs apiece. The only other batsmen to score were A Griffiths with 6 runs and H M Hughes with 2 runs. With eight extras the College score stood at 94 runs.

In reply Llandovery scored 73 runs for three wickets and it looked like the game was over as far as the result was concerned. Llandovery added a further 12 runs but at the cost of another four wickets. Nevertheless Llandovery only needed another ten runs with three wickets remaining. The next man in was bowled for a duck and another wicket fell for just one run added. Llandovery now needed nine runs with just one wicket standing. With the Llandovery score at 91 runs 'Hughes sent down a ball well up on the leg-side. Earlier in the innings it would have been hit, but the anxiety of the position was too much, the batsman played too soon, the ball went up to Price, was held, and the College had won by three runs. The cheers were deafening, hats were seen flying in all directions, and Hughes was tackled by a fellow three-quarter and carried shoulder high.' With one of the Llandovery batsmen being run out the remaining wickets were taken by W H Griffiths 4 wickets, H M Hughes 4 wickets and Willie Llewellyn 1 wicket.

Christ College won their final two matches of the 1896 cricket season, the first against Hereford County College and the final match against Monmouth Grammar School. In the match against Hereford they won by 53 runs and then beat Monmouth Grammar School by 66 runs. Willie Llewellyn put together a good score in the match against Hereford notching 28 runs. He also took a catch. But in the game against Monmouth, although the College won, Willie recorded his fourth duck of the season. He did however take his second wicket of the season in this his final game for the Christ College first eleven.

Edward (Teddy) Morgan came into the first eleven for the games against Llandovery College and Monmouth Grammar School. In a description of the 1896 cricket first eleven *The Breconian* said of Teddy Morgan, 'Worked hard for his place, but only gained it late in the term. Fields excellently, and bats with a freedom which is hardly proportional to his size. Bowled with success for the 2nd XI early in the term. Will make a player when he grows bigger.' This he certainly did; he was a very good cricketer and played six times for Glamorgan County Cricket Club.

As far as sport was concerned this was the end of Willie Llewellyn's Christ College career, with Willie leaving Christ College at the end of the summer term. Nevertheless he would return to Christ College for several social events and play against them on the rugby field.

From as early as 1893 Willie was referred to as W M Llewellyn in *The Breconian*. Willie Llewellyn was actually named as Willie on his birth certificate with no second Christian name. It was while Willie was at Christ College that he started to adopt the second Christian name of Morris and after his time at Christ College he was regularly known as W M Llewellyn. It is generally believed in the family that Willie adopted his mother's maiden name of Morris as his second Christian name.

In the 1861 census Catherine Morris is a nine year old girl living with her mother and step father; Thomas Williams an inn keeper of the Pandy Inn, Clydach Vale. In the 1871 census Catherine is a 19 year old married woman living with her 24 year old husband Richard Thomas, a coal miner, and their 5 month old son Thomas. Sadly Richard died of scarlatina maligna in April 1871, shortly after the census was taken. On Tuesday 26th May 1874 twenty-one year old Catherine, a widow, then married Willie's father, 28 year old Howell Llewellyn. Another name given to Willie Llewellyn while he was at Christ College was his nickname 'Spider', this he acquired because he was believed to have long and agile arms. It seems that nicknames were the order of the day at Christ College: two other Breconians who would feature with Willie in Wales's titanic battle with the 1905 All Blacks were John 'Scethrog' Williams and Arthur Flowers 'Boxer' Harding.

On Tuesday 22nd September 1896 Willie Llewellyn returned to Christ College for the annual Speech Day which had been postponed the previous term. Principal Rhys of Jesus College, Oxford presided and presented Willie Llewellyn with the science prize for forms five and six. Willie also received the modern languages prize for French. Willie Llewellyn and H M Hughes (cricket captain) were joint recipients of the cricket prize for fielding.

Chapter Two

Llwynypia Football Club Invincible Season 1896–97

WILLIE LLEWELLYN went up to Christ College, Brecon at the age of eleven in 1889. He was a young boy with ambition and potential, both sporting and academic. He left Christ College at the end of the summer term 1896 a young man with a great academic pedigree and a brilliant sporting ability. He played four years in the first eleven cricket team and three years in the first fifteen rugby team. He was rugby captain during the 1895–96 season. In his final two years at Christ College he was Victor Ludorum, winning the Christ College Athletics Sports Challenge Cup in 1895 and 1896. It was also while at Christ College Willie Llewellyn learned to play golf and at Easter 1896, together with W H Griffiths, he won the golf competition. He was the consummate sportsman with tremendous ability and a wonderful attitude. He would achieve great things on the rugby field but always remained modest and humble with regard to his achievements.

After leaving Christ College Willie was apprenticed to Mr J W Richards, a pharmacist in Pandy Square, Llwynypia. During this time Willie lived at home with his parents at the Clydach Vale Hotel, Clydach Vale, Rhondda. Willie was employed as a Chemist's Assistant and remained with Mr Richards until he left to complete his pharmaceutical studies at the Royal Pharmaceutical College, Bloomsbury, London in January 1900.

Having played twelve games for Llwynypia during the 1895–96 rugby season, whilst still at Christ College, Brecon, it was natural that Willie would continue that relationship and he played for Llwynypia throughout the 1896–97 season. He continued to play for Llwynypia until the end of the 1899–1900 season despite moving to London and playing for London Welsh. Willie Llewellyn was vice-captain of Llwynypia during the 1897–98 season and captain for the 1898–99 season.

Llwynypia Rugby Football Club was founded in 1891, one of several Rhondda teams to emerge with the industrialisation of the valleys, when the mining of the coalfields led to a mass influx of economic migrants. In the early 1890's Llwynypia, along with other local clubs such as Treorchy, Ferndale and Penygraig, were represented in the newly formed Welsh Football Union.

During the early years Llwynypia were an average team but that all changed during the 1894–95 season. Under the captaincy of Dr Wilfrid Daniel they played 33 games won 25, drew 4 and lost just four. They narrowly lost to Bridgend at home by 2 points, a dropped goal against two unconverted tries. They lost by the same margin away to Llanelly, an unconverted try against a converted try, Llanelly scoring in the last minute of the game. They lost at home to Mountain Ash by a try to a penalty goal and a try. Their heaviest defeat was away to Neath where they lost by a try (3 points) to three goals (15 points) having beaten them by 2 tries (6 points) to nil earlier in the season. With 311 points for and only 81 against they scored more points than any team in Wales. Tom Williams was the top try scorer with 25 tries. Llwynypia were also the possessors of the cup and medals of the Merthyr, Aberdare and Rhondda Valleys League. They were League champions for the first time and out of the 13 League matches played they won 10,

Llwynypia Football Club Cap.
Glamorgan League Champions 1894–95

lost 1 and drew 2. In the last game of the season they defeated Mountain Ash in the final for the Cup at Pontypridd.

The fact that there is a Scottish thistle on the front of the Llwynypia Football Club cap is no coincidence. The association with Scotland goes back to 1863 when Scottish mining engineer Archibald Hood leased land at Llwynypia and sank the Llwynypia No.1 pit. Despite many difficulties Hood continued his endeavours and under the name of the Glamorgan Coal Company had sunk four more pits by 1873. Archibald Hood was a popular figure in the area and his mines became known as the 'Scotch mines' after Hood himself and the number of Scottish miners who followed him to live and work in Llwynypia.

It was a well-known fact in Llwynypia that had it not been for the financial support and assistance of Archibald Hood and his son W Walter Hood, the Llwynypia Football Club and team could not have made the rapid strides and brilliant records which they had done since their formation in 1891. It is no wonder that Llwynypia adopted the Scottish thistle as the emblem for their football cap. Mr W Walter Hood was president of the Glamorgan Football League in 1896 and later became their patron.

These were the glory years of success for Llwynypia; during the 1895–96 season, under the captaincy of W H Mills, they played 39 matches, won 26, lost 10 and drew 3. They scored 435 points for, with 135 against. Tom Williams was again top try scorer with 22 tries. This was the first season Willie Llewellyn played for Llwynypia. Even though he was in his final year at Christ College, Brecon, he played for Llwynypia during the holiday periods. Willie played in twelve matches during the season and scored eight tries. During this season they promised much and defeated several top flight clubs including Neath, Bridgend, Pontypridd, Northampton and Mountain Ash; the Glamorgan League champions.

By 1895 the Welsh selectors began re-evaluating the needs of the Welsh pack and began looking for a more physical style of player. These players would be able to jump and scrummage, but would also be able to take and hand out rough play. This type of forward was found in the valley clubs, strong colliers who would be dubbed the 'Rhondda forward'. This new breed of forward was first represented in 1896 by Treorchy's Sam Ramsey and Penygraig's Dai Evans, and in January 1897 coal cutter Dick Hellings became the first player from Llwynypia Football Club to represent his country.

The 1896–97 season was an excellent one for Llwynypia when they were undefeated. Under the captaincy of Tom Williams they played 33 games, won 32 and drew just one against Mountain Ash. They scored 642 points with just 54 against. They were Glamorgan League champions and defeated some high class opposition including Neath (twice), Swansea, Bridgend (twice), Mountain Ash, Penarth (twice) and Penygraig (three times). This was a year when Llwynypia's success began to attract talent from other clubs and Welsh international forward Jack Evans of Llanelly together with Billy Alexander and Bob Jones of Ferndale joined the club. Willie Llewellyn played in all thirty-three games and scoring in twenty-two of the games he was top try scorer with thirty-eight tries. Tom Williams was next with twenty-four, Isaac Edmunds scored eighteen, Jack Evans scored thirteen, Dick Hellings nine, Billy Alexander eight and Bob Jones scored three tries.

Willie Llewellyn, still only eighteen at the beginning of the season and the youngest member of the team, had come of age and was demonstrating that he could compete with the best at the top of the game. His good form for Llwynypia was rewarded when he was selected to play in the first Welsh international trial match played at Penygraig early in November 1896. Along with fellow Llwynypia teammates Tom Williams, Isaac Edmunds, Andrew Powell, Jack Evans and Dick Hellings he was selected to play for the Mid-District against the West. The West team was made up of players from Neath, Aberavon, Llanelly, Bridgend and Swansea. Despite the Mid-District winning this match by 16 points to four and Willie scoring a try he did not feature in either of the two remaining Welsh trials and was not selected to play for Wales in their only international match of the season, against England, in January 1897.

There were no Llwynypia representatives in the second Welsh international trial match played at Penarth on Wednesday 11th November 1896. In reality there were probably a larger number of refusals than acceptances of the invitations given by the committee of the Welsh Football Union to men whom they thought worthy of a trial. Consequently the sides had to be hastily arranged and with two fairly weak teams the match created practically no interest whatsoever. The Stripes won the encounter beating the Whites by 14 points to nine.

The final international trial match, East v West, took place at Cardiff Arms Park on Saturday 5th December 1896. Although there were some changes from the sides originally chosen the teams were more representative than those for the second Welsh trial. There were three Llwynypia players in the West team; Tom Williams, Jack Evans and Dick Hellings. In a tight game the East were the eventual winners by 17 points to thirteen. When the Wales team to face England at Rodney Parade, Newport, on Saturday 9th January 1897, was announced both Dick Hellings and Jack Evans from Llwynypia were in the side. Tom Williams, together with Owen Badger of Llanelly, was selected as reserve centre. As good a player as Tom Williams was, he was never to gain a Welsh rugby international cap. For Dick Hellings this was the first of nine caps he gained for Wales. For Jack Evans this was the last of three Welsh caps he gained, having won two previously whilst playing for Llanelly.

Dick Hellings who gained nine caps for Wales between 1897 and 1901.

Also playing in the final trial match at Cardiff was Arthur Gould of Newport. In January 1896, following the Wales victory over Scotland, "Old Stager" in his notes on the game in the *South Wales Daily News* suggested that a testimonial fund should be opened in his honour. Arthur Gould made his twenty-fifth appearance for Wales in that game, a record only equalled by Bill Maclagan of Scotland. Maclagan was one of the longest-serving international rugby players during the early development of the sport, and was awarded 25 caps for Scotland. He played international rugby for thirteen seasons, a Scottish record for sixty years and led the first official British Isles team on its 1891 tour of South Africa.

Maclagan's contributions to the early development of rugby were recognised in 2009 with his induction into the IRB Hall of Fame.

Little did "Old Stager" realise what controversy his suggestion was going to cause. The fund opened on Monday 27th January 1896 and by the Wednesday had raised 2,400 shillings (£120). By the beginning of April the value of fund had risen to 10,500 shillings (£525) and at a meeting of the committee responsible for the management of the fund it was reported that the Welsh Football Union had passed a resolution sanctioning the gift (conditionally on it taking the form of a present to Mr Gould of the deeds of his house) and promising themselves to subscribe 1000 shillings (£50) to the fund.

Arthur Joseph Gould, the Newport three-quarter, played rugby for Wales on twenty-seven occasions. He captained them eighteen times.

In March 1896 Arthur Gould captained Wales against Ireland at Lansdowne Road. Wales lost by 8 points to four with Arthur Gould dropping a goal for Wales. At this time there was no hint of the storm that was brewing but by May the question of the Arthur Gould Testimonial Fund entered a new phase. The various other Rugby Unions considered that the fund involved the question of professionalism and a meeting of representatives of the Rugby Unions of the four countries was arranged to discuss the issue. Early in September 1896 Arthur Gould announced his retirement from the game and a few days later the *South Wales Daily Post* ran the following story: 'News has reached us today from a trustworthy source which seems to denote that there is more than meets the eye in Arthur Gould's retirement from Welsh football. It will be remembered that the testimonial fund was got up last season for the benefit of the famous three-quarter and realised between £600 and £700.

The committee charged with the arrangements used the money to purchase a house, in which Arthur Gould now lives as tenant, the lease not having been handed over to him pending the difficulties of the Union authorities. The members of the Welsh Union Committee, when the matter was brought before them, unanimously decided to contribute £50 to the fund. Subsequently, however, when it was found that the action would demand a violation of the rules of amateurism it was decided to appeal for an expression of opinion to the International Rugby Football Board. The latter condemned the proposal in the most emphatic way, whilst acknowledging that no man identified with the game better deserved recognition than Gould.'

When the Welsh Football Union originally put the matter before the International Rugby Football Board, England, Ireland and Scotland were dead against Gould being given the money. After a further meeting with the International Board a communication was sent to the Welsh Committee demanding that the resolution to give a sum to Gould be rescinded or international fixtures with England, Scotland and Ireland would be cancelled. The Welsh Football Union had no option but to withdraw the offer of £50 to the fund. The fact that Arthur Gould had now decided to retire meant that he was at liberty to accept the testimonial in the form decided upon by the promoters of the fund and the question of cancelled Welsh international fixtures between England, Scotland and Ireland would now be resolved.

The fact that Arthur Gould subsequently decided not to retire and continued to play rugby for Newport and was selected for and played in the final Welsh trial at Cardiff complicated matters further. Tensions were heightened when he was subsequently selected to play for and captain Wales against England at Rodney Parade on 9th January 1897 with the issue of his house deeds still not resolved. In February 1897 the Welsh Football Union wrote to the IRFB and withdrew their membership. The Welsh Football Union claimed that they alone had authority over the matter because the IRFB did not have any rules regarding amateurism. Although the fixture with England had gone ahead, Scotland and Ireland refused to play Wales, accusing the Welsh Football Union of 'professionalism'. Arthur Gould retired after the England match and at a banquet at the Drill Hall, Stow Hill, Newport, on Easter Monday 1897,

Sir John Llewellyn, the Welsh Football Union President, presented him with the deeds of his house. Wales did not field another international team until the International Rugby Football Board, supported by the Rugby Football Union (England), recommended that the Welsh Football Union be readmitted into the organisation in February 1898. The Welsh Football Union agreed that they would in future abide by all IRFB by-laws, and that Gould would not be allowed to play in any future internationals. Having already retired from the game Gould accepted the ruling but returned to rugby as a referee and Welsh international selector. Arthur Gould played for Wales on twenty-seven occasions and captained them eighteen times.

As previously stated, Willie Llewellyn played in all thirty-three fixtures for Llwynypia during the 1896–97 season. He scored two tries in the first game of the season when Llwynypia defeated Grangetown at home and another in the second game in the victory over Ebbw Vale.

In the third game of the season against Penarth the Llwynypia line was crossed for the first time. This was the first visit of Penarth to Llwynypia and as both teams had started the season well there was a lot of interest in the game. Penarth were first to score when their captain G W Shepherd crossed for a try which Matthews easily converted. In reply Llwynypia scored two unconverted tries through Williams and Iestyn Thomas. Still it was a very tight game and Llwynypia were leading by just one point at the interval. Late in the second half F Yeoman scored a try which Mills converted to give Llwynypia a six point advantage. Towards the end of the game Llwynypia were awarded a free-kick and Charlie Williams dropped a magnificent goal to put the game out of reach for Penarth with the final score Llwynypia 14, Penarth five.

In the next game at home to Risca both teams were short and played with fourteen men. In wet weather the visitors managed to get to the home twenty-five but Tom Williams, getting the ball after it was heeled, ran three-quarters of the length of the field and passed to Edmunds who scored behind the posts, Williams converting. The game continued in a severe storm which made accurate play almost impossible. With conditions worsening both sides agreed to abandon the game after fifteen minutes of play. Llwynypia thus winning by 5 points to nil.

Willie was back to scoring ways in the next game when Llwynypia played Crumlin away. Early on matters were very even but when Crumlin were awarded a penalty kick for an infringement they were able to take play well into the Llwynypia half of the field. Here Evans of Crumlin made a mark and James scored the goal giving the home team a four point advantage. Almost immediately Llwynypia replied with a try by Willie Llewellyn. George Mills successfully converted. At the interval Llwynypia were ahead by one point and early in the second half Tom Williams dodged several opponents and went over with the second try, which he himself nicely converted. With no further scores Llwynypia were victorious by 10 points to four. At forward the teams were evenly matched but at half-back and three-quarter Llwynypia were without question far superior.

Willie Llewellyn was in outstanding form and scored four tries in the away victory over Morriston. He then scored another four tries in the home victory over Bridgend. Willie scored again in Llwynypia's next game at home against Pontypridd when Llwynypia scored thirty points without reply. After this great performance it was anticipated that a lot of interest would be shown in the forthcoming Welsh trial match played the following Monday. Five Llwynypia men were selected for the Mid-District team to face the West at Penygraig. Willie Llewellyn's great form had earned him a place in the team along with fellow teammates, Tom Williams, Isaac Edmunds, Andrew Powell and Dick Hellings.

This was the first of three Welsh trial matches held before the international against England in January 1897. There was a large and enthusiastic crowd and the game was well above the ordinary as far as trial matches go. There is no doubt that the better team won, everywhere but at forward the Rhondda men were streets ahead of the Westerners. At forward matters were pretty even. The West opened the scoring thanks to a beautiful drop-goal from a mark by Joe Davies. Mid-District replied with a try by Tom Williams after a magnificent run. T Jones failed to convert. In the second half the Mid-District team took control and Dick Hellings scored their second try with three or four of the opposition hanging on his back. Tom Williams converted. A few seconds later the Mid-District crossed again when Bradford scored a splendid try. Tom Williams failed to convert. Towards the end of the game some excellent passing between Phillips, Edmunds and Tom Williams resulted in Willie Llewellyn receiving a scoring pass. Tom Williams converted and with no further scoring the Mid-District team were victorious by 16 points to four.

Despite having a great game and scoring a try Willie Llewellyn did not feature in the remaining two trial matches. Dick Hellings, Tom Williams and Jack Evans, from Llwynypia, were more successful, playing in the East v West final trial match at Cardiff Arms Park on Saturday 5th December 1896. The team to face England was selected at a meeting of the Welsh Football Union immediately following the trial match and both Dick Hellings and Jack Evans were selected to play. Tom Williams and Owen Bader were selected as the reserve centres.

Early in November it had been decided to give caps to all the players taking part in the final trial match, East v West. It was stated that the caps would be very similar in design to the international caps. The chief embellishment being the Prince of Wales feathers together with the letters "E v W".

Following the West v Mid-District Welsh trial match all the Llwynypia men involved in the trial turned out for Llwynypia when they faced Penygraig on the Belle Vue Ground the following Saturday. David Evans, John Rapps and T Jones, who had also played in the trial, turned out for Penygraig. Llwynypia scored two unconverted tries in the first half through Isaac Edmunds and Williams. Just before half-time Willie Llewellyn was unlucky not to score after a good run. With rain falling heavily during the second half Llwynypia scored a further three unconverted tries through Iestyn Thomas, Tom Williams and Jack Evans. The final score was Llwynypia 15 points, Penygraig nil.

Llwynypia had one of their biggest wins of the season in their next game at home against Merthyr. Tom Williams opened the scoring with an unconverted try. Jack Evans was next to score with George Mills converting. Ben Phillips then scored another unconverted try. This was followed by another unconverted try by Willie Llewellyn. Jack Evans then scored his second try of the game followed by another just before half time from Willie Llewellyn. With neither being converted Llwynypia led at the interval by 20 points to nil. In the second half Llwynypia scored a further nine tries, five of which were converted. The final score was Llwynypia 57 points Merthyr nil.

The record of Llwynypia Football Club for the 1896–97 season, reported in the *Evening Express* in May 1897, stated that Willie Llewellyn had scored 38 tries during the season. Although the nine second-half tries scored against Merthyr in this match are unaccounted for it is believed that Willie Llewellyn scored two of them bringing his total for the game to four. Excluding the trial match, this would have brought Willie's total number of tries for the season so far to 17 in just ten games.

The only match of the season Llwynypia didn't win was their next match played away to Mountain Ash. This was always going to be a well contested match. Both teams had played ten games and won them all. Mountain Ash had been League champions the previous year and alongside Llwynypia were second in the table at this point in the season. Treherbert were on top of the league table but with a two game advantage. In some respects this was a disappointing game with very little in the way of open and exciting rugby. The referee did his best to conduct the game in accordance with the rules but there were a number of infringements allowed to go unpunished with the result that players on both sides frequently took advantage with fouls and tackles with more than a suspicion of undue roughness. The Llwynypia three-quarters did most of the attacking, nevertheless, Mountain Ash held out and utilised to better effect their fewer opportunities. The one clear chance in the game fell to Tom Williams but this was missed by him failing to take the ball and as a result the game ended in a no score drawn game.

Willie scored again in the next game at home to Penygraig with George Mills converting. This was the only score of the game which Llwynypia won by 5 points to nil. It was reported in the *South Wales Daily News* that Penygraig were very unhappy with some of the referee's decisions. They claimed that the scoring pass to Willie Llewellyn was at least five yards forwards besides being taken with a knock-on. They also claimed that in the first half they had to play 40 minutes 'against a regular gale of wind' and in the second half, when they had the wind in their favour, they were only allowed to play for 20 minutes.

In the next game, away to Neath, Llwynypia had their line crossed for only the second time thus far into the season. Llwynypia led at the interval by 8 points to nil thanks to a converted try by Mills and an unconverted try by Andrew Powell. In the second half Llwynypia scored two further unconverted tries through Ben Phillips and Edmunds before Neath got on the scoresheet. Charlie Powell, the Neath captain, took advantage of a kick by Hopkins and by following up scored a very clever try. Tom Saunders converted with a superb kick. Towards the end of the game a fine round of passing by the Llwynypia three-quarters resulted in Edmunds running twenty-five yards to cross for a try which Williams converted. With no further scoring Llwynypia won by 19 points to five. A report of the game in the *South Wales Daily News* remarked, 'At forward Neath were immeasurably superior, but it was at three-quarters the Hillmen had matters all their own way. Three of the tries were really the outcome of the smartest combined play ever witnessed on the Neath ground.'

Playing at full-back for Neath in this game was Tom Saunders. Tom had also played in the first Welsh trial at Penygraig, playing at full-back for the West team. The following week when Llwynypia played Ebbw Vale, Tom Saunders was playing full-back for Llwynypia. He also played against Merthyr and toured with the team to Devon where he played against Plymouth and Exmouth. He also played in the game against Penygraig early in January 1897. For some reason, probably injury, Saunders did not play again until the game against Cardiff District towards the end of March. Charlie Williams who had been playing full-back since the start of the season moved to the three-quarters and during Saunders' absence reverted to full-back. A report of a meeting of the Welsh Football Union that appeared in the *Weekly Mail* early in January 1897 confirmed that Tom Saunders had indeed transferred to Llwynypia from Neath.

Following the Neath game it was eight games before Llwynypia had another point scored against them. They defeated Crumlin at home by 8 points to nil and then won five consecutive away games. They defeated Ebbw Vale, Merthyr, Plymouth, Exmouth and Penygraig before defeating Treorky at home. Willie Llewellyn scored six tries in these victories.

Having scored another try in the away win against Penygraig, taking his Llwynypia total for the season to twenty-three, a report in the *Evening Express* the day following the match sang the praises of Willie Llewellyn. The report read, 'Llewellyn, who played right of Tom Williams, is not far off being the fastest amateur in South Wales. One sprint he did on Monday was terrific. He cleared right round half a dozen men when it seemed 100 to 1 against him. His brother told me afterwards that at Brecon

College he won every race he entered for and did the 100 yards in 10.4 secs. Of course that is school timings, which is not often trustworthy. Llewellyn is, I am assured, quite four yards faster now than he was then. That being so, and with any degree of accuracy about the Brecon timing, I should say Llewellyn is not far off being a half-second man, which means that he ought to win the Welsh championship and any number of handicaps.' Praise indeed, Willie Llewellyn was now really getting noticed for his speed and try scoring ability.

As previously stated, the only international match of the 1896–97 season was against England at Rodney Parade, Newport, on Saturday 9th January 1897. Dick Hellings of Llwynypia had been selected for his first Welsh international cap and Jack Evans, also of Llwynypia, had been selected for his third cap. Tom Williams, the Llwynypia captain, had been selected as reserve centre. With a game between Penygraig and Llwynypia on the Monday prior to the international, the Welsh Football Union requested

Wales Team v England 1897

Back Row: W Morris, D Hellings, J Evans, D Evans, J Rapps, F Cornish, H Packer, T Williams (WFU). *Middle Row:* T W Pearson, W J Bancroft, A J Gould (Captain), A W Boucher, E G Nicholls. *Front Row:* C A Bowen, D Jones, S H Biggs.

that players involved in the international should not play in that match. This involved Dick Hellings, Jack Evans and Tom Williams of Llwynypia and David Evans and Jack Rapps of Penygraig. Although David Evans and Jack Rapps stood down from the game, Dick Hellings, Jack Evans and Tom Williams all played for Llwynypia. This did not please the Welsh Football Union and it was thought probable that both Dick Hellings and Jack Evans would be replaced in the team by J H Williams of Swansea and Ivor Griffiths of Aberavon. Subsequently both Dick Hellings and Jack Evans played in the international which Wales won by 11 points to nil.

The Welsh Football Union representative on the far right in the Wales team photograph on the previous page is Tom Williams. He was one of eleven new caps who played against Ireland at Lansdowne Road, Dublin in January 1882. This was only the second international match ever played by Wales who had contested their first match, against England, at Blackheath in February 1881 when they were heavily beaten by 13 tries, 7 conversions and a drop goal to nil. No actual points were awarded in International games until 1891. Wales defeated Ireland by 4 tries and 2 conversions to nil. Robert Gould, the first of three brothers of this famous family to play for Wales, appeared in the Welsh pack as did Hugh Vincent from Trinity College, Dublin, who was knighted in 1924. Tom Jones scored the first ever Wales try in this game. This was Tom Williams' only cap for Wales. Tom Williams, a solicitor, was Willie Llewellyn's uncle; he was the half-brother of Willie's mother. He served on the Welsh Football Union committee as a vice-president and selector and was a representative on the International Board from 1901 until 1908. He refereed the match between England and Ireland in 1904 and appears in several team photographs as a touch judge.

Llwynypia's next game, away to Penarth, was a very close run affair. In a fast and open game the teams were fairly evenly matched but after sustained pressure by Llwynypia they were able to score two unconverted tries before the interval, Jack Evans and Isaac Edmunds being the scorers. In the second half Penarth were the aggressors and were rewarded with an unconverted try by Hudd. Under severe pressure Llwynypia failed to defend their line and W J Evans burst through magnificently between Tom Williams and Isaac Edmunds and scored almost under the posts. An easy conversion put Llwynypia 8 points to six in arrears, and with the second half almost over it looked like their first defeat of the season was on the cards. Try as they might, Llwynypia failed to force Penarth out of their half. Then a fatal mistake by Penarth gave Llwynypia a penalty and a foothold in their quarter of the field. With only three or four minutes remaining Llwynypia gained possession from a scrum and four of the forwards, travelling abreast, beat the home tackling by short passes to one another. The last pass reached Jack Evans who dived over for the try. Although Mills failed to convert, it was enough to give Llwynypia victory by 9 points to eight. Llwynypia won their next four games quite easily. They defeated Penygraig at home by 25 points to nil and then beat Neath at home by 28 points to five. Then two easy away victories against Pontypridd, by 22 points to nine, and Treorky, by 19 points to nil, brought their results for the season to: played 25, won 24, drawn one.

On Thursday 25th February Christ College, Brecon, journeyed to Llwynypia to play a team put together by Christ College Old Boy, Willie Llewellyn. With the rain pouring down all morning prior to the game the state of the ground was not good. Nevertheless Willie Llewellyn's team were able to make the best of the conditions and by the interval they had scored 2 goals and 3 tries (19 points). With the wind in their favour the College played much better in the second half. Mr Thomas scored an unconverted try and then almost immediately after the re-start dropped a magnificent goal. Partridge finished the scoring for the College with an unconverted try. Willie Llewellyn's team only managed to score one try in the second half but still ran out comfortable winners by 22 points to ten.

This was by no means a disgrace. Willie Llewellyn's team was a strong one. Charlie Williams, the Llwynypia custodian, was at full-back and Tom Williams, the Llwynypia captain, was in the three-quarters alongside Willie Llewellyn and his younger brother Evan. Elder brother John Llewellyn, another Christ College Old Boy, was at half-back and the recently capped Welsh international, Dick Hellings, was in the forwards.

There is an amusing story that relates to this game such that the masters and pupils travelled from Brecon to Llwynypia by train and although they arrived safely the return journey home was a different matter. While the boys caught the train back to Brecon and arrived back on time the masters didn't, possibly delayed in a local hostelry. With regard to the trip to Llwynypia the April 1897 edition of *The Breconian* published the following amusing parody:

CHAPTER TWO

LLWYNYPIA

[In Commemoration of Thursday 25th February 1897.]
Tune: Mandalay.

In the rustic Rhondda Valley, where the sun so softly shines,
There are countless railway junctions and endless railway lines;
And an unexpected journey (as you shall shortly hear)
Upset our calculations on the road from Llwynypia.

On the road from Llwynypia, where the skies are bright and clear;
Can't you hear the porters calling, "All change for Merthyr here?"
On the road from Llwynypia, where the skies are bright and clear,
And the boys get back quite safely, but the masters disappear.

Oh, that lovely winter's morning when we caught the early train,
And we reached our destination in a blinding storm of rain?
But we soon forgot our changes and our multitudinous stops
When our famished frames we feasted on a pile of mutton chops.

In the town of Llwynypia where we heard the pitmen cheer,
And they play a sort of billiards that evokes a friendly jeer;
On the road from Llwynypia where the skies are bright and clear,
And the boys get back quite safely, but the masters disappear.

The game – it soon was over, and then 'twas our desire
To excavate our persons from tons of Rhondda mire;
And we recommenced our travels on a somewhat slight repast,
But we didn't watch the stations until Pontypridd was past!

On the road from Llwynypia, "Don't we change for Merthyr here?"
Can't you hear the prefects whisp'ring, "They've missed the train we fear."
On the road from Llwynypia, where the skies are bright and clear,
And the boys get back quite safely, but the masters disappear.

So backward in confusion our laggard steps we traced,
And we urged the festive goods-train to forward us "with haste,"
But as we thought we'd finished our troubles just begin,
For we find we've got to tramp it from the station at Talyllyn.

On the road from Llwynypia "Are you sure the foot-path's here?"
"Can you hear the town clock striking? It's half-past two, or near!"
On the road from Llwynypia, where the skies are bright and clear,
And the boys get back quite safely, but the masters disappear.

Llwynypia's next game was at home to Mountain Ash. Considerable interest was taken in this game on account of the keen manner in which the previous game between these two clubs had been played out earlier in the season. Circumstances were a little different for this game. While Llwynypia had not lost a game since that encounter Mountain Ash had lost several games. When the teams took the field shortly after four o'clock, there were 6,000 spectators present. The first half was evenly contested if not a little rough and the referee had to call the two sides together and admonish them because of the unnecessary roughness of their play. With no score in the first half the game continued to be a close affair until after missing several chances to score Powell got clean away from a scrummage and beating all the opposition, threw to Bob Jones, who struggled over the line to score an unconverted try for Llwynypia. Towards the end of the game Llwynypia scored again when George Mills crossed for a try near the posts which Tom Williams converted. Just before the end of the game the Llwynypia forwards were again attacking and Willie Llewellyn was within an ace of scoring when the final whistle blew, leaving Llwynypia victorious by 8 points to nil.

When the match committee of the Glamorgan League met at the White Hart Hotel, Pontypridd to select the team to play the Monmouthshire League it was no surprise that there were four Llwynypia players in the side. Tom Williams, Willie Llewellyn, Dick Hellings and Jack Evans were all chosen to play while Iestyn Thomas and Billy Alexander were picked in the reserves. On the day Dick Hellings was unable to play and Billy Alexander took his place in the team.

The game took place at Taff Vale Park, Pontypridd and was watched by about 6,000 spectators. The teams were evenly matched and after some fine play by both sides the Glamorgan League were the first to score when Tom Davies of Treherbert rounded his opposite centre and scored behind the posts. Tom Williams failed to convert. Late in the half a mistake by Tom Williams let Tom Lewis in for a try which Sawell, despite a good effort, failed to convert. At the interval the score stood at three points each. In the second half the Glamorgan League side went ahead when Morgan dashed over for a try which Tom Jones failed to convert. Towards the end of the game Jack Evans picked up from a dribble and running strongly scored behind the posts. M'Kenzie converted and with no further scores the Glamorgan League team won by 11 points to three. The win in their next game against Barry put Llwynypia on top of the Glamorgan League table with 23 points. Treherbert and Mountain Ash were second in the table, both with 17 points apiece, albeit that they both had four games in-hand.

In the away match at Bath, Llwynypia had a fine victory by 37 points to five and in their next game against Cardiff District they had their biggest win of the season winning by 63 points to nil. Willie Llewellyn scored four tries and Tom Saunders, playing in his first game since early January, kicked seven conversions.

By the time Llwynypia faced Swansea at St Helen's on Saturday 27th March they had played twenty-nine games, won twenty-eight and drawn one. Swansea were without their international full-back Billy Bancroft, who was laid up with a throat infection and despite being without several other key players including Rice, Tom Jackson and Hopkin Davies, they were still a very strong side. At half-backs they had Evan and David James. They had both been capped by Wales, Evan on four occasions and David on three occasions. Evan gained his first cap against Scotland in 1890 and then the brothers played together against Ireland in 1891 and against Scotland and Ireland in 1892. They

Evan and David James who played for Swansea Rugby Football Club from 1889 until January 1899.

were known as 'the Swansea gems' or 'the curly-headed marmosets'. They first played for Swansea in 1889. Having played for Wales against Scotland and Ireland earlier in the year the brothers apparently played a game for Broughton Rangers in April 1892 and were offered jobs at £2 a week in Manchester. The Rugby Football Union declared them to be professional. As a consequence they were unable to play rugby until they were reinstated by the Rugby Football Union after an appeal by the Welsh Football Union and Swansea Rugby Football Club on 31st January 1896.

Albert Mortimer Jenkin who played for Wales against Ireland in 1895 and England 1896.

After a gap of seven years they played their last international for Wales in the game against England at St Helen's in January 1899. This was the game in which Willie Llewellyn made his debut for Wales and scored four tries in the 26 points to three victory. Three weeks after that match Evan and David James turned professional when they joined Broughton Rangers on 28th January 1899.

Also in the Swansea side to face Llwynypia was Albert Jenkin, who, in the absence of John Prescott, was probably captain on the day. Albert made his debut for Swansea in 1893 and was made captain in 1895–96. He resigned the captaincy in November 1895 because of his professional duties; he was a qualified mining engineer. Billy Bancroft took over as captain for the remainder of the season. Albert Mortimer Jenkin represented Wales on two occasions, in the victory over Ireland at Cardiff in 1895 and in the heavy defeat against England at Blackheath in 1896.

Llwynypia played into a strong wind in the first half and in a hard and vigorous game Swansea were the first to score when A Jones dashed over by the posts for a try which Smith converted. Llwynypia were finding it tough playing against the wind and during the first half their backs only received the ball on one occasion. By contrast every time the Swansea backs got the ball they punted it down field keeping play close to the Llwynypia line. With no further scores in the first half, Swansea were ahead at the interval by 5 points to nil.

Early in the second half, despite the wind being in Llwynypia's favour, Swansea had managed to keep play in the visitor's half of the field. The first chance for Llwynypia came after a free kick, the forwards followed up and twice they nearly scored. Some hard work by the Swansea forwards and some clever play by Evan and David James got Swansea out of danger as they worked their way up to the centre of the field. Nevertheless, the Llwynypia forwards continued to press and they were rewarded moments later when a nice run and transfer by Tom Williams put Willie Llewellyn in with a try. Charlie Williams failed with the conversion. With Swansea still ahead a brilliant piece of work by Tom Williams gave Llwynypia the lead. He shook off several opponents and then passed out to the right where Willie Llewellyn got possession and scored in the corner. Charlie Williams again failed to convert. Time was called shortly afterwards and Llwynypia had won a very close game by 6 points to five.

At forward the teams were fairly well matched but at half-back the brothers James simply smothered the Llwynypia pair. Tom Saunders did not have his best game at full-back and on several occasions fumbled the ball which got Llwynypia into trouble. At three-quarter Llwynypia were too fast and too clever for the Swansea backs. On the Swansea side the brothers James were the most dangerous, whilst for Llwynypia Tom Williams was the perfect centre and Willie Llewellyn took his chances well to score his two tries.

Having defeated Swansea a serious threat to Llwynypia's record had been alleviated. With only four games remaining it looked quite possible that Llwynypia would go the whole season without being beaten. Still there were two tough games to come against Treherbert and there was a possibility that they could lose their unbeaten record and not win the Glamorgan League. Llwynypia won their next two games quite easily, when they defeated Barry at home by 33 points to nil and then defeated Bridgend away by 29 points to five. Willie Llewellyn scored a try in each game.

On Monday 12th April 1897 Llwynypia played the most important game of their season when they faced Treherbert at home in the Glamorgan

League. Victory would mean that they would remain undefeated but more importantly it would make them Glamorgan League champions. Victory would put them top of the table with 29 points and Treherbert in second place with 25 points. With both teams having played fifteen games, defeat in the final League match of the season, scheduled for Thursday 29th April, would make no difference to the League table and Llwynypia would still be champions, although they would of course lose their undefeated status.

The game was played on a pitch which was nothing but mud and mire. There was a dreary downpour the whole of the morning prior to the game and it continued until the teams took the field a few minutes after half-past five. The result of the match was evident right from the start. Pressing hard for the first ten minutes Llwynypia were in control and a couple of minutes later Iestyn Thomas crossed for an unconverted try. Playing against the wind Treherbert found it difficult to get out of their own twenty-five and following a scrummage Tom Williams made a dash for the line and scored in the corner. The conversion was unsuccessful. Llwynypia continued to attack and came close to scoring on several occasions. Treherbert also had their chances but with no further scores Llwynypia were ahead at the interval by 6 points to nil.

In the second half Llwynypia had the wind and rain in their faces but this did not stop them playing some exciting rugby. One minute the ball was in the home twenty-five and the next it was near the visitor's goal line. Then it was Treherbert's time to take control and for a couple of minutes they had much the better of the action. Eventually Andrew Powell dribbled from the half-way line right into the visitors half of the field. Here the Treherbert full-back deliberately and foolishly kicked the ball across his own line. Ben Phillips was up in attack and scored a try which Andrew Powell converted. Treherbert responded courageously and were unlucky not to score. They kept the pressure on Llwynypia right up to the end of the game but sound Llwynypia defence just managed to keep them out. The final score was Llwynypia 11 points Treherbert nil.

The victory was a decisive one and thoroughly deserved and clearly proved that Llwynypia were unmistakably the champions of the League. In spite of the wretched weather and the state of the ground, the game was a very interesting one and far more open than expected. A report in the *Evening Express* made reference to a novel sight towards the end of the game when they reported, 'At the bottom end of the ground is a heap over which the colliers, on their way to the Glamorgan Pit, have to pass. Just before seven o'clock, when the rain was coming down heavily and the twilight gathering, with lowering clouds for the hill tops, on each side, a crowd of colliers with twinkling lamps in their hands and their dusky faces all aglow with excitement, took their stand on the bank previously mentioned. One was almost compelled to pay attention to the strange gathering in preference to the game, especially when, at the close of proceedings, they waved their lamps, which twinkled like so many glow-worms and so paid their silent mead of praise to the teams before they went to the bowels of the earth to commence their weary night's labour.'

Consequently Llwynypia were Rhondda champions for the second time and their unbeaten record was still intact. With one League match remaining, the return match with Treherbert, their unbeaten record could still be taken away from them. A report in the *Evening Express* suggested that there was doubt whether the game would take place and that 'Llwynypia would forego the two points and maintain their record intact.' The paper was however certain that the game would go ahead with Treherbert having prepared a great deal for the final match.

Subsequently the game was abandoned and a report in the *South Wales Echo* on Thursday 29th April read as follows: 'The last of the matches between Llwynypia and Treherbert, which was to have been played this evening, has been cancelled by Llwynypia, several of whose players are either on the sick list or injured. Llwynypia thus give Treherbert two points in the League, but as they are still two points ahead they have won the cup for this season. Last year the cup was held by Mountain Ash and the year before by Llwynypia.'

And so Llwynypia's successful season came to an end. They played 33 games, won 32 and drew just the one against Mountain Ash earlier in the season. They were Glamorgan League cup holders for the second time and could look forward to the coming season with confidence.

Llwynypia's final game of the season against Treherbert was not the last for Willie Llewellyn; he still had one more to play. Along with fellow Llwynypia teammates, Isaac Edmunds, Tom Williams, Jack Evans, Dick Hellings, Bob Jones and Ben Phillips, he was selected to play for the

Glamorgan League against Cardiff on Thursday 22nd April. It was not to be the fairy-tale ending to the campaign that Willie would have wanted. Having played in all Llwynypia's thirty-three games of the season, the first Welsh trial at Penygraig, a match against Christ College, Brecon and the Glamorgan League against the Monmouthshire League, he had not experienced defeat. That was about to change when the Glamorgan League were heavily beaten by a strong Cardiff team at Cardiff. They were beaten by 31 points to nil by a Cardiff team captained by Welsh international scrum-half Jack Elliot. Although only leading by 8 points to nil at the interval, playing with the wind, Cardiff scored four goals and a try in the second half.

The Cardiff team contained no fewer than five Welsh internationals. In addition to Jack Elliot there was Norman Biggs, Selwyn Biggs, Fred Cornish and William John Elsey. Another five of the team would be capped later: John Blake, Tom Dobson, George Dobson, Viv Huzzey and W 'Pussy' Jones. Both Tom and George Dobson went on to play for Llwynypia.

Norman Biggs was, at 18 years and 49 days, the youngest player to be capped for Wales when he played against the New Zealand Natives on Saturday 22nd December 1888. He gained eight caps for Wales between 1888 and 1894. He captained Cardiff in 1893–94 and Bath in 1899–1900. Norman Biggs served as a private in the Glamorgan Yeomanry during the Boer War and was a superintendent in the Nigerian Police. At the age of 37 he was killed by a poison arrow in a native ambush while serving in the Nigerian Police.

This record stood for just under one hundred and twenty-one years and three months. On Saturday 20th March 2010 Tom Prydie of the Ospreys became the youngest player to represent Wales when he played

Norman Biggs became the youngest player to represent Wales when he played against the New Zealand Natives in 1888.

against Italy at the Millennium Stadium, Cardiff. At just 18 years and 25 days Tom Prydie was the only new cap in the Wales team that defeated Italy by 33 points to ten.

The Glamorgan League game against Cardiff brought Willie Llewellyn's 1896–97 season to a close. In his first season of senior rugby Willie had played 37 games and scored at least 39 tries. He had played in a Welsh trial for the first time and played brilliantly for Llwynypia throughout the season. He had made a major contribution to Llwynypia being the only first class team in South Wales to be unbeaten and to them winning the Glamorgan League Cup. He must have looked forward in eager anticipation to the 1897–98 season.

The 1896–97 season will long be remembered in football circles in South Wales because of the wonderful progress made by some of the teams in the Rhondda Valley. The previous season these teams were regarded as being unworthy of fixtures with leading clubs of the Principality such as Llanelly, Cardiff, Neath, Swansea and Newport but that had all changed and now three or four of the Rhondda Valley teams were justifiably worthy of playing such distinguished opposition. Occupying the pre-eminent position was Llwynypia who had brought credit to itself and the Rhondda by going through the season with an unbeaten and brilliant record.

Had Llanelly not lost to Gloucester in the final stages of the season, they too could well have stood shoulder to shoulder with Llwynypia as the only unbeaten sides in Wales. Welsh international forward Jack Evans, formely of Llanelly but now playing for Llwynypia, turned out for a Llanelly side which was weakened by injury and sickness. They lost by the narrowest of margins going down by a goal to a try but the record had gone and it was only Llwynypia who gained the much-coveted title of Invincible.

When Llwynypia played Swansea for the first time at the end of March it was generally considered that this could be the day that the unbeaten record could be taken away from them. In a very close game two Willie Llewellyn tries gave Llwynypia victory by the narrowest of margins when they won by 6 point to five.

Throughout the season the Llwynypia team included two internationals in Dick Hellings and Jack Evans, undoubtedly two of the best forwards that had represented Wales. It is a noteworthy fact that four of the eight forwards that represented Wales in their fine victory over England in January 1897 were players from two adjoining clubs, Llwynypia and Penygraig. David Evans and Jack Rapps were the Penygraig representatives and it is well known what a conspicuous part those four burly Rhondda forwards took in the encounter on that day. Despite losing Yeoman and Hewlett, owing to the depredations of poachers from the Northern Union, the Llwynypia pack remained strong. Billy Alexander and Bob Jones, both formerly of Ferndale, played in all the matches and made a major contribution to the side.

At half-backs Andrew Powell and Iestyn Thomas did sterling work behind the scrum and there was always a perfect understanding between them. Powell proved himself to be a clever scrum-half while Thomas, at outside-half, did some smart things in the most important matches. The three-quarters scored 92 tries between them and that fact in itself shows what a smart quartette they were.

Tom Williams, who so ably captained the team during the season, never represented Wales but was one of the reserve centres chosen for the international against England in January 1897. He went North to Salford before the start of the 1897–98 season and this would have a major impact on the try scoring ability of the Llwynypia team during that season. At right centre he had good speed and great judgement. He had invariably been the top try scorer but that distinction fell to Willie Llewellyn who played on the right wing to Tom Williams during the 1896–97 season. They scored 62 tries between them during the season, Willie Llewellyn with 38 and Tom Williams with 24. Williams' strong point was his ability to make a break and pass to his wing at the right moment. Willie Llewellyn, at nineteen, was the youngest player in the team and with a rare turn of speed and excellent judgement was, even at this early stage in his career, identified as a possible future international. He was quick to utilise the smallest chance and was a very dangerous player whenever near his opponent's goal-line. Ike Edmunds at left centre had great speed and great defence. Some of the eighteen tries he scored during the season were sensational. George Mills on the left wing was also very fast and scored twelve tries during the season. He also had a knack of covering the full-back whenever the goal-line was threatened.

Charlie Williams at full-back was at times safe as a rock and the fact that the Llwynypia line was only crossed on eleven occasions during the season shows that his defensive ability was of the highest order. The team was assisted upon a few occasions by Tom Jenkins of the 2nd XV, Tom and George Dobson of Cardiff, Falcon of Treorky and P C Rees of Pontypridd.

As a result of such an outstanding season Llwynypia were rewarded with a number of excellent fixtures for the following season which included for the first time home and away fixtures with Cardiff, Llanelly and Gloucester. Swansea would only give one date at Swansea but as they would not play at Llwynypia no games were arranged and they did not play each other during the 1897–98 season.

Willie Llewellyn Rugby Games Played 1896-1897 Season					
Willie Llewellyn International Trial Game Played 1896-1897 Season					
Willie Llewellyn Non Llwynypia Rugby Games Played 1896-1897 Season					
Date	Team Played For	Opposition	Venue	Result/Score	W Llewllyn Tries
19/09/1896	Llwynypia	Grangetown	Home	Won 27-0	2
26/09/1896	Llwynypia	Ebbw Vale	Home	Won 11-0	1
03/10/1896	Llwynypia	Penarth	Home	Won 14-5	0
05/10/1896	Llwynypia	Risca	Home	Won 5-0	0
10/10/1896	Llwynypia	Crumlin	Away	Won 10-4	1
17/10/1896	Llwynypia	Morriston	Away	Won 29-0	4
24/10/1896	Llwynypia	Bridgend	Home	Won 30-0	4
31/10/1896	Llwynypia	Pontypridd	Home	Won 30-0	1
02/11/1896	Mid-District	West	Penygraig	Won 16-4	1
07/11/1896	Llwynypia	Penygraig	Away	Won 15-0	0
12/11/1896	Llwynypia	Merthyr	Home	Won 57-0	4
21/11/1896	Llwynypia	Mountain Ash	Away	Drawn 0-0	0
28/11/1896	Llwynypia	Penygraig	Home	Won 5-0	1
05/12/1896	Llwynypia	Neath	Away	Won 19-5	0
07/12/1896	Llwynypia	Crumlin	Home	Won 8-0	1
12/12/1896	Llwynypia	Ebbw Vale	Away	Won 10-0	2
19/12/1896	Llwynypia	Merthyr	Away	Won 11-0	1
25/12/1896	Llwynypia	Plymouth	Away	Won 15-0	0
26/12/1896	Llwynypia	Exmouth	Away	Won 15-0	0
04/01/1897	Llwynypia	Penygraig	Away	Won 9-0	1
16/01/1897	Llwynypia	Treorky	Home	Won 23-0	1
20/01/1897	Llwynypia	Penarth	Away	Won 9-8	0
01/02/1897	Llwynypia	Penygraig	Home	Won 25-0	1
06/02/1897	Llwynypia	Neath	Home	Won 28-5	1
13/02/1897	Llwynypia	Ponypridd	Away	Won 22-9	1
20/02/1897	Llwynypia	Treorky	Away	Won 19-0	1
25/02/1897	W M Llewellyn Esq.'s XV	Christ College, Brecon	Llwynypia	Won 22-10	No record
27/02/1897	Llwynypia	Mountain Ash	Home	Won 8-0	0
01/03/1897	Glamorgan League	Monmouthshire League	Pontypridd	Won 11-3	0
06/03/1897	Llwynypia	Barry	Away	Won 9-3	0
08/03/1897	Llwynypia	Bath	Away	Won 37-5	2
20/03/1897	Llwynypia	Cardiff District	Home	Won 63-0	4
27/03/1897	Llwynypia	Swansea	Away	Won 6-5	2
03/04/1897	Llwynypia	Barry	Home	Won 33-0	1
10/04/1897	Llwynypia	Bridgend	Away	Won 29-5	1
12/04/1897	Llwynypia	Treherbert	Home	Won 11-0	0
22/04/1897	Glamorgan League	Cardiff	Cardiff	Lost 0-31	0
	Games Played by Willie Llewellyn			Llwynypia Points For/Against	Willie Llewellyn Tries Scored
Totals	37			642/54	39

Willie Llewellyn Rugby Games Played and Results 1896–97 Season

Llwynypia "Invincibles" Football Team and Glamorgan League Champions 1896–87

Back Row: J Atkins, W H Alexander, R Jones, J Evans,
D Hellings (Vice-Captain), W Gabe, B T Phillips.
Middle Row: W Jones (Linesman), C Williams, T E Williams (Captain),
D W Royall, G L Mills, D Llewellyn (Hon.-Sec.)
Front Row: W Llewellyn, Iestyn Thomas, A Powell, I Edmunds.

The review of Llwynypia's achievements during the season would not be complete without reference being made of the support given to the club by Mr W W Hood, agent of the Glamorgan Collieries, who took a keen interest in the welfare of the team. At the start of the season he very kindly gave the use of the old Board School, the property of the company, to the team for the purpose of a gymnasium which contributed greatly to the general improvement of the players.

Celebration of the successful football season of 1896–97 finally came to an end at the annual dinner of the Llwynypia and Tonypandy Athletic Club which took place at the Tonypandy Town Hall on Thursday 14th October 1897. The Llwynypia Football Club was actually one of four sections of the Llwynypia and Tonypandy Athletic Club along with sections for cricket, tennis and quoits. The secretary of the club was

Mr David Llewellyn and it was he who helped establish the football section in 1891 having previously been a founder member of the Penygraig Football Club in 1877. During the evening the Glamorgan League cup and medals were presented to the players and in addition the players were also presented with gold Alberts subscribed for by the public of Llwynypia and Tonypandy. With Tom Williams and Charlie Williams having gone North before the presentation their medals were sent on to them. Tom and Charlie Williams were each to have also received a gold Albert but because they had joined the ranks of the professionals the committee decided to withhold them.

In 1894–95 the Llwynypia football team succeeded in winning the handsome cup given by the Glamorgan Football League in the first year of the competition. Mountain Ash won the trophy in 1895–96 and Llwynypia were again winners in 1896–97. In the summer of 1897 the Glamorgan Cricket League was formed and they immediately offered a magnificent silver challenge shield for competition among the clubs affiliated to the League. Determined not to be outdone by their football brethren, the cricketing section of the Llwynypia Athletic Club became possessors of the cricket shield. As a result both the football and cricket sections had won major Glamorgan trophies in the first year of them being offered for competition. Several of the regular players in the football team also played regularly for the cricket section, including Tom Saunders, Andrew Powell and Isaac 'Ike' Edmunds. Willie Llewellyn also played the occasional game.

Chapter Three

Llwynypia Football Club 1897–98 Season

AS EARLY AS November 1896 there were rumours that Tom Williams was about to make a move to the Northern Union. This was fuelled by a visit to Llwynypia by a Northern 'poacher' from Swinton, by the name of Mills. A meeting between Mills and Tom Williams took place at the Ivor Hael Hotel on the evening of Tuesday 10th November with the specific purpose of Swinton Northern Union Club securing the services of Tom Williams. News of the meeting spread quickly through the town and a crowd of between forty and fifty people gathered outside the hotel and ultimately some of them got inside where Mr Mills got a warm reception. He sought the protection of the Llwynypia secretary Mr Dai Llewellyn who helped him get to the railway platform en route to which Mr Mills was subjected to a storm of 'hisses and hooting' and was promised 'an immersion in the works' pond' if he put in another appearance in the locality.

A report in the *Evening Express* on Wednesday 14th July 1897 stated: 'The Northern Union clubs have started importing Welsh players, in view of the work of next season and at a meeting of the Lancashire section, held in Manchester on Tuesday night, several applications for permits were made. Four were granted, as follows: T E Williams of Llwynypia, W

CHAPTER THREE

Morris and J Rhapps of Penygraig, with Salford and E W Porter of Newport, with Oldham.'

A report in the *South Wales Daily News* on Monday 13th September 1897 confirmed what was already suspected, that Tom Williams had indeed gone North but not to Swinton as originally thought but to Salford. Another Llwynypia stalwart who went North that year was full-back Charlie Williams, who joined Huddersfield.

There is no doubt that Tom Williams was severely missed in the Llwynypia three-quarter line. During his year of captaincy 1896–97, the Llwynypia three-quarters scored 92 tries between them, 62 of which were credited to Willie Llewellyn and Tom Williams. Following Tom Williams' departure to Salford the try scoring ability of the team was greatly reduced. The whole Llwynypia team only managed to record 103 tries in the official fixtures for the 1897–98 season and Willie Llewellyn's total was 18 tries compared with 38 tries the previous season when playing outside Tom Williams.

Llwynypia's loss was Salford's gain as Tom Williams continued his brilliant rugby playing career. He soon made a name for himself at Salford, scoring a club record 29 tries in his first season. His 107 points, with the help of 10 goals, was also a club record.

By the end of his first season with Salford he had impressed the selectors sufficiently to be included in the Lancashire side to meet Westmoreland in March 1898. He made six appearances for the County, the last in December 1900 against Cheshire at Stockport. Tom Williams, who captained Salford from 1898 until 1902, began a tradition at Salford for great Welsh captains, which would include Willie Thomas, Jack Gore, Billy Williams, Gus Risman, Alan Edwards, Dai Davies, David Watkins

Courtesy of the Welsh Rugby Union

Tom Williams was captain of Llwynypia during the 1896–97 season. He joined Salford Northern Union Club in September 1897 and captained them from 1898 until 1902.

and David Young. Tom Williams was the first Welshman to lead a Challenge Cup final team when on Saturday 28th April 1900 he captained Salford against Swinton. At Fallowfield Stadium, Manchester a crowd of nearly 18,000 watched as Tom Williams sidestepped his way over the try line to score the opening try of the game. The conversion gave Salford a five points to nil lead but they were eventually defeated by 16 points to eight. It was on Saturday 26th April 1902 that Tom Williams led his team for the second time in a Challenge Cup final when Salford played Broughton Rangers at Athletic Grounds, Rochdale. Broughton Rangers ruined the day with an emphatic 25 points to nil victory thus making it two defeats from two Challenge Cup finals for Tom Williams.

Unfortunately Tom Williams's playing career at Salford was brought to an end when, with twenty-five minutes left to play, he injured his left knee making a tackle in a match with Broughton Rangers on 18th October 1902. Carried from the field, he never played for Salford again. During a five year playing career at Salford Tom Williams made 140 appearances and scored 280 points from 84 tries and 14 goals.

Although no longer playing for Salford but still living up North, Tom Williams was often seen in South Wales. There was a report in the *Evening Express* on Thursday 6th November 1902 that he had been a spectator at the County match between Glamorgan and Devon at Cardiff the previous day. The report specified that 'he was down on a visit to his mother at Llwynypia' and went on to say that he had no intention of making any "captures" for the Northern Union club. Another report in the *Evening Express* on Saturday 15th November stated that 'Tom Williams, the ex-Llwynypia three-quarter, has returned to Salford without having made any "captures." He did not see any player of sufficient merit in the Cardiff district teams to whom he felt inclined to tell the tale.'

In August 1904, it was reported that, although he had returned to live in Llwynypia, Tom Williams had put in a transfer request with Salford. In early 1908 Tom Williams transferred to Swinton Northern Union Club, but due to injury, his comeback was short-lived and he played just one game against Broughton Rangers at the end of the 1907–08 season and two games early in the 1908-09 season against Rochdale Hornets and Hull. In the early part of 1909 he was associated with the Mid-Rhondda Northern Union Club. Mid-Rhondda had several first-rate fixtures during that time when Broughton Rangers, Swinton and Hull all played at Tonypandy. Former Llwynypia stars Tom Williams and Jack Evans made their first appearance for Mid-Rhondda in the game against Barry on Saturday 23rd January 1909. Williams displayed some of his old magic and scored a try in the 16 points to six victory. Tom Williams also played in the games against Broughton Rangers on Saturday 30th January and Hull on Saturday 20th February 1909. After this there is no record of Tom Williams playing rugby again.

In 1915, during the Gallipoli Campaign, Tom Williams died in hospital in Alexandria, Egypt of enteric fever (typhoid), leaving a wife and five children. He is honoured at the Lancashire Landing Cemetery in Turkey where 1800 Lancashire Fusiliers died.

Llwynypia were again victims of Northern poaching when Jack Evans left the club for Swinton Northern Union Club in October 1897. Having previously played for Ammanford and Llanelly, Jack Evans joined Llwynypia at the start of the 1896–97 season. It was while representing Llanelly that Evans was first selected to play for Wales. In the second game of the 1896 Home Championship Evans came into the pack along with four other new caps, Bill Morris and Charles Bowen 'Boomer' Nicholl both of Llanelli, William Davies of Cardiff and William Cope of Blackheath. The selection was a reaction by the Welsh selectors to the terrible defeat to England in the previous game when Wales lost by 25 points to nil at Blackheath. The new players were chosen for their rough physical style of play, and were dubbed 'Rhondda forwards' after the tough coal mining men from that area. Also in the team for his first cap was Gwyn Nicholls the Cardiff centre. Whilst still at Llanelly Jack gained the second of his three caps

Courtesy of Timothy Auty

Jack Evans joined Llwynypia from Llanelly and gained three caps for Wales between 1896 and 1897.

when he played for Wales against Ireland at a muddy Lansdowne Road in 1896. Wales lost by 8 points to four and Ireland won the championship with wins over England and Wales and a drawn game against Scotland. Jack Evans won his third and final cap against England in 1897 whilst playing for Llwynypia. He played his last game for Llwynypia against Cardiff on Saturday 16th October 1897, transferring the following week to Swinton Northern Union Club. After his rugby playing days Jack Evans settled in the Swinton area and had three sons, Jack, Bryn and Harold, all of whom were outstanding rugby league players with Swinton during the 1920's and 1930's.

Despite the serious defections to the Northern Union by Tom Williams, Charlie Williams and Jack Evans, Llwynypia still had a very successful season. In Dick Foster at centre they found an adequate successor to Tom Williams and at full-back both Tom Saunders and J E Jones were more than able replacements for Charlie Williams. Although the back division was for some weeks early in the season unsettled, it was not very long before they were a capable three-quarter line and by the end of the season they were a strong and skilful unit.

In Willie Llewellyn, the Llwynypia vice-captain, though no stranger to the team, they had another young player who had developed into one of the fastest three-quarters in the country. Llewellyn's ability had been recognised with Glamorgan County honours against Gloucestershire and Devon and he was developing so consistently that, although he was light, there were many eyes upon him for international selection.

Another player with Glamorgan County honours was Isaac 'Ike' Edmunds. He was Llwynypia's permanent centre with Dick Foster and having developed so well since the start of the season he was as good a prospect as any centre in the principality.

Llwynypia found another clever youngster in Ben Morgan on the wing, but Morgan's appearances were never certain and Llwynypia often had to rely on players such as J E Jones and George Mills to fill a vacancy. At half-back the club were very strong with the established pairing of Andrew Powell and Iestyn Thomas. Unfortunately there were many occasions, through injury or illness, when they were unable to play together and often on these occasions Llwynypia did not win.

At forward Llwynypia had any amount of talented players and their contribution to the international and county packs was considerable. Both Dick Hellings, the Llwynypia captain, and Billy Alexander represented Wales during the season. Billy Alexander gained the first of his seven caps for Wales alongside Llwynypia club-mate Dick Hellings in the victory against Ireland at Limerick in March 1898. Both Hellings and Alexander then played in the only other international in 1898 when Wales were defeated by England at Blackheath in April 1898. Following the Arthur Gould affair, Scotland did not resume international fixtures with Wales until 1899.

In addition to his Welsh international caps, Billy Alexander also represented Glamorganshire in the games against Gloucestershire (twice), Devon, Cumberland and Yorkshire. Another Llwynypia forward who gained Glamorgan County honours during the 1897–98 season was Bob Jones who played against Devon, Gloucestershire and Cumberland.

Dick Hellings, the Llwynypia captain, represented both Glamorganshire and Devon Counties during what was a very successful season for Llwynypia. They played 40 official games of which they won 27, lost 9 and drew 4. They scored 430 points for with 159 points against. They scored 103 tries of which 41 were converted. In addition they scored 2 field goals, 4 dropped goals and 5 penalty goals. The try scorers were: Willie Llewellyn 18; George Evans 10; Ike Edmunds 9; Iestyn Thomas 8; Ben Morgan 8; D Hellings 5; Andrew Powell 5; Ben Phillips 4; Jack Evans 4; Dick Foster 4; J E Jones 4; George Mills 4; Billy Alexander 3; Gabe 3; Bowen 2; and Andrews, R Evans, Rees, Atkins, Kruger, Huzzey, Bob Jones, W R Williams, E Jones, G Dobson, T Dobson and P Jones one try apiece.

Tom Saunders converted 36 tries, placed 4 penalty goals, 2 field goals and dropped 2 goals. George Evans converted three tries. Willie Llewellyn converted one try. Gibbs converted one try. Ben Morgan dropped a goal. Dick Foster dropped a goal and Huzzey placed a penalty goal.

For the third time in four seasons Llwynypia were again holders of the Glamorgan League Cup. In addition to the forty official games played by Llwynypia they also played three friendly games at the end of the season. They lost to Treorky and the Glamorgan Police and then defeated the Rest of the League by 19 points to six.

Llwynypia played forty official games during the 1897–98 season.

Llwynypia Football Team – Glamorgan League Champions 1897–98

The player with the ball is Llwynypia Captain Dick Hellings. To his right is Willie Llewellyn. To Willie Llewellyn's right is Tom Williams (Committee man). Third from the right in the back row is Billy Alexander.

Willie Llewellyn played in thirty-three of these games and scored 18 tries, he also kicked one conversion. Willie Llewellyn also played in at least two of the three friendly games played at the end of the season. There are no team details for the game against Treorky but he definitely played against the Glamorgan Police and the Rest of the League. Willie scored another try in the friendly game against the Glamorgan Police taking his total number of tries for all games during the season to nineteen.

Although selected as a reserve for the Welsh international trial match at St Helen's, Swansea on Saturday 4th December, Willie Llewellyn did not play but instead captained Llwynypia against Neath in their 8 points to nil defeat. On the same day, Llwynypia captain, Dick Hellings, played for the West team in the Welsh trial match at Swansea. In a very tight game, which the East narrowly won by 14 points to thirteen, the West forwards had the better of their opponents with W E Rees of Pontypridd, David Evans of Penygraig and Dick Hellings of Llwynypia all playing exceptionally well.

Despite not playing in the Welsh international trial match at Swansea, Llwynypia forward Billy Alexander was selected for the first of his seven Welsh international caps when the Welsh team to play against Ireland at Limerick was announced. Also in the side for the game, which took place on Saturday 19th March 1898, was Dick Hellings, gaining his second international cap. A Welsh team containing six new caps defeated Ireland by 11 points to three. For the first time Willie Llewellyn was selected as reserve right wing.

With Scotland still not having resumed international fixtures with Wales there were only two Welsh international matches during the 1897–98 season. When the team was announced for the second international match against England at Rectory Field, Blackheath both Dick Hellings and Billy Alexander of Llwynypia were included. Again Willie Llewellyn was selected as reserve right wing. Despite leading at half-time by 7 points to six Wales eventually lost by 14 points to seven.

Willie Llewellyn started the 1897–98 season in fine style, scoring twice against Maesteg in the opening match of the season. Although he played well and made a few tries, Willie Llewellyn did not score in the 50 points to nil victory over Risca and he did not play in the away victory against Crumlin. Willie Llewellyn returned for the away victory over Bridgend and then played for Llwynypia in their only home defeat of the season against Cardiff on Saturday 16th October.

This game will be remembered for several reasons. Firstly the game was of a far higher standard than expected and despite losing by two goals and a dropped goal (14 points) to a try (3 points), Llwynypia played very well. The home forwards played superbly and the half-backs, Andrew Powell and Iestyn Thomas, did sterling work in containing Selwyn Biggs, the Cardiff captain and scrum-half. Time after time he was caught in possession of the ball and if it had not been for the determined defence of the Llwynypia half-backs the Cardiff score could have been much higher. Playing against each other for the first time in this game were Gwyn Nicholls, the Cardiff centre three-quarter and Llwynypia right wing Willie Llewellyn. Although they played against and with each other on many later occasions, they will be best remembered for playing together for Wales in the famous victory over New Zealand in December 1905.

Gwyn Nicholls played in the centre for Wales on twenty-four occasions and captained them on nine occasions. Willie Llewellyn and Gwyn Nicholls played in the same Welsh team fifteen times, including Willie's last appearance for Wales against New Zealand in 1905. Although Willie Llewellyn had captained Wales to a fourth Triple Crown during the 1904–05 season, Gwyn Nicholls returned as captain for the 1905 game against New Zealand.

The Llwynypia game against Cardiff in October 1897 will also be remembered because of the tragedy that took place during the first half of the game. On the side of the field opposite the grandstand stood an old bandstand which was in a very dilapidated condition. It was crowded with spectators, but many chose to ignore a warning against climbing onto its roof. It was an excellent vantage point and when many more spectators joined those on the already crowded roof the strain became too great and the roof collapsed, burying those beneath in the debris. When the spectators who had been buried underneath were disentangled it was found that two men had been seriously injured. Edward Barrow, who was from Barry and had come up with the Cardiff team, had a compound fracture of his leg and was taken to the Porth Cottage Hospital where he remained for some time. The second man, Evan Haddock, a collier who lived in Llwynypia, received severe internal injuries and died as he was being taken home. He left a wife and eight children, the youngest of whom was born the day before the match.

Mr Dai Llewellyn, the secretary of the Llwynypia Football Club said that something would certainly be done to compensate the family of the deceased man and the unfortunate man who had his leg fractured, and suggested that a charity match should be played between teams selected

Gwyn Nicholls played for Wales on 24 occasions between 1896 and 1906 and captained them 9 times.

Courtesy of the Frederic Humbert Collection

by Selwyn Biggs, the Cardiff captain, and Dick Hellings, the captain of the Llwynypia team. The proposed game with Cardiff was never arranged but a charity match was arranged between Llwynypia and the Bridgewater Club, the proceeds of which were intended for the wife and children of the late Evan Haddock. Despite a guarantee to the Bridgwater Club of £12 they did not honour the arrangement giving financial difficulty as their reason for the non-fulfilment of the fixture. Efforts were then made to secure a fixture with Barry for the charity match but these arrangements also failed. Eventually Llwynypia decided that the proceeds from their Glamorgan League fixture against Mountain Ash on Saturday 11th December 1897 should be given to Mr Haddock's widow and eight children. A share of the proceeds also went to Edward Barrow, the Barry workman, who sustained a fractured leg and to O Powell of Trealaw, who received severe bruising.

In the next game against Morriston Willie Llewellyn was the pick of the Llwynypia three-quarter line. He scored two tries in a game where the home three-quarters were vastly superior to the opposition with the backs scoring seven of the nine tries and Willie Llewellyn kicking the only conversion. The other tries were scored by Ben Morgan (3), Ike Edmunds (2) and George Evans and Iestyn Thomas one apiece.

The Glamorgan League fixture away to Treorky was by no means the runaway victory that the score suggested. It was a ding dong game played at great pace and full of brilliant incidents on both sides. In a tough game Llwynypia were eventually victorious by three goals and a try, 18 points to nil.

A first half try by Billy Alexander and a penalty goal by Tom Saunders were the only scores for Llwynypia in a tough battle in the away game with Ebbw Vale. The home team were totally dominant in the second half and scored a brilliant unconverted try through Scott. Despite continual pressure Ebbw Vale were unable to add to their score and Llwynypia won by 6 points to three.

The home game against Neath was a truly splendid contest. From beginning to end the pace was terrific and until the last ten minutes both teams showed remarkable staying power. Neath held the lead at the interval with an unconverted try by Jack Linnard. In the second half play was fairly even until about the last ten minutes when the heavier

Llwynypia forwards took control. The Rhondda champions were now playing for all their worth and a well-conceived move to the right by Andrew Powell ended with Willie Llewellyn scoring in the corner. The try went unconverted and although Llwynypia finished the stronger team they were unable to add to their total with the result that the game was drawn at 3 points all.

Llwynypia had an equally tough game in their next encounter away to Penarth. A Billy Alexander try which was converted by Foster gave Llwynypia the lead at the interval. Penarth came back strongly in the second half and a try by the Penarth captain Hubert Alexander and a brilliant conversion by Billy Gibbs gave the home team the draw.

Llwynypia suffered only their second defeat of the season when they lost away to Pontypridd. The game was one of the hardest and keenest ever witnessed at Pontypridd. Not having defeated Llwynypia for two years the home team were delighted with their 3 points to nil victory. A second half unconverted try by W E Rees was sufficient to give Pontypridd victory.

On the same day as the Welsh international trial match was taking place at Swansea, Llwynypia were defeated in their return match with Neath at the Gnoll. Dick Hellings was playing for the West against the East in the trial match but both Willie Llewellyn and Billy Alexander, who were reserves for the West team, turned out for Llwynypia. Willie Llewellyn captained a capable Llwynypia fifteen who gave Neath as good a game as had ever been seen on the Neath ground. A first half unconverted try by Neath's J D Davies gave the home team the lead at the interval. In a hard fought second half the Welsh All Blacks scored again through a try by Charlie Steer. Joe Davies converted giving Neath victory by 8 points to nil.

The Llanelly team paid their first visit to Llwynypia on Monday 6th December 1897. The previous week Owen Badger, the four times capped Welsh international centre, went North to play for Norther Union club Swinton. It was generally thought that Badger was, next to Gwyn Nicholls, the best centre in Wales. It was reported in the *Evening Express* that Badger had been tempted to the Swinton Club by a payment of £75 and employment that would bring him £2 10s. per week. These would have been tempting terms for Badger, who, as a steel shearer, would have worked very hard and with youth on his side, would have looked forward to many seasons of football. He played his first game for Swinton against Rochdale on Saturday 4th December 1897, the date he had originally been carded to play for the West in the Welsh international trial match at Swansea. Owen Badger later won two Wales Northern Union caps and his departure left an opening in the centre for Wales that was filled by Gwyn Nicholls who won his first Welsh cap in the next international match against Scotland at Cardiff in January 1896.

It was also thought that Llanelly forward Bill Morris, another Welsh international, had gone North and joined Rochdale. He too had been selected to play in the Welsh international trial match at Swansea but did not appear. Neither did he play in the game against Llwynypia. Despite travelling to Rochdale he failed to come to terms with the Rochdale Club and returned to Llanelly. At a meeting of the Llanelly committee on Monday 20th December it was decided that Bill Morris should once again be picked as one of the club's forwards and he returned to their side for the game against Edinburgh University on Monday 27th December.

The Llwynypia ground was in a terrible state and the players were very soon all covered in mud. Conditions were such that passing of any kind was impossible, nevertheless the game was a very interesting one throughout. Llwynypia were lucky to win for Llanelly failed to score on at least two occasions when tries looked a certainty. The result was due to the superiority of the Llwynypia forwards who were bigger and stronger than the Llanelly eight and Dick Hellings and Billy Alexander were frequently prominent. The only score came early in the second half when Iestyn Thomas crossed for an unconverted try to leave Llwynypia winners of a very tight game by 3 points to nil.

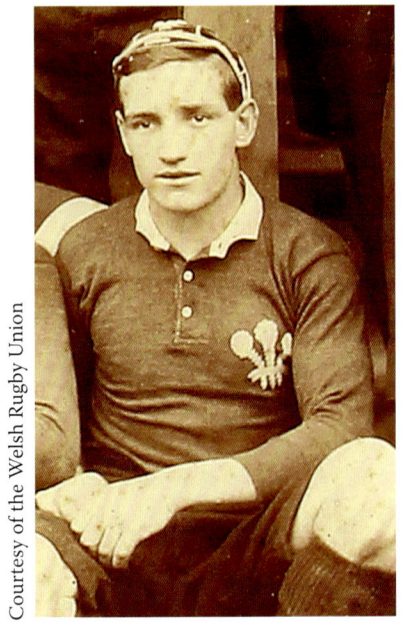

Owen Badger the Llanelly centre who played four times for Wales between 1895 and 1896.

Courtesy of the Welsh Rugby Union

In a fast and open game a dropped goal from a mark was the only score in the game between Llwynypia and Mountain Ash. Just before the interval Ben Morgan made a mark and in a favourable position Dick Foster kicked a splendid goal.

Llwynypia were well represented when the Glamorgan County trial match took place at Treherbert on Monday 13th December 1897. Willie Llewellyn, Isaac Edmunds, Billy Alexander and Bob Jones all played for the East team against the West. Although the East team played as selected, only five of the original West team turned out and as a trial match the game was a farce. The West were well beaten by five unconverted tries to nil. The only score of the first half was an unconverted try by Tom Davies of Treherbert. Further tries in the second half by Walter Phillips of Mountain Ash (2), Bob Jones of Llwynypia and J Jenkins of Treherbert put the game beyond doubt and the East were victors by 15 points to nil.

During the Christmas and New Year period Llwynypia had five hard games. In an exceedingly fast game they defeated Aberavon by 5 points to nil. In the second half a beautiful bout of passing between the Llwynypia backs saw Isaac Edmunds scoring a clever try. Tom Saunders' splendid conversion gave Llwynypia a five point advantage and with Aberavon failing to score Llwynypia were the victors. The day after Boxing Day Llwynypia met Barry in a Glamorgan League fixture. The Llwynypia team contained more second than first fifteen players but were still able to overcome their opponents by 8 points to nil. Barry won the toss and played with the wind. Dick Hellings kicked off for Llwynypia and immediately Barry were under pressure. The forwards took the ball and from a scrummage the Llwynypia backs indulged in a fine round of passing, which ended in Willie Llewellyn rounding the posts for a try which Tom Saunders converted. Late in the second half Henry Kruger cleverly scored in the corner, but Tom Saunders' kick at goal just failed; nevertheless, with no further scores, Llwynypia won the encounter by 8 points to nil.

Llwynypia visited Newport for the first time to fulfil their first engagement with the famous premier Uskside club. The fact that Newport had consented to give the Llwynypia club a fixture had been met with great satisfaction and a crowd of 6,000 spectators turned up to watch the game. Conditions were not brilliant and the ground was in a worse condition than the previous day when Newport drew nil all with Watsonians. Both sides were well represented but with the absence of Andrew Powell, Henry Kruger from the Llwynypia seconds replaced him at scrum-half. Newport fielded a very strong side which included three internationals in Tom Pearson, Bert Dauncey and George Llewellyn Lloyd. In this game Willie Llewellyn renewed his acquaintance with Reg Skrimshire against whom he had played when Christ College, Brecon met Monmouth Grammar School. However this was the first time that Willie Llewellyn had come across Joseph Jehoida Hodges and George Llewellyn Lloyd. They would get to know each other very well as both Hodges and Llewellyn Lloyd played for Wales at the same time as Willie Llewellyn.

Willie Llewellyn and Jehoida Hodges played together for Glamorgan, Newport and Wales. In 1899 they were both debutants along with Reg Skrimshire, John Blake, Fred Scrine, Alfred Brice and Will Parker

Newport Rugby Football Club 1897–98

Back Row: J Hodges, G Jones, W H Williams, J H Dunn, G Boots, M Price.
Middle Row: J Jenkins, A W Boucher, T W Pearson, F H Dauncey (Captain), R T Skrimshire, G Ll Lloyd. *Front Row*: L A Phillips, J B Smithson, M Hannan.

when Wales defeated England at Swansea. Willie Llewellyn and Jehoida Hodges played together for Wales in eighteen out of the twenty games Willie Llewellyn played for Wales, including Willie's last game for Wales against New Zealand in 1905. Jehoida Hodges was capped by Wales on 23 occasions.

Willie Llewellyn and George Llewellyn Lloyd also played together for Wales. Llewellyn Lloyd was capped by Wales on twelve occasions and in nine of those games he played alongside Willie Llewellyn.

With regard to the game it was a great encounter. Despite the soft conditions the game was an exciting one. Llwynypia gave Newport a really hard test. In the first half they did very well, their big forwards going very strong and Llwynypia had slightly the better of the play. However, Llwynypia faded after a scoreless first half. Newport on the other hand raised their game and put Llwynypia under a great deal of pressure. The forward work on both sides was strong and often brilliant, and Dick Hellings of Llwynypia played a wonderfully hard and fine game and stood out as the best scrummager on the field. On the other hand the Rhondda backs were never as good as Newport's. Their passing was seldom clean and accurate. Behind the packs the best player on the field was Tom Pearson who did a lot of fine dribbling over the muddy ground and saved his team on many occasions with his fine defensive play. Two unconverted tries, one each for Tom Pearson and Jehoida Hodges, were the only scores of the game which Newport won by 6 points to nil.

Llwynypia played very well when they met Aberavon on New Year's Day. A converted try in each half was enough to give them victory by 10 points to nil. An interesting feature of Llwynypia's next game against Penygraig was the fact that brothers Fred and Percy Bush were playing in the three-quarters. Fred was on the wing and Percy was in the centre. This was the first encounter between Willie Llewellyn and Percy Bush but they would play against each other on many occasions. They would also play in the same team for Wales. On the occasion of Willie Llewellyn gaining his last cap for Wales against New Zealand in 1905, Percy Bush gained the first of his eight Welsh international caps.

It was while Percy was studying at University College, Cardiff that he played for Penygraig with his brother Fred. They both played for Penygraig between 1897 and 1900. Percy captaining the team for the 1898–99 and

1899–1900 seasons. Legend has it that Gwyn Nicholls invited Percy to play for Cardiff following a game against Penygraig in 1898. Despite being captain of Penygraig during the 1899–1900 season Percy played regularly in the three-quarters for the Cardiff Reserves and also played several games for the first fifteen, scoring four tries in the process. His brother Fred also played for Cardiff during the 1899–1900 season. Percy transferred from Penygraig to Cardiff and from September 1900 was a regular member of the Cardiff first fifteen. He was later captain of Cardiff RFC in the 1905–06, 1906–07 and 1908–09 seasons.

Percy Bush played for the Anglo-Australian Rugby Football Team in Australia and New Zealand in 1904 and gained eight caps for Wales between 1905 and 1910.

Percy Bush and Willie Llewellyn toured with the Anglo-Australian Rugby Football Team to Australia and New Zealand in 1904 (British Lions). Percy was the top points scorer with 97 points and with 5 dropped goals holds the record for most dropped goals for a British Lions player. He played in 19 of the 20 games played including all four Test matches and was top try scorer with 11 tries. Willie Llewellyn played in 15 games and with Teddy Morgan was joint-second among the leading try scorers with 8 each. Teddy Morgan played in 13 games and both he and Willie Llewellyn played in all four Test matches.

The Penygraig game, which was played on the Llwynypia ground, created a great deal of interest and there was an unusually large crowd. Llwynypia were favourites to win and their past record against Penygraig seemed to indicate that they would inflict another defeat upon their rivals and neighbours. In the four matches played the previous season Llwynypia scored 54 tries to Penygraig's nil and out of about ten matches played between the teams Penygraig had only won once. The game was fast and open throughout and both sides demonstrated the keen rivalry that existed between such close neighbours. There was not a great deal of difference between the teams and at the interval Llwynypia were leading by just 8 points to five. An unconverted try by Ben Morgan gave Llwynypia the lead early in the game. Penygraig responded with a try by Lewis and took the lead when Tom Jones converted. Just before the interval Llwynypia three-quarter J E Jones scored a try which Tom Saunders converted to give the home team the lead at the break.

In the second half Llwynypia scored first when Willie Llewellyn very cleverly dodged a couple of men and scored behind the posts. Tom Saunders converted to give Llwynypia an eight point lead. An unconverted try by Fred Bush reduced the deficit but a late try by George Evans which was converted by Tom Saunders gave Llwynypia victory by 16 points to eight. Dick Hellings was the best of the home forwards but Andrew Powell, George Evans, Billy Alexander and Ben Phillips were also in great form. The brothers Bush played a great game for Penygraig and were perhaps the most prominent pair of three-quarters on the field. Both played a splendid defensive game, their kicking and following up being exceptional. Ike Edmunds was conspicuous on the winning side and Willie Llewellyn and Ben Morgan were very dangerous on more than one occasion. The way Willie Llewellyn attempted to cross the line several times in the second half was a treat for the spectators and when he crossed and planted the ball behind the posts the crowd gave him a well-deserved cheer.

When the committee of the Glamorgan County Football Club met at the Walnut Tree Hotel, Aberavon, on Thursday 30th December 1897 for the purpose of selecting the Glamorgan team to meet Gloucestershire at Gloucester on Thursday 6th January 1898, Willie Llewellyn was selected for his first County appearance. Also in the team were Llwynypia teammates Isaac Edmunds and Billy Alexander. The game was not brilliant and reflected poorly on Glamorgan football. The forwards played well enough both in the scrums and the loose but the backs were hopelessly out of sorts. Only Willie Llewellyn and Llewellyn Deere gave decent performances, although Tom Jones at full-back was sound in defence. At forward play was pretty even but at half-back the Gloucestershire pair of Needs and Cummings were much too smart for Alf Jones and Phillips.

Gloucestershire won by 8 points to nil and thoroughly deserved their victory, for on the day's play they were undoubtedly the better team.

Llwynypia won their next three games against Treherbert, Bath and Pontypridd. They had a close victory against Treherbert winning by 5 points to nil and then defeated Bath away by 29 points to three. Although Willie Llewellyn did not play in the Bath game he scored twice in the home victory over Pontypridd before playing his second game for Glamorgan County against Devon at Pontypridd on Thursday 20th January.

The match with Devon involved three Llwynypia players; Willie Llewellyn and Billy Alexander played for Glamorgan County while Dick Hellings played for Devon. Tom Jones kicked off for Glamorgan in drizzling rain and in front of a small crowd. Just before half-time the Glamorgan halves got away and Hubert Alexander, after a brilliant run, scored an unconverted try. Devon had rather the best of the opening exchanges of the second half but afterwards Glamorgan were always superior. Taking the game as a whole, Glamorganshire were the much better team and had there been a better pair of halves behind the forwards, a big score would have been inevitable. With no scores in the second half Glamorgan won the encounter by 3 points to nil.

Two days after playing for Glamorgan against Devon, Willie Llewellyn was back playing for Llwynypia. In a gruelling contest they defeated Treherbert away by 5 points to nil. Llwynypia's next game against Gloucester was one of the most exciting games witnessed on the Llwynypia ground and to the credit of the home crowd, which was one of the biggest of the season, they cheered both teams alike during a contest which was marked by numerous flashes of brilliant and exciting play. In the first half it seemed that Gloucester were going to walk away with a victory. With a good wind behind them they were leading at the interval by 5 points to nil. Willie Llewellyn scored a corner try mid-way through the second half which Tom Saunders just missed converting with a magnificent shot at goal. With only five minutes remaining Llwynypia were still behind, then a clever pick up in the loose by Iestyn Thomas and a pass over the Gloucester forwards' heads gave Willie Llewellyn the chance he had been waiting for. He took the pass beautifully and with a grand dodgy run, he got over in the corner. Tom Saunders, from a very difficult angle, made a good shot for goal but just failed to convert.

This gave Llwynypia the winning point and with Gloucester penned back on their own line for the remaining minutes of the game they were unable to score and Llwynypia were victors by 6 points to five.

A crowd of about 5,000 spectators, which included Lord and Lady Aberdare and some of their family, watched as Llwynypia suffered their fifth defeat of the season away to Mountain Ash. It was a splendid match from start to finish and a try by George Evans which was converted by Tom Saunders and an unconverted try by Bob Jones gave Llwynypia an 8 points to nil advantage at the interval. Despite an unconverted try by Willie Llewellyn, Llwynypia faded in the second half and four tries by the home side, two of which were converted, gave Mountain Ash victory by 16 points to eleven.

In their next game a Llwynypia team, weakened by the absence of Bob Jones, Billy Alexander, Ben Phillips and Andrew Powell defeated Penygraig on their own ground. The Penygraig team, without Frank and Percy Bush, were well beaten. Llwynypia led at the interval by 8 points to nil and two second half unconverted tries gave them victory by 14 points to nil.

There were reports in the *Evening Express* of a Llwynypia mid-week team having been taken to Brecon by Mr Dai Llewellyn, the secretary of the Llwynypia Athletic Club. Although it is stated that 'a strong Llwynypia team won by four tries to nil,' there is no detail of the game or scorers. An amusing report of the after match meal read as follow: 'After the match the team sat down to a rekerky chow-chow. The secretary being late to dinner, Dick Hellings took the head of the table and proceeded to tackle the joint of rosbif. Iestyn Thomas played half-back on the captain's right and passed slabs of juicy meat from the scrum. "Begin on that!" said Captain Hellings, kindly sending a solid five-pound chunk of beef along to Saunders. When the secretary returned, the carving was over: the huge joint had disappeared, distributed in nuggets of varied shape, weighing anything from one pound to six.' Sounds like they had a great time.

Willie Llewellyn only appeared in four of the next nine games played by Llwynypia. He featured in the home victory over Bridgend then missed the away victory over Morriston. He played again in the home victory over Brecon but missed the next two away games against Plymouth and Exmouth. He was unable to get leave from work for the three days required for the Devon tour. Willie Llewellyn was one of five first team regulars who missed the tour. Ben Morgan, Dr Gabe and Iestyn Thomas were unable to make the trip and Dick Foster failed to turn up, his place being taken by his younger brother Tom. Willie Llewellyn returned for the next home game against Penarth which they won by 16 points to nil but then missed the mid-week game against Crumlin. The Llwynypia ground was rendered almost unplayable by the melting of a heavy fall of snow the previous day. Very little interest was taken in the game as Llwynypia were weakly represented, having to play four of their second team forwards. Only twenty minutes were played in each half and the game ended in scoreless draw.

The day following the Llwynypia game against Crumlin the selection committee of the Welsh Football Union met to select the Welsh team to face Ireland in Limerick on Saturday 19th March. There were first caps for William 'Pussy' Jones (Cardiff), Viv Huzzey (Cardiff), Billy Alexander (Llwynypia), Hopkin Davies (Swansea), George Boots (Newport), Tom Dobson (Cardiff) and Joseph Booth (Pontymister). Hubert Alexander (Penarth) was selected as first reserve for either wing and Willie Llewellyn was selected as second reserve for the right wing.

When Llwynypia played Llanelly at Stradey Park on Saturday 12th March the home team were without their captain, Welsh international winger, Evan Lloyd. An effort was made to secure the services of Herbie Morgan the Swansea left wing but he was not available and so the committee had to fall back on Rhys Gabe. J W Lewis, who had been given a few trials on the left wing, failed to come up to scratch and it was hoped that Gabe would be more successful. This was probably the first time that Willie Llewellyn and Rhys Gabe had faced each other on the

Rhys Gabe played for Wales in 24 matches between 1901 and 1908. He also played for the British Team against Australia and New Zealand in 1904.

Courtesy of the Welsh Rugby Union

rugby field. They would get to know each other very well over the years, playing together for London Welsh, the 1904 British Lions and Wales.

This was a strong Llanelly side with no fewer than three Welsh internationals in Ben Davies, Bill Morris and David John Daniel as well as future Welsh internationals Rhys Gabe, James Watts and Nathaniel 'Danny' Walters.

Having lost the previous encounter earlier in the season, Llanelly would have been keen to exact revenge on their home ground. They had several opportunities and crossed the Llwynypia line on several occasions in the first half only to be called back for one infringement or another. The second half was fought out as keen as ever and several Llwynypia opportunities were halted by keen Llanelly tackling. In the dying moments it was Llanelly's turn to put Llwynypia under pressure and Rhys Gabe almost forced his way over for a try. However, he was held up and an exciting game ended with no scores for either side.

On the day that Wales were defeating Ireland at Limerick, Llwynypia were due to play Treorky at home in a Glamorgan League fixture. In the absence of Dick Hellings, who was playing for Wales, Willie Llewellyn was selected to captain the side. The weather was not good and a large crowd waited in the rain for the teams to arrive. The Llwynypia team, after waiting for a long time for their opponents to put in an appearance, drove to the ground to find that only half a dozen of the Treorky men had arrived. The others, they said, were following. The teams and the crowd waited for some time, but no more Treorky men turned up. With time now against them it was decided to cancel the match and the Treorky officials agreed that Llwynypia should be awarded the two points as allowed under the league rules. The result was that Llwynypia, who were practically the winners of the Glamorgan League already and were hot favourites to win this match, were now accredited winners of the Glamorgan League.

Llwynypia met Treherbert on Thursday 24th March at Treherbert having already won the Glamorgan League Cup for the third time. Much to everyone's surprise, the League champions were beaten by 12 points to nil. Neither side was fully representative, Llwynypia were without Willie Llewellyn, Iestyn Thomas and Billy Alexander, while Treherbert were without several of their first team players. An unconverted try in the first half and three unconverted tries in the second half was enough to put the cup holders away as Llwynypia suffered their seventh defeat of the season.

When the Welsh team to face England at the Rectory Field, Blackheath on Saturday 2nd April was chosen Llwynypia forwards Billy Alexander and Dick Hellings were in the side. Hubert Alexander, the Penarth wing was first reserve for either wing and Willie Llewellyn was again second reserve for the right wing.

Willie Llewellyn returned for Llwynypia's next game against Treorky and scored two tries in the 21 points to five victory. Llwynypia won their next two games against Barry and Ebbw Vale before being defeated by Gloucester and Cardiff.

Cardiff wisely chose Llwynypia for their closing match of the season at Cardiff Arms Park on Easter Monday. Despite the rain, which persisted throughout the game, a crowd of between 8,000 and 10,000 spectators were well rewarded with a splendid exhibition of rugby. The home team were strongly represented but Llwynypia were without Dick Hellings, J E Jones, Bowen, Billy Alexander and Bob Jones and this had an inevitable influence on the result. Although Llwynypia played quite well, Cardiff achieved a decisive victory by 13 points to nil and on the day's performance held the advantage in all departments.

With all official fixtures complete Llwynypia finished their season with three friendly games. On the evening of Thursday 14th April, they played an away friendly against Treorky. There is very little detail of the players in this game so it is not known if Willie Llewellyn played. The only Llwynypia players mentioned in a report of the game which appeared in the *Pontypridd Chronicle and Workman's News* were Hadridge, J E Jones, Dick Hellings, Ben Phillips, Iestyn Thomas, Andrew Powell and Abe Lewis. An unconverted try by Teddy Jones late in the game gave Treorky victory by 3 points to nil.

Llwynypia played a home match against the Glamorgan County Police on Thursday 21st April. This was a rearranged fixture of a match postponed the previous December when the Llwynypia pitch was flooded. The Llwynypia backs had several opportunities to score in a contest predominantly confined to the forwards but at the critical moment the final pass went to ground. On one occasion Willie Llewellyn got across for a try, but for some infringement was called back. In a

Date	Team Played For	Opposition	Venue	Result/Score	W Llewellyn Tries
18/09/1897	Llwynypia	Maesteg	Home	Won 26-3	2
25/09/1897	Llwynypia	Risca	Home	Won 50-0	0
02/10/1897	Llwynypia	Crumlin	Away	Won 12-4	Did not play
09/10/1897	Llwynypia	Bridgend	Away	Won 14-0	0
16/10/1897	Llwynypia	Cardiff	Home	Lost 3-14	0
23/10/1897	Llwynypia	Morriston	Home	Won 29-0	2
30/10/1897	Llwynypia	Treorky	Away	Won 18-0	0
01/11/1897	Llwynypia	Ebbw Vale	Away	Won 6-3	0
06/11/1897	Llwynypia	Neath	Home	Drawn 3-3	1
13/11/1897	Llwynypia	Penarth	Away	Drawn 5-5	0
20/11/1897	Llwynypia	Pontypridd	Away	Lost 0-3	0
04/12/1897	Llwynypia	Neath	Away	Lost 0-8	0
06/12/1897	Llwynypia	Llanelly	Home	Won 3-0	0
11/12/1897	Llwynypia	Mountain Ash	Away	Won 4-0	0
13/12/1897	Glamorgan County Trial. East	West	Treherbert	Won 15-0	0
18/12/1897	Llwynypia	Aberavon	Away	Won 5-0	0
27/12/1897	Llwynypia	Barry	Home	Won 8-0	1
28/12/1897	Llwynypia	Newport	Away	Lost 0-6	0
01/01/1898	Llwynypia	Aberavon	Home	Won 10-0	0
03/01/1898	Llwynypia	Penygraig	Home	Won 16-8	1
06/01/1898	Glamorgan	Gloucestershire	Gloucester	Lost 0-8	0
08/01/1898	Llwynypia	Treherbert	Home	Won 5-0	0
13/01/1898	Llwynypia	Bath	Away	Won 29-3	Did not play
15/01/1898	Llwynypia	Pontypridd	Home	Won 11-0	2
20/01/1898	Glamorgan	Devon	Pontypridd	Won 3-0	0
22/01/1898	Llwynypia	Treherbert	Away	Won 5-0	0
29/01/1898	Llwynypia	Gloucester	Home	Won 6-5	2
05/02/1898	Llwynypia	Mountain Ash	Away	Lost 11-16	1
07/02/1898	Llwynypia	Penygraig	Away	Won 14-0	0
10/02/1898	Llwynypia Mid-Week XV	Brecon	Away	Won 12-0	No Detail
12/02/1898	Llwynypia	Bridgend	Home	Won 21-0	1
17/02/1898	Llwynypia	Morriston	Away	Won 3-0	Did not play
19/02/1898	Llwynypia	Brecon	Home	Won 27-9	1
26/02/1898	Llwynypia	Plymouth	Away	Lost 8-11	Did not play
28/02/1898	Llwynypia	Exmouth	Away	Won 12-5	Did not play
05/03/1898	Llwynypia	Penarth	Home	Won 16-0	1
07/03/1898	Llwynypia	Crumlin	Home	Drawn 0-0	Did not play
12/03/1898	Llwynypia	Llanelly	Away	Drawn 0-0	0
24/03/1898	Llwynypia	Treherbert	Away	Lost 0-12	Did not play
28/03/1898	Llwynypia	Treorky	Home	Won 21-5	2
02/04/1898	Llwynypia	Barry	Away	Won 12-7	0
04/04/1898	Llwynypia	Ebbw Vale	Home	Won 14-8	0
09/04/1898	Llwynypia	Gloucester	Away	Lost 3-8	1
11/04/1898	Llwynypia	Cardiff	Away	Lost 0-13	0
14/04/1898	Llwynypia	Treorky	Away	Lost 0-3	0
21/04/1898	Llwynypia	Glamorgan Police	Home	Lost 3-5	1
23/04/1898	Llwynypia	Rest of the League	Home	Won 19-6	0
Totals	Willie Llewellyn Games Played: 40				W Llewellyn Tries: 19

Willie Llewellyn Rugby Games Played and Results 1897–98 Season

forward dominated game both packs worked like Trojans. Hellings, Sweet and George Evans were prominent for Llwynypia, whilst Hockings, Pugsley and Price shone for the police. At half-time there was no score. In the second half a converted try by Rees Davies for the police and an unconverted try by Willie Llewellyn gave the police the victory by the smallest of margins. A report in the *Evening Express* said, 'W M Llewellyn, as usual was the best back on the field, his tackling and kicking being excellent.' One unfortunate consequence of this game was the referee, Mr Morgan, reporting Dick Hellings to the Welsh Football Union for a 'convivial conversation' Hellings had with the referee following the game, the outcome of which was his suspension until the end of October. Dick Hellings' side of the story was never heard by the Welsh Football Union: nevertheless, he missed the first three games of the following season and did not play for Llwynypia until they faced Bridgend on Saturday 15th October.

Llwynypia's last game of the season was against a team composed of players from the other league teams. Llwynypia had a very strong team which was assisted by the inclusion of Gwyn Nicholls and Arthur Ricketts of Cardiff. The teams were equal at forward but Llwynypia were much stronger at half-back and in the three-quarters. The presence of Nicholls and Ricketts in the centre gave Llwynypia a great advantage and they romped to a 19 points to six victory over the visitors. Gwyn Nicholls at centre was the best three-quarter on the field; he played a beautiful game and was the means of getting one of the Llwynypia tries. Ricketts also played well and his tries were beauties. Willie Llewellyn, although he accomplished one or two smart things, was not at his best. George Mills on the other wing showed that he was a fast man and played a good game while Dick Hellings, the captain, and Ben Phillips were the shining lights of the pack.

With rugby over for another season, Willie Llewellyn could look back on another successful campaign. At the age of just nineteen he was vice-captain of Llwynypia, had been reserve for the Welsh trial and represented Glamorgan County for the first time. Willie was also second reserve right wing, behind Hubert Alexander of Penarth, for Wales in their internationals against Ireland and England. Willie played forty games during the season and scored nineteen tries. He was playing with and against the best players in Wales and could look forward to a bright future in Welsh rugby.

Chapter Four

Willie Llewellyn's First Welsh Cap – 1898/1899 Season

LLWYNYPIA PLAYED 35 games during the 1898–99 season, including one friendly game against Christ College, Brecon. Willie Llewellyn, who captained the team, played in 31 of these games. He missed the home game against Neath because he was playing in the Welsh international trial match at Mountain Ash and he also missed the return fixture away to Neath on Saturday 18th February. Willie missed the home game against Ebbw Vale because he was playing for Wales against Scotland at Inverleith, Edinburgh. The only other Llwynypia game Willie Llewellyn missed during the season was the away game against Ebbw Vale in early April 1899.

Of the 35 games Llwynypia played they won 21, lost 8 and drew 6. They scored 353 points for with 113 points against. Llwynypia also won the Glamorgan League Challenge Cup for the fourth time in the five seasons since its inception in 1894–95. The Glamorgan League was established to improve the standard of rugby football in the Rhondda and clubs which were virtually unknown in South Wales, had, over two or three seasons, become household names. Not only had these clubs become better known but the instigation of the League had been instrumental in considerably improving the quality of the game in the Rhondda.

The clubs which were affiliated to the Glamorgan League were Llwynypia, Pontypridd, Mountain Ash, Treherbert, Penygraig, Treorky, Barry, Pontyclun and Ferndale. All these clubs benefited from inclusion in the League but Llwynypia possibly more than the others. Having won the League in its first year and subsequently every year since, with the exception of 1895–96 when it was won by Mountain Ash, Llwynypia became the Rhondda club to play for and many excellent players were attracted to the club.

Winning the Glamorgan League in 1898–99 was not accomplished without a severe struggle and the issue was in the balance until the game against Penygraig on 27th April. Had Llwynypia lost that game they would have effectively been out of the competition. However, the narrow victory over Penygraig and the victory over Pontyclun in the last game of the season gave Llwynypia the Glamorgan League title for a third consecutive year.

The first League match of the season was away to Treherbert and was unquestionably a very rough game which resulted in a home win for Treherbert by just one unconverted try to nil. This game started a series of injury misfortunes for Llwynypia which hindered them throughout the first half of the season. Iestyn Thomas sustained a knee injury in the game against Treherbert which kept him out of the game until Llwynypia played Penygraig in December. Unfortunately in this game he was knocked unconscious in the first half and had to retire. He did not play again during that season. A fortnight later Ike Edmunds' season was ended when he dislocated his shoulder in the game against Aberavon. Sometime later Charlie Wood, another centre, broke his arm whilst assisting Penygraig and did not play for Llwynypia again that season. Then on December 5th, J E Jones, who had played a consistently safe and reliable game at full-back from the start of the season fractured his leg at Penygraig. To add to Llwynypia's injury worries, R P Lewis and J Coombes, two reserve three-quarters, whose services were requisitioned more than once, were also consigned to the injured list. It may well be imagined therefore that these unfortunate incidents had a detrimental impact upon the team and caused the officials of the club no end of selection problems especially at three-quarters and half-back.

Eventually, however, by reshuffles and recruitment, a good side was secured. At three-quarters Willie Llewellyn, Dick Foster, Ben Phillips and Ben Morgan formed a formidable back line. Willie Llewellyn and Ben Morgan were on the wings with Dick Foster and Ben Phillips between them. Ben Phillips having been taken out of the forwards to fill the vacancy at centre. George Mills turned out a few times for his old club and showed that he had lost none of his pace on the wing. Unfortunately he was unable to play regularly and Ben Morgan was chosen for the right wing. He did fairly well but during the closing matches of the season was replaced by Max Williams of Cardiff. Henry Kruger, also of Cardiff, was tried at half-back, but he eventually left to play for Huddersfield and later Rochdale. In December, Hillman, formerly of Mountain Ash, joined the team, followed on March 4th by Stephens of Llandaff. From that time onwards they played together at half-back and proved themselves to be a reliable pair. Before the end of the season Tom Saunders was recalled from Pontypridd and during the latter part of the season was seldom caught napping, his long kicks to touch and solid defence were invaluable on many occasions. He was at that time without question one of the finest custodians in Wales.

Amongst the forwards were veterans Dick Hellings and Billy Alexander, two of the finest and strongest internationals that had ever played for Wales. There was also Bob Jones, Rowley Thomas (who had transferred from Pontypridd), Albert Powell, J Bowen, Evan Jones, William Rhys Williams, Rees Jenkins and Arthur Harding. Harding, who was a fellow student with Willie Llewellyn at Christ College, Brecon joined the club a few weeks before the end of the season and made an immediate impact on the team, Llwynypia winning all five games he played in. With Willie Llewellyn gaining his first Welsh cap in the international against England at Swansea in January 1899, this was the first season that the Rhondda had provided an international three-quarter and Llwynypia had the unique distinction of having three international players during the same year.

Home and away matches were played with Cardiff and the heaviest defeat of the season was sustained at the Cardiff Arms Park where the Welsh Metropolitans piled on a score of 21 points to nil. A couple of months later, however, Cardiff barely escaped a defeat. Each side scored a try but those who witnessed the game agreed that the Rhondda men certainly deserved to win. On that occasion Gwyn Nicholls was unable to play for Cardiff. The first encounter against Neath ended in a pointless draw but in the return game at Neath the home team won by three penalty goals to nil. Both games against Llanelly were drawn and it is interesting to note that out of the previous four matches with Llanelly three were drawn and the other resulted in a victory for Llwynypia.

Much disappointment was felt when the home match with Gloucester was abandoned due to the bad weather that prevailed in February 1899. Between the end of December 1898 until the middle of February 1899 Llwynypia only played one game, the away defeat to Cardiff. There was considerable interest in the game when Llwynypia played away to Gloucester at the end of March. Gloucester had beaten Cardiff, Newport, Swansea and Llanelly and there were high hopes that the Rhondda men would be able to put a stop to their series of victories over Welsh teams. Llwynypia, who were without Billy Alexander and Bob Jones, played well in a hard fought game but a first half converted try by the home team was enough to give them victory.

Llwynypia was renowned as a club where there was an excellent relationship between players and the officials. They had recognised that thorough organisation and good feeling, in addition to constant training was necessary if any measure of success was to be attained. The untiring and zealous work of the long term club secretary, Mr Dai Llewellyn, who was skilfully assisted by enthusiastic colleague and treasurer Mr Ted Hughes, kept the club on a solid organisational footing. In addition, the services of Mr Tom Williams, of the Welsh Football Union, who had been one of the mainstays of the club over many years cannot be overestimated. In their president for the season, Dr Morgan of Clydach Vale, they had a patron who showed a lively interest in the welfare of the team and had been the means of enthusing many of the leading residents of the district in a similar manner. Finally the support of Mr Archibald Hood and his son Mr W Walter Hood, owners of the Glamorgan Colliery, was instrumental in the success of Llwynypia Football Club over many years.

This was without doubt the season when Willie Llewellyn came of age. The previous season, as vice-captain of Llwynypia, he had gained Glamorgan County honours, been reserve for the Welsh international trial match and been selected as a reserve wing for both of Wales' internationals against Ireland and England. Owing to his remarkable turn of speed, his coolness, judgment and brilliant try scoring ability, he was looked upon as a promising future Welsh international.

This potential was realised during the 1898–99 season when Willie Llewellyn was selected to play for Wales for the first time. When the Welsh team was selected to play against England at St Helen's, Swansea on 7th January 1899, he was chosen as left wing. At just twenty-one years of age many did not approve of his selection as it was thought he was too young, light and not stylish enough. However, he had a dream debut scoring a record four tries in a 26 points to three victory.

Willie Llewellyn gained the first of his twenty Welsh caps six days after his twenty-first birthday.

As captain of Llwynypia for the 1898–99 season, Willie led his team to a third consecutive Glamorgan League title, played again for Glamorgan County, played in the Wales international trial match at Mountain Ash and in addition to his first Welsh cap against England he also played for Wales against Scotland and Ireland. Willie Llewellyn had become known throughout the football world as one of the best wings Wales had ever possessed.

In addition to the two Llwynypia practise matches Willie Llewellyn played thirty-seven games during the 1898–99 season including thirty-one games for Llwynypia, two games for Glamorgan County, one Welsh international trial match and three internationals. Excluding the try Willie Llewellyn scored in the second trial match he scored thirty-four tries including four against England, one against Scotland, two against Somerset and three against Cornwall. He also scored four tries for Llwynypia in the game against Mona.

Prior to the start of the season Llwynypia played two practise matches, one on Saturday 10th September and one the following Saturday on 17th September. Only twenty-two players turned out for the first practise match. The match was scheduled to start at five o'clock but did not actually start until 6 o'clock owing to a heat wave, which made it necessary to play in the cool of the evening. Before a good number of spectators, an eleven aside match was played between Dick Hellings' team and Willie Llewellyn's team. A fast and spirited game was the result; although no match details were recorded. Llwynypia's final trial match on the whole was very disappointing. After the poor turn out of players the previous Saturday it was expected that at least thirty players would take the field. This was not the case and only twenty-eight players turned out and the game was played between twelve of the first team and sixteen of the district. The day's play gave hardly any insight into the form of any of the first team. No player shone throughout the game but now and again a brief flash of brilliant play was shown by several players, notably Charlie Wood, Ike Edmunds, Willie Llewellyn, Dick Hellings and Billy Alexander. Willie Llewellyn scored one of the seven tries in a three goals and four tries (27 points) to nil victory.

Llwynypia started the 1898–99 season with a narrow victory over Maesteg and then comprehensively beat Abertillery at home by 41 points to nil. Willie Llewellyn scored two of the eleven tries and converted the final try which was scored by George Evans.

The first defeat of the season came when Llwynypia played Treherbert in the first League match of the season. It was the first game of the season for both Dick Hellings and Billy Alexander and this was evident by the fact that the Llwynypia forwards were well beaten by the Treherbert pack. It was a fierce game and the referee, Mr Gavin Henry, had to interrupt the game on several occasions because of rough play. Early in the game Iestyn Thomas was injured and Ben Phillips had to be taken out of the forwards to play at half-back and then in the three-quarters. It was a pity for Llwynypia that they had to play with only fourteen men for nearly three-quarters of the game but that did not detract from Treherbert's victory. With their forwards in total control and the Llwynypia halves playing behind a beaten pack of forwards there was very little chance for the Llwynypia three-quarters to shine but on the very few occasions when they did have the ball they acquitted themselves in splendid fashion. The game was not a pretty one and with no striking features a first half unconverted try by J Jenkins for Treherbert was sufficient to secure victory for the home team.

Llwynypia returned to winning ways in their next game against Bridgend. An unconverted try by Willie Llewellyn in the first half and three unconverted tries, one by Ben Phillips and two by Dick Hellings, in the second half, gave Llwynypia victory by 12 points to nil. A feature of the visitors play was the sturdy defence presented by them to the vigorous onslaught of Llewellyn's men.

In the next game an unconverted try by Billy Alexander late in the game gave Llwynypia a narrow away victory over Aberavon. For fully three-quarters of the game there was hardly anything to choose between the two sides but during the closing stages of the game the Llwynypia forwards took control and through Alexander scored the winning points.

Willie's next game was for Glamorgan against Somerset at Cardiff on Wednesday 26th October. Willie, who played on the left wing, lined up in the three-quarters with Welsh internationals Gwyn Nicholls and Viv Huzzey of Cardiff with fellow Llwynypia teammates Dick Hellings and Billy Alexander in the forwards. Charlie Powell of Neath opened the scoring for Glamorgan with a try that Viv Huzzey failed to convert. Somerset replied with a magnificent drop goal by Sealey. Then just before half-time Dan Jones, Aberavon's first international player, got the ball ten yards from halfway on the Somerset side and started a spectacular three-quarter movement. When looking certain to be tackled Jones passed to Viv Huzzey who passed on to Dan Rees, the Swansea centre. Rees showing excellent judgement drew the opposing right wing and transferred to Willie Llewellyn who crossed wide out for an excellent try. With the try going unconverted Glamorgan led at the interval by 6 points to four.

Early in the second half Glamorgan added to their score when Powell darted over for a try which Gibbs converted. Shortly afterwards Powell fielded very smartly and passed to Dan Jones who passed on to Gwyn Nicholls after he had slipped past the Somerset left centre. The Cardiff captain handed-off Somerset's left wing and cleverly drawing the left centre passed to Dan Rees who took the ball splendidly and gave a model pass to Willie Llewellyn enabling him to cross for another brilliant try.

Gibbs again converted and Glamorgan now led by 16 points to four. It was now clear that Somerset were well beaten and a further unconverted try by Sam Davies put the result beyond doubt. Another late try by Viv Huzzey which was converted by Gibbs brought the game to an end with Glamorgan winning by 24 points to four.

The League match with Barry that was due to be played at Llwynypia on Saturday 29th October did not go ahead. Barry turned up short of players and when they went to the ground claimed that it was in an unplayable condition because of a small pool of water in front of the goal-posts. The ground was very sodden after heavy rain the previous fortnight and considerable discussion took place between the teams. Barry however, persisted with their assertions and the match was abandoned. As a result of the game not being played a very amusing story appeared in the *Evening Express* the following Tuesday. It read as follows: 'There are 89 million gallons of Scotch whisky lying idle in bond owing, Mr Dewar says, to the difficulty finding a sufficient supply of suitable water with which to mix the spirit. Yet if word were passed round for the release of that whisky from its bond, rescuers to bring their own water, it would not have to languish long. Barry refused to play their League fixture with Llwynypia last Saturday, just because a pool of water stood in front of the goal-posts. It was seriously suggested that a few gallons of whisky put into the pool would alter their opinion. There was no doubt about it and here there's whisky idly waiting for water! Ah! the inequalities of life!'

Llwynypia continued their campaign with their next game away to Morriston. The home team were winning by two unconverted tries to nil at the interval and Llwynypia looked as if they were unable to get back into the game. Morriston started the second half strongly but Llwynypia managed to get an unconverted try when George Evans caught the ball in a line-out and dashed over for a try. Morriston were again on the attack and the home forwards brought off another of their loose rushes which took them to the Llwynypia twenty-five. Here Willie Llewellyn pulled the match out of the fire with a magnificent bit of play. Receiving a long pass from a melee just inside his quarter, he took the ball on the run and in an instant had skipped past wide, round the full-back and was making for the line with a clear field in front of him. There was not a man in Morriston to overtake him and though they tried hard, he left them far behind in a run three-quarters the length of the field. He scored behind the posts and Foster easily converted. Llwynypia were now leading and encouraged by their success they pulled themselves together and when the ball was again free their forwards passed in an irresistible fashion and covering half the length of the field Jones scored. The kick at goal failed but Llwynypia were now well on top and during the final few minutes before the end of the game they were able to do as they liked. When the final whistle came Llwynypia were leading by 11 points to six.

The following Monday Willie Llewellyn played his second County game of the season when he played for Glamorgan against Cornwall at Cardiff. He again lined up with Welsh internationals Gwyn Nicholls and Viv Huzzey in the three-quarters together with future Welsh international Dan Rees the Swansea centre. Although both Dick Hellings and Billy Alexander were selected to play neither appeared on the day. This was a great day for Willie Llewellyn who crossed for three of the eight tries scored. Glamorgan were on top from the start and an early try by Gwyn Nicholls, which Billy Bancroft failed to convert, gave Glamorgan an early lead. Willie Llewellyn was the next to score after some clever play by Dan Rees and Gwyn Nicholls. The try went unconverted. Nevertheless, Cornwall responded well and Glamorgan were not getting things all their own way. Then within three minutes Glamorgan scored two tries, both scored by Willie Llewellyn wide out. The first came when Charlie Powell, having run to the centres, transferred to Dan Rees, who beat his man and gave the ball trickily to the Llwynypia sprinter who dashed over for an unconverted try wide out. The second came about when Gwyn Nicholls managed to get a pass away out of the tackle to Dan Rees who subsequently gave a well-timed pass back to Gwyn Nicholls. The Cardiff captain forged his way over the line and taken down by the legs lost the ball which Willie Llewellyn picked up and carried behind the posts. Billy Bancroft, the Swansea and Wales international full-back, easily converted and Glamorgan led at the interval by 14 points to nil.

Cornwall gave the spectators a surprise early in the second half. The whole of the halves and three-quarters handled the ball and Thomas scored a brilliant try in the left-hand corner after dragging Viv Huzzey ten yards with him. The attempt at goal failed. Another fine try by Viv Huzzey which was converted by Bancroft gave Glamorgan a sixteen point lead. Emlyn Lewis and Charlie Powell at half-backs kept the Glamorgan three-quarters continually in motion and eventually Fred Cornish scored a try which Bancroft converted. Two further tries by Charlie Powell and Viv Huzzey, one of which was converted, brought the scoring to an end and Glamorgan were victorious by 32 points to three.

Willie Llewellyn captained Llwynypia in their next game, their third encounter against Llanelly at Stradey Park, on Saturday 12th November. The weather was miserable with rain falling almost continually throughout the game. Llanelly took the field with only fourteen men, pending the arrival of their full-back Alf Roberts. W J Thomas came out of the pack to take his place but barely ten minutes had elapsed before Alf Roberts arrived and took up his usual position. Before Alf Roberts' arrival Willie Llewellyn almost scored but was forced into touch by the temporary full-back Thomas. With Roberts turning up Thomas returned to the pack. From a scrum at the centre the Llwynypia forwards went away with a dangerous rush which took play close to the Llanelly goal-line. Llanelly relieved the pressure but from the next scrum the Llwynypia backs were set in motion from which Foster scored a fine try. With the try converted Llwynypia took the lead by 5 points to nil. After this the Llanelly backs had several good runs and just failed to score on a few occasions. Just before half-time the Llanelly backs were again on the move and after a series of passes Rhys Gabe scored a brilliant try for Llanelly. Evan Lloyd, the Welsh international winger, kicked the conversion and the game was drawn at 5 points all at the interval. Although Llanelly were pressing for much of the second half Llwynypia concentrated on keeping the ball amongst their forwards to prevent the home team from scoring. Despite Llwynypia being on the defensive for almost the whole of the second half they kept their line intact and the game ended in a draw.

At a meeting of the match committee of the Welsh Football Union held at the Queen's Hotel, Cardiff on Thursday 17th November Willie Llewellyn was selected to represent the Whites against the Stripes in the Welsh international trial match to be played at Mountain Ash on Saturday 3rd December. Also in the Whites three-quarter line were current Welsh internationals Gwyn Nicholls and Viv Huzzey together with the uncapped Reg Skrimshire of Newport. Fellow Llwynypia teammate Dick Hellings was in the Whites pack while Billy Alexander was selected in the Stripes forwards. Willie's selection was recognition of the fact that he was in tremendous form; he had already scored nine tries from the ten games he had played so far during the season. The teams selected were as follows:

Whites: Back, W J Bancroft (Swansea); three-quarters, G Nicholls and V Huzzey (Cardiff), R T Skrimshire (Newport) and W Llewellyn (Llwynypia); half-backs, D James (Swansea), G Ll Lloyd (Newport); forwards, D Hellings (Llwynypia), W Parker (Swansea), A Brice (Aberavon), F Scrine (Swansea), J Blake (Cardiff), W Gibbs (Penarth), Sam Davies (Neath) and Rev. E T Davies (Mountain Ash).

Stripes: Back, J Davies (Neath); three-quarters, G Davies and D Rees (Swansea), M Williams (Llanelly), and Hubert Alexander (Newport); half-backs, C Powell (Neath) and S Biggs (Cardiff); Forwards, W H Alexander (Llwynypia), J Hodges (Newport), D J Daniel (Llanelly), Tom Dobson (Cardiff), W E Rees (Pontypridd), J Matthews (Bridgend), A Sawtell (Cwmbran) and F Cornish (Cardiff).

Willie Llewellyn scored another three tries when Llwynypia defeated Penarth at home by 17 points to nil. Willie opened the scoring with an unconverted try. This was followed by a try for George Mills which was converted by George Evans. Just before the interval Billy Alexander added another unconverted try which gave Llwynypia an interval lead of 11 points. Two second half unconverted tries for Willie Llewellyn completed the scoring.

The most important match in the Rhondda on Saturday 26th November was the League match between Llwynypia and Pontypridd and a large crowd turned out to watch the game. Willie Llewellyn was again on form and scored two tries in the 30 points to nil victory. George Mills opened the scoring for Llwynypia with an unconverted try. Shortly afterwards Foster got the ball and clearing the centre passed to Willie Llewellyn, who took the pass at full-speed and slipped round behind the posts. George Evans converted and the crowd were 'sent into ecstasies of delight.' Llwynypia scored again when George Mills rounded Saunders and scored behind the posts. George Evans failed to convert. Despite having a goal and two tries scored against them in the first fifteen minutes Pontypridd did not lose heart and up until the interval they played some good rugby and prevented Llwynypia from scoring. Before half-time J E Jones, the

Llwynypia custodian was injured and had to leave the field and Llwynypia were forced to play the remainder of the half with fourteen men. When the half-time whistle blew Llwynypia were leading by 11 points to nil.

Shortly after the restart J E Jones returned for Llwynypia and they were back at full strength. Llwynypia picked up where they had left off in the first half and it was not too long before Ben Phillips dodged his way home and scored close to the posts. George Evans converted. Despite Pontypridd playing well in patches Llwynypia were too good for them and when Foster dashed into a loose scrum and picked up, Llwynypia were off again. Foster passed to Rhys Williams who passed on to Willie Llewellyn. He took the ball splendidly with one arm and ran round every man half the length of the field and grounded behind the posts for a magnificent try. The kick for goal failed when George Evans struck the cross-bar and the ball bounced back into the field. However, in three minutes Ben Phillips got the ball and dodging through scored again. George Evans once again failed with the conversion. Shortly afterwards Willie Llewellyn, in the thick of his opponents, threw out a beautiful long pass to Foster who ran on and passed to Ben Phillips. Phillips showed the Pontypridd left wing a clean pair of heels and scored his third try behind the posts. Andrew Powell converted. Just before the final whistle Bob Jones scored an unconverted try and immediately afterwards time was called with the score, Llwynypia 30 points, Pontypridd nil.

On the day Llwynypia were playing Neath at home Willie Llewellyn, Dick Hellings and Billy Alexander were all playing in the Welsh international trial match at Mountain Ash. The decision of the Welsh Union Committee to alter the title and scope of the old East v West trial, which produced nothing but discord between the respective districts, and to substitute it for a trial of presumably the best thirty players in the clubs of the Principality, without regard to their territorial position, was met with great approval throughout Wales.

There were several alterations in the teams from those originally selected. David Davies of Bridgend and David Davies of Llanelly filled vacancies caused by the absence of David James of Swansea and Selwyn Biggs of Cardiff. Louis Phillips, the Newport scrum-half, occupied the position which was assigned to Llewellyn Lloyd. The teams lined up as follows:

Whites: Back, W J Bancroft (Swansea); three-quarters, Gwyn Nicholls (Cardiff) right centre, R T Skrimshire (Newport) left centre, V Huzzey (Cardiff) right wing and W Llewellyn (Llwynypia) left wing; half-backs, D Davies (Bridgend) and L A Phillips (Newport); forwards, D Hellings (Llwynypia), W Parker (Swansea), A Brice (Aberavon), F Scrine (Swansea), J Blake (Cardiff), W Gibbs (Penarth), Sam Davies (Neath) and Rev. E T Davies (Mountain Ash).

Stripes: Back, J Davies (Neath); three-quarters, George Davies and D Rees (Swansea) centres, Morgan Williams (Llanelly) right wing, and Hubert Alexander (Newport) left wing; half-backs, Charlie Powell (Neath) and David Davies (Llanelly); Forwards, W H Alexander (Llwynypia), J Hodges (Newport), D J Daniel (Llanelly), Tom Dobson (Cardiff), W E Rees (Pontypridd), J Matthews (Bridgend), A Sawtell (Cwmbran) and F Cornish (Cardiff).

Contrary to expectations the game was vigorously contested throughout and of a higher than average standard for a trial match. Brilliant back play was almost impossible owing to the sorry state of the ground, due to heavy and continuous rain. The conditions greatly hampered the Whites' three-quarters who were far superior to their counterparts in the Stripes back line. The Stripes forwards were undoubtedly the stronger, but the Whites pack contained several prominent individuals. Neath forward Sam Davies opened the scoring with a fine try which Billy Bancroft just failed to convert. Reg Skrimshire was the next to score after Viv Huzzey made ground and kicked across the field. Skrimshire, showing great pace, gained the ball and scored. Billy Bancroft landed the conversion to give the Whites an 8 point lead. Though the Stripes forwards were still prominent their side was not comparable to the Whites. Just before the interval a break by Gwyn Nicholls made an opening for Viv Huzzey. Beating Alexander for pace Huzzey ran up to the opposition twenty-five where he passed back to the forwards. Scrine got possession, but the Swansea forward passed back to a colleague who mulled the ball, but Brice, fielding the ball, galloped over for a try. Billy Bancroft was again successful with the conversion and the Whites led at the interval by 13 points to nil.

In the second half, despite being given many opportunities by their forwards, the Stripes three-quarters failed to score. Skrimshire did very good work in defence as did Nicholls and Llewellyn, but it was generally not a case of stopping the backs but saving forward rushes. Tom Dobson and Fred Cornish then led a dangerous looking dribble for the Stripes with Jehoida Hodges in close attendance. This took play to the Whites' twenty-five and George Davies, getting a rebound off Nicholls, passed towards his forwards. In a general melee W E Rees, the Pontypridd forward, scored a try for the Stripes. Joe Davies, the Neath custodian, converted from an easy position. Despite the Whites nearly scoring on several occasions there were no more scores and the Whites were victorious by 13 points to five.

The best of the Stripes forwards were Billy Alexander, Tom Dobson, Jehoida Hodges, Fred Cornish and David Daniel. For the Whites Dick Hellings, Alfred Brice, Jere (John) Blake, Will Parker and Fred Scrine were the pick of the forwards. Although both sets of half-backs played well it was felt that the selection of the international half-backs for the game against England on Saturday 7th January 1899 would be David James, the Swansea half-back, and whoever was playing the best between Selwyn Biggs (Cardiff) and George Llewellyn Lloyd (Newport). David James had demonstrated beyond doubt in recent matches for Swansea that he was a tremendous half-back, even when playing without his famous brother Evan as a partner. Evan was not considered for the trail match and not thought to be in contention for selection for the Welsh match against England because he was injured. At three-quarters it was thought that the Whites quartette of Viv Huzzey, Gwyn Nicholls, Reg Skrimshire and Willie Llewellyn were not likely to be improved on as they were infinitely a better side on the day. Reg Skrimshire showed himself to greater all round advantage than his most formidable rival, Dan Rees, of Swansea, who on the day was eclipsed by his fellow club-mate, George Davies. Everything seemed to be in place for Reg Skrimshire and Willie Llewellyn to take their places in the Welsh team for their first caps against England at St Helen's. At full-back Billy Bancroft was still without a peer and his place looked certain in the Welsh team.

Although selected for the Glamorgan League team to play the Monmouthshire League the following Monday, Willie Llewellyn, Dick Hellings and Billy Alexander all stood down to take part in the important Glamorgan League fixture against Penygraig to be played on the same evening at Belle Vue Park, Penygraig. The game was one of the best games seen at Penygraig for a long time with several passages of exciting play being witnessed on both sides. The only score of the game came in the first half when Harry Morgan dropped a goal for Penygraig. An injury to one of the Llwynypia players resulted in the visitors having to play the remainder of the match with only fourteen men. Severely handicapped, Llwynypia were unable to break down their opponents and lost the game by 4 points to nil. Following the match Llwynypia launched a protest to the Glamorgan League committee on the grounds that the Llwynypia team were kept waiting at the ground for their opponents 15 minutes after the advertised start time and as a result the game was stopped five minutes too soon in consequence of the darkness. At a meeting of the Glamorgan League committee on Friday 16th December, Mr Tom Williams, Llwynypia, Welsh Football Union, presiding, the referee, Mr Gil Evans of Swansea, confirmed these statements and despite a vigorous protest by Mr Moses Jenkins, the Penygraig secretary, the committee ordered the game to be replayed at Penygraig on a date to be mutually agreed upon.

On Thursday 8th December the Welsh Football Union Committee met to select the Welsh team to play against England at St Helen's, Swansea, on Saturday 7th January 1899. When the team was announced Willie Llewellyn had indeed been selected to play his first game for Wales and gain his first Welsh international cap. In addition to Willie Llewellyn there were another five new caps in the side, Reg Skrimshire (Newport), Will Parker (Swansea), Alfred Brice (Aberavon), Jehoida Hodges (Newport) and Fred Scrine (Swansea). Evan and David James of Swansea were chosen at half-back, Evan having recovered from the injury that threatened his selection.

Willie Llewellyn celebrated his selection in the Welsh team by scoring a try in Llwynypia's next game away to Mountain Ash. The visit of the Rhondda champions to Mountain Ash was always regarded as the game of the season. Additional interest was taken in this game because both teams had lost two League matches and since the launch of the League competition the fight for honours had always featured these two sides, Mountain Ash winning once and Llwynypia winning three times. The game was refereed by Arthur Gould and throughout the first half play was open and exciting. Mountain Ash opened the scoring with an unconverted try by Linton. A short while later after some even play, Ben Phillips put in a good kick to the Mountain Ash backs who returned into touch. Then Hillman made a fine run, breaking through beautifully, but he was not backed up. From a series of passes amongst the Llwynypia three-quarters Willie Llewellyn got possession and crossed for a spectacular try. George Evans took the kick at goal and made a splendid effort but the ball hit the upright and rebounded into the field of play. With the Llwynypia forwards getting the upper hand in the open Foster received a pass in a good position and dropped a well-judged goal. Things remained pretty even between the two sides and with no more scoring the whistle went for half-time with Llwynypia leading by 7 points to three. Here things stayed and with no scoring in the second half Llwynypia won this important League encounter.

The committee of the Glamorgan County Football Club met on Thursday 16th December to select the Glamorgan team to play Devon on Wednesday 28th December. When the team was announced there were only five men different from the fifteen selected to represent Wales against England at Swansea. Jere Blake (Cardiff) and Sam Davies (Neath) took the places of Hodges (Newport) and Daniel (Llanelly) in the forwards, Selwyn Biggs (Cardiff) and Charlie Powell (Neath) replaced the brothers James at half-back, whilst George Davies replaced Reg Skrimshire (Newport) at left centre. This would have been an ideal opportunity for at least ten of the Welsh side to practise prior to the game against England but unfortunately the game was cancelled.

Llwynypia drew their next game against Bridgend. Andrew Powell scored a try in the first half which Tom Saunders failed to convert. An unconverted try in the second half by Bennett brought the scores level and for a while it was anyone's game. Each side attacked in turn but nothing further was scored and the game ended in a draw.

Willie Llewellyn had a brilliant game in Llwynypia's next encounter against Treorky in the Glamorgan League. There was a great deal of interest in this the first League match of the season between the two sides. Early in the game, after fast and open play, the home backs started a bout of passing which ended in Willie Llewellyn, after receiving from Foster, eluding White and Davies to score at the corner flag.

Tom Saunders failed to convert. Willie scored again when Hellings, receiving from a line-out threw out wide to Foster who gave a scoring pass to Willie Llewellyn. This time Tom Saunders was successful with the conversion. Treorky responded with a try of their own when White made a strong burst and passed wide at the right moment to D R Thomas, who, without a second's delay, threw to Lewis Lewis, who scored a well-deserved try by the corner flag. Tom Jones converted from a difficult angle. The game was then evenly contested for about fifteen minutes. After Tom Saunders had figured prominently in some fine defensive work, Llwynypia again assumed aggressive tactics. Having reached the Treorky twenty-five Ben Phillips got possession and smart passing between himself, Foster and Llewellyn ended in the international wing scoring his third try. Saunders again converted and Llwynypia led at the interval by 13 points to five.

Two second half tries by Ben Phillips, the first of which was converted by Tom Saunders brought the scoring to an end and Llwynypia were victors by 21 points to five. The game was keenly contested throughout and the League champions thoroughly deserved to win. Long before the close of the game it was apparent that the visitors were clearly beaten although they tried hard right up to the final whistle.

Llwynypia travelled to Leicester for their next game on Boxing Day. About 10,000 spectators were present to witness a hard fought game that ended in a nil all drawn game. The teams were evenly matched and although the game flagged a little towards the close, interest in it was maintained throughout. Llwynypia acquitted themselves very well in every respect. Their attack was smart and clean, while in defence they proved themselves impregnable.

Three hard games in four days proved too much for Llwynypia and they narrowly lost their next match against Northampton. Llwynypia decided to play exactly the same team that had performed so well the previous day at Leicester. A second-half try which Simmonds scored and converted himself was the only score of the game. Following the Northampton score Llwynypia attacked strenuously but they lost innumerable chances and the game ended with Northampton winning by 5 points to nil. Although Llwynypia were superior at forward they made bad use of their opportunities and when near the goal-line invariably spoiled their chances. Lewis, Hellings and Llewellyn all played well but

Newport Rugby Football Club 1897–98

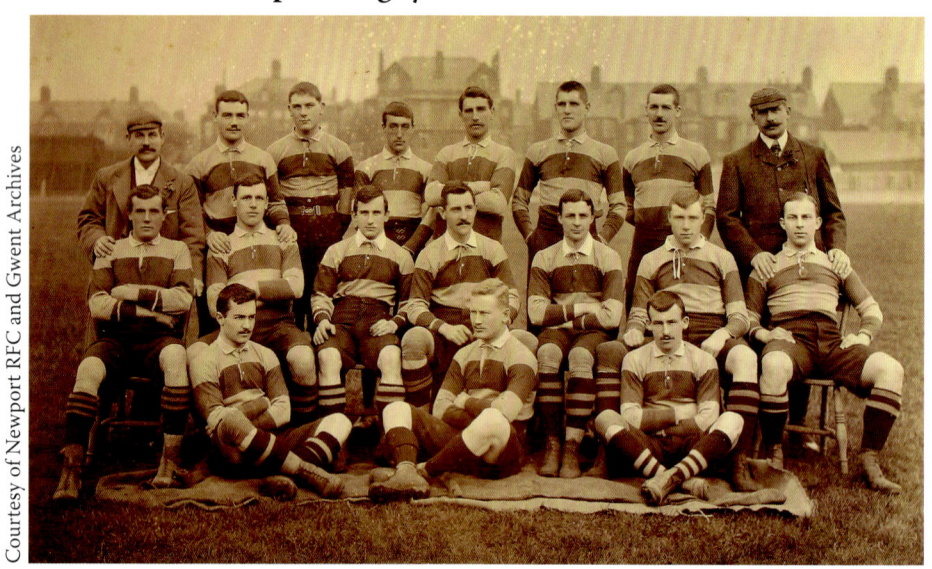

Back Row: G Thomas (Trainer), A Inns, H S Williams, W Carrol, W Parfitt, J H Dunn, M Price, Harry Packer. *Middle Row*: J J Hodges, G Boots, G Ll Lloyd, A W Boucher (Captain), H G Alexander, W H Williams, J E C Partridge.
Front Row: L A Phillips, C D Phillips and P Doran.

Tom Saunders was not in his usual good form. The game was not as pleasant as that against Leicester while the referee's decisions were often incomprehensible to the spectators.

When the Newport team to play the Monmouthshire League on Saturday 31st December was announced Willie Llewellyn had been selected on the left wing. Jones of Chepstow stood down to allow Willie Llewellyn to play with Reg Skrimshire prior to them playing together for Wales against England at Swansea the following week. The clear intention was to give both players the opportunity of practising what they should to do against the English team at St Helen's. Unfortunately the match was declared off in consequence of the ground at Newport being in an unfit condition. Keen disappointment was felt among the League clubs, for the players had looked forward to the match with much interest and in addition the game would have provided the opportunity for Reg Skrimshire and Willie Llewellyn, who formed the left wing in the three-quarter line for Wales, to develop their style of play, the Llwynypia captain being on the spot ready to fill the position kindly arranged for him by the Newport Committee.

The Newport team selected for the match against the Monmouthshire League was as follows: Back, T Thomas (Blaina); three-quarters, W Llewellyn (Llwynypia), R T Skrimshire, A W Boucher and H G Alexander; half-backs, G Ll Lloyd and L A Phillips; forwards, J Hodges, M Price, W H Williams, A Inns, W Parfitt, J E C Partridge, A Brown and S White. If the game had been played not only would it have enabled Willie Llewellyn to play alongside fellow Wales' debutants Reg Skrimshire and Jehoida Hodges but also alongside seasoned Welsh international Arthur Boucher and George Llewellyn Lloyd who had gained the first of his twelve Welsh caps against Ireland in 1896. Willie would also have been playing with future Welsh international Louis Phillips and future South Africa international J E C 'Birdie' Partridge who played for South Africa in the first test against the 1903 British Lions.

An article in the *Sporting Life* criticised the selection of the Welsh team to face England at Swansea on Saturday 7th January 1899. Firstly there was doubt about the selection of the brothers James at half-back in place of Selwyn Biggs and George Llewellyn Lloyd. Although there was agreement that behind a strong pack they were clever and determined it was felt that if the Welsh pack was beaten, as they expected it to be, and the brothers were rushed, they did not have the physique to stem the tide. The article stated, 'They are in fact, a typical part of the works in the Welsh game, demonstrative but not defensive.' The article went on to say, 'Lloyd and Biggs are to our mind players of a very much better school and though we regret that neither of them has this year earned the distinction of representing his country, we feel from their absence in the team a great deal more confidence as to the result of our game at Cardiff.' Of Billy Bancroft it was thought that he was a marvellous kicker but a weak tackler and of Skrimshire it was recognised that he had improved greatly but was reckless and speculative. The article concluded by saying, 'W Llewellyn of Llwynypia has a great reputation for grace and strength; Hellings, by no means a finished player has been chosen presumably for robustness but we have not, so far, seen anything terrorising in his play. T Dobson, with pugilistic physiognomy, is a very thorough player. The Swansea forwards we have not yet had an opportunity of seeing. We are bold enough to think we could have improved very much in this side from the available material.' Having beaten Wales in the Home Nations Championship the previous year England possibly had every right to be optimistic with regard to the outcome of the game but they were in for a terrible shock.

Wales had faced England on fifteen previous occasions and had only managed three victories, the first away at Dewsbury in 1890 and two at home; Cardiff in 1893 and Newport in 1897. There was only one change from the team originally selected and John 'Jere' Blake of Cardiff replaced Llwynypia's Dick Hellings who had not recovered from a severe sprain received in the game against Leicester. With Jere Blake making his debut for Wales this brought the total number of debutants in the Welsh team to seven. England also had seven new caps in their team. The teams lined up as follows:

Wales: W J Bancroft (Swansea, Captain); H V P Huzzey, E G Nicholls (Cardiff), *R T Skrimshire (Newport), *W M Llewellyn (Llwynypia); E James, D James (Swansea); *J Blake, T Dobson (Cardiff), W H Alexander (Llwynypia), *F G Scrine (Swansea), *A B Brice (Aberavon), D J Daniel (Llanelly), *J J Hodges (Newport), *W J Parker (Swansea). (* Wales debut)

England: *H T Gamlin (Devonport Albion); *R Forrest (Wellington), P W Stout (Richmond), P M R Royds (Blackheath), G C Robinson (Percy Park); R O' H Livesay (Blackheath), A Rotherham (Richmond, Captain); H W Dudgeon, F Jacob, *J Daniell (Richmond), *C H Harper (Exeter), *W Mortimer (Marlborough Nomads), *G R Gibson (Northern), *J Davidson (Aspatria), R F Oakes (Hartlepool Rovers). (* England Debut)

Referee: Adam J Turnbull (Scotland).

In great weather a crowd of 25,000 saw Wales defeat England in grand style. Willie Llewellyn opened the scoring for Wales. After Gwyn Nicholls had found touch near the English twenty-five yard line Wales got possession and Willie Llewellyn, Gwyn Nicholls and Reg Skrimshire had hard lines in not scoring. Still they pegged away right on the English line and eventually, a kick by Royds being charged down, Willie Llewellyn went over in the corner with a beautiful try which Billy Bancroft just failed to convert. The Welsh forwards were now scrummaging very well and time after time the ball was coming out to the Welsh backs. Evan James was holding his shoulder and obviously in a lot of discomfort but he

Wales Team v England 1899

Back Row: T Dobson, F Scrine, W Parker, J J Hodges, A Bryce, J Blake, D J Daniel.
Middle Row: R T Skrimshire, H V P Huzzey, W J Bancroft (Captain),
W Llewellyn, E G Nicholls, W Alexander.
Front Row: G Bowen (Linesman), Evan James and David James.

played on. Although England tried hard and despite having the wind in their favour they could not get out of their own half. Just before the interval, after a few minutes of loose play between the forwards, the game settled down just outside the English twenty-five. Here from a scrummage David James, popping round on the short side, ran right up to Gamlin and threw to Willie Llewellyn who, chased by a couple of English players, scored the second try for Wales. Billy Bancroft failed with the conversion and immediately afterwards half-time was called.

Leading by 6 points to nil Bancroft started the second half with the little wind there was now in favour of Wales. After Billy Bancroft had narrowly missed a shot at goal from a mark by Skrimshire England were penalised from the drop-out. From a scrummage on the English twenty-five the ball was sent to Gwyn Nicholls who ran between Rotherham and Royds and bearing to the right, threw out to Huzzey, who slipped past Gamlin and scored a beautiful try. Billy Bancroft converted from a difficult angle and Wales were ahead by 11 points to nil.

Having so much of the ball there seemed to be no question as to Wales winning. The Welsh forwards were now winning nine out of every ten scrummages and with so much possession were soon to score again. Nicholls getting a pass from Skrimshire slipped past Royds and running up to Gamlin, threw out to Huzzey, who beat the English custodian and scored a try which Bancroft again converted. It was a beautiful effort from the start, especially in the case of Nicholls, who took an awkward pass with one hand when nearly on his knees.

At length England managed to work their way up to the Welsh twenty-five, but a scrummage and a couple of line-outs and a punt from Huzzey brought play back to halfway. Here Willie Llewellyn and Reg Skrimshire started an attack that was joined by a couple of their forwards. They got down to the English goal-line, where Llewellyn got his pass back and crossed in the corner for his third try. Bancroft again converted with a magnificent kick. Once again the Welsh forwards got the better of the English pack and getting down to halfway the Welsh backs got away. They were checked and the ball came back to Bancroft who, racing round to the right, punted to the centre. Willie Llewellyn got the better of a race with Forrest and scored his fourth try. Bancroft easily converted and Wales were 26 points without reply. Losing their concentration for a moment, weak Welsh defence allowed Royds to slip past Gwyn Nicholls and pass to Robinson who crossed for the try. Stout failed with the conversion. This woke the Welsh team up and they were soon back in the English half of the field but with no further scoring the final whistle went and Wales were victorious by 26 points to three.

Just six days after his twenty-first birthday Willie Llewellyn had a dream debut for Wales. He scored four tries and was unlucky not to score a few more. No Welsh player before him had scored more than two tries in a match. All six tries came from the wings, with Viv Huzzey scoring the other two tries and Billy Bancroft converting four of them. Evan James managed to outwit the opposition, despite being handicapped by a dislocated shoulder. The James brothers played really well after a seven-year absence, but somehow the Welsh selectors never really appreciated them and neither played for Wales again. In February 1899, just six weeks after his last game for Wales, David James joined Broughton Rangers Northern Union Club.

This Welsh victory was the start of something very special with regard to games against England. Having lost to Wales in this match England did not defeat Wales again until they won at Twickenham in January 1910. Wales won the next four encounters and then drew 14 points all at Welford Road, Leicester in 1904. Wales then won five consecutive matches before they lost at Twickenham in 1910. During this time Wales were Home Nations champions on six occasions, sharing with Ireland in 1906. Between 1899 and 1911 Wales won six Triple Crowns and three Grand Slams. Wales won their first Triple Crown in 1893 and then won Triple Crowns again in 1900, 1902, 1905, 1908, 1909 and 1911. They played France for the first time in 1908 and won by 36 points to four, giving them their first Grand Slam. They subsequently won Grand Slams in 1909 and 1911. This was truly the first Golden Era of Welsh rugby.

Llwynypia lost their next game against a very strong Cardiff fifteen at Cardiff Arms Park. The Llwynypia colours being exactly the same as Cardiff, the Welsh Metropolitans turned out in white jerseys with a broad dark blue stripe. In the Cardiff side were Welsh internationals Gwyn Nicholls, William 'Pussy' Jones, Selwyn Biggs, Tom Dobson, Jere Blake and Fred Cornish. Also in the side was Bert Winfield at full-back who later played five times alongside Willie Llewellyn for Wales. The Llwynypia side contained only two Welsh internationals, the newly capped Willie Llewellyn and Billy Alexander, Dick Hellings having still not recovered from the injury received in the game against Leicester. This was Llwynypia's heaviest defeat of the season, going down by 21 points to nil. Two unconverted tries by Wayne Morgan and a try apiece for Arthur Ricketts and Jere Blake, both converted by Bert Winfield, gave Cardiff a 16 point lead at the interval. The only score of the second half was a try by William 'Pussy' Jones converted by Bert Winfield and when the final whistle went Cardiff were victors by 21 points to nil.

The match committee of the Welsh Football Union met at the Royal Hotel, Cardiff on Thursday 12th January 1899 and selected the same Welsh team to play against Scotland at Inverleith on Saturday the 28th January with the exception of the injured Evan James. Selwyn Biggs of Cardiff was selected to partner David James at half-back. George Llewellyn Lloyd was picked as first reserve. There was a feeling that if David James was selected, consideration should also have been given to select his younger brother Sam James as his partner, as both had played well together for Swansea in the absence of the injured Evan James. There was some doubt over the fitness of Viv Huzzey and if unavailable Billy Trew of Swansea would fill the left wing position with Willie Llewellyn moving to the right wing. Dick Hellings had recovered from the injury he sustained in the game against Leicester and was chosen as first reserve for the forwards.

The committee of the Glamorgan County Football Club met at the Royal Hotel, Swansea on Saturday 21st January to select the team to face Gloucestershire at Cardiff on Wednesday 8th February. They picked a very strong team that contained only three uncapped players, George Davies (Swansea), Charlie Powell (Neath) and Sam Davies (Neath). This was a very experienced side and at full-back was the twenty-five times capped Billy Bancroft. At centre and scrum-half were Gwyn Nicholls and Selwyn Biggs, both having been capped six times by Wales. Dick Hellings had four caps for Wales and Viv Huzzey, Billy Alexander and Tom Dobson had all been capped three times for Wales. The remainder of the team were Willie Llewellyn, Will Parker, Fred Scrine and Jere Blake all of whom had gained first caps in the January international against England.

The weather in January and February 1899 was particularly wretched with rain and frost accounting for many games. The Glamorgan fixture against Gloucestershire was one such casualty. The international rugby match between Wales and Scotland at Inverleith, Edinburgh, which was scheduled to take place on Saturday 28th January, was postponed four times because of a frozen Inverleith pitch. It was eventually played in the snow on Saturday 4th March. Llwynypia lost five fixtures with the games against Mountain Ash, Gloucester, Aberavon, Pontypridd and Penygraig all being cancelled because of the weather. In fact following the game against Cardiff on Saturday 14th January Llwynypia did not play again until their friendly match against Christ College, Brecon on Thursday 16th February.

An interesting newspaper report in the *Evening Express* on Friday 13th

January 1899 stated that Willie Llewellyn had gone North. The article read as follows: 'A Manchester correspondent, telegraphing on Thursday night says: – It is well known that Salford have for some time had in view the acquisition of a prominent three-quarter. Tonight it was stated that they had secured Llewellyn of Llwynypia, the man who scored four tries for Wales against England last Saturday, and he is expected to turn out in the important match against Widnes a week next Saturday. This is one of the most important captures ever made by a Northern Union club. It is rumoured that they have also obtained another brilliant player, whose name has not transpired.' The report went on to say, 'The suggestion of Llewellyn joining the Salford Club is so wildly improbable that a denial of the above statement is hardly needed. Willie Llewellyn in the first place is a home bird that maternal ties bind most strongly. Again his apprenticeship to a Rhondda chemist does not expire until September next and it is particularly unlikely that he will prejudice his future, probably of an analytical chemist, by taking any such step.' When approached the Welsh Football Union dismissed the rumour as completely false and stated there was probably confusion as there were many good players in Wales with the surname Llewellyn. Whether there was any truth in the rumour or not the fact remains that Willie Llewellyn did not go North and played all his rugby under Rugby Union rules.

There were other rumours at the time implicating additional Welsh players. It is said that before he was capped by Wales Billy Trew of Swansea had considered terms offered by Broughton Rangers. It was suggested that he had been offered £75 down and £2 a week and seriously considered accepting the offer. A report in the *Evening Express* on Wednesday 25th February stated that Trew intended leaving Swansea on the Tuesday morning but missed the 11.40 train. The report went on to

Billy Trew was a legend of Welsh rugby. He gained twenty-nine caps between 1900 and 1913.

say, 'On Tuesday afternoon he joined the local international players and reserves in a practise game, but unless sufficient pressure is brought to bear he will be up North in a few days' time.' Billy Trew never went North and became a true legend of the game in Wales. Trew first played for Swansea at Penarth on 8th October 1897 and soon established himself in the team playing in a variety of positions in the backs. He played for Wales on 29 occasions between 1900 and 1913, scoring 39 points (11 tries, 1 conversion and a drop goal), playing in three different positions, namely wing, stand-off and centre. He captained Wales in 14 matches between 1907 and 1913. Billy Trew was a member of the Triple Crown sides of 1900, 1908, 1909 and 1911 as well as winning the Grand Slam in 1908, 1909 and 1911. Willie Llewellyn and Billy Trew played together for Wales on six occasions.

George Davies, the Swansea centre and full-back was another player rumoured to be going North. His growing reputation meant he was hunted by Northern Union clubs. It is said that he went as far as travelling to Manchester to discuss terms with Oldham, along with his Swansea teammate Dan Rees. Fortunately for Swansea neither played in a Northern Union trial match which would have branded them professional players and therefore made them ineligible to play in the Union game. George Davies was first selected to play centre for Wales against England in 1900 and held on to that position for the next two internationals against Scotland and Ireland. He played in all three internationals the following season but with the growing partnership between the Cardiff pair of Gwyn Nicholls and Rhys Gabe at centre and Bert Winfield at full-back he did not

George Davies played centre and full-back for Swansea and Wales and gained nine caps for Wales between 1900 and 1905.

Courtesy of the Welsh Rugby Union and Gwent Archives

play at centre for Wales again. He returned to the Welsh team following solid performances at full-back for Swansea in their "Invincible" season of 1904–05. It was in this position that he won his last three caps for Wales in the 1905 Triple Crown side. Willie Llewellyn played in all the nine games in which George Davies played for Wales and captained the 1905 Triple Crown side.

Certainly the most famous capture by the Northern Union clubs was that of Evan and David James of Swansea, who signed for Broughton Rangers in January 1899. Both had played well for Wales in the victory over England at Swansea earlier in the month and although Evan was injured, David was selected to play for Wales in their next international against Scotland at Inverleith. A report in the *Evening Express* on Wednesday 18th January confirmed that inducements were being offered to Swansea players to go North. The report stated, 'The whole James family are on the point of moving.' Evan James remarked in an interview that he had found work very uncertain in Swansea and in addition to a large money bonus he was also offered a public-house if he signed for Broughton Rangers. To add to all this speculation a report in the *Evening Express* the following day confirmed that David James had written to Walter Rees, secretary of the Welsh Football Union, to say he would not play for Wales against Scotland.

A report in the *South Wales Daily Post* on Thursday 19th January, gave an account of an interview with Evan James which gave the details of the offer that Broughton Rangers had made. The terms of the offer were that the whole family, consisting of the father, mother, the younger three boys together with David, Evan and their children, would be relocated to Broughton. They would receive a

Evan James played half-back for Swansea and was capped by Wales on five occasions between 1890 and 1899.

CHAPTER FOUR

Courtesy of Swansea Rugby Football Club

David James played half-back for Swansea and was capped by Wales on four occasions between 1891 and 1899.

lump sum of £200 down, whilst David and Evan would be found work worth £2 a week, with Evan being given the management of a public-house. When questioned about his younger brothers Evan made the following comment: 'We'll start with Sam; he, of course, is already pretty well known. Then there's Will, who is about a year or so younger than Sam; he's coming on and bids fair to make a good half. After him comes young Claude, whose age is thirteen and I have no hesitation in saying that he'll make the best of the bunch. His trickiness is beyond telling, even now.'

A report in the *South Wales Daily Post* on Wednesday 25th January, confirmed the news which every Swansea rugby supporter had been expecting, that Evan and David James had signed for Northern Union Club, Broughton Rangers. The report confirmed that 'the fatal step' had been taken at a meeting in Manchester the previous evening when the committee of the Northern Union Lancashire Senior Competition met to grant playing permits for the four James brothers. In a conversation with a *South Wales Daily Post* reporter Evan confirmed that all arrangements with Broughton Rangers had been completed and that he and David had signed on their own behalf and they had also agreed terms on behalf of their brothers Sam and Will. When asked about the money the following conversation took place between Evan and the reporter: "Oh, that's all right," said Evan, "What do you mean by 'all right'?" asked the reporter. Evan replied, "I mean that Dai and I brought it back with us." "What in cheques?" "No, in bright golden sovereigns, my boy." Evan then confirmed that he had his share and that David had his but they still had to divide it with the 'old people.'

Before turning professional Evan James had played five times for Wales between 1890 and 1899, playing with his brother David on four occasions. David played four times for Wales between 1891 and 1899. The brothers' journey up North was unfortunately not a happy one with Evan falling ill and dying soon afterwards in August 1901. Swansea Rugby Football Club helped the James family financially upon their return to their home district in St Thomas. David died in Bonymaen in January 1929. Younger brother Claude played inside right for the Swansea East XI, a forerunner of Swansea Town and in the 1904 season, when the side played and won over twenty games, he scored thirty-two goals. Sadly Sam died of consumption in 1909.

After four consecutive weeks without a match because of the weather Llwynypia eventually played a friendly game against Christ College at Brecon on Thursday 16th February. Willie Llewellyn scored three tries in a game that saw a strong Llwynypia side defeat a Christ College fifteen that included future Welsh international wing, Teddy Morgan. Llwynypia were better in the tight scrummages and had a very smart pair of half-backs who got the ball away repeatedly. Willie Llewellyn's pace succeeded in eluding all the opposition on several occasions and Llwynypia were comfortable winners by 17 points to nil. Without Willie Llewellyn Llwynypia then lost their next game away to Neath by 9 points to nil. On Willie's return they lost away to Plymouth by 6 points to nil.

Two days before Wales faced Scotland in the rearranged international rugby match at Inverleith, Llwynypia played their rearranged Glamorgan League fixture against Mountain Ash. Played at Llwynypia, a brilliant first-half unconverted try by Llewellyn Deere gave Mountain Ash a three points to nil interval lead. A beautiful drop goal by Tom Saunders in the second half was enough to give Llwynypia victory by 4 points to three. Despite being picked to play for Wales against Scotland two days later, Dick Hellings, Billy Alexander and Willie Llewellyn, Llwynypia's three internationals, turned out for the club.

Having been postponed on four occasions, the international between Wales and Scotland eventually took place in the snow at Inverleith on Saturday 4th March. There were just two changes from the team original selected with George Llewellyn Lloyd of Newport taking the place of David James who had gone North to Broughton Rangers and Dick Hellings of Llwynypia taking the place of the injured David John Daniel of Llanelly.

The teams lined up as follows:

Wales: W J Bancroft (Swansea, Captain); H V P Huzzey, E G Nicholls (Cardiff), R T Skrimshire (Newport), W M Llewellyn (Llwynypia); S H Biggs (Cardiff), G Ll Lloyd (Newport), W H Alexander, D Hellings (Llwynypia), W J Parker, F G Scrine (Swansea), T Dobson, J Blake (Cardiff), A B Brice (Aberavon), J J Hodges (Newport).

Scotland: *H Rottenburg; H T S Gedge, D B Monypenny (London Scottish), *G A W Lamond (Kelvinside Acads), T L Scott (Langholm); J W Simpson (Royal HSFP), R T Neilson (West of Scotland); M C Morrison (Royal HSFP, Captain), W M C McEwan (Edinburgh Acads), H O Smith (Watsonians), G C Kerr (Durham City), R C Stevenson, A MacKinnon (London Scottish), J M Dykes (Glasgow HSFP), *W J Thomson (West of Scotland). (* Scotland Debut)

Referee: Michael G Delaney (Ireland).

Early in the game Wales struggled to get out of their own half and after constant pressure by the Scottish team one of the Scottish halves

Wales Team v Scotland 1899

Back Row: Tom Schofield (WFU, Touch-judge), J J Hodges, F Scrine, W H Alexander, A B Brice, H V P Huzzey, E G Nicholls, Walter E Rees (Secretary WFU). *Middle Row*: W Llewellyn, W J Parker, R T Skrimshire, W J Bancroft (Captain), T Dobson, D Hellings, J Blake. *Front Row*: G Ll Lloyd and S H Biggs.

picked up just outside the Welsh twenty-five and threw a pass out to Gedge. He ran clean through the Welsh defence and scored a try beside the posts. Lamond failed to convert. After the re-start Wales were again under pressure and after Wales were penalised Lamond just failed with a kick at goal. Following some fine play by the Scottish forwards the Welsh defence was again sorely tried. Lloyd saved cleverly a minute later. Then, just on their own twenty-five, the Welsh three-quarters brought off a beautiful round of passing. When the ball reached Willie Llewellyn he put in a kick to the centre and Hodges following up was dropping on the ball to score when Scott kicked the ball from under his hands. This brought play right to the Scottish goal-line. There the Welsh forwards charged down a kick and set to work scrummaging, with the result that Lloyd got a pass from Biggs and nipped through the Scottish defence in beautiful fashion and scored a try wide out which Bancroft converted from a difficult angle. After some aggressive manoeuvres by the Scottish forwards had been dealt with, Dick Hellings got the ball from a line-out and passed to Tom Dobson. He started the Welsh three-quarters moving and at the finish Willie Llewellyn received on the wing and dashing over scored a try right in the corner. Billy Bancroft again converted. Despite being under pressure for a considerable portion of the first half Wales went in at the interval leading by 10 points to three.

Things changed dramatically in the second half and Scotland scored eighteen unanswered points to win the game by 21 points to ten. An unconverted try by Monypenny opened the second half scoring for Scotland. Then from a line-out in the Welsh twenty-five Smith made a mark and William Thomson kicked the goal. With the scores equal Scotland continued to press and while Reg Skrimshire was getting a punch in the face from a Scottish forward, the Scottish three-quarters got the ball and Lamond, on the far wing, took a left footed shot and dropped a goal. The pace now quickened and both sides were playing a rough and tumble game. Willie Llewellyn stopped a rush of the Scottish forwards and they repaid him by putting their boot into his ribs while he was still on the ground. Another penalty against the Welsh forwards seemed to take the heart out of the whole Welsh team. The ball was placed for William Thomson on the centre line. Gwyn Nicholls received but his kick was charged down and Harry Smith scrambled over for a try which

Thomson just failed to convert. About ten minutes from the end Gedge got possession and dropped an excellent goal. With the game now lost by Wales play was fairly even until the final whistle went and Scotland were victorious.

The report of the game in the *Evening Express* seemed to suggest that the referee allowed the Scottish forwards to get away with a lot of foul play and often penalised the Welsh forwards when the Scottish forwards were to blame for one infringement or another. Nevertheless, the Scottish forwards were allowed to play this rough style to good effect and with many incidents completely disregarded by the referee; they were superior on the day.

On the same day as Wales played Scotland at Inverleith, Llwynypia played Ebbw Vale at home and won by 10 points to nil. This was an excellent victory for Llwynypia considering three of their best players, namely Dick Hellings, Billy Alexander and Willie Llewellyn were all playing for Wales against Scotland in Edinburgh. Dick Foster opened the scoring for Llwynypia with a first-half try which was converted by Tom Saunders. Another first-half try by Ben Phillips, again converted by Tom Saunders completed the scoring and with no scores in the second half Llwynypia were victorious by 10 points to nil.

Just two days after losing to Scotland, Willie Llewellyn and Dick Hellings were back playing for Llwynypia at home against Llanelly. Billy Alexander did not play as he was playing for Glamorgan against Lancashire at Cardiff Arms Park. This was incredible commitment from all three players who had played three hard games in just five days. Firstly they had all played in the Glamorgan League match against Mountain Ash on Thursday 2nd March. Then all three had played for Wales against Scotland at Inverleith on Saturday 4th March and finally Billy Alexander played for Glamorgan against Lancashire on the same day Willie Llewellyn and Dick Hellings played in the important fixture against Llanelly on Monday 6th March, Willie Llewellyn having driven up from Cardiff on the return journey from Scotland just in time for the match. From beginning to end the match against Llanelly was memorable. Brilliant attack from the visiting three-quarters and equally sterling defence from the home three-quarters made it a very exciting game. Llanelly were the first to score when the League champions were penalised for off-side. Williams easily landed the goal. Dick Hellings re-started and subsequent play was more even, until Willie Llewellyn, the home skipper, sneaked a pass on the half-way line and beat the Llanelly defence to score a spectacular try wide out. Tom Saunders just failed to convert. Just before half-time P J Thomas of Llanelly fractured one of his ribs and had to retire.

With the scores equal Daniel restarted for Llanelly and almost immediately another disaster befell the visitors. Evan Lloyd, the Welsh international wing, fell awkwardly and injuring his ankle was laid up for the rest of the game. The home forwards were now completely beating the Scarlets pack, but the backs were prevented from doing much by the offside tactics of the Llanelly quartette. Usher now made the best run of the day but despite beating all opposition he unfortunately stumbled just short of the line. A moment later, however, he made amends by creating a splendid opening thus enabling Morgan to score an unconverted try for Llwynypia. From the kick out the Llwynypia backs made a terrible mistake which enabled Rhys Gabe to cross for an unconverted try in the corner. With no further scores the game ended in a draw at 6 points all.

Willie Llewellyn was selected to play for Glamorgan against Lancashire but instead turned out to captain Llwynypia in their important home fixture against Llanelly. A strong Glamorgan side defeated Lancashire by three goals and a try to nil. A first-half try by George Dobson which was converted by Selwyn Biggs gave Glamorgan a 5 point lead at the interval. Early in the second half clever passing between Selwyn Biggs, Dan Rees and George Davies saw the latter score a clever try near the posts which Selwyn Biggs again converted. Viv Huzzey had hard lines when he crossed for a try which the referee disallowed. George Davies had better luck a moment later when George Dobson started a movement which ended with George Davies beating two or three men to score an unconverted try. The final try of the game resulted in a hat trick for George Davies when he scored a try which Selwyn Biggs converted to give Glamorgan victory by 18 points to nil.

When Glamorgan played Somerset at Bridgewater on Thursday 9th March only five of the players originally selected to play actually turned out; they were Viv Huzzey, George Davies, Emlyn Lewis, Will Parker and Jere Blake. Billy Bancroft, Willie Llewellyn, Dan Rees, Selwyn Biggs, Dick Hellings, Billy Alexander, Alfred Brice, Tom Dobson, Fred Scrine and

Sam Davies all cried off. Glamorgan lost the game by 11 points to ten. The Glamorgan points came from a dropped goal by George Davies and unconverted tries by George Davies and Jere Blake.

On Wednesday 8th March the Selection Committee of the Welsh Football Union met at the Royal Hotel, Cardiff, to select the team to represent Wales against Ireland at Cardiff Arms Park on Saturday 18th March. There were only two changes from the Welsh team that had been defeated by Scotland. D J Daniel and George Boots took the places of Will Parker and T Dobson in the pack. Tom Dobson was relegated to the reserves.

A week before the final Welsh international match of the season against Ireland, Llwynypia played Cardiff at home. On show were seven of the Welsh international players who would play against Ireland the following week: Viv Huzzey, Selwyn Biggs, Fred Cornish and Jere Blake of Cardiff and Willie Llewellyn, Billy Alexander and Dick Hellings of Llwynypia. Tom Dobson, who had played for Wales against England and Scotland, was captain of the Cardiff side. With the Llwynypia jersey exactly the same as those of Cardiff, the home side played in the black and amber colours of Mountain Ash. A first-half unconverted try by one of the Cardiff forwards gave the visitors a 3 points to nil lead at the interval. A second-half try by Billy Alexander, which Tom Saunders failed to convert, brought the score level and with no further scores a hard fought game ended in a draw.

When Wales met Ireland at Cardiff Arms Park on Saturday 18th March there was only one change from the side originally selected, Fred Cornish replacing the injured Fred Scrine. This was the last of four Welsh caps for the Cardiff forward. In August 1899 Cornish joined Hull Northern Union Club.

An interesting article in the *South Wales Daily Post*, published on the Thursday before the game, referred to the instructions sent to the players by Mr Walter Rees, secretary of the Welsh Football Union. It read as follows: 1. You will dress at the Grand Hotel, where lunch will be provided for players and officials at 12.30 p.m. 2. You must be there no later than 12.30. 3. You will play in navy knicks and international jersey. 4. The teams will be photographed at 2.35 p.m. 5. Kick-off 3.00 p.m. 6. The dinner will take place at the Royal Hotel at 5.30 p.m. Morning Dress. 7. The committee hope you will do your utmost to get fit for the 18th as every effort must be made to win the match. The instruction concluded by saying, 'Should anything happen to prevent you playing please wire me without delay to my Neath address up to noon on Friday; after that to the Royal Hotel, Cardiff.' The teams for the game lined up as follows:

Wales: W J Bancroft (Swansea, Captain); H V P Huzzey, E G Nicholls (Cardiff), R T Skrimshire (Newport), W M Llewellyn (Llwynypia); S H Biggs (Cardiff), G Ll Lloyd (Newport); W H Alexander, D Hellings (Llwynypia), J Blake, F H Cornish (Cardiff), D J Daniel (Llanelly), J G Boots, J J Hodges (Newport), A B Brice (Aberavon).

Ireland: P O'Brien-Butler (Monkstown); G P Doran (Lansdowne), G Harman (Dublin U), C Reid (NIFC), E F Campbell (Monkstown); L M Magee (Bective, Captain), G G Allen (Derry); W G Byron, J E McIlwaine (NIFC), *C C H Moriarty (Monkstown), M Ryan, J Ryan (Rockwell Coll), J Sealy, A W D Meares (Dublin U), T J Little (Bective). (* Ireland Debut)

Referee: Adam J Turnbull (Scotland).

Wales Team v Ireland 1899

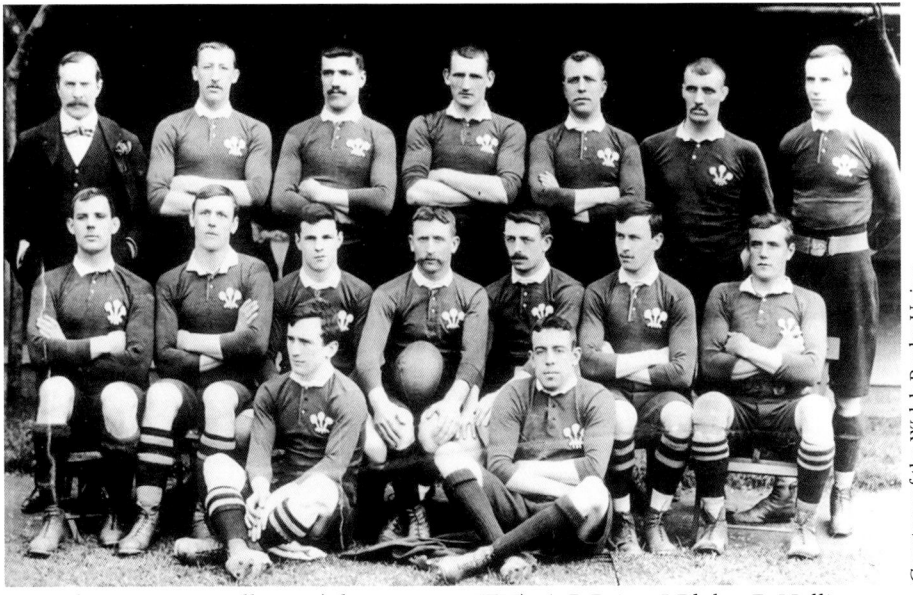

Back Row: Tom Williams (Llwynypia, WFU), A B Brice, J Blake, D Hellings, W H Alexander, D J Daniel, E G Nicholls. *Middle Row*: F H Cornish, J G Boots, W Llewellyn, W J Bancroft (Captain), H V P Huzzey, R T Skrimshire, J J Hodges. *Front Row*: G Ll Lloyd and S H Biggs.

A record crowd of 40,000 spectators watched Wales play Ireland at Cardiff Arms Park on Saturday 18th March. Spectators took advantage of every vantage point they could with youngsters on the roof of the stand and every tree surrounding the ground festooned with fifteen to twenty spectators. All viewing points were taken and spectators were everywhere; the balcony of the County Club, the Grand Hotel, Grand Theatre and all adjoining warehouses were simply packed. People were on the roofs, in windows and even up telegraph poles. With the spectators spilling onto the pitch, the match was delayed for a good twenty minutes whist the field was cleared.

Bancroft started the game for Wales and play was just about even when Ireland were awarded a penalty in a kickable position. The Welsh forwards, through several hard scrums, had worked their way out of danger, moving play from their own goal-line to just outside their twenty-five yard line, where they were penalised for an infringement. The ball was placed in a fairly easy position for one of the Irish backs but the Welsh forwards managed to charge the ball down and play was brought back to the centre of the field. Shortly afterwards, just twenty-five minutes into the game, Billy Bancroft was injured after running the Irish forwards around a bit and punting down to touch just inside the visitors half of the field. There were reports that Micky and John Ryan had thrown Bancroft into the crowd, but whatever happened the result was that Billy Bancroft was seriously injured and had to leave the field. As a result Alfred Brice came out of the forwards and took Billy Bancroft's place at full-back forcing Wales to play the majority of the game with just fourteen men and only seven forwards. Play was then held up for some time after the crowd had come over the rails.

Just before the interval the Irish forwards upped their game and with a series of forward rushes, got right up to the Welsh goal-line. Here Allen picked up from the back of a scrum and running round on the right passed to Gerry Doran who scored an unconverted try. This was the only score of the game and Wales were defeated by 3 points to nil.

Walter Rees, secretary of the Welsh Football Union, and many of the Welsh players that day felt that the defeat was entirely due to the injury to Billy Bancroft, and had he not been injured and forced to retire from the game, Wales would have won the match. A report in The *South Wales*

Daily Post suggested that Wales threw away a golden chance to score when Reg Skrimshire was tackled on the Irish goal-line and failed to get a pass to Willie Llewellyn who was unmarked. This was harsh criticism as a similar incident had happened in the second half with Gwyn Nicholls. A report in the *Evening Express* was a little kinder when it stated that although Reg Skrimshire had played better than he did against Scotland he was still not up to the form he had shown against England earlier in the season. Whatever the case may be this was Reg Skrimshire's last game for Wales and the following season the preferred centre partnership was George Davies (Swansea) with either Gwyn Nicholls or Dan Rees (Swansea). Despite not being selected by Wales again Reg Skrimshire was the only Welshman on the 1903 British Isles tour to South Africa and was top points and try scorer with 59 points. As well as appearing in all twenty-two games he scored a try in the first international.

The Wales game against Ireland was Billy Bancroft's twenty-seventh consecutive cap for Wales and marked the occasion when he equalled Arthur Gould's record of twenty-seven international caps for Wales. Not that this was much consolation to the Wales and Swansea captain who suffered two injured and one broken rib in the game against Ireland. As a result of this injury Billy Bancroft did not play rugby again during the 1898–99 season. Nevertheless, he finished the season with an impressive record for Swansea where he scored 8 tries, kicked 73 conversions, 4 dropped goals and 3 penalties. Billy Bancroft returned to play for Wales the following season and went on to achieve thirty-three consecutive caps for Wales between 1890 and 1901. This record was not broken until Ken Jones did so in 1954. Ken Jones went on to win forty-four caps for Wales, forty-three of them consecutively, between 1947 and 1957.

Willie Llewellyn and Dick Hellings returned to club rugby when they played for Llwynypia in their away fixture with Gloucester. Llwynypia were without Dick Foster and Ben Morgan but had useful replacements in Usher of Pontypridd and Deere of Mountain Ash. Billy Alexander and Bob Jones were also Llwynypia absentees. In a hard fought game Gloucester took the lead just before the interval when England international forward Frank Stout scored a try which his brother Percy, also an England international, converted. Llwynypia did very well in the first half to keep the scoring down when playing against the wind. It was mainly a forward game with Gloucester getting the better of the argument but Llwynypia, with the wind in their favour, did well in the second half and for the last five minutes of the game looked like scoring on more than one occasion. However, they were well marked and failed to score with the result that Gloucester were triumphant by 5 points to nil.

Willie Llewellyn scored his twenty-eighth try of the season when Llwynypia defeated Barry in a Glamorgan League match at home. Llwynypia won by 25 points to nil. Four tries in the first half by Willie Llewellyn, Hillman, Dick Hellings and Ben Morgan, all converted by Tom Saunders, gave Llwynypia a twenty point lead at the interval. Play was much more even in the second half and the only score was a try for Llwynypia by Evan Jones. Tom Saunders converted and with no further scores Llwynypia picked up another two League points.

Having narrowly lost earlier in the season, Llwynypia were keen to secure the Glamorgan League points in their next game at home to Treherbert. With the game only a few minutes old the referee had to rebuke more than one player for rough tackling after Billy Alexander had been fouled by an opposing player. The game was played at a terrific pace and the sides were very fairly matched, although Llwynypia had done most of the attacking. Llwynypia were the first to score when Ben Phillips finished off a round of passing and scored in an easy position for Tom Saunders to convert. Just before the interval Tom Saunders had a kick charged down with the result that Hanbury scored an unconverted try for the visitors. Early in the second half Llwynypia were having the better of the play and almost scored on several occasions. Ben Phillips almost dropped a goal with half a dozen men around him and an instant later Tom Saunders got the ball and dropped a beautiful goal from a long way out. Just before the final whistle Ben Phillips scored a try in the corner which Tom Saunders failed to convert. The final score was Llwynypia 12 points, Treherbert three.

Willie Llewellyn scored four tries in a game for the second time in the season when Llwynypia defeated the touring Isle of Man side, Mona, on Easter Monday. Willie Llewellyn opened the scoring with an unconverted try very early in the game. Dick Foster was the next to score a try which Tom Saunders converted. Then Foster, after a tricky run, made an opening for Ben Morgan, who easily scored in the corner. Tom Saunders failed with the conversion. The best try of the half was scored after Stephens, having beaten half-a-dozen of the Manxmen, threw to Dick Foster. He transferred to Willie Llewellyn who ran beautifully across and scored in a position which enabled Tom Saunders to easily convert. In the second half two tries apiece for Willie Llewellyn, Dick Foster and Ben Morgan, three of which were converted by Tom Saunders, gave Llwynypia an easy victory by 40 points to nil.

Although selected Willie Llewellyn did not play in the next Llwynypia game against Ebbw Vale but returned for the Glamorgan League fixture against Pontypridd. Rain had fallen heavily throughout the day and the ground was like a quagmire. An open game was impossible and play was almost entirely confined to the forwards. The game was vigorously contested throughout and Llwynypia had the best of the struggle, winning by 20 points to nil. Just before the interval Rhys Williams scored a try which Tom Saunders converted. In the second half Billy Alexander scored a try which Tom Saunders converted and almost immediately afterwards dribbled over the line and scored another try which Tom Saunders again converted. George Warlow, the Pontypridd full-back, claimed he had touched the ball at the same time as Billy Alexander and as a result of an argument with the referee, Mr J H Bowen, was ordered off the field for using bad language. Ben Phillips scored the final try of the game which Saunders again converted.

Llwynypia's next game was a Glamorgan League fixture at home against Barry. The significant feature of this game was Arthur Harding playing his first game of the season for Llwynypia. Harding featured in all five remaining games of the season when Llwynypia were undefeated. Two unconverted tries, one by Dick Hellings and the other by Bob Jones, were the only scores in the game which Llwynypia won by 6 points to nil.

A great deal of interest was shown in Llwynypia's next home game which was the final Glamorgan League fixture between Llwynypia and Penygraig on Thursday 20th April. The game was practically to decide the championship of the League for the season. Unfortunately the referee, Mr Harry Bowen, of Llanelly, failed to make an appearance, having lost his connection with the Rhondda and Swansea Bay Railway at Aberavon. Despite some of the best referees in Wales being present at the ground including Mr W M Douglas, Cardiff and Mr Ack Llewellyn, Pontypridd, who were willing to referee the game, Penygraig objected to the match being a League fixture and after a long discussion it was agreed to play a friendly game instead and that the League fixture should be played the following Thursday on the Llwynypia ground. Willie Llewellyn captained the home team while Percy Bush captained the visitors. The game was a spectacular one for the large crowd that had assembled to watch the encounter. Penygraig were superior at forward while Llwynypia held the advantage behind. In the first half Hillman broke clear from a scrummage on his own side of halfway and passed to Stephens. His fellow half then threw to Willie Llewellyn who passed on to Dick Foster who gave Ben Phillips the opportunity of making a determined dash for the line, which he crossed to score a try which Tom Saunders converted. Billy Alexander got the final try which Tom Saunders again converted. Arthur Harding got a mention in the *South Wales Echo* when they reported, 'Harding, an ex-Brecon collegian and contemporary of Willie Llewellyn did particularly well.' Llwynypia won by 10 points to nil.

Llwynypia finished the season with three consecutive League matches. A first-half try by Dick Hellings which was converted by Tom Saunders was the only score of the away game against Treorky.

The re-arranged League game with Penygraig was played on Thursday 27th April at Llwynypia. Percy Bush and his brother Fred played in the three-quarters for Penygraig and Llwynypia were strengthened by the inclusion of W 'Pussy' Jones and Tom Dobson both of Cardiff. The game was not as good as the game the previous week. There was much more rough play and less real skill. The referee Mr Harry Bowen kept the players well in hand and on a couple of occasions he administered prompt cautions, which checked the unsportsmanlike tactics of both sides. All the points of the game were scored in the first half. Within six minutes of the start Willie Llewellyn kicked into the open and Percy Bush picking up dropped a beautiful goal. A short while later W 'Pussy' Jones, the Cardiff wing, scored a try after a fine deceptive run. Tom Saunders failed to convert. Percy Bush almost dropped another goal but it was charged down by Bob Jones. Llwynypia scored again when Billy Alexander picked up in the open and gave a scoring pass to W Williams on the right wing. Tom Saunders failed to convert. With the score at 6 points to four in favour of Llwynypia the whistle blew for half-time.

The Llwynypia forwards played much better than they did the previous week with Harding providing some inspirational individual play. In a hard fought second half both sides had opportunities to score but last minute defence saved the day and the game ended with a win for Llwynypia by 6 points to four. As a result of this victory Llwynypia were once again holders of the Challenge Cup and were Glamorgan League champions for the third successive year.

Following the game the Penygraig Club made a protest against Llwynypia and claimed the two League points because the cup holders were assisted by W 'Pussy' Jones and Tom Dobson of Cardiff. Both were Welsh internationals with W 'Pussy' Jones gaining his two Welsh caps against Ireland and England in 1898 and Tom Dobson, the Cardiff vice-captain, having been capped by Wales on four occasions. A special meeting of the Glamorgan Football League was held at the White Hart Hotel, Pontypridd on Thursday 18th May to consider the protest. The meeting was held at a quarter past six and as the Penygraig Club were not represented judgement went by default against them. A few minutes after the meeting had finished Mr Morgan Rees and Mr Moses Jenkins, Penygraig's treasurer and secretary respectively, made an appearance and it transpired that the card convening the meeting which had been sent to Mr Moses Jenkins stated that the meeting would be held at 8.15 p.m. As a result another meeting was arranged.

Subsequently a second meeting was held on Tuesday 13th June with Mr Tom Williams in the chair. The two points claimed by Penygraig against Llwynypia for playing Jones and Dobson (Cardiff) at the last League fixture was considered. It was pointed out that Penygraig had played J Lewis of Treherbert, whose transfer had not been confirmed. It was also pointed out that there was no rule by which the matter could be dealt with and the claim was accordingly dismissed and thus confirmed Llwynypia as Glamorgan League champions with still one League match to play.

Feelings of rivalry had run high in many of the League matches during the season and this keenness had been accentuated by the fact that the champion club was rewarded by home and away fixtures with Cardiff which meant a substantial addition to the finances of the champion club. It was felt by many that far too much rough play had distinguished the contest and squabbling on and off the field had become a regrettable feature of the competition. There was popular opinion that the League competition should be abandoned. This opinion was reinforced by the fact that the friendly game played between Penygraig and Llwynypia the previous week was a much better spectacle with regard to the fact that there was much less rough play and more skill. Despite strong opinion that the Glamorgan League competition should be discontinued this was not the case and the following season the Glamorgan League Challenge Cup was won by Treorky.

Llwynypia's last game of the season was their final Glamorgan League fixture against Pontyclun. The clubs were due to play two League fixtures but with Pontyclun unable to provide a ground for their home fixture they conceded the two League points to Llwynypia. Willie Llewellyn scored two tries in a runaway victory for Llwynypia by 29 points to nil.

Willie Llewellyn without a doubt had become one of the most popular rugby players in the Glamorgan League. At just 10st. 10lb in weight and 5ft. 7ins in height, he gained his first Welsh cap just six days after his twenty-first birthday. Willie Llewellyn had originally played on the right wing but changed to the left wing position where he played in the Welsh trial match at Mountain Ash and was subsequently selected in that position to represent Wales against England at Swansea in January 1899. Willie had a dream debut and scored four tries, more than any other Welsh international before him. He really must have enjoyed the celebration dinner at the Royal Hotel, Swansea on the evening of the match.

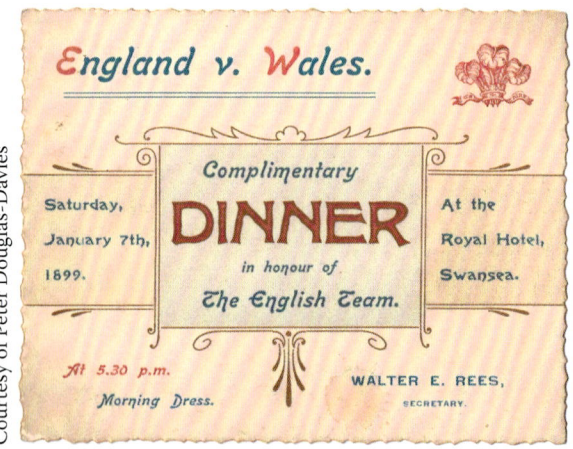

Dinner invitation for the after match celebration dinner at the Royal Hotel, Swansea.

Willie Llewellyn Rugby Games Played and Results 1898–99 Season

Date	Team Played For	Opposition	Venue	Result/Score	W Llewellyn Tries
	**Willie Llewellyn Llwynypia Rugby Games Played 1898-1899 Season**				
	Other Llwynypia Rugby Games Played 1898-1899 Season				
	**Willie Llewellyn Welsh International and Welsh Trial Rugby Games Played 1898-1899 Season**				
	**Willie Llewellyn Glamorgan County Rugby Games Played 1898-1899 Season**				
	Llwynypia Friendly Games 1898-1899 Season				
10/09/1898	Llwynypia 1st trial Match	Only 22 Players	Home	Unrecorded	Unrecorded
17/09/1898	2nd Trial Match	District	Home	Won 27-0	1
24/09/1898	Llwynypia	Maesteg	Home	Won 5-3	0
01/10/1898	Llwynypia	Abertillery	Home	Won 41-0	2
08/10/1898	Llwynypia	Treherbert*	Away	Lost 0-3	0
15/10/1898	Llwynypia	Bridgend	Home	Won 12-0	1
22/10/1898	Llwynypia	Aberavon	Away	Won 3-0	0
26/10/1898	Glamorgan	Somerset	Cardiff Arms Park	Won 24-4	2
29/10/1898	Llwynypia	Barry	Game Not Played		0
05/11/1898	Llwynypia	Morriston	Away	Won 11-6	1
07/11/1898	Glamorgan	Cornwall	Cardiff Arms Park	Won 32-3	3
12/11/1898	Llwynypia	Llanelly	Away	Drawn 5-5	0
19/11/1898	Llwynypia	Penarth	Home	Won 17-0	3
26/11/1898	Llwynypia	Pontypridd*	Home	Won 30-0	2
03/12/1898	Welsh Trial - Whites	Stripes	Mountain Ash	Whites 13-5	0
03/12/1898	Llwynypia	Neath	Home	Drawn 0-0	Did not play
05/12/1898	Llwynypia	Penygraig*	Away	Lost 0-4	0
10/12/1898	Llwynypia	Mountain Ash*	Away	Won 7-3	1
17/12/1898	Llwynypia	Bridgend	Away	Drawn 3-3	0
24/12/1898	Llwynypia	Treorky*	Home	Won 21-5	3
26/12/1898	Llwynypia	Leicester	Away	Drawn 0-0	0
27/12/1898	Llwynypia	Northampton	Away	Lost 0-5	0
07/01/1899	Wales	England	St Helen's	Won 26-3	4
14/01/1899	Llwynypia	Cardiff	Away	Lost 0-21	0
16/02/1899	Llwynypia	Christ College	Away	Won 17-0	3
18/02/1899	Llwynypia	Neath	Away	Lost 0-9	Did not play
25/02/1899	Llwynypia	Plymouth	Away	Lost 0-6	0
02/03/1899	Llwynypia	Mountain Ash*	Home	Won 4-3	0
04/03/1899	Wales	Scotland	Inverleith, Edinburgh	Lost 10-21	1
04/03/1899	Llwynypia	Ebbw Vale	Home	Won 10-0	Did not play
06/03/1899	Llwynypia	Llanelly	Home	Drawn 6-6	1
11/03/1899	Llwynypia	Cardiff	Home	Drawn 3-3	0
18/03/1899	Wales	Ireland	Cardiff Arms Park	Lost 0-3	0
25/03/1899	Llwynypia	Gloucester	Away	Lost 0-5	0
31/03/1899	Llwynypia	Barry*	Home	Won 25-0	1
01/04/1899	Llwynypia	Treherbert*	Home	Won 12-3	0
03/04/1899	Llwynypia	Mona	Home	Won 40-0	4
08/04/1899	Llwynypia	Ebbw Vale	Away	Lost 5-13	Did not play
13/04/1899	Llwynypia	Pontypridd*	Away	Won 20-0	0
15/04/1899	Llwynypia	Barry*	Away	Won 6-0	0
20/04/1899	Llwynypia	Penygraig	Home	Won 10-0	0
22/04/1899	Llwynypia	Treorky*	Away	Won 5-3	0
27/04/1899	Llwynypia	Penygraig*	Home	Won 6-4	0
06/05/1899	Llwynypia	Pontyclun*	Home	Won 29-0	2
		*League Games			
	Willie Llewellyn Games Played				W Llewellyn Tries
Totals	39				35

Willie Llewellyn Rugby Games Played and Results 1898–99 Season

As captain of Llwynypia, Willie Llewellyn had led his team from the front. He played in thirty-one of the thirty-five games played by Llwynypia during the 1898–99 season and not including the two trial matches scored twenty-four tries. Llwynypia had a very successful season. Of the 35 games played they won 21, lost 8 and drew 6. After a very close finish to the Glamorgan League they just edged out Penygraig whom they

CHAPTER FOUR

Willie Llewellyn's Welsh Trial Cap.

Courtesy of Dr Michael Jones

defeated in the penultimate League game of the season to win the Glamorgan League Challenge Cup for the third consecutive season.

In addition to the games Willie played for Llwynypia he also played twice for Glamorgan County, the Welsh trial match and in all three Welsh international matches against England, Scotland and Ireland. In total, not including the two Newport trial matches, Willie Llewellyn played thirty-seven games during the season and scored 34 tries. Changing from the right wing to left wing had not dimmed his brilliance in any way and he gave as fine an exposition of wing play as ever in this position.

Willie Llewellyn had matured into a very fine international rugby player. He was exceedingly fast, very tricky and able to take passes with either hand. He was an excellent tackler and was a fine tactician. Willie was the complete rugby player and the first three-quarter to attain international honours from the Rhondda clubs. He could look back on the 1898–99 rugby season with pride and look forward to a very promising future as a Welsh international wing three-quarter.

The Christ College Old Boys were representing the College very well on the rugby field during the 1898–99 season. Willie Llewellyn was the standout player having played so well for Llwynypia and representing Wales in all three internationals against England, Scotland and Ireland. The 1898 December edition of *The Breconian* said the following with regard to Willie Llewellyn: 'Another pleasure as great as our Llandovery win has just been accorded us by the information that our old and popular football captain, W. M. Llewellyn, has been chosen in the Welsh International XV to play against England. Good old "Spider"! We wish you joy and hope you may long be spared to notch tries galore for the Principality.' Arthur Harding was also doing well and although he only played in the last five games of the season for Llwynypia he had made a significant contribution to the team. Several other Old Boys were also doing well with W Ll Thomas and C D Phillips playing for Newport, T J Thomas playing for Cardiff, T P Thomas playing for Guy's Hospital, M T Williams playing for London Hospital, M H Ll Williams playing for Jesus College, Oxford and J H Evans playing for London Welsh.

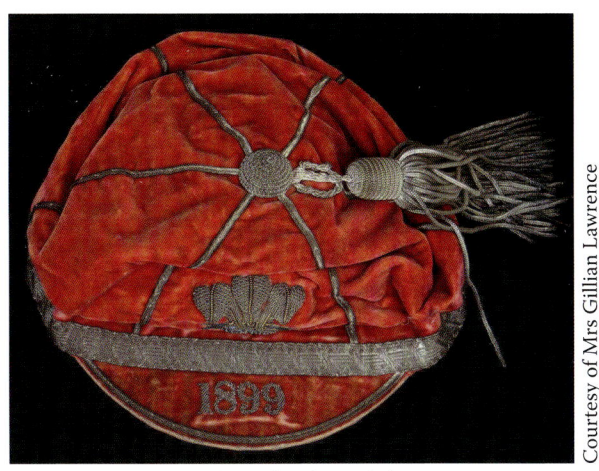

Willie Llewellyn's Welsh Cap.

The Old Boys were doing very well and there was also no shortage of new talent coming through the ranks by way of the 1898–99 Christ College rugby 1st XV. Three exceptional players were Edward (Teddy) Morgan, John Frederick Williams and Hopkin Maddock. All three were regular first team players and all were highly respected by the College. Teddy Morgan was a fast and clever wing three-quarter who not only scored plenty of tries but also took kicks at goal and was very safe in defence. He scored three tries in the 40 points to nil victory over Monmouth Grammar School and another two in the victory over old rivals Llandovery College. In a biography of the first team players in *The Breconian* the following was written about Teddy Morgan: 'E Morgan (right wing three-quarter). – A brilliant runner, good kick and fine tackler; the most dangerous scorer in the team. Injured for part of the season, but turned out better than ever.' There were plaudits too for Hopkin Maddock and J F Williams and the same article said the following of both players: 'H T Maddock (back). – A sound player, tackles brilliantly considering his weight and an accurate kick who always finds touch. Cool to a fault: though he has made many excellent saves; has too many kicks charged down. J F Williams (forward). – Unfortunately absent a good deal through injuries, but greatly improved since last year. His dash is undeniable and

Christ College Brecon, Rugby First XV 1898–1899

Back Row: J L Phillips, E Morgan, A E C Morgan, P R Bartlet Esq.,
R B Lattimer Esq., H E Powel-Jones, L M Thomas, F H E Nicholls.
Middle Row: W Simpson, R H Gibbon, R L Evans, R L Partridge (Captain),
J F Williams, P B Jones, E D Brown.
Front Row: H T Maddock, T J David, W P Williams.

his tackling sound. Improved as a scrummager.' All three would go on to play with distinction for London Welsh and Wales. Hopkin Maddock captained London Welsh 1909–10 and 1911–12 and gained six caps for Wales between 1906 and 1910. Teddy Morgan gained sixteen caps for Wales and played for the British Isles on their 1904 tour to Australia and New Zealand. He also scored fourteen tries for Wales including the one against New Zealand in 1905 which gave Wales victory by 3 points to nil. J F Williams gained four caps for Wales and toured Australasia with the Anglo-Welsh in 1908. He captained London Welsh during the 1907–08 season. John Frederick 'Scethrog' Williams was also one of the victorious Welsh team that defeated New Zealand in 1905.

Chapter Five

Willie Llewellyn moves to London – 1899/1900 Season

UNDER THE CAPTAINCY of Billy Alexander, Llwynypia played 39 matches during the 1899/1900 season. They won 18, lost 15 and drew six. They scored 358 points for with 253 points against. Llwynypia scored 35 converted goals, 53 tries, 4 penalties, 2 goals from a mark and 1 dropped goal. Their opponents scored 20 converted goals, 43 tries, 4 penalties and 3 dropped gaols. Of the 39 games played by Llwynypia, Willie Llewellyn played in 25 matches and scored 8 tries.

Willie Llewellyn only missed two Llwynypia games between the first game of the season against Tredegar and the away game at Leicester on Boxing Day 1899. He missed the home game against Penygraig on Saturday 2nd December because he was playing in the Welsh trial at Newport and he missed the Christmas Day game against Cardiff Mackintosh. During this time Willie also played for Cardiff in their away game against Cambridge University.

Llwynypia had a fairly good season considering that on many occasions they were unable to field their strongest side because of injury. Llwynypia captain, Billy Alexander, missed six weeks of the season because of injury. In addition, Willie Llewellyn left the district to pursue his studies at the Pharmaceutical College, Bloomsbury (now University College London, School of Pharmacy). Having played in the away game against Leicester on Boxing Day, Willie did not play again for Llwynypia until 24th March 1900, when he played in the away game against Plymouth. During this period Willie played international rugby for Wales against England, Scotland and Ireland, County rugby for Glamorgan and club rugby for Swansea and London Welsh. Having returned from London, Willie then played for Llwynypia in all their nine remaining games of the 1899/1900 season.

As a result of injury and absence the Llwynypia committee had no alternative but to call upon the services of younger players and were fortunate in securing Oscar and Joe Williams and Wyndham Jones from the Merthyr Vale district. At half-back Llwynypia occasionally engaged Billy Jones and Jack Davies from the junior teams, both of whom played well for the senior team. Jack Davies tipping the scales at 12st was considered a senior team player of the future. With regard to the forwards the club was fortunate to retain the services of Dick Hellings, Bob Jones, Billy Alexander, William Rhys Williams, Jack Bowen and J H Reynolds who were the bedrock of the pack. In addition, they had the sterling player Joe Hellings, brother of Welsh international forward, Dick Hellings. Arthur Harding, who had studied at Christ College with Willie Llewellyn, was also an important member of the Llwynypia pack. Harding having been appointed cashier for John Aird and Co., Pontypridd, at once found a place in the Llwynypia team and played several games towards the end of the previous season. During the 1899/1900 season he was an established member of the team and played regularly for the Llwynypia first team. He was also selected as a reserve for the Welsh trial match at Newport. He played for Llwynypia against Bridgend on Saturday 20th January but this was his last game for the club. In February 1900 he volunteered for the Glamorgan Division of the Imperial Yeomanry and served in the Boer War in South Africa until July 1901. On his return from South Africa, Arthur Harding played rugby for Cardiff and gained his first Welsh cap against England in 1902.

Having won the Glamorgan League Challenge Cup for four out of the five seasons since its inception and for three consecutive years between 1897 and 1899, Llwynypia withdrew from the competition in the 1899/1900 season. A report in the *Evening Express* on the 17th April 1900 suggested that Llwynypia had not played so well since they had left the Glamorgan

League; nevertheless, with Llwynypia no longer involved, interest in the competition gathered new momentum and on the Llwynypia ground on Saturday 19th May, Treorky and Penygraig met to decide the final of the Glamorgan League championship. Chant for Penygraig and J Thomas, L Lewis and S Muxworthy of Treorky, scored tries in the first half. L Lewis scored another try after the interval and thus Treorky became Glamorgan League Challenge Cup holders for the first time.

In September 1899, as Willie Llewellyn's sparkling rugby career continued, his younger brother George was just starting his education at Christ College, Brecon. Following in the footsteps of his elder brothers Willie and John, George attended Mr Morton's House. Similar to his brothers, George would have an equally distinguished sporting career as a Christ College student.

An interesting article in the *Western Mail* on Friday 22nd September 1899 read as follows: 'A meeting of the general committee of the Welsh Rugby Union was held at the Queen's Hotel, Cardiff, for the purpose of considering applications made by T Dobson, W Jones and W Williams for transfers from Llwynypia to Cardiff. It will be remembered that at the end of last season these players obtained transfers to assist the hill club (Llwynypia) in one of their league matches, and now wish to return to the old love. The committee resolved to grant the application.' All three players had played for Llwynypia against Penygraig in the Glamorgan League match played on Thursday 27th April. A narrow victory for Llwynypia, by two tries to a dropped goal, gave Llwynypia the Glamorgan League Challenge Cup for the third consecutive year. Despite a protest being lodged by Penygraig, a special meeting of the Glamorgan Football League decided in favour of Llwynypia and the result stood. Both Tom Dobson and W 'Pussy' Jones had previously been Llwynypia players and it appears they were quite happy to return to their old club to help out whenever needed.

Llwynypia started the 1899/1900 season very well, winning all their first five games against Tredegar, Rest of the League, Abertillery, Treorky and Pontyclun. Willie played in all five games and scored three tries in their 62 points to nil victory over Pontyclun. The visitors were nothing like as fast as Llwynypia but were quite as heavy and strong. Llwynypia, however, were in such excellent form that they would have beaten almost

CHAPTER FIVE

William Henry Thomas was the first Welsh player to play for the British Isles. He was capped eleven times by Wales between 1885 and 1891.

World Rugby Museum, Twickenham

any team on the day's form. Dick Hellings, Billy Alexander and Joe Williams were outstanding and on the whole the quality of play gave Llwynypia optimism for the coming season.

Despite this optimism, Llwynypia narrowly lost their next game, at home to a weakened Cardiff side. This was Cardiff's third visit to Llwynypia and although they had Welsh internationals, Viv Huzzey, W 'Pussy' Jones and Jere Blake in the side they were without Arthur Ricketts in the three-quarter line, regular scrum-half Cecil Sweet-Escott and forward George Dobson. They were also without their captain Gwyn Nicholls, who was on tour with British Team in Australia. Nicholls had the honour of being the first Welsh player to appear in an international for a British Isle side and was also the first person to score a try against Australia in that country's first international in 1899. He also scored a try in the second international and was top try scorer with twelve tries. Although Gwyn Nicholls was the first Welsh player to appear in an international for a British Isle side he was not the first Welsh player to play for a British Isle side. This honour belongs to William 'Willie' Henry Thomas of Fishguard, Cambridge University and London Welsh, who toured Australia and New Zealand with the first British Isles team in 1888. This unofficial tour did not involve any international matches and therefore no Test caps were awarded. Gwyn Nicholls did not return from Australia until Friday 12th January 1900 and therefore missed the Welsh trial match at Newport and the first Welsh international of the season, against England at Kingsholm, Gloucester on Saturday 6th January.

At full-back for Cardiff was future Welsh international Bert Winfield.

This was the second time Willie Llewellyn and Bert Winfield had faced each other, but over the next six years they would become very familiar rugby opponents and contemporaries. They would play together for Wales on five occasions, the last being when Wales defeated New Zealand in 1905.

Bert Winfield had a wonderful game and his accurate kicking kept Llwynypia pinned back in their half for long periods of the game. Winfield had become a regular in the Cardiff first team and was beginning to demonstrate his future potential. During the 1899/1900 season he gained County honours with Glamorgan, played for the Whites in their victory over the Stripes in the Welsh trial at Newport and was reserve to Billy Bancroft for Wales in all three internationals against England, Scotland and Ireland. However, Bert Winfield did not gain his first Welsh cap until the game against Ireland in 1903. After Billy Bancroft's retirement in 1901, it was a straight fight between Bert Winfield and John Strand-Jones for the Welsh full-back position for the first international of the season against England. Strand-Jones got in by a six to five majority vote and retained his position for the next four internationals.

Bert Winfield played full-back for Wales on fifteen occasions between 1903 and 1908. He was Cardiff captain between 1901 and 1903.

On the eve of the game against England in January 1901, Bert Winfield was called up to play at full-back for Wales instead of the chosen Billy Bancroft; who was also selected as captain. A telegram purporting to come from Bancroft, addressed to Walter E Rees, the secretary of the Welsh Football Union, read, 'Regret cannot play tomorrow; influenza – Bancroft'. Gwyn Nicholls was made captain and the cards listing both teams, with Bert Winfield at full-back, were printed. It transpired that the telegram was a hoax; Billy Bancroft took his place at full-back and the disappointed Bert Winfield had to wait until March 1903 before winning his first cap for Wales against Ireland.

Llwynypia fielded a strong team which included Welsh internationals Willie Llewellyn, Billy Alexander and Dick Hellings. Unfortunately they were without Arthur Harding, who had damaged his wrist in a practise match at Pontypridd the previous Thursday. Although originally selected for the game, they were also without Rowley Thomas who, at his own request, was given his transfer back to Pontypridd.

In the absence of Gwyn Nicholls the Cardiff team was captained by Viv Huzzey. In a very even first half both teams attacked strongly but were unable to score. Bert Winfield missed a few drop goal attempts and Tom Saunders missed a penalty kick for Llwynypia. Early in the second half Ivor Jones made a mark and Bert Winfield narrowly missed the kick at goal from the halfway line. It had the required length but not quite the direction and only a minor resulted. Viv Huzzey narrowly failed to score on a couple of occasions and with the Cardiff forwards now playing better than at any time in the game Llwynypia were under a great deal of pressure. From a scrum, Kestell, Sweet-Escott's replacement, got the ball away to Hughes who passed on to Ivor Jones who managed to get over the Llwynypia line for a try which Bert Winfield just failed to convert. Although under a great deal of pressure, Llwynypia managed to prevent Cardiff from scoring any further points, but they were still defeated by 3 points to nil.

Llwynypia's next game was the first of four fixtures they played against Mountain Ash during the season. Llwynypia were strongly represented with Dan Rees of Treherbert playing full-back instead of Tom Saunders, and P C Boulton of Penygraig and P C Rees, of Pontypridd, both of whom had transferred to Llwynypia, among the forwards. Welsh international Billy Alexander captained the team and fellow Welsh internationals, Willie Llewellyn and Dick Hellings, were also in the side. Nevertheless, Llwynypia were defeated by a goal and a try to a penalty goal, with all the points coming in the first half.

Llwynypia returned to winning ways in their next game with a narrow home victory over Aberavon by 6 points to three. Arthur Harding then returned to the Llwynypia side for the away game against Neath but they still lost by 8 points to nil. There were three Christ College, Brecon

Old Boys in the Llwynypia team that day, Willie Llewellyn, his brother John and Arthur Harding.

Willie Llewellyn played his first County game of the season when Glamorgan played Yorkshire at Castleford. The original team chosen by Glamorgan was almost a Welsh international fifteen, but two changes were necessary after Billy Bancroft withdrew because of injury and Dick Hellings was unavailable. Bert Winfield took the place of Billy Bancroft at full-back and J Jenkins, the Treherbert captain, took the place of Dick Hellings in the forwards. The Glamorgan team was as follows: Back, Bert Winfield (Cardiff); centres, George Davies and Dan Rees (Swansea); wings, Viv Huzzey (Cardiff) and Willie Llewellyn (Llwynypia); half-backs, W Jones (Aberavon) and G Hughes (Cardiff); forwards, J Jenkins (Treherbert), Billy Alexander (Llwynypia), Robert Thomas and Hopkin Davies (Swansea), Jere Blake (Cardiff), J Thomas (Neath), V Jones (Aberavon) and J Matthews (Bridgend).

Glamorgan played with the sun and wind behind them in the first half but despite this advantage Yorkshire were the first to score. Within ten minutes of the start, with the Yorkshire forwards taking control, they were awarded a scrum under the Glamorgan posts. From here the ball was passed out quickly to the Yorkshire three-quarters. Shepherd received and passed to Robinson, who then passed on to Hammond, who crossed for an unconverted try. After this Glamorgan settled down and played much better and some fine kicking by Bert Winfield kept the home team pinned in their own half. A good passing round by Jones, Hughes and Davies was checked by Taylor, after which Bert Winfield was again conspicuous with some fine kicking. Just before half-time Yorkshire made good ground into the Glamorgan half but their stay was short and Dan Rees, receiving from his half-backs, tricked his opponent and passed out to George Davies. The Swansea centre completed a clever movement by scoring a try which Bert Winfield converted. Glamorgan held the lead at the interval and with no further scores won the game by 5 points to three. On the whole the game was very evenly contested. The Glamorgan backs showed the shrewder combinations and were generally the more skilful, while the home forwards counter-balanced the encounter with their good all-round play.

Llwynypia drew their next game away to Penarth. Just before the interval Joe Williams crossed for a try with two men hanging on his legs. From an easy position, Arthur Harding failed with the conversion and thus Llwynypia were leading at the interval by an unconverted try to nil. Penarth equalised in the second half with a try by Warburton their captain, Thornley, failed to convert. The match generated plenty of excitement and when Penarth pressed hard, Whale was unlucky to miss a scoring opportunity a yard from the try line. The Llwynypia forwards then broke away with Arthur Harding repeatedly leading the charge. The Breconian was doing great things in the loose, while Dick Hellings was doing the lion's share in the pack. It was clear that Llwynypia had plenty of energy in reserve but Penarth did not relent and try as they did Llwynypia failed to score again and the game ended drawn at 3 points all.

In their next game, without their usual full-back and Harding missing from the forwards, Llwynypia lost to Mountain Ash for the second time in the season. Although Llwynypia were losing by 13 points to nil at the interval it was generally felt that they should at least hold their own in the second half with a strong wind behind them. Unfortunately they failed to do that and their punishment during the last 40 minutes was, if anything, more severe than during the first half. Despite playing with a lot of spirit right up to the end they never really looked like scoring and Mountain Ash scored another two tries in the second half to give them victory by 19 points to nil.

At last, having lost four of their last six games, Llwynypia defeated Penarth at home by 17 points to five. Play was in Llwynypia's favour throughout and the score just about represented the state of play. In the first half Joe Williams scored a try and kicked a conversion and a penalty goal for Llwynypia, whilst Dai Bowen, the replacement full-back, also scored an unconverted try. In the second half Dick Hellings scored two unconverted tries while Allison scored a try for Penarth which Thornley converted.

Having played for Llwynypia on the Saturday, Willie Llewellyn travelled to Cambridge the following day and played for Cardiff in their game against Cambridge University on the Monday. On the same day as Willie was playing for Llwynypia, Cardiff lost heavily to an undefeated Swansea side at Cardiff Arms Park. Several Cardiff players were injured in that game and others were unable to get away from business. The Swansea side put Cardiff to the sword. George Davies dropped two goals and scored a try, and fellow centre Dan Rees scored a try which gave Swansea the 14 points to nil victory. The Cardiff team was without Viv Huzzey, W 'Pussy' Jones, Arthur Ricketts, Hughes and Bert Winfield. Llewellyn Deere (Mountain Ash) and Willie Llewellyn (Llwynypia) volunteered their services to replace Ricketts and Huzzey. For the other positions the club drew upon their reserves. Playing for Cambridge University was David Revell 'Darkie' Bedell-Sivright. Willie Llewellyn would get to know him very well as Bedell-Sivright would be chosen to lead the British Team on their tour of Australia and New Zealand in 1904. Willie Llewellyn also made the tour and played in fifteen games including all three test matches against Australia and the single test match against New Zealand.

George Dobson opened the scoring for Cardiff with a try which Ivor Jones failed to convert. Before the interval F H Fasson scored a try for Cambridge. G E Sisterson took the conversion from an easy angle, but it was charged down by Willie Llewellyn. Early in the second half John Sagar dropped a goal for Cambridge and T A Cook scored a try which Sisterson failed to convert. Cardiff replied with another try by Llewellyn Deere, but George Dobson failed to convert and Cardiff were still four points adrift. With only a minute of time remaining Cardiff made desperate efforts to cross the Cambridge line and only good defence prevented Ivor Jones from scoring. In the last seconds of the game Daniell got possession for the Cantabs and with a brilliant run scored behind the posts. Sisterson converted easily and immediately afterwards time was whistled leaving Cambridge victorious by 15 points to six.

Having not scored for nine games, Willie Llewellyn at last got on the score sheet when Llwynypia defeated Pontymoile at home by 34 points to six. Such a dearth was unusual for Willie Llewellyn who was a prolific try scorer, but despite playing well in many of the games his scoring prowess seemed to have deserted him. He corrected that to some extent when he scored the opening try of the game. Arthur Harding converted and Llwynypia were five points ahead. Before the interval Harding scored a try which he converted himself, he then converted a try scored by Joe Williams. The angle, though difficult, was safely negotiated by Harding. The reserve trial forward's goal-kicking powers came as a complete surprise to the spectators who heartily applauded. Not downhearted,

Pontymoile returned to the attack and Bunney scored a try in the corner which went unconverted leaving the score at the interval; Llwynypia 15 points Pontymoile three.

In the second half Pontymoile started strongly and made a determined onslaught on the Llwynypia line, but yet again Harding played brilliantly, breaking through a scrummage with the ball at his toes and, ably supported by Billy Alexander and Rhys Williams, they took the ball to the centre of the field. Seeing Joe Williams in a favourable position, the Breconian, with a soccer pass, sent the ball to the three-quarter. Williams dribbled in fine style, keeping onwards until the line was crossed and scored a great try. For a fourth time Harding sent the ball over the bar. Wyndham Jones then scored two unconverted tries in quick succession followed shortly afterwards by another unconverted try by Stephens. Jack Bowen scored Llwynypia's last try which Harding successfully converted. With the light fading fast, Morgan brought the scoring to an end with an unconverted try for Pontymoile.

Such a performance could not have come at a better time for the Llwynypia men, several of whom had been selected for the Welsh trial match scheduled for the following Saturday. The determination brought to the game by Bob Jones, Billy Alexander, Arthur Harding and Dick Hellings was well worth witnessing. This quartette of forwards played a remarkable game. Harding especially shone but he was closely followed by the dashing play of Bob Jones. Willie Llewellyn, as usual, proved himself to be a tower of strength to his side, his attacking and defensive powers being above reproach. Rarely had the home spectators seen such brilliant play as that shown by the players chosen for the forthcoming trial match.

Of the original thirty players chosen for the Welsh trial at Newport three were unavailable. Billy Bancroft of Swansea, and Gwyn Nicholls and Jere Blake both of Cardiff. David J Boots of Abercarn replaced Billy Bancroft, Dan Rees of Swansea replaced Gwyn Nicholls and Dai Harris of Swansea came in for Jere Blake. Arthur Harding of Llwynypia remained in the reserves and did not play. The distribution of the thirty players into the Whites and Stripes sides was not made until an hour before kick-off and when the teams took the field they lined up as follows:

Stripes: Back, D J Boots (Abercarn); three-quarters, F Simmonds (Northampton), J A Gould (Portsmouth), W Llewellyn (Llwynypia) and L Deere (Mountain Ash); half-backs, G Ll Lloyd (Newport) and L A Phillips (Newport); forwards, F Scrine (Swansea), D Hellings (Llwynypia), F Miller (Mountain Ash), J J Hodges (Newport), D Harris (Swansea), J Foley (Brynmawr), D Walters (Llanelly), and Green (London Welsh).

Whites: Back, H B Winfield (Cardiff); three-quarters, G Davies (Swansea), D Rees (Swansea), M Williams (Llanelly) and W Trew (Swansea); half-backs, C Sweet-Escott (Cardiff) and R Jones (Swansea); forwards, A Brice (Aberavon), G Boots (Newport), G Dobson (Cardiff), R Thomas (Swansea), A Bolton (Penygraig), F Kirby (Penarth), W H Williams (Pontymister) and G Matthews (Bridgend).

Referee: Mr W M Douglas, Cardiff.

With regard to Green of London Welsh, a report in *The Cambrian* on Friday 22nd December 1899 by a London correspondent stated that Green had never played for London Welsh and was in fact a member of the Richmond team. The London Welsh Secretary confirmed that Green had been asked to play for London Welsh but had refused. The club were very angry that he played in the trial as a "London Welsh" representative while two of their best players, Livingston Davies and Johns, were overlooked.

The Stripes were outplayed in the first half, Alfred Brice of Aberavon opening the scoring for the Whites with a try which Bert Winfield converted. George Davies of the Whites was injured while tackling Dick Hellings and had to leave the field. Before the interval Billy Trew added another try which Bert Winfield failed to convert, but the Whites were leading at the break by 8 points to nil. In the second half Cecil Sweet-Escott crossed for a try but appeared to knock-on as he attempted to gather the ball. Nevertheless, the referee awarded the try, much to the dissatisfaction of the crowd. Bert Winfield failed with conversion. Following the kick-out the Stripes carried play to the Whites' end of the field and J A Gould and Llewellyn Deere took the ball over the line and claimed a try, but the referee only awarded a minor. A short while later the referee disallowed a free-kick for an off-side by Sweet-Escott. Again the crowd were annoyed and the shouts of disapproval became so loud that the referee stopped the game until order was restored and the crowd became calm. The Whites increased their lead when Morgan Williams crossed for another try which Bert Winfield converted and late in the game Dan Rees went over for the Whites, Bert Winfield again converting. Just before the final whistle J A Gould scored a try for the Stripes but he failed with the conversion. The outcome of the game was that the Stripes were well beaten by 21 points to three.

Following the trial there was a lot of speculation with regard to who may or may not represent Wales in their international at Gloucester on 6th January. Although he did not play in the trial at Newport, Billy Bancroft was still the favourite to take the full-back position. Despite playing very well in the trial it was thought that Bert Winfield had not shown the form that he displayed for Cardiff during the season, but he was certainly the first player to threaten the previously unchallenged position of the legendary Welsh captain and full-back, Billy Bancroft. It was disappointing that George Davies was injured early in the game as many felt he was in great form and ready to step up to international honours. If available, Gwyn Nicholls would be a certainty for selection; otherwise Dan Rees of Swansea, whose try was the best individual effort of the trial match, would be a more than able replacement. At centre for the Stripes team the combination of Frank Simmonds and Joseph Augustus 'Gus' Gould, brother of the famous Arthur Gould, was a complete failure. Despite having plenty of possession they were quite unable to take advantage of their fast wings, Willie Llewellyn and Llewellyn Deere. There was plenty of competition for the wing positions, Billy Trew playing exceptionally well in the trial, as did Llewellyn Deere. Willie Llewellyn often showed glimpses of his brilliance both in attack and defence but his selection in the Welsh team was by no means certain. At half-back, G Llewellyn Lloyd and Louis Phillips both played well for the Stripes but Cecil Sweet-Escott was the pick of the four half-backs in attack and defence and stood a real chance of being selected for the Welsh team. Dick Jones of Swansea had his best game of the season to make selection of the Welsh half-backs for the England game very difficult. Most prominent of the forwards were Alfred Brice, Jehoida Hodges, Dick Hellings and George Boots while George Dobson, Fred Miller, William Henry 'Buller' Williams, Bob Thomas and Danny Walters all played extremely well. Another player who performed well in the trial was Jack Foley of Brynmawr who, according to a report of the match in *The South Wales Daily News* was, 'a player who could hold his own in any club team.'

One disappointing aspect of the Welsh trial match at Newport was the omission of Reg Skrimshire. Although he did not play his best rugby in the international matches of 1899, it was considered that his worst form was greatly superior to that shown by the men given preference over him. It was generally presumed that Skrimshire had been penalised for playing for Blackheath rather than London Welsh, and was not selected despite the fact that he was playing very well for his new club. All the selection speculation would be concluded on Thursday 14th December when the selection committee of the Welsh Football Union met in Cardiff to select the Welsh team and reserves for the game against England at Gloucester.

The week after the trial match, Llwynypia faced Llanelly at Stradey Park. Llwynypia had the better of matters during the initial stages of the game. Their forwards, headed by their captain Billy Alexander, played magnificently and up until the interval neither side had scored. However, the Llwynypia forwards could not keep up their superiority and with more possession, the Llanelly backs played splendidly. Early in the second half Alcwyn Jones picked up and made a brilliant burst, scoring the first try in magnificent style. Evan Lloyd converted. Half-back Ben Davies added to the score with an unconverted try. With the Llanelly backs now playing with great confidence several rounds of passing culminated in Ben Davies scoring his second try of the match. Evan Lloyd converted. Although there was very little passing on the Llwynypia side, Willie Llewellyn and Arthur Harding were brilliant in defence and with Llwynypia improving towards the end of the game they kept play in the Llanelly half until the final whistle blew. Nevertheless, Llanelly were the better side on the day and were victorious by 13 points to nil.

On the Thursday following the Llwynypia game against Llanelly the match committee of the Welsh Football Union met at the Queen's Hotel, Cardiff and selected the Welsh team to face England at Gloucester on Saturday 6th January 1900. The following team was selected:

Wales: Back, W J Bancroft (Swansea); three-quarters, E G Nicholls (Cardiff), right centre, George Davies (Swansea), left centre, W Llewellyn (Llwynypia), right wing, W Trew (Swansea), left wing; half-backs, G Ll Lloyd (Newport) and L A Phillips (Newport); forwards, D Hellings (Llwynypia), A Brice (Aberavon), G Boots (Newport), F Miller (Mountain

Ash), W H Williams (Pontymister), J R Thomas (Swansea), J J Hodges (Newport) and J Blake (Cardiff).

Reserves: Back, H B Winfield (Cardiff); three-quarter backs, right centre, D Rees (Swansea), left centre, W Jones (Cardiff), right wing Ll Deere (Mountain Ash) and left wing, M Williams (Llanelly); half-backs, C Sweet-Escott (Cardiff) and R Jones (Swansea); forwards, G Dobson (Cardiff), F Scrine (Swansea), D J Walters (Llanelly), and A Bolton (Penygraig).

With Gwyn Nicholls still not back from Australia it was generally believed that Dan Rees of Swansea, would partner his club-mate, George Davies, if the Cardiff captain did not play. The Newport halves, probably because they had played so long and well together, were chosen ahead of Cecil Sweet-Escott of Cardiff and Dick Jones of Swansea. Six places in the forwards were regarded as filled after the trial match. Alfred Brice, Dick Hellings, George Boots, Jehoida Hodges, Jere Blake and Fred Scrine were popularly believed to be indispensable. The committee, however, gave preference to Bob Thomas, who, after years of being close to gaining his first Welsh cap, finally got selected in place of his colleague Fred Scrine.

Fred Miller was given another chance having gained his first cap for Wales in their defeat against Ireland at Lansdowne Road in 1896. Miller was considered as being the best forward next to Dick Hellings in the Glamorgan League. William Henry 'Buller' Williams of Pontymister was selected purely for his brilliant display in the trial match.

Swansea were certainly well represented with regard to the number of players chosen in the Welsh team and reserves. They were unquestionably playing wonderful rugby, only losing one of their thirteen games thus far into the season. In addition to Billy Bancroft gaining his twenty-eighth consecutive cap for Wales, overtaking the legendary Arthur Gould with twenty-seven caps, first caps were richly deserved for George Davies, Dan Rees, Billy Trew, and Bob Thomas. Dick Jones, the Swansea outside-half would have to wait another year for his first cap and Fred Scrine would be capped just once more for Wales against Ireland in 1901.

Having lost to Llanelly, Llwynypia faced a monumental task in their next game against Swansea at St Helen's. Swansea had played thirteen games and won twelve. They had scored 187 points with only 19 against. Only Newport, Neath and Llanelly had scored against them. Swansea had lost their only game of the season the previous week when they lost to Llanelly at Stradey Park by 8 points to three. This was never going to be an easy encounter for Llwynypia, and so it proved, Swansea winning by 30 points to nil. The defeat by Llanelly was to be the only game lost of the 32 Swansea played that season as undisputed Welsh club champions. They scored 586 points with only 57 points against. Billy Trew scored 31 tries and he and Billy Bancroft were top points scorers with 93 points apiece. Club captain Billy Bancroft also captained the Welsh team, who secured their second Triple Crown in 1900. Billy Trew, George Davies, Dan Rees and Bob Thomas all made their debuts for Wales in the first international of the season against England at Gloucester.

As the score suggests, the game was very one-sided with Swansea being far superior to their opponents, and throughout the match there was scarcely a noticeable bout of passing by the Llwynypia three-quarter line. Their forwards, however, did play a really good game and frequently

Swansea RFC 1st XV 1899–1900 Season

Back Row: Harry Ball (Trainer), F E Perkins (Sec.), A Jones, W Parker, W Joseph, D Harris, J A Smith, F Scrine, Sam Rice (Touch Judge).
Middle Row: R Thomas, F G Gordon, D Rees, W J Bancroft (Captain), G Davies, W J Trew, H Davies. *Front Row*: S Bevan, R M Owen and R Jones.

cleared their line when danger threatened. Three first half unconverted tries by Frank Gordon, Dan Rees and Hopkin Davies gave Swansea an interval lead of 9 points to nil.

In the second half Swansea continued where they left off in the first and early in the half Dan Rees scored his second try of the afternoon. The kick at goal failed. Then, after Swansea had kept Llwynypia pinned in their twenty-five for quite a while, George Davies very cleverly dropped a goal with his left foot. Swansea now led by 16 points to nil and it was evident that the game was lost and won as the Swansea men kept attacking in brilliant style. Shortly afterwards a kick by Dickie Owen culminated in Arthur Jones getting possession and scoring a try which Billy Bancroft converted. By way of a change Llwynypia rallied in astonishing style and Willie Llewellyn, with a really fine run, nearly succeeded in scoring. He was tackled in the middle of the home twenty-five by Billy Trew and the ball was sent to Arthur Jones, who failed to field, but Dan Rees, cleverly scooping the ball up, had a clear run in and scored his third try of the afternoon. Billy Bancroft converted. Towards the end of the game Billy Bancroft brought the scoring to an end when he dropped a fine goal to give Swansea victory by 30 points to nil.

With regard to the players, all the Swansea three-quarters were in good form whilst Dickie Owen, ably supported by Dick Jones, was particularly smart behind the scrummage. Although Billy Bancroft played well, it took him some time to find his kicking boots. For Llwynypia, Dick Hellings, Arthur Harding and Tom Dobson were the pick of a really good pack. Willie Llewellyn was by far the best of the Llwynypia three-quarter line.

Llwynypia's third successive defeat in three games came in their Boxing Day away match against Leicester. Willie Llewellyn scored the only points for Llwynypia when he crossed for a splendid try in the 9 points to three defeat. The second match of Llwynypia's Christmas tour was against Northampton. At the last moment Willie Llewellyn stepped down in favour of Joe Williams and the game ended in a draw with both sides failing to score.

With Gwyn Nicholls not expected back from Australia until after the international between Wales and England at Gloucester, Dan Rees, the Swansea centre, was called up from the reserves to take his place in the Welsh team. In preparation for the international against England, Willie

Llewellyn was asked to play in the Swansea match against Old Wesley, Dublin. This would enable Willie Llewellyn and his new international partner Dan Rees to become familiar with each other's playing style. With Billy Bancroft absent, Lockman played at full-back. Billy Trew played left wing with Frank Gordon at left centre. Dan Rees played right centre inside Willie Llewellyn on the right wing. George Davies did not play. Dickie Owen and Dick Jones were the half-backs. The forwards were Fred Scrine, Will Parker, Bob Thomas, Hopkin Davies, Will Joseph, D Harris, J A Smith and A Jones.

Having narrowly defeated the Old Wesley by 16 points to twelve a few days previously, Swansea had a more convincing victory in their return match, winning by 23 points to nil. Just before the interval Willie Llewellyn scored an unconverted try to give Swansea a three point lead. In the second half Swansea played really well. Will Joseph was the first to score when he picked up in the loose and ran through half a dozen opponents to score a brilliant try which Lockman converted. On several occasions Swansea got right up to the Old Wesley goal line but the passing was poor and the tackling was good. Following some fierce forward rushes both the Old Wesley wings were injured when they collided with each other while attempting to tackle Frank Gordon. Both received severe cuts to the head and had to retire. With only thirteen men the visitors showed considerable courage but time after time they were forced back to their own goal line where only determined defence prevented the home team from scoring. At last a better scoring chance was obtained by Swansea and when Dan Rees passed to Billy Trew the latter ran over easily and scored. Lockman converted. Then Willie Llewellyn got in very cleverly on the wing after a nice pass from Dan Rees. Receiving the ball on the twenty-five yard line, Llewellyn sprinted around four or five opponents in international style and scored in a good position for Lockman to convert. This was Willie Llewellyn's best effort so far, but directly afterwards he started a round of passing which did not finish until Jones got in on the other wing. Lockman again converted and immediately afterwards time was called with Swansea victors by 23 points to nil.

The experiment of playing Willie Llewellyn outside Dan Rees for Swansea was deemed an unequivocal success and all eyes now focussed on the forthcoming international between England and Wales at Kingsholm,

Wales Team v England 1900

Back Row: *W H Williams, J Blake, J G Boots, F Miller, J J Hodges, A B Brice.
Middle Row: Mr W E Rees (Sec. WFU), W M Llewellyn, D Hellings, *D Rees, W J Bancroft (Captain),*G Davies, *W J Trew, Mr A J Davies (Touch Judge).
Front Row: *R Thomas, G Ll Lloyd and *L A Phillips. (* Wales Debut)

Gloucester, on Saturday 6th January 1900. There was only one change from the team originally selected, Dan Rees at centre replacing Gwyn Nicholls who had not returned from his trip to Australia with the British Isles team.

This was the seventeenth meeting between Wales and England. The odds historically were very much in England's favour having won eleven of the sixteen games played. Wales had only won four games and there was just the one pointless drawn game at Stradey Park, Llanelly in 1887. For this match a crowd of between 30,000 and 35,000 spectators turned up to watch the game, half of them Welsh. On the morning of the game there were rumours that George Dobson would take the place of Dick Hellings. It appeared that Hellings had played in a practise match on the Thursday prior to the international thus breaking the Welsh Football

Union's unwritten law that no selected player should turn out during the week of an international. There was also some concern over Alfred Brice, who had also played a game on the Monday prior to the international. With regard to Brice, a wire was sent by Mr Walter E Rees, Secretary of the WFU, prohibiting Brice from turning out. However, there was no change in the Welsh side and both teams turned out as selected. England won the toss and a minute or two before 2.30 the Royal Standard was hoisted and the band played 'God Save the Queen'. And for the first time at an international match the huge concourse joined in signing the anthem with the utmost enthusiasm.

England: H T Gamlin (Devonport Albion); *S F Coopper, *G Gordon-Smith (Blackheath), *A T Brettargh (Liverpool OB), *E T Nicholson (Birkenhead PK); R H B Cattell (Captain, Moseley), *G H Marsden (Morley); *F J Bell, *R W Bell (Northern), *W Cobby (Hull), *A Cockerham (Bradford Olicana), *J W Jarman (Bristol), *S Reynolds (Richmond), *C T Scott (Blackheath), *J Baxter (Birkenhead Park). (* England Debut)

Referee: Adam J Turnbull (Scotland).

Following the anthem Billy Bancroft led his men on to the field. Dick Cattell, the English captain, at the head of the Englishmen, followed immediately afterwards. Just after 2.30 Billy Bancroft kicked off for Wales into a strong wind. Early in the game Dick Hellings got injured and play was held up for several minutes while he was treated. He still looked groggy, did not attempt to take his place in the line-out that followed and shortly afterwards left the field. Even without Hellings the Welsh pack held the upper hand and when he returned they successfully wheeled a scrum and took play to just inside the English twenty-five. Here the ball was released and Hellings picking up made a desperate dash for the line and got over for a try beneath the goal posts. Billy Bancroft converted. There was no doubt that Dick Hellings was badly hurt because he played outside the scrum more as a fifth three-quarter than anything else. Before the interval Brettargh was badly injured and had to leave the field and during the wait Hellings left the field again.

Wales led by 5 points to nil at the break but early in the second half England worked their way to well inside the Welsh twenty-five where Billy Bancroft brought off a save at the critical moment. He had a gruelling by the English forwards, but he stuck to it just the same and saved an almost certain try. Having put the Welsh team under pressure for some time the English three-quarters created an opportunity and with the ball moving from the left, Brettargh got the ball away to Nicholson who rounded Billy Trew and scored a beautiful try which Gamlin failed to convert. Following the try England played with a lot more enthusiasm and at least half a dozen times their three-quarters attacked the Welsh line. On each occasion they looked very dangerous but the Welsh defence just managed to keep them out. Then it was the Welsh three-quarters' time to attack and after a couple of bouts of passing it looked certain that Willie Llewellyn would cross for a try, but Gamlin brought off one of his characteristic tackles and put Llewellyn in touch about six yards from the line. From the line-out one of the Welsh forwards got the ball away to the three-quarters. Dan Rees and George Davies handled and the latter, running up to Gamlin, passed to Billy Trew who scored behind the posts. Billy Bancroft converting. George Davies was injured and left the field for a short while and Wales were still handicapped by the injury to Dick Hellings, whose left arm just hung by his side. Towards the end of the game the Welsh three-quarters where well on top of their opponents and several times just failed to score. Wales were not left long without being rewarded and when England were penalised Billy Bancroft dropped a magnificent penalty goal. When time was called immediately afterwards Wales were victorious by 13 points to three. It was discovered after the match that Dick Hellings had played most of the game with a broken arm.

The Welsh team played exceptionally well, particularly taking into account the injury to Dick Hellings. Willie Llewellyn had another sound game, well served by Dan Rees; he never failed to make ground.

Billy Bancroft made his first club appearance for Swansea against Newport on 5th October 1889. He played for Swansea for his entire rugby career.

Courtesy of Newport RFC and Gwent Archives

Although beaten by Coopper once or twice in the first half, in the second half there was no question that Willie Llewellyn was far superior to his opposite number rounding him time after time and never letting Coopper get near him.

The most conspicuous player on the field was Billy Bancroft. He had an outstanding game on the occasion he became the most capped Welsh rugby player of all time with twenty-eight caps. In the game against Ireland in 1899, Bancroft had equalled the record of Arthur Gould, who was capped by Wales on twenty-seven occasions. Billy Bancroft won his first cap for Wales against Scotland in 1890. Playing for Swansea in his first season of senior rugby, Bancroft was originally selected as the reserve full-back to Tom England of Newport. Tom England was injured playing for Newport against Penarth the Saturday prior to the international and was unable to play, leaving the reserve, Billy Bancroft, to fill the position. Two weeks later Tom England was back playing for Newport in their game against St Thomas's Hospital. Unfortunately, however, the opportunity of winning a Welsh cap had passed him by, for although selected as reserve full-back for the final international of the season against Ireland at Lansdowne Road, on St David's Day, Tom England never played international rugby for Wales.

Billy Bancroft played for Wales on thirty-three consecutive occasions. Although Bancroft would only win two out of his first nine Welsh games, he was part of the Wales team that won their first Triple Crown in 1893. The first game of that season saw Wales face England at the Cardiff Arms Park. With little time left to play and Wales losing 9–11, they were awarded a penalty near touch, 30 yards from the England goal line. The Welsh captain, Arthur Gould called Bancroft over and told him to kick

Tom England played 180 games for Newport between 1887 and 1895. Injury cruelly denied him a Welsh international cap.

(from the ground) for goal. Bancroft insisted on dropping for goal, but his captain forbade it. The two began arguing in front of the home crowd until, Gould threw the ball to the ground in frustration and walked away only to find that Bancroft had coolly drop-kicked the penalty goal. Not only had Bancroft won the match, he had scored the first penalty goal kicked in international rugby.

The week after the international against England the following article appeared in *The Rhondda Leader*: 'Mr Willie Llewellyn, Clydach Vale Hotel, left the district on Monday with the 1.15 p.m. train for London to complete his chemical studies. His play at the recent international match at Gloucester drew from all English critics unstinted praise, nearly all crowning him as "best man on the field." In addition to his recent presentation from admiring friends, he was the recipient of a handsome gift from his late employer, Mr J W Richards, chemist. His loss will be an irreparable one to the local team, but the London Welsh will be greatly benefited by his presence. The homesters are anxiously looking forward to his holidays when they hope to see some of his brilliant runs once more.'

Willie Llewellyn travelled to London on Monday 8th January to pursue his studies at the Pharmaceutical College, Bloomsbury, London. Early in December Willie had been the recipient of a magnificent gold watch presented to him by his many admirers at a special evening at the Clydach Vale Hotel on Thursday 7th December 1899.

Willie had been selected to play for Glamorgan in their game against Durham at Cardiff Arms Park on Wednesday 10th January. As he was already in London, Willie did not play. The team originally selected was almost a full Welsh international side. The full-back and three-quarters were the same as the Welsh team that played against England at Gloucester and the half-backs were the Welsh reserves for that game, namely Cecil Sweet-Escott and Dick Jones. The forwards were Alfred Brice, Bob Thomas, Fred Miller, Jere Blake, George Dobson, A Bolton, Fred Scrine and F Kirby. Brice, Thomas, Miller, Blake and Scrine were all full internationals. The remaining three had all played in the victorious Whites team in the Welsh trial at Newport and George Dobson and A Bolton were reserves for the Wales team that played against England the previous week-end.

This was Glamorgan's first game against Durham and for several players the game was considered as a trial for the international match against Scotland. The selection committee of the Welsh Football Union were meeting immediately after the game to select the Welsh side. As it transpired the selection committee would learn nothing from the full-back and three-quarters as Billy Bancroft, George Davies, Dan Rees, Billy Trew and Willie Llewellyn all withdrew from the game. Their places were taken by Bert Winfield, Viv Huzzey, W 'Pussy' Jones and Percy Bush, all from Cardiff, and Llewellyn Deere from Mountain Ash. The half-backs were as selected: Cecil Sweet-Escott of Cardiff and Dick Jones of Swansea. The only change in the forwards was J Wheeler of Cardiff who replaced Bob Thomas. Glamorgan won the game which was more difficult than the score suggests. Kirby opened the scoring for Glamorgan with a try that Bert Winfield failed to convert. Shortly afterwards Percy Bush took an indifferent pass and running straight up the touchline to his opposite number gave a try scoring pass to Viv Huzzey. Bert Winfield again failed with the conversion. Percy Bush was again instrumental in providing a second try for Viv Huzzey. This time Bert Winfield added the extra points. Just before the interval Smith scored an unconverted try for Durham. In the second half Dick Jones got the ball away to Viv Huzzey, who passed on to his centre and Percy Bush, with a brilliant effort, scored a try. Bert Winfield converted and Glamorgan were victorious by 21 points to three.

The subsequent deliberations of the selection committee of the Welsh Football Union who met at the Queen's Hotel, Cardiff, took barely thirty minutes. When the team to meet Scotland at Swansea on Saturday 27th January was announced there were only two changes from the side that defeated England at Gloucester: Gwyn Nicholls replaced Dan Rees and George Dobson replaced the injured Dick Hellings. The committee, while honouring the famous Cardiff centre with the first refusal of the position, endorsed their appreciation of Dan Rees' display at Gloucester by choosing the Swansea right centre as first reserve to Nicholls. The reserves selected were as follows: Back, H B Winfield (Cardiff); three-quarters, Ll Deere (Mountain Ash) right wing; Dan Rees (Swansea) right centre; W Jones (Cardiff) left centre; and M Williams (Llanelly) left wing; half-backs, C Sweet-Escott (Cardiff) and C Powell (Neath); forwards N 'Danny'

Walters (Llanelly); R Jones (Llwynypia); F Kirby (Penarth) and Hopkin Davies (Swansea).

Arriving in London on Monday 8th January 1900, Willie Llewellyn did not waste any time getting involved with his new rugby club. On Saturday 13th January Willie was playing his first game for London Welsh in the away fixture with Twickenham. Willie had a dream debut scoring both the tries in a one goal and one try to nil victory. The following week he was at his very best again and scored another two tries when London Welsh defeated Rovers at Acton by 12 points to nil.

On Saturday 27th January Wales played their second international rugby match of the season against Scotland at St Helen's, Swansea. Welsh selector Arthur Gould had stated that Wales were not strong enough to beat Scotland, but they did, in front of almost 40,000 spectators, including those in a temporary stand behind the goal-posts on the cricket pitch. The Welsh team was as selected with Gwyn Nicholls playing at centre instead of Dan Rees, and George Dobson playing at forward in place of the injured Dick Hellings. Following in his brother Tom's footsteps, George Dobson won his only Welsh cap that day. The teams were as follows:

Wales: Back, W J Bancroft (Swansea, Captain); three-quarters, E G Nicholls (Cardiff), right centre, George Davies (Swansea), left centre, W M Llewellyn (Llwynypia), right wing, W Trew (Swansea), left wing; half-backs, G Ll Lloyd (Newport) and L A Phillips (Newport); forwards, *George Dobson (Cardiff), A Brice (Aberavon), J G Boots (Newport), F Miller (Mountain Ash), W H Williams (Pontymister), J R Thomas (Swansea), J J Hodges (Newport) and J Blake (Cardiff). (* Wales Debut)

Scotland: Back, H Rottenburg (London Scottish); three-quarters, T L Scott (Langholm), A B Timms (Edinburgh Wdrs.), *W H Morrison, *J E Crabbie (Edinburgh Acads.); *F H Fasson (Edinburgh U), J I Gillespie (Edinburgh Acads.); M C Morrison (Royal HSFP, captain), W M C McEwan (Edinburgh Acads.), W J Thomson (West of Scotland), J M Dykes, *F W Henderson (London Scottish), G C Kerr (Durham City), T M Scott (Hawick), *D R Bedell-Sivright (Edinburgh U). (* Scotland Debut)

Referee: A Hartley (England).

Scotland won the toss and had a strong wind in their favour during the first half. They missed an early chance to take the lead when T M Scott failed with a penalty kick from a favourable position, and wasted another chance when another penalty kick just missed the post by inches. The Welsh forwards, having been under pressure for a while started to take control and holding out in their own twenty-five Louis Phillips received the ball. He transferred to Llewellyn Lloyd, who passed on to Gwyn Nicholls. The Welsh centre passed to Willie Llewellyn who cleared several forwards, the half-backs and a couple of three-quarters. Running with terrific speed and judgement he easily eluded Rottenburg at full-back and scored a magnificent try. Billy Bancroft, with a fine kick, just failed to convert. Wales continued to put Scotland on the defensive and for quite some time Wales were in control until a mistake by Billy Bancroft presented Scotland with an easy try. Johnny Dykes chased the ball over the line and scored a simple try after it had passed through the Welsh custodian's legs. Fortunately for Wales, the conversion was missed and the scores were level at three points all. Wales responded well and after defending their line for a short while a magnificent rally, started and finished by Gwyn Nicholls, resulted in the Cardiff captain scoring a try. Billy Bancroft again missed the conversion and minutes later half-time was called.

In the second half, with the Welsh forwards gaining a lot of possession, the backs were performing splendidly and Scotland did well to prevent them from scoring. Repeatedly the Welsh three-quarters were up on the Scottish line but Rottenburg's tackling was superb. Twenty minutes of the second half passed with Scotland under constant pressure and only fine tackling prevented Wales from scoring. Then at last their defence was penetrated and a fine round of passing by the Welsh backs enabled Gwyn Nicholls to put Willie Llewellyn cleverly over for a try which again Billy Bancroft failed to convert. Scotland were now badly beaten and, although they did manage to get into the Welsh half, they were soon on the defensive again with the Welsh forwards rushing up the field. A mistake by the Scottish three-quarters gave George Boots a chance to snap up a corner try when least expected to do so. Billy Bancroft again missed the conversion but Wales were victorious by 12 points to three. This was an outstanding performance by a Welsh team that was expected to struggle against a strong Scottish pack which contained D R 'Darkie' Bedell-Sivright winning the first of his twenty-two caps. Wales now faced the prospect of winning their second Triple Crown when they played

Ireland in the last international of the Home Nations Championship at Balmoral, Belfast, on Saturday 17th March.

Willie returned to club rugby at London Welsh after the Scottish international. For three consecutive Saturdays there was no game. The first was due to the international at Richmond between England and Ireland, while the weather accounted for the other two. The game against Saracens on Saturday 17th February was cancelled on the day of the match because the Saracens' ground was under water. With everything in place for the next fixture against St Mary's Hospital, fate played its part again and the Hospital cancelled the fixture the day prior to the game because of the injuries the team had sustained playing a cup tie against St Thomas' Hospital earlier that week. However, St Mary's sent a scratch team down to Acton and London Welsh did likewise; the result of a hard fought game was in favour of London Welsh by three tries to one. Although there is no mention of Willie Llewellyn it is assumed that he played in this game.

The following weekend Willie Llewellyn played for London Welsh in their home game against Berkshire Wanderers. Within the first five minutes of the game Willie Llewellyn intercepted a pass and, running the length of the field, scored behind the posts, Williams converting. Shortly afterwards the Welsh forwards dribbled up the field and Walter Davies scored an unconverted try. Heywood, the London Welsh captain, received from the kick off and eluding everybody, he scored the third try of the match. Four more tries were added by Llewellyn, Williams, Walter Davies and Heywood respectively and the Welsh won a one-sided game by one goal and six tries (23 points) to nil.

The following week Willie Llewellyn travelled down from London to play for Glamorgan in their match against Gloucester at Cardiff Arms Park. There were several changes from the team originally selected. None of the chosen Swansea players turned out and Swansea people in fact took very little interest in the match, a protest at Glamorgan County's refusal to stage its games there. The only player from Swansea who did eventually turn out was Will Joseph who had originally been selected as a reserve. He replaced club-mate Hopkin Davies. Billy Bancroft was replaced by Bert Winfield of Cardiff (not for the first time this season). Ivor Jones of Cardiff came in for George Davies, Llewellyn Deere of Mountain Ash replaced Billy Trew and Bob Thomas was subbed by Billy Alexander of

Llwynypia. With G Llewellyn Lloyd, the Newport outside half, getting injured playing for Kent in their game against Devon at Blackheath, it was intended that Selwyn Biggs of Cardiff and Charlie Powell of Neath should play as half-backs and that the better player would be chosen to replace Lloyd in the Welsh team to face Ireland at Balmoral, Belfast. This idea was generally criticised as it left Cecil Sweet-Escott (Cardiff), who had been selected as the reserve half-back for the two previous internationals, out in the cold. However, Selwyn Biggs cried off and Cecil Sweet-Escott and Charlie Powell were the half-backs for Glamorgan. Although he did not play, Percy Bush of Cardiff featured in the reserves, an indication of his growing prominence in the game (although he would have to wait another five years for the honour of gaining his first Welsh cap). The full team was as follows:

Glamorgan: Back, H B Winfield (Cardiff); three-quarters, W M Llewellyn (Llwynypia), E G Nicholls, Ivor Jones (Cardiff), Ll Deere (Mountain Ash); half-backs, C Powell (Neath) and C Sweet-Escott (Cardiff); forwards, A Brice (Aberavon), F Miller (Mountain Ash), R Jones (Llwynypia), D H Davies (Neath), W Joseph (Swansea), J Blake (Cardiff), W Alexander (Llwynypia) and F Kirby (Penarth).

The game was refereed by Arthur Gould and played in front of 6,000 spectators. Play was fast and even for the first twenty minutes. Gwyn Nicholls then gained a mark right in front of the Gloucester post and Bert Winfield placed the goal. Just before half-time Ivor Jones received from Willie Llewellyn and scored a wonderful try. Bert Winfield failed to convert but Glamorgan were leading at the interval by 7 points to nil. Early in the second half Charlie Powell received a pass from Sweet-Escott and, after beating two or three men, struggled over the line to score a fine try. Bert Winfield kicked the conversion. Gloucester were by no means out of the game and responded with some good attacking play which resulted in a fine try by J Lewis which was converted by Oates. With the Gloucester forwards showing a marked superiority, they rushed play into the Glamorgan half. Just outside the Glamorgan twenty-five a pass from the Glamorgan scrum was intercepted by Oswell who threw out to Lockley who scored a well-earned try which Oates had hard lines in not converting. Just before the final whistle Ivor Jones, running very strongly, transferred to Llewellyn Deere and the Mountain Ash man scored another unconverted try for the home side. Shortly afterwards time was called with Glamorgan winning a well contested game by 15 points to eight.

Willie Llewellyn returned to the London Welsh team for their Saturday fixture against Olney after playing for Glamorgan. The Welsh won the toss and playing with the wind scored an unconverted try by means of Hughes within the first five minutes. From the kick off Jones received and returned to the opposition's twenty-five. From the line-out Livingston Davies passed to Willie Llewellyn who, eluding everybody, scored a brilliant try which James converted. Shortly before half-time Heywood, after a brilliant round of passing amongst the Welsh backs, scored a third try which James again converted. London Welsh, facing the wind in the second half, scored tries through Williams, Treharne and W S Williams. Just before the final whistle Olney scored from a forward rush, but the kick at goal failed. A one-sided but interesting game thus ended in favour of London Welsh by 3 goals and 3 tries to 1 try (24–3).

Willie Llewellyn had only played five games for the Exiles since arriving in London but they had won them all and his contribution had been immense, scoring 7 of the club's nineteen tries. Under the captaincy of J A Heywood, London Welsh finished the season having played 19 matches, of which they had won 10, drawn 4 and lost 5. There was no hint of the team's hidden strength early in the season when London Welsh lost four of their first seven games. But from December 2nd 1899 until the end of the season they only lost once when Sutton won at West Acton. Efforts to re-establish the club certainly bore fruit during the 1899–1900 season. The generosity of the Welsh Football Union and the ability of the club to attract international players of the calibre of 22 year old Willie Llewellyn proved a turning point in the history of London Welsh. Two months after Willie Llewellyn joined them Teddy Morgan, a medical student at Guy's Hospital, linked up with the club. He ran in a match-saving try at Bedford on the day Willie Llewellyn was playing for Wales against Ireland at Belfast. Both Old Breconians, Willie Llewellyn and Teddy Morgan would be instrumental in the club's rise to fame over the next few seasons, although Teddy Morgan would have to wait another two years before winning his first Welsh cap against England in 1902.

On St Patrick's Day 1900 Willie Llewellyn celerbrated his sixth cap for Wales with his first Triple Crown success and Wales's second having won their previous one in 1893. The team selected by the Welsh Football Union on Thursday 1st March contained only one change from the side that defeated Scotland at St Helen's, Swansea; Dick Hellings, who had been badly injured in the game against England, returned at the expense of George Dobson. Although G Llewellyn Lloyd of Newport was selected, he had been injured playing for Kent against Devon at Blackheath and his place was taken by Selwyn Biggs of Cardiff. This was the last of nine Welsh caps gained by Selwyn Biggs. The teams turned out as follows:

Wales: Back, W J Bancroft (Swansea, Captain); three-quarters, E G Nicholls (Cardiff), right centre, George Davies (Swansea), left centre, W Llewellyn (Llwynypia), right wing, W Trew (Swansea), left wing; half-backs, S H Biggs (Cardiff) and L A Phillips (Newport); forwards, D Hellings (Llwynypia), A Brice (Aberavon), J G Boots (Newport), F Miller (Mountain Ash), W H Williams (Pontymister), R Thomas (Swansea), J J Hodges (Newport) and J Blake (Cardiff).

Ireland: Back, J Fulton (NIFC); three-quarters, E F Campbell (Monkstown), B R Doran (Lansdowne), J B Allison (QCB), I G Davidson (North of Ireland); L M Magee (Captain, Bective), J H Ferris (QCB); T J Little (Bective), M Ryan, J Ryan (Rockwell Coll.), A W D Meares, P C Nicholson, *T A Harvey (Dublin U), C E Allen (Derry), S T Irwin (QCB). (* Ireland Debut)

Referee: Adam J Turnbull (Scotland).

Ireland played a sterling forward game and their defence was so good, that the Welsh team, who had so easily disposed of England and Scotland, could only win by a single unconverted try. Although the Welsh victory was a narrow one, they had very much the better of the play and despite occasionally being under pressure from the Irish pack their forwards worked very well together and were much better in the tight scrummages. Ireland's tactic, which was seldom effective, was to break up the scrummage and use their feet in the open. The Welsh half-backs and three-quarters played splendidly and only powerful tackling kept the Welsh score within the smallest possible limit. Wales scored their only try in the second half when, from a scrummage in midfield, Louis Phillips obtained the ball and passed to Gwyn Nicholls who made a wonderful opening for George Davies to burst over the line and score. He knew very little of what happened after being knocked unconscious by a kick in the mouth as he scored. However, he was able to resume a few minutes later. Billy Bancroft took the kick which went wide. From this time onwards Ireland made tremendous efforts to score but the game finished with Wales victorious by 3 points to nil. Wales, playing splendid football, both in the scrummages and behind, had the distinction of winning all three of their international matches and secured their second Triple Crown.

With the international season over and Willie Llewellyn home from college, he ended the season playing in all nine remaining games for Llwynypia. He returned to the side for the away game against Plymouth, who had lost only once up to that point in the season (against the Glamorgan Police in January). This was a brutal game and after Plymouth had scored an unconverted try in the first half Bob Jones was ordered off the field by the referee for unnecessary rough play. Llwynypia started well in the second half but Plymouth responded with another unconverted try. With Llwynypia unable to score Plymouth won the game by 6 points to nil.

On the day that Bob Jones played for Llwynypia against Ebbw Vale a meeting of the Welsh Football Union decided to suspend him for a fortnight for the sending off against Plymouth. Consequently he did not feature in the game against Bridgend the following week, but returned for the match with Cardiff only eleven days after his suspension.

Following their defeat against Plymouth, Llwynypia played Mountain Ash for the fourth and final time during the season. Having lost two and drawn one, Llwynypia were keen to get at least one victory under their belt against their old rivals. However, this was not to be and two unconverted tries in the first half and a goal in the second gave Mountain Ash victory by 11 points to nil.

Llwynypia returned to winning ways in their next game against Pontypridd. Willie Llewellyn's' first home game since his return from college was greeted with a round of applause. An unconverted try in the first half by Joe Williams gave Llwynypia the lead at the interval. Ten minutes from the final whistle Whale of Pontypridd was penalised for off-side and W 'Pussy' Jones, taking a penalty kick close to the halfway line, scored a beautiful goal from a difficult angle.

Willie Llewellyn scored a try in each of Llwynypia's next two games against Ebbw Vale and Bridgend. Bob Jones opened the scoring with an unconverted try in the home game against Ebbw Vale. Just before the interval, Willie Llewellyn, with a brilliant run from beyond the halfway line, scored a try behind the posts. Jones again failed to convert. In the second half a fine round of passing by the Llwynypia quartette almost ended in a try but W 'Pussy' Jones, having beaten his man, fell. A moment later he made amends by scoring a fine try which was not converted. This was the end of the scoring and Llwynypia won a well contested game by 9 points to nil.

In the away game against Bridgend, George Stephens opened the scoring for Llwynypia with a second-half try. Llwynypia scored again when W Jones crossed for a try but Bridgend responded positively by making an onslaught on the Llwynypia goal line and only clever defence by Willie Llewellyn prevented a score. Willie Llewellyn then scored Llwynypia's third try to extend Llwynypia's lead to 11 points to nil. Towards the end of the game Bridgend made a good stand against a strong rush by the Llwynypia forwards and George Ball secured the leather and dropped an exceedingly smart goal for them. Play was very fast and even right up to the finish of the game and Llwynypia were the winners by 11 points to four.

Having narrowly lost to Cardiff at home earlier in the season, Llwynypia played the return fixture at Cardiff Arms Park on Easter Monday. This was Cardiff's last game of the season and attracted a crowd of about 7,000 spectators. Despite the absence of Percy and Fred Bush, who were on the injured list, and Bert Winfield, who was unwell, Cardiff were still strongly represented. Welsh internationals Gwyn Nicholls, Selwyn Biggs, Jere Blake and George Dobson were all included while Llwynypia also fielded a strong team with their Welsh caps Willie Llewellyn, Dick Hellings, Billy Alexander and Tom Dobson all taking the field.

Early in the game Arthur Ricketts opened the scoring for Cardiff after cleverly kicking ahead and following at speed to score a stunning try which Gwyn Nicholls failed to convert. Dick Hellings replied for Llwynypia when he scored an excellent try which Dot Williams failed to convert. Llwynypia were now on top of their game and five minutes later Willie Llewellyn made the best move of the game so far. Snatching a pass within ten yards of the halfway line the international wing set off at incredible pace and outstripping all his opponents, scored a beautiful try in a favourable position. Again Dot Williams failed with the conversion but within a few seconds of half-time Selwyn Biggs got away smartly and scored an unconverted try in the far corner to level the scores at the interval.

Cardiff started the second half with a bang and a clever passing movement between Griff Hughes, Selwyn Biggs, Jim Williams and Gwyn Nicholls almost resulted in a try for the home team. The defence, however, was stubborn and a minute later Willie Llewellyn ran away in fine style and kicked over the halfway line. Another good tackle by Willie Llewellyn prevented Arthur Ricketts from scoring. Llwynypia then worked their way into the Cardiff twenty-five, but their stay was only a short one Jim Williams, receiving in his own twenty-five, got away smartly and had the goal-line at his mercy when Willie Llewellyn, who had tackled like a demon all through the game, brought his man down and saved a certain try. Towards the end of the game Cardiff were having the better of the play with the Llwynypia defence being tested on numerous occasions. Cardiff now made repeated efforts to score and on one occasion only a brilliant tackle by Oscar Williams prevented Jim Williams from scoring. Ultimately, the Llwynypia defence was broken when Griff Hughes started a movement which ended with Arthur Ricketts forcing his way over for his second try of the game, a timely shove from Gwyn Nicholls keeping him clear of the touch-line. The conversion failed but Cardiff won this exciting encounter by 9 points to six. Willie Llewellyn was again the shining light for Llwynypia. His defence in defeat was superb and during the greater part of the game he put in the work of two ordinary players.

The following week Llwynypia played their return match against Llanelly at home. Llanelly were strongly represented with Welsh internationals Evan Lloyd and Ben Davies in the side. They also had a strong pack of forwards which included future Welsh internationals James Watts and Dan Walters. Llwynypia had a few of their regular players missing but were strengthened by the inclusion of Cecil Biggs and George Dobson of Cardiff. Making his debut for Llwynypia was Teddy Morgan of Guy's Hospital. Old Breconian Teddy Morgan was a very close friend of Willie Llewellyn and they would go on to play many times together for London Welsh, Wales and the British Isles. In addition to Willie Llewellyn, Billy

Alexander and Dick Hellings, three of Llwynypia's Welsh internationals, was young Joe Hellings, brother of Dick. At just seventeen or eighteen years of age he was a very promising prospect and was expected to have an equally successful football career as his famous elder brother.

Joe Hellings opened the scoring with a try which George Stephens converted to give Llwynypia an early lead. Moments later Joe Hellings almost scored again when Llwynypia rushed the ball up field. A kick sent the ball into the visitors' quarters and it was a race for possession between Joe Hellings and one of the Llanelly three-quarters. The ball struck the post and rebounded into Hellings' hands and he had a clear run in. Unfortunately, as he was crossing the line the ball slipped from his grasp and Bob Richards, the visiting custodian, was able to concede a minor. In the ensuing play the ball was fed to the Llanelly three-quarters who indulged in a pretty bout of passing. Rhys Gabe made a brilliant run but was pushed into touch by Dick Hellings when in the home twenty-five. Moments later Gabe was off again and, going strong for the line, he was tackled from behind by Willie Llewellyn. After this the game was exceptionally fast and up to the interval the home forwards were obliged to defend courageously against clever attacks of the visiting backs.

Early in the second half Llwynypia were kept in their own twenty-five by the aggressive attacks of their opponents. After the hard first half, the Llwynypia forwards were showing signs of weakness and two minors were conceded in quick succession. However, Llwynypia fought back and when George Stephens got possession he was able to invade the visitors' quarter by running along the touch-line. Trailed by A W Jones he was easily able to get over the line to score a sensational try which Teddy Morgan converted. Llwynypia now had a comfortable lead of ten points to nil but Llanelly never gave up. At length, Ben Davies secured the ball from a scrum and fed his three-quarters. The ball was sent to Morgan Williams who almost crossed for a try, but moments later another three-quarter move did result in Rhys Gabe scoring Llanelly's first try. Bob Richards converted from a difficult angle and Llanelly were very much back in the game. Llwynypia were now continually under pressure and when Rhys Gabe got the ball he was almost over again. Just before the end of the game, Thomas scored a try for Llanelly which Bob Richards again converted and a hard fought game ended in a ten points all draw.

This was the best match of the season at Llwynypia. Games between these old rivals were traditionally always splendidly contested and this one was no different. The pace from start to finish was exceptional and all thirty players looked thankful when the referee, Mr Douglas, blew the final whistle. The Llwynypia forwards were in magnificent form, their greater weight considerably testing the Llanelly pack. Joe Hellings was the best forward on the field while Thomas played a very hard and strong game for Llanelly. Ben Davies and Lodwig, the Llanelly half-backs, were far superior to the Llwynypia pair, Ben Davies' experience being a critical factor in the game. In the three-quarters Llanelly held a slight advantage but their efforts were invariably nullified by the Llwynypia forwards. There was very little difference in the custodians, both playing a sound game, although Bob Richards did let George Stephens in for his try. Willie Llewellyn was given very few chances but in defence he proved a thorn in the side of Rhys Gabe. Altogether it was a fine game played in a great spirit, and a draw was a fair result.

Llwynypia finished the season with games against Treherbert and Ebbw Vale. Having lost to Treherbert at home in March, their fortunes were no better in the return fixture at Treherbert. Two first half unconverted tries for the home team gave them a six point lead at the interval. The second half was a repetition of the first and two goals and two unconverted tries with no reply gave Treherbert the victory by 22 points to nil. Llwynypia's final game of the season resulted in a draw with Ebbw Vale at the Beaufort Arms ground. Ebbw Vale had the lead at the interval with an unconverted try by Jack Davies. In the second half George Stephens equalised and with his try being unconverted the game ended in a draw at 3 points all.

Although Willie Llewellyn only played 25 of Llwynypia's 39 matches during the 1899–1900 season he made a significant contribution to the games in which he appeared. Of the 25 games Willie played, Llwynypia won 11 lost 11 and drew 3, including the important stalemate against Llanelly. Willie scored 8 tries including three in the game against Pontyclun. All told, Willie Llewellyn played 38 games during the 1899–1900 season and scored 19 tries. He certainly spread himself about, playing club rugby for Llwynypia, London Welsh, Cardiff and Swansea. He also played for Glamorgan County, the Stripes in the Welsh Trial at Newport, and in all three internationals for Wales.

Willie Llewellyn Llwynypia Games Played 1899-1900 Season					
Willie Llewellyn London Welsh Games Played 1899-1900 Season					
Willie Llewellyn Welsh International and Welsh Trial Games Played 1899-1900 Season					
Willie Llewellyn Glamorgan County Games Played 1899-1900 Season					
Other Games Played by Willie Llewellyn during the 1899-1900 Season					
Date	Team Played For	Opposition	Venue	Result/Score	W Llewellyn Tries
16/09/1899	Llwynypia	Tredegar	Home	Won 17-0	0
21/09/1899	Llwynypia	Rest of the League	Home	Won 5-0	0
23/09/1899	Llwynypia	Abertillery	Home	Won 14-8	0
30/09/1899	Llwynypia	Treorky	Away	Won 5-0	0
07/10/1899	Llwynypia	Pontyclun	Home	Won 62-0	3
14/10/1899	Llwynypia	Cardiff	Home	Lost 0-3	0
19/10/1899	Llwynypia	Mountain Ash	Home	Lost 3-8	0
21/10/1899	Llwynypia	Aberavon	Home	Won 6-3	0
28/10/1899	Llwynypia	Neath	Away	Lost 0-8	0
30/10/1899	Glamorgan	Yorkshire	Castleford	Won 5-3	0
04/11/1899	Llwynypia	Penarth	Away	Drawn 3-3	0
11/11/1899	Llwynypia	Mountain Ash	Away	Lost 0-19	0
18/11/1899	Llwynypia	Penarth	Home	Won 17-5	0
20/11/1899	Cardiff	Cambridge University	Away	Lost 6-15	0
25/11/1899	Llwynypia	Pontymoile	Home	Won 34-6	1
02/12/1899	Welsh Trial -Stripes	Whites	Newport	Whites 21-3	0
09/12/1899	Llwynypia	Llanelly	Away	Lost 0-13	0
23/12/1899	Llwynypia	Swansea	Away	Lost 0-30	0
26/12/1899	Llwynypia	Leicester	Away	Lost 3-9	1
30/12/1899	Swansea	Dublin (Old Wesley)	St Helen's	Won 23-0	2
06/01/1900	Wales	England	Gloucester	Won 13-3	0
13/01/1900	London Welsh	Twickenham	Twickenham	Won 8-0	2
20/01/1900	London Welsh	Rovers	West Acton	Won 12-0	2
27/01/1900	Wales	Scotland	Swansea	Won 12-3	2
24/02/1900	London Welsh	St Mary's Hospital	West Acton	Won 9-3	Unknown
03/03/1900	London Welsh	Berkshire Wanderers	West Acton	Won 23-0	2
07/03/1900	Glamorgan	Gloucester	Cardiff Arms Park	Won 15-8	0
10/03/1900	London Welsh	Olney	Olney	Won 24-3	1
17/03/1900	Wales	Ireland	Belfast	Won 3-0	0
24/03/1900	Llwynypia	Plymouth	Away	Lost 0-6	0
29/03/1900	Llwynypia	Mountain Ash	Away	Lost 0-11	0
31/03/1900	Llwynypia	Pontypridd	Home	Won 6-0	0
05/04/1900	Llwynypia	Ebbw Vale	Home	Won 9-0	1
14/04/1900	Llwynypia	Bridgend	Away	Won 11-4	1
16/04/1900	Llwynypia	Cardiff	Away	Lost 6-9	1
21/04/1900	Llwynypia	Llanelly	Home	Drawn 10-10	0
26/04/1900	Llwynypia	Treherbert	Away	Lost 0-22	0
28/04/1900	Llwynypia	Ebbw Vale	Away	Drawn 3-3	0
	Willie Llewellyn Games Played				W Llewellyn Tries
Totals	38				19

Willie Llewellyn Rugby Games Played and Results 1899–1900 Season

Willie Llewellyn had now played six times for Wales and scored seven tries. He was a prolific try scorer and during the four seasons since leaving Christ College had notched 111 tries. Not only was he excellent in attack but he was equally good in defence and his devastating tackling prevented many a try being scored against whichever team he was representing. Willie Llewellyn had developed into an excellent rugby player and he could look forward to an exceptional rugby career which would culminate in victory over the 1905 All Blacks.

Not only was the 1899–1900 season a significant year in the development of Willie Llewellyn but it was also an important year in the development of the other fourteen players who would take the field for Wales against New Zealand in December 1905.

BERT WINFIELD – The regular full-back for Cardiff during the 1899–1900 season, Bert Winfield was a prolific goal kicker. During the season he kicked 39 conversions, 5 penalties and 1 drop goal. He played for the victorious Whites in the Welsh Trial at Newport and several times for Glamorgan County. He was also reserve full-back to Billy Bancroft for Wales in all three internationals of the 1899–1900 season.

GWYN NICHOLLS – Already an accomplished rugby player, Gwyn Nicholls had ten Welsh caps to his credit. He was captain of Cardiff Rugby Football Club in 1898–1899 and 1899–1900, although for the first half of the 1899–1900 season he was away playing for the British Isles in Australia where he appeared in all four test matches and was leading try scorer with twelve tries.

RHYS GABE – Although missing many games during the early part of the season because of important examinations Rhys Gabe was a key member of the Llanelly three-quarter line. He had shown brilliant form playing on the wing during the season and was joint top try scorer with Morgan Williams, both with 13 tries apiece.

TEDDY MORGAN – Studying Medicine at Guy's Hospital, Teddy Morgan played regularly for the hospital first fifteen. He also played for London Welsh and guested for Llwynypia in their drawn game against Llanelly. Teddy Morgan was an exceptionally fast wing three-quarter and in addition to his club rugby he represented Surrey County on several occasions during the season.

PERCY BUSH – Having played at centre three-quarter for Penygraig for several seasons and captaining them during the 1898–1899 and 1899–1900 seasons, Percy Bush started playing for Cardiff Rugby Football Club in December 1899. He played with distinction for both the Cardiff first and reserve teams. Percy Bush also played for Glamorgan County during the season and was developing into a very skilful rugby player.

DICKIE OWEN – Swansea were the Welsh champions during the 1899–1900 season and Dickie Owen was their first choice scrum-half. Registered as Owens he is often referred to as Owen. Although a small man at just 5ft 2 inches and barely 9st 7lb he confounded defences and at a time when the game was as rough as ever it was, he helped guide Swansea to their second championship season.

WILL JOSEPH – A cousin of Dickie Owen, Will Joseph was also a member of the 1899–1900 Swansea side that won the unofficial Welsh championship. Well over six feet tall and around thirteen stones, he was an outstanding forward in an outstanding pack. Not only noted for his brilliant work in the tight, as a tall man, he was also very good at the line-out. Another essential forward skill was dribbling and Will Joseph was very adept at it. He could also tackle with deadly certainty.

JEHOIDA HODGES – Another player who was already a Welsh international, Jehoida Hodges won his first Welsh cap on the same day as Willie Llewellyn and he had also played in all six internationals since the game against England in January 1899. Hodges had only played first team rugby for Newport for two years before he gained his first Welsh cap. Jehoida Hodges played twenty-six games for Newport during the 1899–1900 season, several times for Glamorgan County, for the Stripes in the Welsh Trial at Newport and three times for Wales.

GEORGE 'TWYBER' TRAVERS – A tough scrummager, a fine tackler and good in the line-out, George Travers was playing regular first team rugby for Pill Harriers during the 1899–1900 season.

CLIFF PRITCHARD – Playing his first season of senior rugby for Newport, Cliff Pritchard appeared twenty-four times for Newport at centre and scored eleven tries.

CHARLIE PRITCHARD – At seventeen years of age, Charlie Pritchard was studying at Long Ashton School, Bristol. He would not make his debut for Newport until the game against Swansea in January 1902.

DAI 'TARW' JONES – David Jones gained his nickname Tarw (Welsh for bull) from his imposing stature: He scaled 6 feet 1 inch in height and weighed in at around 16 stone. During the 1899–1900 season David Jones was playing regular first team rugby for Treherbert in the Glamorgan League.

JOHN 'SCETHROG' WILLIAMS – Known as 'Scethrog' because he was born in Scethrog near Brecon. He studied at Christ College, Brecon where at a meeting held at the beginning of the Autumn Term 1899, he was elected captain of the first fifteen. During that term he passed the London University Matriculation examinations and left Christ College at Christmas 1899 to pursue his studies in London, where he initially played rugby for Richmond. The December 1899 edition of *The Breconian* provided the following pen-pic: 'J F Williams (Captain, forward) – The most useful man in the team, both in attack and defence. As a captain has done all that he possibly could to stimulate interest in the game and have it played in a sportsmanlike fashion. Might have asserted himself more prominently on the field by advising his team.' J F Williams was the youngest Welsh player in the match against New Zealand in 1905.

ARTHUR FLOWERS 'BOXER' HARDING – Also a past captain of the Christ College first fifteen, Arthur Harding played rugby for Llwynypia during the first part of the 1899–1900 season. He was an exceptional forward who was a surprisingly nimble player with a good running and passing style. He also possessed excellent kicking ability and was selected as a reserve for the Welsh trial at Newport. He played his last game for Llwynypia against Bridgend on Saturday 20th January 1900 after which he served with the Glamorgan Division of the Imperial Yeomanry in the Boer War in South Africa. Returning from South Africa in July 1901, Arthur Harding played rugby for Cardiff and gained his first Welsh cap against England in 1902.

Regarding Arthur Harding's Boer War experiences, the following letter which he sent to the students at Christ College, Brecon in May 1900 makes interesting reading.

Ladybrand
Orange Free State
May 18th 1900

Having come right through the Orange Free State, we are at present here doing Police work practically. At West Beaufort we came across the V. Welsh and it was quite a meeting of old friends. I should have told you we passed the S. W. B's just before, amongst whom I saw J. Walters, who was at one time I think our groundsman and whom I remember as a football player.

Early on Sunday morning we started riding from Norvals Pont and so we went on till we reached Bloemfontein on the first of May. We did on the average about 2 and 20 miles a day and were very glad to see Bloemfontein in sight. As we rode into Bloemfontein I saw Geo. Seaton of the C.I.V., an old Brecon boy who got his colours. He had some cigarettes and chocolate waiting for Percy Ward and me. He looked very well and was one of Lord Roberts' orderlies, so he is very lucky. We were only there 3 hours but during that time we had a good feed and look round. What I saw was mostly hospitals, and there were 300 patients being brought in there in one day.

We had the English mails there to take on with us and that night we marched out to Springfield; during our stay there we saw Lord Kitchener and Lord and Lady Roberts. Lord Roberts inspected us and spoke very favourably to the Major. From Springfield we went to the Waterworks where we stayed a day or so. We had a good wash there in a tributary to the Modder, the first really decent one we have had since leaving Cape Town, so you may guess how glad we were to be able to get it. From there we went to Thaban' Chu and we were there 24 hours when we went into action under General Brabant. We went out with Artillery and Infantry and with a good many Yeomanry. The guns opened fire but we soon put theirs out of action. During the time we were in action however they made it decidedly awkward for us and one began to realize that small as the action was, fighting is not all beer and skittles, though of course we know nothing of the pleasures of a bayonet charge.

We went out the next day in the hope of having more fun but we could not see a Boer for miles around. During our action only one of us, a man named Humphries, got hurt. He was wounded in the arm by some shrapnel. We left Thaban' Chu a couple of days afterwards and went out to a camp called Egypt. The first night we were there we ate all the chickens and ducks in the place as well as anything worth eating we could lay on to. It seemed like a house supper over again. We went from there to Olivier's farm, one of the Boer generals' places. The beauty of the place was a large reservoir and excellent drinking water. From there we gradually came on until here we are at Ladybrand, the garden of the O.F.S. We marched in here the other night and met with a tremendous reception as we are the first English soldiers to come in and stay, the Hussars going through and back once at a gallop. They gave us tea and coffee here, and the stores also being open we are able to buy at very fair prices considering everything, bread, butter, tea, sugar, cigarettes, etc, etc, while the farmers round bring in poultry to the camp every day. To-day I am on guard over prisoners who are coming in daily and laying down their arms. I hope the College is doing well, as the cricket season must now have started.

I remain,
Sincerely yours,
ARTHUR F. HARDING.

All the games that Rhys Gabe lost during the 1899–1900 season because of his studies paid off handsomely as this report from the *Evening Express* testifies: 'Gabe, the Llanelly three-quarter back, whose right wing play against Cardiff was an outstanding feature of the game, excels not only in sport, but also in the scholastic profession which he follows. He passed, a fortnight since, the Queen's Scholarship Examination and as the topmost Welshman in the list of successful candidates, won the Neale Exhibition, a much-coveted scholarship which is awarded to the Cymro who attains to that position. He will enter Borough Road Training College, London, for a course of Study and although his removal to the Metropolis will mean a distinct loss to the tin-platers, his location will be welcomed with joy by the London Welsh, into whose ranks he will throw in his lot.'

Rhys Gabe was just one of a group of good Welsh rugby players who were studying in London, Teddy Morgan was at Guy's Hospital, J F Williams at London University and of course Willie Llewellyn was studying at the Pharmaceutical College in Bloomsbury. And it was with only a handful of games for London Welsh under his belt that the trainee pharmacologist was now elected as the club captain for the 1900–1901 season, a position he was to hold for three seasons.

Significantly, too, the Welsh Football Union readily accepted Willie Llewellyn's recommendation that any Welshman playing and living in London would only be considered for a Welsh cap as long as they played for London Welsh. This development had an immediate impact on the club and for the start of the 1900–01 campaign London Welsh recruited four players of immense importance: Rhys Gabe, Wallace Watts, a powerful forward from Newport, J F Williams and the brilliant Hopkin Maddock. With Teddy Morgan also able to play between six and eight games during the season, Willie Llewellyn could look forward to the forthcoming season with a great deal of confidence.

Chapter Six

The London Welsh Years 1900–1903

AT THE ANNUAL MEETING of the London Welsh Rugby Football club in September 1900, Willie Llewellyn, having only played five games for London Welsh during the previous season, was elected captain for the 1900–1901 season. Livingstone Davies, the old Swansea veteran, was elected vice-captain. Among the many new recruits at London Welsh at the beginning of that season was Wallace Watts of Newport. Born in Chipping Sodbury, he was affectionately known as 'Chippy'. A tall, heavy and fast forward, Wallace Watts started playing for Newport in 1889 and played 157 games for the club between 1889 and 1906, often playing for them when he returned to Wales. He was capped by Wales on twelve occasions between 1892 and 1896 and was a member of the Welsh team that won their first Triple Crown in 1893. Watts continued

Wallace Watts played for Wales on twelve occasions between 1892 and 1896.

to play for London Welsh until 1911 when he was forty-one years old and was Honorary Secretary during the 1912–1913 season. His son David was chairman of London Welsh Rugby Football Club from 1968 until 1975.

Another influential player to join London Welsh that season was Rhys Gabe. The personal invitation of Willie Llewellyn was largely responsible for Gabe joining London Welsh while he was studying at Borough Road Teacher Training College. The influence of Christ College, Brecon also had a big impact on London Welsh during the season. In addition to Willie Llewellyn, Teddy Morgan, Hop Maddock, J F 'Jack' Williams, Arthur Harding, T P Thomas, W G Hodge and F G Williams were all old boys of the famous Welsh College that played for London Welsh during the season.

London Welsh played 19 games during the 1900–1901 season of which they won 9 lost 7 and drew three. They scored 129 points for with 86 against. Willie Llewellyn played in seventeen of these games only missing the first game of the season away to Bedford and the game against Leytonstone in February when he was playing for Wales in the international against Scotland.

The start of the 1900–1901 season was anything but auspicious. Despite a fine try by Tom James, Bedford were rarely extended and won by 22 points to three. The London Welsh three-quarter line played poorly and their forwards were rarely a match for the opposing eight. Willie's first game of the season was the away game against Streatham, then among the strongest sides in London. Streatham scored within the first ten minutes after which London Welsh settled down and more than held their own. During the second half Rhys Gabe, playing his first game for London Welsh, scored a beautiful try from a lovely pass right across the field by Willie Llewellyn. This was immediately followed by Livingstone Davies putting Sparrow in for a try. Although they played well, Streatham were the stronger team and Willie Llewellyn, receiving poor service from his halves, was marked out of the game by the spirited Streatham backs.

In their next game Hopkin Maddock, 'feinting beautifully', scored on his debut in the 22 points to nil rout of Saracens. In the first half Tom James, following up smartly, scored in the corner and Jerred placed a magnificent goal. Shortly afterwards Willie Llewellyn scored and Jerrad again converted. Just before the interval T B Johns scored an unconverted try. Early in the second half Hop Maddock scored his wonderful try which was followed by tries from Tom James and Jerred. With none of the second half tries being converted a one-sided game ended in favour of London Welsh.

Hop Maddock would continue to delight the London Welshmen with his exemplary sportsmanship and prodigious scoring feats right up to the outbreak of the First World War. He captained London Welsh in 1909–10 and again in 1911–12. On two occasions he scored five tries in a game, the first time was against Ilford Wanderers in September 1906 and then he did the same thing in the game against Oxford University in February 1909. During the fourteen years Hop Maddock played for London Welsh he played 275 games and scored 170 tries. On two occasions he was top try scorer; with 25 tries from 22 games during the 1905–06 season and 26 tries from 30 games during the 1908–09 season. His great talent was not recognised by Wales until 1906 when he gained his first Welsh cap against England at Richmond. In the six games he played for Wales between 1906 and 1910 he scored six tries. For the game against England in 1906 he was one of only two changes from the Welsh side that had defeated New Zealand the previous December. Harry Watkins of Llanelly was the other change, winning his sixth and final cap, he replaced the injured J F Williams. Hop Maddock died at the age of forty from the effect of wounds sustained during the First World War. He served in the Royal Fusiliers (Public Schools Battalion) and the Machine Gun Corps.

The week following their victory over Berkshire Wanderers, London Welsh were without a fixture. Willie Llewellyn never missed a chance to

Hopkin Maddock was another Christ College old boy who played for Wales. He gained six caps between 1906 and 1910. Maddock captained London Welsh in 1909–10 and again in 1911–12.

Courtesy of Christ College, Brecon

play and took the opportunity to play his first game for Newport in their away game at Blackheath. The game gave Willie time to catch up with his old Welsh international colleague and often opponent Reg Skrimshire, who played centre for Blackheath. On the day it was Willie who came out on top with Newport winning by 14 points to nil. Willie opened the scoring when he dodged past three men to score a great try in the corner, George Boots just failing to convert. Twice Willie just failed to score when he was held up on the line after some fine passing by the three-quarters. Eventually Newport scored again when Jehoida Hodges crossed for another unconverted try. Just before the interval Llewellyn Lloyd crossed for a try which he converted himself. The only score of the second half was another great try by Willie Llewellyn, which again went unconverted. With no further scoring Newport were superior in all departments and won handsomely.

On Monday 29th October Willie Llewellyn was selected to play for Glamorgan in their game against Yorkshire at Cardiff. Willie wrote to the selection committee expressing his regret at being unable to travel from London to play in consequence of his studies. Even without Willie Llewellyn Glamorgan were in fine form and won the game by 52 points to three.

Willie Llewellyn was back to his brilliant best for London Welsh in their next game away to Northampton. Dick Hellings played for the Welsh and Willie Llewellyn's excellent first half try gave London Welsh an interval lead of three points to nil. Only a late second half penalty goal for Northampton saved the game for them and the match ended in a draw at 3 points all.

On a dull and depressing day Willie Llewellyn played his first County game for Surrey in their match against Hampshire at Crystal Palace. The result did nothing to cheer the Surrey side with them going down by 8 points to nil. Unfortunately, old habits die hard and discipline remained a problem for London Welsh. Following a no score drawn game against Stroud, several Welsh players arrived late for the game against Harlequins at Finchley and as a consequence only twenty minutes were played each way, with the game ending in near darkness. Nevertheless, London Welsh had the best of the game. Tries were scored by Willie Llewellyn after a brilliant run more than half the length of the field and by Wayne Morgan after a splendid dribble by Wallace Watts. With both tries being converted London Welsh won the game by 10 points to nil.

Having lost away to Streatham earlier in the season by just two points, London Welsh lost by exactly the same margin when they played them at home on December 1st. The ground was exceedingly heavy and the Welsh three-quarters never got a chance throughout the game. Tom James scored for London Welsh but because two men handled the ball the kick at goal was disallowed. Streatham, having converted their try won by 5 points to three. On the same day as Willie was playing for London Welsh against Streatham he was selected to play in the Welsh international trial match at Neath. Willie was one of ten players originally selected for the trial match that for one reason or another were unable to play.

On the Thursday before London Welsh celebrated the opening of their new ground at Lower Welsh Harp in Hendon Willie Llewellyn was playing his second County game for Surrey against Eastern Counties at Ilford. Alongside Willie Llewellyn was London Welsh and Guy's Hospital wing Teddy Morgan. Also in the team was J E C 'Birdie' Partridge of Blackheath and Newport who had also played in Willie's first game for the County against Hampshire. Seth Smith opened the scoring for Surrey and Teddy Morgan placed the goal. Eastern Counties replied with an unconverted try but before the interval Teddy Morgan scored a smart try which went unconverted. In the second half Teddy Morgan, after a clever run, scored his second try of the afternoon which he converted himself. The Counties attacked on several occasions but were always met with strong defence and with no further scoring Surrey won by 13 points to three.

The Saturday after the Surrey game London Welsh played London Irish in a game that celebrated the opening of their new ground at Lower Welsh Harp in Hendon. It was London Irish that had provided the opposition in the first match at Cambrian Park, Hampstead in November 1898. London Welsh only played at Cambrian Park for one season after which they moved to Toley's Athletic Ground, Acton. They stayed there for two seasons but moved to Lower Welsh Harp in December 1900 because of the onerous rent at Toley's Athletic Ground. It was a splendid contest and in the words of *The Sportsman*, 'It was a treat to see Llewellyn (the popular captain) and the Morgans, and it seldom falls to the lot of the ordinary Rugby follower to witness such combination work as they played all through. Throughout the game was very fairly played, was exceedingly fast and characterised by excellent combination work, especially by the Welshmen, who so fittingly and well represented gallant little Wales.' London Irish were the first to score when after fifteen minutes Magee crossed for a try which Dyas failed to convert. This was the end of the scoring for the Irish and from this point onwards London Welsh took control. With the wind at their backs the Welsh forwards were very smart on the ball and gained considerable ground. Willie Llewellyn had a brilliant game and scored all three tries. In the first half he crossed for a try which Wayne Morgan converted to give the Welsh the lead at the interval. Playing against the wind in the second half James made an opening and all the Welsh three-quarters handled before Willie Llewellyn crossed for his second try of the game. Shortly afterwards Willie Llewellyn scored again after another fine run. Wayne Morgan failed to convert either try but nevertheless London Welsh were victorious by 11 points to three.

Willie Llewellyn missed his second Glamorgan County game of the season when he was unable to travel down from London to Gloucester for the game against Gloucestershire on Thursday 13th December. Billy Bancroft and Gwyn Nicholls also cried off but Glamorgan were still the victors by 13 points to nil.

Willie scored again when London Welsh played Saracens at Muswell Hill on Saturday 15th December. Due probably to their previous win over Saracens by 22 points to nil earlier in the season, many of the usual team cried off and five reserves were called into the side. The game started punctually as advertised and resulted in a win for London Welsh by 1 goal and 1 try to nil. This score would have been increased considerably were it not for the fact that Willie Llewellyn and one of the forwards had to leave at half-time in order to get to Paddington to catch the train to South Wales. The second half consisted of thirteen Welshmen keeping their opponents at bay, but with only six forwards, they were unable to act on the offensive and the ball never came out to the backs. Willie Llewellyn and D J Thomas scored tries while Wayne Morgan kicked a conversion.

Christmas was a busy time for Willie Llewellyn, on the Saturday, having played only half a game against Saracens, he travelled by train from Paddington to South Wales. On the Monday he travelled up to Christ College, Brecon for the Old Boys' rugby match and the annual

Christ College, Brecon v Old Boys XV 1900

Group photograph of the Christ College past and present teams with masters.
Willie Llewellyn is third from the right in the front row.
Teddy Morgan is on his left.

Old Boys' dinner and on the Thursday he was selected to play for Wales against England at Cardiff on Saturday 5th January 1901. The following Saturday he played for London Welsh against Bristol in the first of three Christmas tour matches. The second game against Mountain Ash was played on Christmas Eve with the final game against Aberavon being played on Christmas Day. In total he played five games, or actually four and a half games, in a period of ten days, just amazing commitment.

For the Christ College Old Boys' match the Old Boys had got a strong team together, including as it did both Willie Llewellyn and Teddy Morgan. Also in the team was Willie's elder brother John. The report of the game in *The Breconian* read as follows: 'It was practically an exhibition game, as we were outclassed in all departments of the game; ten minutes elapsed before the first score; E. Morgan had made several sprints up the wing, and at last punted across the field to Llewellyn, who shook off one or two of his opponents and scored a pretty try, which, however, was not converted. The next try was scored by J. H. Llewellyn, who broke through the backs and planted the ball behind the posts. E. Morgan scored the third with a clear run, also the fourth. Four more tries were scored before half time, two of which were converted. Half-time score: Old Boys, 2 goals, 6 tries; Christ College, nil. Immediately after the restart, J. P. Jones nearly dropped a goal for the Present. A little later Twyning secured the ball from a line out and ran half the length of the field and scored. Then E. M. James scored for the Present a try which Hodge converted. R. L. Evans retaliated by putting on another try for the Old Boys, after a run from midfield. Twyning scored once again, and towards the close of the game J. P. Jones scored a pretty try for the College. Final score: Old Boys, 3 goals, 8 tries; Christ College, 1 goal, 1 try.'

The teams were as follows:

Old Boys: Back, Leyshon; three-quarters, W M Llewellyn, E Morgan, T Morgan, and R L Evans; half-backs, D F H Williams and J H Llewellyn; forwards, J H Williams, G S Seaton, Twyning, A E C Morgan, F E Thomas, C T Davis, G Francis, T G Phillips.

Christ College: Back, Stephens; three-quarters, E W A Thomas, C Dyke, J P Jones, C J C Davies; half-backs, C Rich and W Ll Morgan; forwards, W G Hodge, E M C Denny, F Davis, C H M Nixon, H G Williams, W L Arthur, E M James and either P Spencer-Smith or E J Hughes.

Twenty players made themselves available for the London Welsh Christmas tour which started with their first ever game against Bristol at the County Ground. The huge crowd were treated to a magnificent open game in which Bristol did all the scoring in the first half. At the interval London Welsh were down by 9 points to nil the result of a penalty goal by Oates and two unconverted tries, one by Baker and the other by Vaughan. London Welsh were much better in the second half and two unconverted tries, one by Willie Llewellyn and the other by D J Thomas, was not quite enough and they lost the game by 9 points to six.

London Welsh proceeded from Bristol to Cardiff where they made their headquarters at the Queen's Hotel. On Christmas Eve, in front of their biggest crowd of the season they were well beaten by Mountain Ash. At the interval Mountain Ash were winning by a goal and a try to nil and they scored exactly the same in the second half to win the game by 16 points to nil. Although Mountain Ash were to a great extent disorganised they played very well and were well worth their 16 point victory. Although on the losing side Willie Llewellyn was the pick of the three-quarters of both sides.

In their final game of the Christmas tour London Welsh lost a hard fought game against Aberavon. An unconverted try late in the game was sufficient to give Aberavon victory by 3 points to nil. The Welsh three-quarters were almost up to international standard with Maddock, Willie Llewellyn, Gus Gould, Rhys Gabe and Teddy Morgan but a weak pack could not win enough possession and the opportunity of watching these brilliant backs in action was lost.

The first half of the year had been disappointing for London Welsh; they had played 13 games, won 5, lost 6 and drawn 2. Although seldom fielding their full strength side they won four of their remaining six games with one loss and one drawn game. Considering they had only played at home on six occasions their record of nine wins, seven defeats and three drawn games was a worthy achievement. Several games were cancelled because of the death of Queen Victoria in January 1901 and Willie often spoke of how he had watched the funeral while he was in London.

On Saturday 5th January 1901 Willie Llewellyn gained his seventh Welsh cap when he played against England at Cardiff Arms Park. There was only one change from the team originally selected with John 'Bala' Jones of Aberavon taking the place of the injured Louis Phillips of Newport. Phillips badly strained his ankle playing for Newport against Cork the day after Boxing Day and had not sufficiently recovered to be able to play in the international match against England. 'Bala' Jones was a scrum-half who played club rugby for Aberavon and Devonport Albion and county rugby for Glamorgan and Devon. This was his only Welsh international cap. For the fourth consecutive international Bert Winfield was reserve full-back to Billy Bancroft. Rhys Gabe was also making an impact with regard to gaining international honours and he was chosen as reserve left wing. Billy Alexander, the Llwynypia forward who had already gained six Welsh caps was also reserve for this game. The teams lined up as follows:

Wales: W J Bancroft (Swansea, Captain); W M Llewellyn (Llwynypia and London Welsh), E G Nicholls (Cardiff), G Davies (Swansea), W J Trew (Swansea); G Ll Lloyd (Newport), *J 'Bala' Jones (Aberavon); D Hellings (Llwynypia), A B Brice (Aberavon), F Miller (Mountain Ash), J G Boots

(Newport), J J Hodges (Newport), J Blake (Cardiff), R Thomas (Swansea), W H 'Buller' Williams (Pontymister). (* Wales debut)

England: *J W Sagar (Cambridge U); *E W Elliott (Sunderland), J T Taylor (Castleford, Captain), *E J Vivian (Devonport Albion), *C C Smith (Gloucester); *E J Walton (Castleford), R O Schwarz (Richmond); H Alexander (Birkenhead Pk), A F C Luxmoore (Richmond), C T Scott (Blackheath), *N C Fletcher (OMT's), *D Graham (Aspatria), *C O P Gibson (Northern), *E W Roberts (RNC Dartmouth), *A O'Neill (Torquay). (* England Debut)

Referee: Adam J Turnbull (Scotland).

On the eve of the game Bert Winfield was called up to replace Billy Bancroft. A telegram had been received by Walter Rees, the WFU secretary, allegedly from Billy Bancroft, saying he was unable to play because he had influenza. Gwyn Nicholls was named as captain and the cards listing both teams were printed. It emerged that the telegram was a hoax and Billy Bancroft was reinstated as full-back and captain. The disappointed Bert Winfield had to wait another two years before he gained

Wales Team v England 1901

Back Row: Ack Llewellyn (WFU), A Brice, W H Millar, J Blake, W H Williams, R Thomas, W M Llewellyn, J G Boots, J J Hodges.
Middle Row: W J Trew, W J Bancroft (Captain), G Davies, E G Nicholls, D Hellings. *Front Row*: G Ll Lloyd and J 'Bala' Jones.

his first Welsh cap against Ireland in March 1903. The only change in the English team was the withdrawal of John Daniel through injury, his place being taken by Arthur O'Neill. The Welsh team was very experienced and successful. The previous season they had won their second Triple Crown and apart from the absent Louis Phillips this was exactly the same team. England on the other hand were a new combination with ten debutants in the team, three of whom; C C 'Whacker' Smith, Charles Gibson and David Graham would never play for England again.

The weather, though chilly, was brilliantly fine and in the region of 40,000 spectators witnessed a hard fought and exciting game. Bancroft kicked off and within the first couple of minutes Wales almost scored after a brilliant round of passing. Shortly afterwards Elliott Vivyan was

Billy Bancroft (far right), leads the Welsh team onto the field.
Willie Llewellyn in on the far left.

Lemons being passed around at half-time.

injured and had to leave the field. It was while Vivyan was off the field that Wales scored their first try. Jere Blake and other forwards got the ball to the English twenty-five where a fine round of passing by the Welsh three-quarters culminated in Gwyn Nicholls crossing for a try. Billy Bancroft kicked the conversion and with less than a quarter of an hour played Wales were winning by 5 points to nil. England retaliated and a mark in a favourable position by Elliott Vivyan looked a certain four points, however, he missed the drop-kick attempt at goal. Afterwards England pressed very hard and on two or three occasions were very close to scoring. After being in grave danger for some time, Wales reached the other end and two determined attacks by George Davies and Billy Trew were repelled by sound defence. With Wales right on the English line half-time was called.

During the first half the contest had been fairly even but Wales started to take control in the second half. Wales attacked time after time but the English defence was sound and although Wales got right up to the English line on many occasions the English defence just managed to prevent them from scoring. Wales should have added to their score but Billy Bancroft missed a penalty kick from a fairly easy position. England again forced play into the Welsh half but Wales worked their way up field and a brilliant cross kick by Llewellyn Lloyd resulted in a try by 'Buller' Williams. Billy Bancroft missed the conversion. A minute or two later a mistake by Elliott Vivyan gave Wales possession which culminated in Jehoida Hodges crossing for a try. This time Billy Bancroft was successful with the conversion and Wales took a thirteen point lead. With less than ten minutes remaining England tried hard to redress the balance and fought right up to the end of the game. On one occasion Elliott Vivyan ran around Billy Bancroft but still England failed to score and with Wales keeping their line intact they won by 13 points to nil.

The general opinion in the local press was that the game was disappointing and that Wales did not deserve to win by such a large margin. A report in *The Cambrian* stated, 'It is important that a few changes should be made for the Scotch and Irish matches. Scrine should most certainly be selected.'

An interesting article in *The Sportsman*, in reference to the match included fascinating pen pictures of the players. Of Willie Llewellyn, it remarked: 'Is captain of his club and has done much to bring them this season into great prominence. He is a fine all-round athlete and holds the record for the long jump at Brecon College. He is wonderfully fast, a splendid kick and tackles like a tiger. He is twenty-three years of age, weighs 10st. 10lb. and stands 5ft. 8ins. tall.' Paul Beken and Stephen Jones in their exceptional book, *Dragon in Exile, The Centenary History of London Welsh RFC*, added to this biography by saying that 'Willie Llewellyn was also one of life's gentlemen, modest, kindly and always ready to give encouragement to the many who sought his advice. His speed and guile were celebrated throughout the game. Dummies he could sell by the score, but for a relatively small man he could also pack a tremendous punch when opting to run straight and hard. Often he would run right through the opposition and the crowds loved it all, no less his fearless tackling. He was one of the brightest stars in the first golden era of Welsh rugby.'

A bright star he certainly was and following the international Willie returned to London Welsh for their home game against Park House. An unconverted try in the first half by W G Hodge and a similar by A G Merry, a Swansea reserve player, in the second, gave London Welsh victory by 6 points to nil. There were twelve old Breconians and Llandoverians playing in this game. Four of these were past captains of Christ College, Brecon: T P Thomas, W Llewellyn, J F Williams and W G Hodge.

The only defeat London Welsh suffered after Christmas was in their next game against Catford Bridge. Catford had been strengthened by the inclusion of some players from the defunct Wickham Park Club and no fewer than five Kent County players were included in their ranks. In addition, Holywell, the Cumberland County three-quarter was also included in their team. London Welsh were also strongly represented with Hop Maddock at full-back and Willie Llewellyn, Wayne Morgan, Gus Gould and Rhys Gabe in the three-quarters. Nevertheless, early in the game it was apparent that Catford were stronger at forward which restricted the opportunities for the Welsh backs. London Welsh had a few chances to score but a missed penalty by Gus Gould and an unsuccessful drop at goal by the same player robbed them of two good chances. Nevertheless, London Welsh were the first to score when Gus Gould crossed for an unconverted try. Playing strongly from this point onwards,

Catford scored a try through A E Lord which Francis Helder converted. Willie Llewellyn nearly scored on more than one occasion but Catford held out and won by 5 points to three.

On Thursday 10th January the committee of the Welsh Football Union met at the Queen's Hotel, Cardiff and selected the Welsh team to play against Scotland at Inverleith, Edinburgh on Saturday 25th January. When the team was announced there were three changes from the team that had defeated England. Louis Phillips returned to the side at scrum-half in place of John 'Bala' Jones and in order to strengthen the forwards, Billy Alexander (Llwynypia) and Hopkin Davies (Swansea) replaced W H 'Buller' Williams and Bob Thomas. Bert Winfield was again reserve full-back to Billy Bancroft and Rhys Gabe reserve right wing. Gus Gould was the other reserve three-quarter covering the right centre and left wing positions. John 'Bala' Jones and W Needs (Bristol) were the reserve half-backs while Bob Jones (Llwynypia), Edwin Thomas Maynard (Known as 'Beddoe' Thomas, Newport), D J Walters (Llanelly) and Will Joseph (Swansea) were the reserve forwards. The game was scheduled to take place on Saturday 25th January but because of the death of Queen Victoria the game was postponed until Saturday 9th February. The Welsh team played as selected and there were no debutants in the Welsh side. The teams lined up as follows:

Wales: W J Bancroft (Swansea, Captain), W M Llewellyn (Llwynypia and London Welsh), E G Nicholls (Cardiff), G Davies, W J Trew (Swansea); G Ll Lloyd and L A Phillips (Newport); D Hellings (Llwynypia), A B Brice (Aberavon), F Miller (Mountain Ash), J G Boots (Newport), J J Hodges (Newport), J Blake (Cardiff), H Davies (Swansea), W H Alexander (Llwynypia).

Scotland: *A W Duncan (Edinburgh U); W H Welsh, A B Timms, *P Turnbull (Edinburgh Acads), *A N Fell; F H Fasson (Edinburgh U), J I Gillespie (Edinburgh Acads); M C Morrison (Royal HSFP, Captain), J M Dykes (Glasgow HSFP), *A B Flett, *A Frew, D R Bedell-Sivright (Edinburgh U), *J Ross (London Scottish), *J A Bell (Clydesdale), *R S Stronach (Glasgow Acads). (* Scotland Debut)

Referee: Rupert W Jeffares (Ireland).

Considering Wales had strengthened their pack of forwards for this game the result was very disappointing with Scotland winning by

18 points to eight. In seventeen outings Wales had only managed to beat Scotland on four occasions and only once away from home at Raeburn Place, Edinburgh in 1893 when they won their first Triple Crown. They had managed a no score drawn game in Glasgow in 1885 when William 'Willie' Henry Thomas from Llandovery College made his debut at the age of 18 years and 10 months. He later became the first Welshman to play on a British tour when he toured New Zealand and Australia in 1888. The early exchanges were fairly even but Wales were having the worst of the whistle with the referee awarding four free kicks against them in the first seven minutes. When Wales did get away A W Duncan, on his debut at full-back, was having a brilliant game and prevented Wales from scoring on several occasions with his wonderful tackling. Wales were really having the better of the play and had been very close to scoring on a dozen occasions with only sound Scottish tackling or the referee's whistle preventing them from crossing the Scottish line. Then, against the run of play, weak Welsh defence allowed Johnnie Gillespie to cross for a try which he converted himself. Before the interval Scotland scored again through Andrew Flett and with Gillespie again converting they were 10 points to nil ahead.

In the second half Scotland continued to put Wales under pressure and after some fine play by Phipps Turnbull, Johnnie Gillespie scored his second try of the afternoon. Flett added the extra points with a magnificent kick from wide out. Scotland scored again when Turnbull, receiving the ball on the half-way line, ran half the length of the field to score a brilliant try which Flett failed to convert. Wales were now a badly beaten team but with about seven minutes of the game remaining they did manage to score a try when, after some clever play, Billy Trew gave a scoring pass to Llewellyn Lloyd. Billy Bancroft kicked the conversion. In the final two or three minutes Wales scored again when George Boots got possession and after a strong burst crossed for an unconverted try. But it was too little too late and immediately afterwards time was called with Scotland victorious by 18 points to eight.

Bearing in mind that Scotland had five debutants in their pack, for a large proportion of the game, they completely outplayed the Welsh eight. Wales were not only beaten at forward they were also beaten at three-quarters and the score was a true reflection of the superiority of the Scottish team. At half-back Gillespie played a magnificent game and debutants Duncan and Fell played well in their first international match. This was Scotland's first game of the 1901 Home Nations Championship and they went on to beat Ireland by 9 points to five and England by 18 points to three winning their third Triple Crown.

On the day Wales were beaten by Scotland, London Welsh defeated Leytonstone by 6 points to nil. The following Wednesday both Willie Llewellyn and Teddy Morgan were selected to play for Surrey against Middlesex at Crystal Palace. Willie Llewellyn was also selected to play for Glamorgan against Devon on the same day. Since he was already up in London Willie Llewellyn decided to play for Surrey but unfortunately the game was called off because of the hard state of the ground. Even without Willie Llewellyn Glamorgan won by 8 points to nil.

Willie Llewellyn returned to club rugby with London Welsh in their next game against St Mary's Hospital. He was in blistering form and scored four tries in the 23 points (1 goal and 6 tries) to nil victory. It was a good day for the Welsh with Rhys Gabe scoring two of the other three tries.

Willie Llewellyn was very keen to maintain his links with Christ College, Brecon and would take every opportunity to visit or to play for or against his old college. On Wednesday 27th February Willie captained a team of Old Breconians in their game against Eastbourne College at Eastbourne. The report of the game in *The Sportsman* read as follows: 'Eastbourne started in good fashion but the strength of the visiting three-quarter line manifested itself before the interval in a score of three tries, all by Teddy Morgan from passes by Willie Llewellyn. The same players were also responsible in the second half for scoring three more tries, one of which was converted, so that the visitors won by 20 points to nil.' *The Eastbournian* recorded that Teddy Morgan scored five tries and Willie Llewellyn one.

Willie Llewellyn brought his London Welsh try tally for the season to fourteen when he scored two tries in their victory over the Civil Service at Richmond. London Welsh were handicapped by the absence of two of their regular three-quarters and three of their regular forwards and as a result they were lucky to win a scrambling game by a goal and a try to two tries. Early in the game Rhys Gabe carved on opening and running from his twenty-five passed to Willie Llewellyn who raced away and scored behind the posts. Rhys Gabe added the extra points. Before the interval some fine work by the home forwards resulted in an unconverted try. Two minutes into the second half Willie Llewellyn cleverly intercepted a pass in mid-field and with practically no opposition ran in another try which Rhys Gabe failed to convert. The Civil Service made determined efforts to bring the scores level and although they scored another try before the end of the game they missed the conversion and lost a hard fought game by 8 points to six.

Willie Llewellyn was really on top of his game and in his next match, playing for Glamorgan against Gloucestershire at Cardiff, he scored another three tries. Glamorgan scored eight tries and Bert Winfield kicked five conversions and a penalty goal to give Glamorgan victory by 37 points to nil. This was a very strong Glamorgan side with Bert Winfield at full-back and Willie Llewellyn, Gwyn Nicholls and W 'Pussy' Jones in the three-quarters. At half-backs were the Swansea pair of Dick Jones and Dickie Owen. Swansea were Welsh Club Champions for the third consecutive year in 1900–01 and this was recognised in the original selection of the Glamorgan team which included seven Swansea players. Those chosen were: George Davies, Billy Trew, Dick Jones, Dickie Owen, Fred Scrine, Will Joseph and Hopkin Davies. The fact that Bert Winfield was chosen over Billy Bancroft was an indication that he was at last coming to the end of his illustrious career or it may well have been the fact that Billy Bancroft often relinquished the opportunity to play for the County after he had been chosen. However, of the seven Swansea players originally selected only four actually played. Billy Trew was injured and George Davies and Fred Scrine withdrew. W 'Pussy' Jones of Cardiff replaced George Davies and J Moors of Pontypridd replaced the injured Billy Trew. At forward Bob Jones of Llwynypia and D Jones of Neath came into the Glamorgan side to replace Fred Scrine (Swansea) and Jere Blake (Cardiff). Will Joseph, Hopkin Davies (Swansea), Alfred Brice (Aberavon), Fred Miller, W T Osborne (Mountain Ash) and Billy Alexander (Llwynypia) all played as selected.

This County game had an important bearing on the team to be selected to represent Wales against Ireland at St Helen's, Swansea on Saturday 16th March. A meeting of the match committee of the Welsh Football Union had be arranged to take place at the Queen's Hotel, Cardiff immediately after the game with the purpose of selecting the Welsh team to face Ireland. The team selected was as follows:

Wales: Back, W J Bancroft (Swansea); three-quarters, E G Nicholls (Cardiff), W Llewellyn (London Welsh), George Davies, W Trew (Swansea); half-backs, R Jones and R Owen (Swansea); forwards, A Brice (Aberavon), J G Boots (Newport), J Hodges (Newport), Fred Miller (Mountain Ash), W H Alexander (Llwynypia), R Jones (Llwynypia), J Blake (Cardiff), and H Davies (Swansea).

The Glamorgan County committee may well have thought that Billy Bancroft was at the end of his career but the Welsh selection committee were happy to select him once more for Wales. However, this would be his final swansong and his last international for Wales. He had been a brilliant servant to his country and played in thirty-three consecutive international matches for Wales. The unlucky Bert Winfield, who had played brilliantly for Glamorgan, was again selected as reserve to Billy Bancroft. The other Welsh reserves were Dan Rees (Swansea – right centre), W 'Pussy' Jones (Cardiff – left centre), R Gabe (Llanelly/London Welsh – left or right wing), J A 'Gus' Gould (second reserve either wing); half-backs, G Ll Lloyd and W Needs to play failing either of the Swansea half-backs; forwards, F Scrine (Swansea), E Thomas (Newport), W H 'Buller' Williams (Pontymister), and H Beere (Mountain Ash) in the order named.

The only alterations in the team from the side that had played against Scotland was that Bob Jones replaced his Llwynypia team-mate Dick Hellings and Dickie Owen and Dick Jones replaced the Newport half-backs G Ll Lloyd and Louis Phillips. Unfortunately Dick Hellings and Louis Phillips had played their last games for Wales when they played in the international match against Scotland. Dick Hellings won nine caps for Wales between 1897 and 1901 and Louis Phillips won four caps for Wales between 1900 and 1901. Will Joseph who had played well for Glamorgan was unlucky not to be selected in the reserves but his chance would come the following year.

On the Wednesday prior to the international Billy Trew withdrew because the knee injury he sustained playing for Swansea against Leicester at the end of February had not improved. Walter Rees, the secretary of the Welsh Football Union, then brought Rhys Gabe into the team as Trew's replacement. The only other change in the team was Fred Scrine replacing Jehoida Hodges who cried off the day before the game with influenza. The teams lined up as follows:

Wales: W J Bancroft (Swansea, Captain), W M Llewellyn (Llwynypia and London Welsh), E G Nicholls (Cardiff), G Davies (Swansea), *R T Gabe (Llanelly/London Welsh); *R H Jones and *R M Owen (Swansea); A B Brice (Aberavon), F Miller (Mountain Ash), F G Scrine, H Davies (Swansea), J G Boots (Newport), J Blake (Cardiff), W H Alexander (Llwynypia), *R (Bob) Jones (Llwynypia). (* Wales Debut)

Ireland: C A Boyd (Wanderers); A E Freear, B R W Doran (Lansdowne), J B Allison (QCB), I G Davidson (NIFC); A M (Louis) Magee (Bective, Captain), *H H Ferris (QCB); M Ryan, J Ryan (Rockwell Coll), C E Allen (Derry), F Gardiner (NIFC), T A Harvey (Dublin U), P Healey (Limerick), J J Coffey (Lansdowne), S T Irwin (QCB). (* Ireland Debut)

Referee: George H Harnett (England).

There were four new caps in the Welsh side that faced Ireland and between them they would amass seventy-five caps for Wales between 1901 and 1912. Dickie Owen was the most capped with thirty-five followed by Rhys Gabe with twenty-four. Dick Jones gained fifteen caps for Wales bewteen 1901 and 1910 and in all his internationals was partnered by Dickie Owen. This was Bob Jones' only international cap for Wales.

Richard Morgan 'Dickie' Owens (his name was always shortened to Owen in his lifetime) was born on November 17th 1876 in Swansea. He remains one of probably the three greatest scrum-halves that Wales have ever produced, along with Gareth Edwards and Haydn Tanner.

A diminutive figure at just 5ft 2 inches tall and barely 9st 7lb at best, his achievements are the greater for the

Dickie Owen held the record for the number of Welsh caps until he was surpassed by Ken Jones of Newport in 1954.

Courtesy of the Frederic Humbert Collection

CHAPTER SIX

difficulties his lack of physical presence presented, in an age when the game was as rough as it has ever been. Yet Dickie Owen confounded defences and along with his club partner Dick Jones, helped guide Swansea through an unprecedented period of success for the club in the early years of the 20th century. Owen was a superb reader of the game but his supreme skill was as an innovator of scrum-half play. Dickie Owen gained 35 Welsh caps winning 5 Triple Crowns and captaining Wales for the first time against England in 1907 at his home ground of St Helens. He played for Wales with Dick Jones as his half-back partner 15 times. The Welsh selectors had teamed him up with Cardiff's Percy Bush on occasions, notably in the 1905 All Blacks match. They were paired together again against England in 1906 and South Africa the following year, but they were both innovative and influential in their own right and never gelled well together. The South Africa match was the last time they played together although Percy Bush went on to gain a further five Welsh caps. At the age of thirty-four, Dickie Owen played his last game for Wales against Scotland at St Helen's in 1912. Having captained Wales in the previous game against England he was also captain for his last game. The little giant was carried from the field on the shoulders of delirious supporters after a final victory in the Welsh jersey. Dickie Owen was given the captaincy of Swansea in this his last season of 1911–12 as Billy Trew stood aside for him after five consecutive seasons at the helm.

Like Dickie Owen, Dick Jones came into the Swansea side after the brilliant James brothers went North to Broughton Rangers in 1899. Known as the 'Dancing Dicks', Dick Jones and Dickie Owen created one of the most devastating half-back pairings to play for Swansea.

Jones was a brilliant runner who could dodge, jink and swerve very

Dick Jones partnered Dickie Owen in all his fifteen appearances for Wales.

cleverly. His kicking also marked him out for he was one of the first halves to mix running with kicking in offence. But it was his judgement that made him stand out for he was a greater thinker than many players who had more ability than he had. Gradually, Owen and Jones were able to anticipate immediately and intuitively the others' forthcoming move. Both were always looking for new ways of doing things; so much so that opponents never knew what to expect of them. With the Welsh selectors preferring to play club pairings at half-back and Newport's Louis Phillips breaking down in the Scottish match, Dick Jones and Dickie Owen were called up for their first caps against Ireland in 1901. It was the first of fifteen appearances together for Wales; a record not beaten until Barry John and Gareth Edwards in 1970. Wales were fortunate to win and the Swansea pair hardly distinguished themselves. Jones and Owen played against England in 1902 but then Jones was dropped in favour of G Ll Lloyd of Newport whose form was such that the advantage of club pairing was not enough.

Although Dick Jones continued to play brilliantly for his club and Glamorgan he was not picked again for Wales until 1904, when he proved his class by some superb kicking to defeat Scotland and some magnificent running and support play against Ireland. 1904–05 was the year of the Swansea Invincibles and Dick Jones, with Dickie Owen, was at the top of his form. His superb running carved out opening after opening against England, and Wales ran in seven glorious tries. But two weeks later at Newport, Dick Jones broke his instep in a club game and he did not play rugby again until November 1907. Dick Jones returned against France in 1908 and then starred in the Triple Crown decider against Ireland by making the winning try. 1908–09 brought Wales five wins; against Australia and the four Grand Slam matches. Dick Jones and Dickie Owen were instrumental in them all and masterminded some excellent play. It was a year in which the pack struggled for parity but superb back play ensured enough scores for victory. 1910 brought a sad final Welsh game for Dick Jones. After taking France apart on New Year's Day, Wales headed for Twickenham, where England beat Wales for the first time in twelve years. Dick Jones and Dickie Owen were dropped and while Dickie Owen returned in 1911, a serious accident ended Jones' career prematurely.

The only other debutant to be originally selected to play for Wales against Ireland was Bob Jones of Llwynypia. The match was played at Swansea's St. Helen's Ground and Jones took his place in the squad with fellow Llwynypia teammates Billy Alexander and Willie Llewellyn. This was Bob Jones' only cap for Wales and although he continued to play rugby for Glamorgan County he never played for Wales again. In his later career, Jones played for top flight Welsh club, Cardiff and as an officer in the Glamorgan Constabulary he also represented Glamorgan Police on the rugby field. (See Llwynypia team photograph on page 67.)

Rhys Gabe won his first cap for Wales as a result of Billy Trew withdrawing because of injury. Fred Scrine was also called up to replace Jehoida Hodges who had influenza. Fred Scrine had already won two Welsh caps against England and Scotland in 1899. His cap against Ireland was his last for Wales.

Rhys 'Rusty' Gabe was born in Llangennech and played his early rugby with the local club. He made his debut for Llanelly at the age of seventeen. Rhys Gabe played his first game for London Welsh in the match against Streatham in October 1900 after moving to London to study at Borough Road Training College. Although he won his first cap playing on the left wing, for all his remaining caps he played in the centre. It was while he was at London Welsh that Willie Llewellyn persuaded him to move to centre and this he did with brilliant effect. After qualifying as a mathematics teacher, he took a teaching post in Cardiff and joined the Cardiff club, where he formed a devastating centre combination with Gwyn Nicholls for both club and country. He played for Cardiff between 1902 and 1910, captaining the club in the 1907–08 season. He scored 51 tries for Cardiff in 115 appearances.

Rhys Gabe's 24 caps for Wales included the famous 1905 victory

Courtesy of the Frederic Humbert Collection

Rhys Gabe played 24 times for Wales between 1901 and 1908. He was just twenty years of age when he first played for Wales against Ireland in 1901.

against New Zealand. He only captained Wales on one occasion in the 1907 match against Ireland. He toured Australasia with the British Isles team of 1904 and played in seventeen out of the twenty games, including all four test matches. Gabe was an impressive try scorer; he scored six tries for the British Isles and scored 11 tries for Wales during his international career. In 1906 he appeared four times against the touring Springboks; for Glamorgan, Wales, Llanelly and Cardiff. Rhys Gabe retired in 1908, but still appeared occasionally for Cardiff. He was a fine club cricketer and played occasionally for Glamorgan. He also captained Radyr Golf Club, and played at Cardiff Golf Club well into his eighties.

The game against Ireland was a hard fought affair and Wales could consider themselves very lucky that they were the eventual winners. With Ireland outscoring Wales by three tries to two it was only the goal kicking of Billy Bancroft that saved the day. Wales didn't play well and often their defence was penetrated; the general opinion in the press was that the better side lost. Within six minutes of the start Ireland were in front. From a scrummage on the Welsh twenty-five Louis Magee got the ball away and with the Welsh defence in a heap behind the scrummage Jack Ryan forced his way over in the extreme corner and scored an unconverted try. Wales were continually under pressure and a mistake by the half-backs allowed Ireland to take control of a loose rush which resulted in Arthur Freear crossing for Ireland's second unconverted try. Wales just could not cope with the frequent rushes of the Irish forwards and within 23 minutes of the start of the game Ireland scored their third unconverted try when Ian Davidson crossed the line with three or four Welsh players hanging on his back. Again Ireland missed the conversion and this was to be Wales' saving grace. Just before the interval a rare mistake by Boyd, the Irish full-back, brought play right up to the Irish goal line. From a scrummage Willie Llewellyn eventually received and kicked across field to his forwards and Billy Alexander crossed for a try right behind the posts. Billy Bancroft made no mistake with the conversion and at half-time Ireland were leading by 9 points to five.

Early in the second half, with the Irish forwards getting the ball from the scrummage on nearly every occasion, it was attack after attack by the Irish three-quarters. Only determined tackling by Gwyn Nicholls, George Davies and Willie Llewellyn prevented disaster. For a full five or ten minutes it looked like Ireland would score. Eventually Wales were able to clear their lines when Dickie Owen got possession and kicked down field. Billy Bancroft was not having a good game and after another fumble Freear just failed to gather when a try looked certain. Against the run of play Wales managed to get within fifteen yards of the Irish goal line. The ball went out to Rhys Gabe on the left wing and he did the same trick as Willie Llewellyn and kicked into the centre of the field near the posts. As luck would have it Billy Alexander was there again and a desperate race between him and one of the Irish backs resulted in Alexander getting there first and scoring his second try of the game right under the posts. Again Billy Bancroft made no mistake with the conversion and Wales were one point ahead. Wales played much better in the closing stages of the game and although they won by 10 points to nine, it could have been, possibly should have been, a victory for Ireland. Nevertheless Wales were victorious and the victory earned them second place in the Home Nations Championship. Scotland won the championship outright and gained their third Triple Crown with comfortable victories over Wales, Ireland and England.

After thirty-three consecutive caps Billy Bancroft probably had his worst game for Wales in what was his last international. Including Billy Bancroft seven Welsh players had their last game for Wales in this international. Billy Alexander of Llwynypia played in seven internationals between 1898 and 1901. Jere Blake of Cardiff had gained nine Welsh caps between 1899 and 1901. Hopkin Davies of Swansea played in four internationals between 1898 and 1901. For Bob Jones of Llwynypia this was his only international appearance. Fred Miller was capped seven times between 1896 and 1901 and finally Fred Scrine had played just three times for Wales between 1899 and 1901.

With the Home Nations Championship over for another season Willie Llewellyn returned to club rugby and the week after the international he played for London Welsh in their final game of the season against Upper Clapton. Played at Clapton it was a fast and even game and both teams nearly scored on several occasions however, when the final whistle went neither side had managed to get any points on the score sheet and the game ended in a draw. In their report of the game *The Sportsman* made the following comments: 'For Clapton Talbot, Treloar and Milne did well behind, while all the forwards were good, with Reynolds, McNeill and Bell the most prominent. For London Welsh, Llewellyn, Gabe and Morgan (Teddy) behind and Watts and Williams forward were best.'

Having played 19 games, they won 9, lost 7 and drew 3, scoring 129 points for, with 86 against. With the season now over for London Welsh it was reported in the *Evening Express* that 'Willie Llewellyn would assist Llwynypia for the remainder of the season.' Although information on the Llwynypia team for the final few games of the 1900–01 season is sparse Willie Llewellyn definitely played for Llwynypia in their Glamorgan League game against Treherbert on Saturday 6th April. The *Evening Express* stated, 'Willie Llewellyn, the clever London Welsh wing,

Date	Team Played For	Opposition	Venue	Result	W Llewellyn Tries
29/09/1900	London Welsh	Bedford	Away	Lost 3-22	Did not play
06/10/1900	London Welsh	Streatham	Away	Lost 6-8	0
13/10/1900	London Welsh	Saracens	Home	Won 22-0	1
20/10/1900	London Welsh	Berkshire Wanderers	Away	Won 11-6	0
27/10/1900	Newport	Blackheath	Away	Won 14-0	2
03/11/1900	London Welsh	Northampton	Away	Drawn 3-3	1
14/11/1900	Surrey	Hampshire	Away	Lost 0-8	0
17/11/1900	London Welsh	Stroud	Away	Drawn 0-0	0
24/11/1900	London Welsh	Harlequins	Away	Won 10-0	1
01/12/1900	London Welsh	Streatham	Home	Lost 3-5	0
06/12/1900	Surrey	Eastern Counties	Away	Won 13-3	0
08/12/1900	London Welsh	London Irish	Home	Won 11-3	3
15/12/1900	London Welsh	Saracens	Away	Won 8-0	1
17/12/1900	Christ College Past	Christ College Present	Brecon	Won 39-8	1
22/12/1900	London Welsh	Bristol	Away	Lost 6-9	1
24/12/1901	London Welsh	Mountain Ash	Away	Lost 0-16	0
25/12/1900	London Welsh	Aberavon	Away	Lost 0-3	0
05/01/1901	Wales	England	Cardiff Arms Park	Won 13-0	0
12/01/1901	London Welsh	Park House	Home	Won 6-0	0
19/01/1901	London Welsh	Catford Bridge	Away	Lost 3-5	0
09/02/1901	Wales	Scotland	Inverleith, Edinburgh	Lost 8-18	0
09/02/1901	London Welsh	Leytonstone	Away	Won 6-0	Did not play
23/02/1901	London Welsh	St Mary's Hospital	Home	Won 23-0	4
27/02/1901	Old Breconians	Eastbourne College	Eastbourne	Won 20-0	1
02/03/1901	London Welsh	Civil Service (Richmond)	Away	Won 8-6	2
06/03/1901	Glamorgan	Gloucestershire	Cardiff Arms Park	Won 37-0	3
16/03/1901	Wales	Ireland	St Helen's, Swansea	Won 10-9	0
23/03/1901	London Welsh	Upper Clapton	Away	Drawn 0-0	0
06/04/1901	Llwynypia	Treherbert	Away	Drawn 3-3	0
20/04/1901	Treherbert	Gloucester	Home	Drawn 3-3	0
25/04/1901	Llwynypia	Treorky	Home	Won 14-3	0
29/04/1901	Llwynypia	Penygraig	Home	Won 19-0	0
04/05/1901	Llwynypia	Treherbert	Home	Drawn 0-0	0
11/05/1901	Llwynypia	Maesteg	Home	Drawn 0-0	Did not play
	Willie Llewellyn Games Played				W Llewellyn Tries
Totals	31				21

Willie Llewellyn Rugby Games Played and Results 1900–1901

had few chances at Treherbert last Saturday. The Treherbert supporters were somewhat sarcastic in shouting "Good old Llwynypia and London Welsh." A Llwynypia man in the train last Saturday evening said, "Why, the blooming women were worse than the youngsters" he added as he filled his pipe with the strongest shag.' Complain they did, on the field and afterwards and with regard to this game the secretary of the Glamorgan League received a letter from Mr Mainwaring, Treherbert, claiming that the two points should be awarded to Treherbert on the grounds that Llwynypia played Willie Llewellyn who they claimed was not eligible to play in League matches. At a meeting of the Glamorgan Football League at Pontypridd on Wednesday 17th April with Mr Tom Williams, Welsh Football Union, in the chair, the Treherbert protest was considered. After a great deal of discussion Mr Mainwaring, who was representing Treherbert, withdrew the protest.

There was obviously no lasting bad feeling between the two clubs because a fortnight later three of Llwynypia's Welsh internationals; Willie Llewellyn, Billy Alexander and Bob Jones, all played for Treherbert in their home game against Gloucester. In the first half Treherbert were let down by their centres who ruined a handful of opportunities by not being able to combine with their wings. Gloucester were by far the better side and an unconverted try by Cook gave them a three point lead at the interval.

The second half was the reverse of the first and Treherbert were the better team. The report of the second half in the *Western Mail* read as follows: 'In the second half Treherbert pressed nearly all through, their forwards playing a magnificent game. Bob Jones soon dashed over in the corner but the kick at goal was a poor one. Try as they would afterwards the homesters could not pierce the defence, although they came desperately near to it on a number of occasions and one of the most exciting games and one of the best exhibitions of rugby football ever seen in the Rhondda ended in a draw.'

Although the *Evening Express* had stated that 'Willie Llewellyn would assist Llwynypia for the remainder of the season' there is very little Llwynypia team detail for the last four games of the season. Other than the fact that Willie Llewellyn did not play in the last game of the season against Maesteg he could well have played in the games against

Treorky, Penygraig and Treherbert. If he did then Willie Llewellyn played thirty-one games during the 1900–01 season and scored twenty-one tries. He played in all three Welsh international matches and represented both Surrey and Glamorgan at county level. In addition to his seventeen games for London Welsh he also played for Newport, Llwynypia and Treherbert. Willie also maintained his links with Christ College, Brecon by playing for the Old Boys team against the Present team and the Old Breconians against Eastbourne College. This had been another very successful season for Willie Llewellyn; he had shown once again his brilliant try scoring ability with four tries for London Welsh in their game against St Mary's Hospital and three tries for the same team against London Irish. He also scored three tries for Glamorgan in their game against Gloucestershire. At the general meeting of the London Welsh Football Club at the White Horse Hotel, Holborn on Saturday 27th April, the secretary of the club in his report referred to the success the club had attained during the season and stated it was mainly, if not entirely, due to the captaincy of Willie Llewellyn. Not surprisingly therefore at the same meeting Willie Llewellyn was once again elected as captain for the forthcoming season with Wallace Watts as his vice-captain.

The Welsh fifteen that would face New Zealand on Saturday 16th December 1905 was also developing nicely. In addition to Willie Llewellyn, Gwyn Nicholls and Jehoida Hodges, who were seasoned internationals, Rhys Gabe and Dickie Owen had now joined the Welsh international fraternity by gaining their first Welsh caps in the final international of the season against Ireland. With Bert Winfield the regular reserve to Billy Bancroft it looked likely that he would be the natural successor to Bancroft who had played his last game for Wales. There was however, another big disappointment coming Bert Winfield's way before he would get that elusive Welsh cap. Will Joseph, having been chosen as reserve forward for the Scotland match was unlucky not to be named in the reserves for the international against Ireland but it was only a matter of time before he would gain his first Welsh cap. Teddy Morgan was also playing very well for Guy's Hospital and London Welsh and was not far away from his first Welsh cap. The 1901–02 season would see another four of the Welsh side that defeated New Zealand in 1905 gain Welsh international caps; Teddy Morgan, Will Joseph, Arthur Harding and

Dai Jones all gained their first Welsh caps during that season. The remaining six: Bert Winfield, Percy Bush, George Travers, Cliff Prichard, Charlie Pritchard and John 'Screthog' Williams would all have to wait a little longer before they joined the exclusive international club.

With subscriptions and membership doubling it was with great delight that the London Welsh committee were able to announce that for the 1901–02 season fixtures had been resumed with Newport, Swansea and Oxford University. Another feature of the approaching season was the visit of the formidable Devonport Albion and a first meeting with Gloucester on the Easter tour. The tour games against Mountain Ash and Aberavon were also eagerly anticipated.

London Welsh Rugby Football Club 1901–02 Season
London Welsh played 22 games during the 1901–02 season. They won 10 lost 10 and drew two. They scored 201 points for with 153 points against. Of the twenty-two games they played nine games were at home and eleven games were away. Of the home games seven were played at the Lower Welsh Harp, Hendon while the games against Devonport Albion and Swansea were played at the Athletic Ground, Richmond. Willie Llewellyn played in 17 of the twenty-two games, he missed the away game against Berkshire Wanderers because he was playing for Glamorgan against Yorkshire. Willie missed the game against St Mary's Hospital because it was a week before the international against Scotland. He missed the games against Oxford University and Berkshire Wanderers because of the injury he sustained playing in the international against Scotland. The only other game Willie missed was the game against the Welsh Wanderers when he was playing for Wales in the international against Ireland at Lansdowne Road, Dublin.

Willie Llewellyn opened his 1901–02 campaign with the first game of the season for London Welsh in their away game against Newport. Both sides were well represented with Welsh internationals George Llewellyn Lloyd, George Boots and Jehoida Hodges in the Newport side and fellow internationals Willie Llewellyn and Wallace Watts playing for London Welsh. Also in the Newport side was Cliff Pritchard, playing his second season of senior rugby for Newport. This was the first time Willie Llewellyn and Cliff Pritchard had faced each other on the rugby field, they would however, get to know each other very well playing together for Newport and Wales, including the famous victory over New Zealand in 1905.

Newport had the edge in this game but London Welsh battled hard and despite being under immense pressure they were only three points adrift at the interval with an unconverted try by future Welsh international D P 'Ponty' Jones. Early in the second half some good passing between Cliff Pritchard and Wyatt Gould, saw the brother of the famous A J Gould, race round with a try behind the posts that Llewellyn Lloyd easily converted. London Welsh were now clearly beaten and further tries by William Williams, Jehoida Hodges and Cliff Pritchard, the latter converted by Newport captain Llewellyn Lloyd, gave Newport victory by 19 points to nil.

Next up for London Welsh were the mighty Devonport Albion. The previous season Davenport had won thirty-six and drawn two of their thirty-nine games, only losing to Swansea at home in November by 7 points to three. In the return match at St Helen's they drew 3 points all. Having defeated Leicester the previous week by 13 points to three expectations were high for this encounter. London Welsh were certainly not overawed and they gave a wonderful display in holding the visitors to a drawn game. With regard to the game *The Sportsman* remarked: 'The London Welsh, who had certainly whipped up a strong team for the occasion, had much the best of a drawn game with Devonport Albion; indeed, as a matter of a fact they were rather unfortunate in not coming away victorious.' The London Welsh team included Welsh internationals Willie Llewellyn, Rhys Gabe and W H 'Buller' Williams while Devonport Albion had English internationals Herbert Gamlin at full-back and E J Vivyan at centre. A crowd of over 2,000 watched a thrilling match and an evenly fought first half saw the interval arrive with neither side being able to score. Immediately on changing ends the Welsh attacked in the most vigorous fashion with Willie Llewellyn, Rhys Gabe and Teddy Morgan in sparkling form and only sound defence prevented both Wayne Morgan and Willie Llewellyn from scoring. Eventually, after pressing hard, Rhys Gabe ran behind the posts to score a try which he converted himself, much to the delight of the London Welsh supporters. A few minutes before the end of the game 'Buller' Williams was injured and had to leave the field with a nasty scalp wound. A minute after he had left the field J Peard broke away from a line-out and making a clever run scored a try which Vivyan converted. With no further scores an exhilarating game ended in a draw at 5 points all.

London Welsh were without a victory in their first two games and things did not get better when they lost away to Streatham by 10 points to three. A second half unconverted try by J F Williams the only score for the Welsh. At last in their fourth game of the season London Welsh registered their first victory when they defeated Saracens by 8 points to six. The score should have been much higher but London Welsh were unfortunate enough to lose two of their three-quarters at the start of the game which resulted in them playing with just six forwards for the remainder of the game. In the first half the Saracens took the lead with an unconverted try. This had the effect of shocking the Welshmen into action and from a line-out close to the line Wallace Watts struggled over for a try which Hodge converted. Early in the second half Hodge dropped a goal from a penalty to extend the lead to 8 points to three. After some fierce attacking the Saracens scored another unconverted try but London Welsh held on to their lead and won by 8 points to six.

The following week Willie Llewellyn was back playing with his old Llwynypia and Wales team mate Bob Jones when they both played for Glamorgan in the game against Yorkshire at Castleford. It wasn't a happy reunion with Glamorgan going down by 10 points to six. The only consolation was that Bob Jones scored one of Glamorgan's two unconverted tries. The other was scored by J Lewis of Treherbert.

On the same day as Glamorgan were defeated by Yorkshire, London Welsh had a wonderful victory over Berkshire Wanderers at the County Ground, Reading. Neither side was at full strength but nevertheless the teams were well matched. In addition to Willie Llewellyn, London Welsh were also without Rhys Gabe, D J Thomas and R B Sparrow. Two first half unconverted tries by L E Silcox gave London Welsh a six point lead at the interval. Early in the second half W L Evans scored a try for the Welsh and for the first time in the game W G Hodge was successful with the conversion. Although eleven points down Berkshire Wanderers did not give up and two unconverted tries and a drop goal brought them right back into the game. It was however, not quite enough and losing by 11 points to ten they suffered their first defeat of the season.

The London Welsh Rugby Football Club

Back Row: A Bevan, J F Williams, W L Davies, R Griffiths, J Bookless, H G Lloyd. *Middle Row*: J Dawson, T Morgan, G Evans, F G Williams, M T Williams, R F Williams, E Morgan. *Front Row*: S C Brown, W M Llewellyn (Captain), W G Hodge and R Seaton.

The photograph titled the 'London Welsh Rugby Football Club' above appeared in the 6th November 1901 issue of *The Tatler*. Although it is described as a London Welsh team this group of players never played for the same team at London Welsh. Many of the players in the photograph are Christ College Old Boys and there are possibly one or two Llandovery College Old Boys in the photograph as well. The December 1900 edition of *The Breconian* made reference to the fact that a group of past pupils had arranged a few games and reported, 'We hear that a team of London Old Boys intends touring in Sussex in the Easter holidays. Matches have been arranged with Eastbourne College and other clubs.' We know the game against Eastbourne College took place in February 1901 but there is no record of any other games taking place. The Eastbourne College game was reported in both *The Breconian* and *The Eastbournian* but reference is made in *The Eastbournian* to T P Thomas (Old Breconian) who does not appear in the photograph so it is unlikely to be that team. If they did play another game it is possible that this is a photograph of that team. In the photograph R Seaton is wearing his Christ College blazer.

Willie Llewellyn returned to captain London Welsh in their next game against Sutton at Hendon. Although the result was a win for the Welsh there is no record of whom or how the three points were scored. On the same day Teddy Morgan was playing for Newport in their away game at Blackheath. He had a wonderful afternoon; in front of 8,000 spectators he scored three tries in the 22 points to four victory. Blackheath's only points came from a drop goal by Welsh international Reg Skrimshire.

Having not scored in his first six games, Willie Llewellyn scored his first try of the season when London Welsh defeated the Civil Service at Hendon by 3 points to nil. Having at last got on the score sheet Willie went into the London Welsh record books when he scored five tries in his next game for London Welsh at home to Park House. Reports of the actual score vary between 54 points and 60 points to nil but the general consensus is that they won by 8 goals (1 dropped) and seven tries to nil. Willie Llewellyn was in tremendous form and crossed for five tries while Wallace Watts crossed for three. Hop Maddock equalled Willie's achievement when he did the same against Ilford Wanderers in September 1906 and then went one better by doing it again against Oxford University in February 1909.

Willie Llewellyn and Teddy Morgan were both selected in a strong Surrey side to face Middlesex at West Kensington on Wednesday 13th November. However, neither played and with about seven changes in the Surrey team it is not surprising that they were defeated by 22 points to nil.

Probably the biggest game of the season for London Welsh was when they played Swansea at Richmond Athletic Ground. Swansea had been Welsh champions for the previous three seasons and arrived in London undefeated. They brought with them a very strong team which included Welsh internationals George Davies, Dan Rees, Dickie Owen, Dick Jones, Fred Scrine and future Welsh internationals Sid Bevan, David John Thomas and Will Joseph. Also in the side was Arthur Freear, the Irish international wing who had moved to Swansea at a time when he was able to temporarily replace the injured Billy Trew. Freear played for Swansea between 1901 and 1905 after which he went North to Hull Kingston Rovers.

London Welsh were also strongly represented with Willie Llewellyn, Wayne Morgan, Rhys Gabe and Teddy Morgan in the three-quarters and W H 'Buller' Williams, J F Williams, J C Jenkins, M T Williams,

Tom James, W C Roberts, F Clay and W G Hodge in the forwards. London Welsh also had the assistance of J Thornley (Llwynypia) at full-back and N L James (Cardiff) at half-back.

A crowd of about 3,000 spectators watched a fast but scrambling game at the Richmond Athletic Ground. The report of the game in *The Sportsman* read as follows: 'Though by no means a great game, it was nevertheless thoroughly interesting from beginning to end. The home brigade were by no means disgraced, indeed, to a certain extent, they covered themselves with glory in running such a crack organisation as Swansea to within 8 points. The play for the first quarter of an hour was in favour of the Welsh, Gabe, Llewellyn and Wayne Morgan being very prominent. The tackling, too, was magnificent, Clay, W H Williams and Jenkins doing great work.' The only score in the first half was an unconverted try by Sid Bevan just before the interval. In the second half a try by Cole which was converted by Lockman put the game to bed for Swansea and although they attacked right up until the end of the game the London Welsh defence was sound and prevented any further scoring.

Swansea, who went on to win twenty-five of the thirty-two games they played during the season; losing just three games with four drawn they were Welsh club champions for the fourth consecutive year.

On Wednesday 20th November the Welsh Football Union held a preliminary trial match at Cardiff Arms Park to enable them to pick strong representative sides for the final trial to be played at Treherbert on Saturday 7th December. The committee purposely ignored the better known players in South Wales with the sole object of seeing what other talent was available other than those who were considered 'probables' for the international team. The two sides were classified as 'A' and 'B' and there were quite a few notable players in the teams. The 'A' team was captained by the already capped W 'Pussy' Jones of Cardiff. Also in the 'A' team were the uncapped Teddy Morgan, Arthur Harding and George Travers. Cliff Pritchard, the Newport centre, was selected but was unable to play. The 'B' team, captained by Cardiff forward D L Bowen, also included J Strand-Jones of Oxford University and Llanelly at full-back, Percy Bush of Cardiff in the centre and Dai 'Tarw' Jones of Treherbert in the forwards.

The 'B' team scored all their points in the first half and the 'A' team all their points in the second half. The game ended in a draw at 12 points all and although it may have helped the Welsh Football Union to select the Possibles against the Probables it was of very little use with regard to the selection of the Welsh team to play England at Blackheath in January 1902. The *Evening Express* reported, 'Out of the thirty men who turned out there were only two who materially enhanced the reputations which they have gained in club matches and those two were Strand-Jones and Percy Bush. The former impressed everyone with the sterling soundness of his back play, while Bush gave another demonstration of the knack which he possesses in an abnormal degree of doing things which few other players would care to attempt and doing them well. His single handed try, if I may so term it, was the brightest individual effort in the whole game and in giving him credit for his clever display it must not be forgotten that he was playing out of his accustomed position in the Cardiff team, being relegated to the centre, instead of the left wing.' John Strand-Jones and Percy Bush were both rewarded for their fine display when after the match the selection committee of the Welsh Football Union included both players in the Possibles team for the final Welsh trial.

Following their defeat against Swansea, London Welsh returned to winning ways in their next game against London Irish, Willie Llewellyn leading the side to a 12 points to 5 victory. Their next game at home against Streatham was a disappointing affair with injuries too frequent on the Welsh side, at one point they were down to twelve men. In the first half unconverted tries were scored by E T Hancock for Streatham and J F Williams for the Welsh. The highlight of the six points all drawn game was Willie Llewellyn's try. Picking the ball up in his own twenty-five, he ran through all his opponents and scored a brilliant try between the posts which Wayne Morgan failed to convert. Another unconverted try by Hancock levelled the scores.

Willie's next game was playing for the Probables in the final Welsh trial at Treherbert. There were several changes from the teams originally selected. For the Probables, Tom Samuel of Llanelly was promoted from the Possibles to take the place of George Llewellyn Lloyd and Harry Jones of Penygraig took the place of Alfred Brice in the forwards. In the Possibles W 'Pussy' Jones took the place of fellow Cardiff teammate Percy Bush on the left wing and Arthur Williams of Penygraig replaced Dan Rees of Swansea at right centre. J Lewis of Treherbert came into the side at half-back in place of the promoted Tom Samuel. The teams took the field as follows:

Probables: Back, H B Winfield (Cardiff); three-quarters, Gwyn Nicholls (Cardiff), George Davies (Swansea), Rhys Gabe and Willie Llewellyn (London Welsh); half-backs, Tom Samuel (Llanelly) and Dick Jones (Swansea); forwards, Harry Jones (Penygraig), Jehoida Hodges and George Boots (Newport), Arthur Harding (Cardiff), Will Osbourne (Mountain Ash), Dai Jones (Treherbert), E Thomas (Newport) and Will Joseph (Swansea).

Possibles: Back, J Strand-Jones (Oxford University and Llanelly); three-quarters, W 'Pussy' Jones (Cardiff), Arthur Williams (Penygraig), Teddy Morgan (London Welsh), and Cliff Pritchard (Newport); half-backs, J Lewis (Treherbert) and Jack Hillman (Newport); forwards, Danny Walters and Isaac Lewis (Llanelly), D Thomas (Cardiff), George Travers (Pill Harriers), A G Brown (Newport), D Davies (Mumbles), G Thomas and D Thomas (Newport).

Drizzling rain fell steadily throughout the game and made the outlook gloomy and miserable. However, the match turned out to be one of the most interesting trial games ever played under the auspices of the Welsh Football Union. Despite all the rain the pitch was in fairly good condition and there was every chance of a fast and open game. Initially the Probables were the stronger side and put their opponents under considerable pressure and only fine defensive play by the Possibles kept them out. Then against the run of play Cliff Pritchard got possession in his own twenty-five and running well, punted across field. Teddy Morgan followed up well and beating all his opponents from the half-way line, scored a brilliant try. The kick at goal failed but at the interval the Possibles were leading by 3 points to nil. The Probables had their chances in the first half but Bert Winfield had an off day with the boot and missed three kicks at goal. Just before the interval Dick Jones got away beautifully and when within ten yards of the line gave to Dai Jones but he was tackled by Strand-Jones before he could get to the line.

In the second half the Probables were finding that in the other side they had men who, as a combination, were quite their equals and play generally pointed to the fact that it was going to be difficult for the Welsh selection committee to select absolutely the best team to face England.

After some fairly mediocre play by the Probables they eventually rose to the challenge and Willie Llewellyn got smartly away after receiving the ball from Dick Jones on the touch-line and scored a superb try. At last Bert Winfield got his kicking boots on and converted with an excellent kick to put his side two points ahead. In the closing stages of the game the Probables were attacking continuously and Willie Llewellyn was brought down five yards from the line. With the Probables forwards now playing better than at any other point in the game their three-quarters were kept continually on the move. On three or four occasions in rapid succession Gwyn Nicholls and George Davies made herculean efforts to break through but the tackling of Cliff Pritchard and Strand-Jones in particular was as deadly as ever and with no further scores the Probables won an exciting contest by 5 points to three.

The Welsh Football Union had originally intended to select the Welsh team to face England immediately after the trial but such was the difficulty of their task that it was decided to defer the selection of the team until Wednesday 18th December. In the meanwhile Willie Llewellyn returned to London Welsh for their game against R. I. E. College at Egham. The ground was very slippery which made accurate play very difficult and with the aid of their forwards R.I.E.C. won this game by two tries (6 points) to nil.

As expected the Match Committee of the Welsh Football Union met at the Queen's Hotel, Cardiff on Wednesday 18th December to select the Welsh team for the first international of the season against England at Blackheath on Saturday 11th January 1902. Once again there was a massive disappointment for Bert Winfield. Having been Welsh reserve to Billy Bancroft on so many occasions and playing in the winning side in the final Welsh trial at Treherbert he could well have expected to have been selected at full-back for the game against England. Unfortunately this was not to be and with a six to five vote against him he once again found himself as reserve full-back; but this time to the uncapped John Strand-Jones of Oxford University and Llanelly. Bert Winfield, the Cardiff captain, who was born in Nottingham, was especially unlucky as having played for Midland Counties and for the Rest of England against Devon in the English trial match he also stood a chance of being selected for England. This was again not to be and the six times capped English international Herbert Gamlin of Devonport Albion and Somerset was preferred by the English selectors. Gamlin would remain as England's full-back until the end of the 1904 international season.

In addition to John Strand-Jones there were first Welsh caps for Teddy Morgan (Guy's Hospital and London Welsh), Will Joseph (Swansea), Dai 'Tarw' Jones (Treherbert), Will Osborne (Mountain Ash), Arthur Harding (Cardiff) and Nathaniel 'Danny' Walters (Llanelly).

Having been selected for his tenth consecutive Welsh cap, Willie Llewellyn returned home from his studies for the Christmas period. During the Christmas break he played three times for Newport. On three consecutive days he played against Watsonians, Moseley and the Barbarians. It was a good vacation for Willie; Newport won all three games and Willie scored one try in the victory over Watsonians and two in the victory over Mosely. The game against the Barbarians took place in pouring rain on a quagmire of mud and it was agreed to play just twenty-five minutes each way. There was no score right up until the final minutes of the game when on one occasion the game was stopped for a minute for Willie Llewellyn to wipe the mud out of his eyes. Soon afterwards he made a clever mark but George Llewellyn Lloyd's kick went wide. Newport continued to press and Willie Llewellyn, passing to Charlie Lewis, the latter dropped a goal which brought the extraordinary game to a close. This was Willie Llewellyn's first game against the Barbarians and although he played against them on a few occasions surprisingly he never played for them. The game against Watsonians was only the second game Willie Llewellyn had played for Newport having previously played against Blackheath in October 1900. During his career Willie would play forty-seven games for Newport.

A report in the *Evening Express* on Tuesday 31st December 1901 stated that Gwyn Nicholls the Welsh international and Cardiff centre had transferred from Cardiff to Newport. The report read as follows: 'Last evening the committee of the Cardiff Football Club received a formal application from E Gwyn Nicholls for his transfer to Newport. Needless to say the committee at once acceded to the request. Thus Nicholls follows in the wake of H T Day, T W Pearson and J B Smithson and in this instance it may truly be said that Cardiff's irreparable loss is Newport's inestimable gain.' Gwyn Nicholls played his first game for Newport in the no score drawn match with Devonport Albion. He played in all eleven fixtures right up until the end of the season during which time Newport did not lose a game. Gwyn Nicholls returned to play for Cardiff the following season and captained the club for the fourth time during the 1903–04 season.

On Saturday 11th January 1902 Wales played England at the Rectory Field, Blackheath in the first international of the season. The team fielded as selected with no changes. Gwyn Nicholls, now playing for Newport, captained the side for the first time. For the seventh consecutive international Bert Winfield was reserve full-back. Having been understudy to Billy Bancroft for two seasons he now found himself as reserve to debutant John Strand-Jones. Billy Bancroft continued to be available for Swansea despite having called it a day on his International career after 33 consecutive caps at full-back (11 times as captain). In fact the irrepressible Bancroft was again to end the season as Swansea's top points scorer. As previously mentioned there were also first caps for Teddy Morgan, Will Joseph, Dai Jones, Will Osborne, Arthur Harding and Danny Walters. Dan Rees of Swansea was first reserve for either centre position and Cliff Pritchard of Newport was second reserve. Although selected in the centre, Rhys Gabe was also first reserve for either wing with Cecil Biggs of Cardiff second Reserve. The reserve half-backs were George Llewellyn Lloyd and Jack Hillman, both of Newport. The reserve forwards in the following order were Harry Jones of Penygraig, George Travers of Pill Harriers, P C Stacey of Llanelly and Edwin 'Beddoe' Thomas of Newport.

England: H T Gamlin (Devonport Albion); *P L Nicholas (Exeter), *J E Raphael (OMT's), J T Taylor (Castleford), *S F Coopper (Blackheath); P D Kendall (Birkenhead Park), B Oughtred (Hartlepool Rvs); H Alexander (Birkenhead Park, Captain), *D D Dobson (Newton Abbot), *L R Tosswill (Exeter), *S G Williams (Devonport Albion), *T J Willcocks (Plymouth), *J Jewitt (Hartlepool Rvs), *G Fraser (Richmond), J J Robinson (Headingley). (* England Debut)

Referee: Rupert W Jeffares (Ireland).

A crowd of around 15,000 spectators watched Wales defeat England at the Rectory Field, Blackheath. Wales, who had lost on all the four previous occasions when they played England at the famous Blackheath ground, eventually recorded their first victory on the celebrated enclosure. In the previous eighteen meetings between the two countries Wales had

Wales Team v England 1902

Back Row: *J Strand-Jones (Llanelly), *N Walters (Llanelly), *A F Harding (Cardiff), A Brice (Aberavon), J S Jones WFU (Touch-judge), *D Jones (Treherbert), *W T Osborne (Mountain Ash), *W Joseph (Swansea).
Middle Row: J J Hodges (Newport), G Boots (Newport), E G Nicholls (Cardiff, Captain), R T Gabe (Llanelly), W M Llewellyn (London Welsh).
Front Row: R M Owen (Swansea), *E Morgan (Guy's Hospital and London Welsh), R H Jones (Swansea). (* Wales Debut)

only managed to win on six occasions and only two of those victories away from home. Wales started really well and ten minutes into the game Rhys Gabe scored a great try. The movement started when Strand-Jones, receiving a kick in his own half, ran round the English forwards and beating them all got a pass away to Rhys Gabe in the English twenty-five. The Llanelly man, running well, fairly beat Gamlin and scored a magnificent try. Strand-Jones missed the conversion but Wales were in the lead by 3 points to nil. Wales continued to attack but England rallied and after some clever play Denys Dobson scored under the posts and Alexander kicked the conversion. Despite some fine play by Wales, England continued to attack and some accurate kicking often put Wales on the defensive.

The English forwards were now playing well and within ten yards of the Welsh line John Robinson picked up and forced his way over the line for a try. Arthur Harding charged down the conversion but the referee allowed it to be retaken without a charge. Nevertheless, the kick went wide but England were ahead at the interval by 8 points to three.

England started the second half where they had left off in the first and were continually on the attack but they failed to make the most of their opportunities. Some fine play by the Welsh three-quarters took play well into the English half and after the Welsh forwards had the better of the argument from a scrummage Will Osborne crossed for a try which Strand-Jones failed to convert from a difficult angle. Still two points behind Wales did everything in their power to secure a score but time after time they were denied, the English defence stood firm. Time was running out and Wales, making a final effort, took the ball to the English line, where a knock on at the last moment, robbed them of a try. However, a moment later, Dickie Owen lured Bernard Oughtred offside and John Strand-Jones drop kicked a magnificent penalty to give Wales the narrowest of leads. The final minutes of the game were tremendously exciting with both sides having opportunities to score. On one occasion Willie Llewellyn was over the line but was tackled before he could ground the ball. Wales were determined not to lose the advantage and with the crowd singing 'Hen Wlad fy Nhadau' and 'Sospan Fach' the final whistle blew and Wales were victorious by 9 points to eight.

The report of the game in the *Evening Express* paid tribute to Rhys Gabe when it said, 'after all the anxieties concerning our left wing, R T Gabe was the hero of the Welsh three-quarter line. In attack and defence he was magnificent and shared with Taylor the honours of the day. Nicholls was too closely watched in his aggressive work to be as effective as he usually is, but his defence was sound as a bell. Willie Llewellyn had two chances of beating Gamlin but was tackled each time. Just a little swerve would have done it but Gamlin collared grandly. Otherwise Llewellyn's play was very fine. Teddy Morgan, on the other wing, was too hard pressed every time he received the ball to display his powers to the fullest extent.' Wales, to a man, had fought hard for the victory and although England played well it was the superior play of Dickie Owen and Dick Jones at half back which gave Wales the edge.

With regard to the forwards the report continued, 'there are men on the Welsh side who are entitled to special recognition. Brice, Hodges and Harding stood out as a great triumvirate in the Welsh pack, their play being consistently brilliant throughout the game. There were no shirkers in the pack and the least that can be said of every one of the eight is that he played a hard and honest game.'

This was Nathanial 'Danny' Walters only cap for Wales and he was one of only two changes in the Welsh team to play against Scotland in the next international. Danny Walters was replaced by Harry Jones of Penygraig. Walters continued to play rugby for Llanelly long after his international career was over and he captained them during the 1901–02, 1902–03 and 1906–07 seasons. The only other change in the team to face Scotland was George Llewellyn Lloyd of Newport returning to the Welsh team in place of Dick Jones. After only two internationals Dick Jones would have to wait another two seasons before returning to the Welsh team.

Of the seven new caps in the Welsh side four would go on to be immortalised as members of the Welsh team that defeated New Zealand in 1905; Teddy Morgan, Will Joseph, Arthur Harding and Dai 'Tarw' Jones, all of whom had their first Welsh caps in the 1902 international against England. Nine of that famous 1905 team were now Welsh internationals: Gwyn Nicholls, Willie Llewellyn, Rhys Gabe, Teddy Morgan, Dickie Owen, Will Joseph, Jehoida Hodges, Dai 'Tarw' Jones and Arthur Harding.

The result was vindication for the selectors because when the team was announced there

Teddy Morgan — Courtesy of Frederic Humbert

Will Joseph — Courtesy of Swansea RFC

Arthur Harding — Courtesy of Christ College, Brecon

Dai 'Tarw' Jones — Courtesy of the Welsh Rugby Union

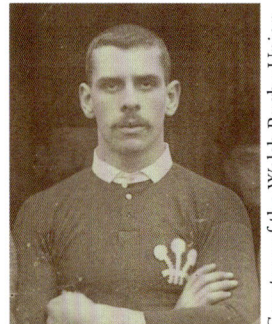

was great disappointment that George Davies, the Swansea centre three-quarter, had been replaced by Rhys Gabe and the general feeling was that the selection committee had made a mistake. There was also regret that Billy Bancroft was no longer considered for international honours. Nevertheless, John Strand-Jones had an excellent game at full-back, playing well throughout the game and being very instrumental in the Rhys Gabe try. As previously mention, Rhys Gabe had a brilliant game and the Swansea half-backs of Dickie Owen and Dick Jones outplayed their opponents all the way through the match. After this sensational victory Wales could look forward with a great deal of optimism to their next encounter against Scotland.

With Willie Llewellyn still home from College he took the opportunity to play for his old club, Llwynypia, in their game against Ebbw Vale the Saturday following the international. He was once again on form and scored a try in the 8 points to six victory. It was reported in the *Evening Express* that Willie would also play in Llwynypia's next game against Mountain Ash, but this was not the case and with the game against Scotland the following week Willie withdrew from the team.

On the same weekend London Welsh, without the assistance of Willie Llewellyn and Rhys Gabe, were victors in their game against St Mary's Hospital. Playing with six reserves the Welsh pressed from the outset and were eventual winners by 11 points to nine.

The previous Thursday the Welsh Football Union had announced the Welsh team that had been selected to play against Scotland at Cardiff Arms Park on Saturday 1st February. There were two changes from the team that had played so well against England. There was no real surprise that Harry Jones of Penygraig had replaced Danny Walters of Llanelly. Although a fine forward, Walters was considered to be quite light and the bigger and stronger Harry Jones was preferred to face the big Scottish forwards. The second change in the team was a complete surprise with Newport's George Llewellyn Lloyd replacing Swansea's Dick Jones at outside half. This was a shock selection and although Lloyd was an accomplished outside half with seven Welsh caps to his name he had never played alongside Dickie Owen. Dick Jones must have been bitterly disappointed particularly having played such a key role in the defeat of England. The reporter of *The Cambrian* was incensed and wrote the following with regard to the selection of Lloyd over Dick Jones: 'I scarcely know what to say of the other change. I suppose we must regard it as yet another instance of the idiosyncrasies of the "powers that be." Yet one would have thought the gentlemen who form the Selection Committee would have had sufficient intelligence to see that it is taking too much risk to play two halves who have never turned out together, especially in the light of what was witnessed at Blackheath a few weeks ago. The wisdom of playing two club-mates, who of necessity, know each other's programme, was on that occasion proved beyond a shadow of a doubt and yet the committee deem it wise to upset so effective a combination! Well I am afraid they'll regret it and that bitterly. As I never placed much faith in the abilities of the Union members as a whole, I am not at all surprised at their continuing to ignore Bancroft and Dan Rees.' This reporter was not the only one who thought that the Welsh team would struggle against the current Home Nations champions; there were several newspaper reports that gave Wales little chance of winning.

The team selected was as follows: Back, John Strand-Jones; three-quarters, Gwyn Nicholls, Rhys Gabe, Willie Llewellyn and Teddy Morgan; half-backs Dickie Owen and G Ll Lloyd; forwards, Alfred Brice, George Boots, Jehoida Hodges, Will Joseph, Dai Jones, Will Osborne, Arthur Harding and Harry Jones. Bert Winfield was again reserve full-back with Dan Rees, Cliff Pritchard and Cecil Biggs reserve three-quarters. Dick Jones and Tom Samuel were the reserve half-backs. The reserve forwards were George Travers, Stacey and E Thomas.

A few days before the international against Scotland rumours were circulating that Will Osborne of Mountain Ash had signed professional papers for Northern Union club Hull. It was also rumoured that J Aikman Smith, secretary of the Scottish Union, had, or was about to notify the Welsh Football Union that the Scottish team would not play against Will Osborne. The Welsh Football Union interviewed Will Osborne with regard to him signing Northern Union forms, a claim that Will Osborne emphatically denied. Osborne confirmed that Fred Miller, the old Mountain Ash and Welsh international, had approached him and offered him a substantial amount of money to sign for the Hull club. The offer amounted to a down payment of £50 with a promise of a remunerative job. Osborne confirmed that he had firmly declined the offer and that he had told Fred Miller that no inducement could tempt him to go North. All the members of the Welsh Football that had interviewed Will Osborne at the Queen's Hotel, Cardiff were satisfied that Osborne 'had not committed himself to professionalism' and unless there was proof that he had done so he would still represent Wales in the match against Scotland the following Saturday. No proof was forthcoming and Will Osborne duly took his place in the Welsh team as selected.

In July 1903 it was reported that Mountain Ash had suffered a severe blow when three of their players were tempted to travel North to play for various Northern Union clubs. Wing three-quarter Reuben Carpenter, previously of Newport, joined Oldham, full-back Tom Walton joined Huddersfield and after gaining six Welsh caps, Will Osborne also joined Huddersfield. Will Osborne made his debut for Huddersfield Northern Union Club on 5th September 1903 after moving from South Wales where he had worked as a collier and a police officer. He transferred to Hull Northern Union Club in October 1906.

On the Wednesday afternoon before the international against Scotland the Welsh team had a practise game at Cardiff Arms Park. Their opposition was made up of Cardiff Collegians and members of the Hayes club. All the Welsh players were present with the exception of John Strand-Jones, Rhys Gabe, Teddy Morgan and Dai Jones. Attention was mainly given to scrummaging in order that George Llewellyn Lloyd and Dickie Owen could get to know each other's play at the base of the scrum. The forwards also had line-out practise, while Gwyn Nicholls and Willie Llewellyn were kept moving as often as possible on the right wing. All that was now needed was for the ground to be protected from the frost and everything was in place for the eighteenth encounter between Wales and Scotland.

Scotland: A W Duncan; W H Welsh, A B Timms (Edinburgh U), P Turnbull (Edinburgh Acads), A N Fell; F H Fasson (Edinburgh U), J I Gillespie (Edinburgh Acads); M C Morrison (Royal HSFP, Captain), *J V Bedell-Sivright, D R Bedell-Sivright (Cambridge U), J R C Greenlees (Kelvinside Acads), J Ross (London Scottish), J A Bell (Clydesdale), A B Flett (Edinburgh U), *W E Kyle (Hawick). (* Scotland Debut)

Referee: P B Gilliard (England).

There were certainly doubts whether the game against Scotland would go ahead because a heavy frost for several days before the game had

Wales Team v Scotland 1902

Back Row: Sir John Llewellyn Bart, A F Harding, W T Osborne, *H Jones, D Jones, A Brice, W Joseph, P B Gilliard (Referee). *Middle Row*: W M Llewellyn, J G Boots, E G Nicholls (Captain), J J Hodges, E Morgan, A J Davies, WFU (Touch-judge). *Front Row*: R T Gabe, R M Owen, J Strand-Jones, G Ll Lloyd. (* Wales Debut)

affected the ground to such an extent that it was decided to cover the hardest parts of the ground with straw in order to protect it from the frost. The thick layer of straw did its job and by eleven o'clock on the day of the match the ground was in perfect condition.

The *Evening Express* reported that 'A departure was made from the orthodox football programme by the introduction of the Welsh marseillaise 'Sospan Fach' with the stipulation that the chorus should be sung upon the entry of the Welsh team. There was also the Scottish evergreen "Auld Lang Syne" and just half a verse of "Hen Wlad fy Nhadau," which for the first time in the history of Welsh national music had to play second fiddle to the "Sospan".' As it turned out Auld Lang Syne was sung as the Scotsmen took the field and a minute later the Welshmen followed to the tune of Hen Wlad fy Nhadau. Having won the toss, Gwyn Nicholls elected to play with the wind, towards the river end.

At precisely three o'clock George Boots kicked off for Wales. Play was

Menu card for the complimentary dinner held at the Queen's Hotel, Cardiff after the international between Wales and Scotland 1902.

very fast from the beginning and within five minutes of the start, with the ball moving right along the Welsh three-quarter line, Willie Llewellyn scored a try for Wales. Alfred Brice failed to convert from a difficult angle. Wales were often on the attack and on several occasions were stopped just short of the Scottish line. Eventually, from a scrummage, Dickie Owen got the ball away to George Llewellyn Lloyd and with one of his brilliant burst he got straight through the Scottish backs. Getting close to the Scottish line he passed to Willie Llewellyn at just the right moment and Willie crossed in the corner for his second try of the match. Again the kick at goal was unsuccessful but Wales were ahead by six points to nil. The Welsh forwards were on the top of their game and the ball continually came out of the scrummage on the Welsh side. Although the Scottish half-backs tried all they could to stop Dickie Owen, time after time he managed to successfully get the ball away to Llewellyn Lloyd. Following a scrummage ten yards from the Scottish line, Lloyd, receiving from Dickie Owens, passed to Gwyn Nicholls, who ran beautifully and provided the perfect pass for Rhys Gabe who crossed for a brilliant try. John Strand-Jones made a good attempt at the conversion but the ball fell a couple of feet short of the cross-bar.

The Welsh forwards were having things all their own way and continually won possession from the scrums. Scotland were again under pressure and Duncan was forced to minor after Gwyn Nicholls had kicked ahead. From the kick-out, Arthur Harding, picking up in a loose scramble, kicked over Duncan's head and Teddy Morgan, gathering the ball, beat Fell and, running up to Duncan, passed to Rhys Gabe who crossed for another brilliant try. This time Strand-Jones made no mistake with the conversion and Wales were ahead by 14 points to nil. Just before the interval Gillespie and Fasson got the ball away beautifully and following some brilliant passing Willie Welsh crossed for a magnificent try which John Gillespie converted. Immediately afterwards half-time was called with Wales leading by 14 points to five.

All the scoring was done in the first half and the second half was a great battle with each side striving for superiority. The Welsh three-quarters probably had the better of things but were unable to cross the Scottish line. Just before the end of the game Willie Llewellyn was injured and left the field for a short while. He did, however, return but was limping badly. Immediately after his return Wales made a final effort to add to their formidable score but this was not to be, nevertheless, they were worthy winners by 14 points to five. The two tries scored by Willie Llewellyn brought his international total number of tries to nine. However, there was a heavy price to pay. The injury he sustained in the last minutes of the game was serious enough to keep him out of the game for four weeks. He missed the London Welsh games against Oxford University and Berkshire Wanderers and the Glamorgan game against Somerset.

As was to be expected when the Welsh Football Union met to select the team to face Ireland at Lansdowne Road, Dublin on 8th March they named an unchanged side. With the possibility of a third Triple Crown at stake the selection committee stayed faithful to the side that had beaten Scotland so convincingly a few weeks earlier. Bert Winfield was again reserve full-back with Cecil Biggs and Dan Rees reserve three-quarters with Dick Jones reserve half-back. The reserve forwards were George Travers, Stacey and Edwin 'Beddoe' Thomas.

The injury Willie Llewellyn sustained in the closing moments of the game against Scotland was still a concern and several newspaper reports stated that he was unlikely to be fit enough to play against Ireland. As late as 24th February the *Evening Express* reported, 'We learn from London that there exists some doubt as to whether Willie Llewellyn will be able to play against Ireland. Llewellyn is suffering from an injured knee and is being treated by a London specialist. If he should be unable to play Cecil Biggs will get his cap.' The following day another report in the *Evening Express* stated that Willie Llewellyn had informed Walter Rees, the secretary of the Welsh Football Union, that he was unable to play because of the knee injury. However, the report went on to say that 'Willie Llewellyn's brother received a letter from him stating that he was perfectly fit and never looked forward to playing any match with greater pleasure.' The report continued: 'This is good news, as the London Welsh captain's services are too valuable to be lost to the Welsh team and that his many friends will be glad to know that his injured knee has ceased to give him any serious trouble.' Having missed two games for London Welsh and one for Glamorgan because of injury, a week before the international Willie was selected to play for London Welsh in their away game against Northampton. A crowd of over 4,000 watched Willie prove his fitness despite London Welsh losing narrowly by 5 points to three.

With no injury worries Willie Llewellyn was able to take his place in the Welsh team to face Ireland and win his twelfth international cap. This was unfortunate for Cecil Biggs, brother of Welsh internationals Norman and Selwyn Biggs, although he had played for the Barbarians in 1899 and captained Cardiff during the 1904–05, Cecil never gained his Welsh international cap. He was regarded as one of the greatest uncapped Welsh players. With Willie once again fit the Welsh team that faced Ireland was as selected. The Ireland team was also as selected. Of the sixteen matches played between the two countries since 1882, Wales had won nine and Ireland six with the 1890 game at Dublin drawn at three points all. There was a great deal of excitement with regard to the game and the outcome was by no means a foregone conclusion. Wales had beaten England by just one point at Blackheath and then convincingly beaten Scotland at Cardiff. Ireland on the other hand had narrowly lost to England at Leicester by 6 points to three and then defeated Scotland, the reigning Home Nations champions, at Belfast by 5 points to nil. Several days before the game all the seating accommodation had been booked and on the day of the game every available space was taken. By the time the game started there were 12,000 spectators eagerly awaiting the outcome of the match.

Ireland: J Fulton (NIFC); G P Doran, B R Doran (Lansdowne), J B Allison (QCB), I G Davidson (NIFC); A M Magee (Bective, Captain), H H Corley (Wanderers); F Gardiner (NIFC), J J Coffey (Lansdowne), A Tedford (Malone), S T Irwin (QCB), T A Harvey (Dublin U), P Healey (Limerick), J C Pringle (RIEC/NIFC), G T Hamlet (Old Wesley).

Referee: J Crawford Findlay (Scotland).

Wales Team v Ireland 1902

Back Row: Ack Llewellyn WFU (Touch-judge), A F Harding, J Strand-Jones, H Jones, W T Osborne, D Jones, W Joseph, W M Llewellyn, Walter E Rees (WFU).
Middle Row: A B Brice, J G Boots, E G Nicholls (Captain), J J Hodges, R T Gabe.
Front Row: G Ll Lloyd, R M Owen, E Morgan.

The weather in Dublin during the week of the match had been fine and the ground was in perfect condition but on the day of the game the weather was not ideal with a strong wind and slight rain. Gwyn Nicholls lost the toss and Ireland decided to play with the wind at their backs. In the first half the Irish forwards were having the better of play but the Welsh backs outplayed their opponents. Despite having the wind advantage Ireland were unable to score and the interval arrived with neither side registering a point.

The second half was a different matter altogether. With Ireland under pressure they were penalised and Strand-Jones narrowly missed a drop at goal. Wales began to assert themselves and when Llewellyn Lloyd made an opening for Gwyn Nicholls, the Welsh captain promptly dropped a goal with his left foot. Shortly afterwards Wales were on the attack again and a fine pass from Dickie Owen put Willie Llewellyn over in the corner. Strand-Jones failed with the conversion but the next score wasn't far away. From a scrummage near the Irish line, Dickie Owen handed the ball to Llewellyn Lloyd who dived over for a clever try which Alfred Brice converted from a difficult angle. Wales were now fully in control and their third Triple Crown was secure. Wales continued to attack vigorously and five minutes from the end Gwyn Nicholls raced in at the right-hand corner for a try which Brice failed to convert. Shortly afterwards the final whistle went and Wales were victorious by 15 points to nil.

With regard to the Welsh performance *The Sportsman* made the following comments on the Welsh players: 'Not a little of the credit of the victory is due to the captain, who, in addition to displaying masterly generalship, played a grand game. Llewellyn, on the right wing, made good use of the opportunities afforded him of showing his great turn of speed and Morgan also did finely. A better exposition than that given by Strand-Jones at full-back has not been seen in Ireland for a long time and truly Bancroft's mantle has fallen on worthy shoulders. The half-backs both proved very clever. Owen, if anything, proving the superior and though their vis-à-vis, Magee and Corley, were not by any means outclassed, the Welsh pair were slightly ahead of them. Nothing but praise can be written of the forwards, who often proved as good as the opposing eight in the loose and if they were beaten in the first half, they fairly wore down the Irish pack towards the end. Brice, Hodges, H Jones and Harding were perhaps the pick.' Praise indeed and for the fourth time Wales had secured the Home Nations Championship and won their third Triple Crown. Although Wales won the Home Nations Championship outright in 1893, 1900 and 1902 they shared the 1888 championship with Ireland and Scotland with each team winning one game apiece. England were excluded from the 1888 competition because of their refusal to join the International Rugby Football Board.

On the day Willie was playing for Wales against Ireland, London Welsh were defeated by the Welsh Wanderers. London Welsh had fielded a very weak team and the report in the *Evening Express* stated that 'the Welsh Wanderers played with eighteen men.' The report also said, 'The whole of the back division of the London Welsh reserves played for the Wanderers.'

Willie played in all five remaining games of the season for London

Welsh. They lost their away game to Catford Bridge playing most of the game with effectively six forwards. Within five minutes of the start one of the Welsh forwards was kicked in the thigh and was 'absolutely useless' for the remainder of the game. Before the interval another Welsh forward injured his collar-bone and retired from the game. The report in the *Evening Express* stated, 'The six forwards played up pluckily and time after time beat the opposing eight. Gabe, Strand-Jones, Llewellyn, Evans, Wallace Watts and J F Williams all being held up within a yard of the line time after time.' The most amazing thing in the whole match was a dropped penalty goal from near the touch-line between the Welsh twenty-five and half-way by W G Hodge. After some brilliant passing, Evans scored a try between the posts but the kick was charged down. In the last five minutes of the game Catford scored two dubious tries, one at least of which should never have be allowed by the referee, even the spectators laughed. Nevertheless, awarded they were and with one of the tries converted London Welsh were defeated by 8 points to six.

Willie added to his try tally in the next game against Upper Clapton. There was no score in the first half but Rhys Gabe, Willie Llewellyn and Evans all scored unconverted tries in the second half to give the Welsh victory by 9 points to nil.

London Welsh brought their 1901–02 season to a close with an Easter tour to Gloucester and Wales. They lost against Gloucester by 14 points to three but won their next match against Mountain Ash. The Gloucester half-backs of Hall and Goddard assisted the Welsh in their first victory in Wales for quite some time. Within five minutes of the start Hall got the ball out to Goddard, who ran through and passed to E D Evans. Running smartly on the greasy ground, Evans put Willie Llewellyn in for a magnificent try. Teddy Morgan failed to convert. Mountain Ash replied with an unconverted try by O'Neill and the scores were level. Another unconverted try shortly afterwards by Windham Jones gave Mountain Ash the lead. Before the interval W J Evans ran to the line and unselfishly passed to Willie Llewellyn who crossed for his second try of the afternoon. The conversion failed and at half-time the scores were equal at 6 points all.

For quite a while in the second half Mountain Ash had the better of the game but the London Welsh defence was too good and prevented any scoring by the home team. At one point Willie Llewellyn got away and only fine tackling prevented an almost certain try. Mountain Ash also had their chances but missed two penalty kicks at goal. After quite some time London Welsh were awarded a penalty and Teddy Morgan kicked the goal that gave London Welsh a well-deserved victory by 9 points to six.

Willie Llewellyn captained London Welsh in their final game of the season against Aberavon. London Welsh had a strong team with Rhys Gabe the only absentee. From the outset Aberavon were the stronger team and only sound defence by the Welsh prevented further tries being scored. The report of the game in the *Western Mail* read as follows: 'At Aberavon. Harris dropped two goals and James scored a try. An immense crowd witnessed an interesting and pleasant game. The homesters were superior to the visitors all round. The visitors were smart in the loose rushes and the defence was very sound.' The final score was Aberavon 11 points, London Welsh nil. This game brought the London Welsh season to a close. They had played 22 games, won 10, lost 10 and drawn two. They scored 201 points for with 153 against. Willie played in seventeen games and scored ten tries.

Willie's last game of the season was on Easter Tuesday for Newport against Rockcliff. This was his fourth game in five days and he took the place of Cliff Pritchard who stood down with an injured knee. Wallace Watts also played for Newport, taking the place of A G Brown. Newport were too good for the visitors and won by 27 points to nil. Gwyn Nicholls was in fine form and scored a try and dropped a goal. Although selected for Newport's next game against Leicester, Willie stood down because he had a bad cold. He was no better four days later when he also stood down from the Glamorgan match against Devon. With no further mention in any of the match reports for Newport or Llwynypia it is safe to say that Willie Llewellyn's season came to an end with the game for Newport against Rockcliff.

Willie had played twenty-seven games during the season and scored eighteen tries. He played club rugby for Llwynypia, Newport and London Welsh, county rugby for Glamorgan and in addition to the Welsh trial match at Treherbert he played in all three internationals. Along with Gwyn Nicholls, Rhys Gabe, Dickie Owen and Jehoida Hodges he had become a permanent member of a successful Welsh team. Another four members of the Welsh team that defeated New Zealand in 1905 had also progressed to the international ranks. Teddy Morgan, Will Joseph, Dai 'Tarw' Jones and Arthur Harding all gained their first Welsh caps in the first international of the season against England and all retained their places for the games against Scotland and Ireland. Bert Winfield of Cardiff, George Travers of Pill Harriers and Cliff Pritchard of Newport had all played in the final Welsh trial match with Winfield and Travers selected as Welsh reserves for all three internationals. Cliff Pritchard was a reserve three-quarter for the England and Scotland games but injury prevented his selection as reserve for the game against Ireland. Bert Winfield and George Travers were capped the following season but Cliff Pritchard would have to wait until the 1904 game against Scotland before he gained his first Welsh cap.

Of the remaining six members of the 1905 Welsh team who played against New Zealand only Percy Bush had been selected to play in the final Welsh trial match. Although he had played in the preliminary trial match at Cardiff he was unable to play in the final trial match at Treherbert because of the ankle injury he sustained playing for Cardiff against Newport in November. Subsequently he was not considered as a reserve for any of the international matches. The injury effectively kept him out of the game for the remainder of the season.

Of the remaining two players Charlie Prichard had made his first team debut for Newport in their victory over Swansea in January 1902 and was a regular member of the Newport first team for the remainder of the season. He played in all ten remaining games of the season, during which time Newport only lost one game; the home game against Cardiff. Charlie Pritchard played in the Newport game against Rockcliffe which was Willie Llewellyn's last game of the season. This was the first time Willie and Charlie had played alongside each other but they would become teammates for both Newport and Wales over the next few seasons. John 'Scethrog' Williams, also referred to as Jack Williams, was a regular member of the London Welsh team and although not yet playing representative rugby, the youngest member of the 1905 Welsh team, he would eventually play for the Barbarians, Glamorgan, Middlesex and international rugby for Wales.

An article in the *Athletic News* on Monday 28th April 1902 made reference to the influence Public Schools in Wales were having on the rugby game in

Wales, a fact, 'not duly appreciated by the average enthusiast, or even those in higher circles.' Christ College, Brecon was strongly represented during the 1902 international season. Arthur Harding and Teddy Morgan joined Willie Llewellyn in the Welsh team for the first international of the year against England. The Old Boys were not forgotten by their College, in fact they were celebrated and *The Breconian* of April 1902 in a report of the Old Breconians annual dinner of December 1901 said the following: 'The evening opened auspiciously, for just before dinner Mr. Morton received a telegram stating that three O.B.'s, viz: W. M. Llewellyn, E. Morgan, and A. F. Harding had been selected to play for Wales against England on January 11th at Blackheath. This welcome news was enthusiastically received and gave an additional zest to the proceedings.' Mr Morton must

Date	Team Played For	Opposition	Venue	Result	W Llewellyn Tries
Willie Llewellyn London Welsh Games Played 1901-1902 Season					
Willie Llewellyn Welsh International and Welsh Trial Games Played 1901-1902 Season					
Willie Llewellyn Glamorgan and Surrey County Games Played 1901-1902 Season					
Willie Llewellyn Newport Games Played 1901-1902 Season					
Willie Llewellyn Llwynypia Games Played 1901-1902 Season					
28/09/1901	London Welsh	Newport	Rodney Parade	Lost 0-19	0
30/09/1901	London Welsh	Devonport Albion	Home	Drawn 5-5	0
05/10/1901	London Welsh	Streatham	Away	Lost 3-10	0
12/10/1901	London Welsh	Saracens	Away	Won 8-6	0
19/10/1901	Glamorgan	Yorkshire	Castleford	Lost 6-10	0
19/10/1901	London Welsh	Berkshire Wanderers	Away	Won 11-10	Did not play
26/10/1901	London Welsh	Sutton	Home	Won 3-0	Unknown
02/11/1901	London Welsh	Civil Service	Home	Won 3-0	1
09/11/1901	London Welsh	Park House	Home	Won 60-0	5
18/11/1901	London Welsh	Swansea	Home	Lost 0-8	0
23/11/1901	London Welsh	London Irish	Away	Won 12-5	0
30/11/1901	London Welsh	Streatham	Home	Drawn 6-6	1
07/12/1901	Welsh Trial - Probables	Possibles	Treherbert	Won 5-3	1
14/12/1901	London Welsh	R.I.E.C.	Away	Lost 0-6	0
26/12/1901	Newport	Watsonians	Rodney Parade	Won 9-5	1
27/12/1901	Newport	Moseley	Rodney Parade	Won 12-0	2
28/12/1901	Newport	Barbarians	Rodney Parade	Won 4-0	0
11/01/1902	Wales	England	Blackheath	Won 9-8	0
18/01/1902	Llwynypia	Ebbw Vale	Home	Won 8-6	1
25/01/1902	London Welsh	St Mary's Hospital	Home	Won 11-9	Did not play
01/02/1902	Wales	Scotland	Cardiff Arms Park	Won 14-5	2
05/02/1902	London Welsh	Oxford University	Away	Lost 0-3	Did not play
22/02/1902	London Welsh	Berkshire Wanderers	Home	Won 36-4	Did not play
01/03/1902	London Welsh	Northampton	Northampton	Lost 3-5	0
08/03/1902	Wales	Ireland	Lansdowne Road	Won 15-0	1
08/03/1902	London Welsh	Welsh Wanderers	Home	Lost 13-18	Did not play
15/03/1902	London Welsh	Catford Bridge	Away	Lost 6-8	0
22/03/1902	London Welsh	Upper Clapton	Away	Won 9-0	1
28/03/1902	London Welsh	Gloucester	Away - Easter Tour	Lost 3-14	0
29/03/1902	London Welsh	Mountain Ash	Away - Easter Tour	Won 9-6	2
31/03/1902	London Welsh	Aberavon	Away - Easter Tour	Lost 0-11	0
01/04/1902	Newport	Rockcliff	Home	Won 27-0	0
Totals	Willie Llewellyn Games Played				W Llewellyn Tries
	27				18

Willie Llewellyn Rugby Games Played and Results 1901–1902 Season

Christ College Old Boys Willie Llewellyn, Arthur Harding and Teddy Morgan.

have been especially proud as all three boys were members of his House while at Christ College. Later in the document *The Breconian* commented, 'We offer our congratulations to W. M. Llewellyn, A. F. Harding, and 'Teddie' Morgan on their being chosen to represent Wales in all three International Rugby football matches this season, and especially on their three brilliant wins. *Palmam qui (Let he who merits).*'

Other Public School Old Boys who played for Wales during the 1901–02 season were John Strand-Jones of St David's College Lampeter and George Llewellyn Lloyd who attended The Leys School, Cambridge.

The same article in the *Athletic News* did not forget the contribution made by Llandovery College and remarked, 'The list of Llandovery boys is a much longer one and space will only allow the mention of a few. W H 'Willie' Thomas of Cambridge and Welsh international fame, gained his first cap while playing for his school, a unique occurrence in the history of the Welsh game. Conway Rees, who captained the Oxford team and represented Wales on three occasions, is a Llandoverian; while C B Nicholls, who rivals W H Thomas for the best forward ever turned out of Wales, learnt all his football at the same school. Teddy Bishop, who played for Swansea and gained his cap against Scotland in 1889 and D W Nicholls, who appeared against Ireland in 1894 are others, but the most distinguished athlete connected to the school is C P Lewis, who figured in the second Welsh international team and whose connection with 'Varsity' football and cricket can yet be remembered.'

Public School Old Boys had certainly made a massive contribution to Welsh rugby at that time. This was very much mirrored at London Welsh where so many Breconians and Llandoverians now played. No fewer than seven Christ College Old Boys played for London Welsh during the 1901–02 season. This heritage would continue into the 1902–03 season when the Wales and Cardiff forward Arthur Harding joined the club.

London Welsh Rugby Football Club 1902–03 Season
Willie was again selected as captain of London Welsh for the 1902–03 season, with Arthur Flowers 'Boxer' Harding as his vice-captain. London Welsh played 29 games during the season winning 8, losing 19 with 2 drawn games. They scored 156 points for with 325 against. With regard to this season Paul Beken and Stephen Jones, in their book *Dragon in Exile, The Centenary History of London Welsh RFC* made the following comment: 'The arrival of the powerful Cardiff and Wales forward, Arthur Harding, at the start of the 1902–03 season was another major boost. He was immediately appointed vice-captain to Willie Llewellyn and became one of the most influential forwards in the club's history. In fact, Harding's first season did not produce an upturn in results. Although the overall record of eight wins and two draws from 29 games may be disappointing from a side bristling with such talent, great difficulties were experienced in fielding anything like a settled combination. Because of frequent representative calls and a heavy injury list, 74 players were called into the first team; 40 of them in only one or two fixtures.' This was not a good season as far as Willie was concerned. He was injured playing for Newport against Edinburgh University on Christmas Eve 1902 and didn't play again until he played for Glamorgan against Somerset at the end of February 1903. In total he only played 13 games for London Welsh during the season, missing eleven games through injury and another three because of representative duties. Willie was unavailable for the game against Upper Clapton in December 1902 and missed the game against Rosslyn Park because he was playing for Newport against Blackheath. During his long

absence because of injury, he also missed the two internationals against England and Scotland and the Glamorgan game against Cornwall.

London Welsh now had an enviable fixture list and attracted enormous crowds. In addition to playing most of the leading English clubs during the 1902–03 season they also had home and away fixtures with Llanelly, Swansea and Mountain Ash and single fixtures with Newport, Cardiff and Aberavon. The opening game of the season was the home fixture against Newport. The *Evening Express* reported, 'At Queen's Club, West Kensington, the London Welsh were at home to Newport. The latter were hardly at full strength.' In their report of the game *The Sportsman* elaborated a little more on the matter of the Newport team when they commented, 'The visitors were by no means at full strength, having half a dozen of their regular players away, three being under suspension and the remainder ill.'

The interesting comment was 'three being under suspension.' Early in September a touring team known as the Welsh Barbarians had played two games in the North of England against West Hartlepool and Castleford. The arrangement of the fixtures was a total disregard of a resolution passed by the Welsh Football Union prohibiting such tours, the Union believing that any player taking part in such outings would receive a monetary benefit and therefore contravene their amateur status. At a meeting of the general committee of the Welsh Football Union on Wednesday 17th September all the players included in the Welsh Barbarians were suspended for a fortnight. This included Dickie Owen, Dick Jones, Fred Scrine, Dan Rees and Frank Gordon of Swansea, David Boots, Reuben Carpenter, Jehoida Hodges, Cliff Pritchard, C Jenkins and Trevor Beard of Newport and Williams, Gunter and Hill of Pontymister. Effectively the suspension really meant a one week ban as the season did not really start in earnest until Saturday 27th September.

With regard to the tour, in front of a crowd of about 5,000 spectators the Welsh Barbarians won their first game against West Hartlepool by 8 points to six. Reuben Carpenter scored a try which Hill converted and Dan Rees scored an unconverted try. West Hartlepool scored an unconverted try and kicked a penalty. In the second game the Welsh Barbarians were again victorious when they defeated Castleford by 19 points to eight. Tries were scored by Trevor Beard, Dan Rees, Cliff Pritchard, Reuben

Carpenter and Jehoida Hodges. Carpenter converted his own try and that of Hodges. Castleford's reply was a converted try and a penalty goal.

Returning to the London Welsh game against Newport, despite having so many players absent, Newport still fielded a strong side which included Welsh internationals Tom Pearson, George Llewellyn Lloyd and George Boots. Also in the Newport side were future internationals Jack Jenkins, Harry Uzzell and J E C 'Birdie' Partridge. While Jack Jenkins only had one Welsh cap against South Africa in 1906, Harry Uzzell gained fifteen Welsh caps between 1912 and 1920. Joseph Edward Crawshay 'Birdie' Partridge was a Welsh born British army officer and international rugby union player who was capped for South Africa in the first test against the 1903 British Lions. He was also a member of the Barbarians in that side's first international, played against Wales in 1915. London Welsh were by no means the rookies in comparison to their experienced Welsh rivals and despite not having played together for any amount of time they

London Welsh v Newport – September 1902

Courtesy of The Tatler

Back Row: Dr Pryce Jenkins (Linesman), A F Harding, M T Williams, J F Williams, W C Roberts, W G Hodge, W S Hughes, W Ll Davies (Honorary Secretary). *Middle Row*: F H Clay, W J Evans, W H Watts, Willie Llewellyn (Captain), E D Evans, R T Gabe, E Morgan. *Front Row*: H T Maddock and R Russell.

nevertheless were a talented group of players. In addition to old Welsh international Wallace Watts the London Welsh side included current Welsh internationals Willie Llewellyn, Rhys Gabe, Teddy Morgan and Arthur Harding. Also in the side were Christ College Old Boys and future Welsh internationals Hop Maddock and J F 'Jack' Williams.

In glorious weather, a crowd of 3,000 spectators watched the opening game of the season at the Queen's club. Despite the game being evenly contested in the early stages the superiority of the Newport halves paid dividends before the interval. An unconverted try by 'Birdie' Partridge gave Newport the lead but London Welsh were not downhearted and a spectacular run by Evans and Llewellyn almost ended in a score. The London Welsh forwards were playing strongly and took play right up to the Newport line but the visitors managed to relieve and forced play back to the centre where neither side were able to take complete control. The Newport half-backs of Jack Hillman and Llewellyn Lloyd were too good for the London Welsh pair of Evans and Russell and just before the break Llewellyn Lloyd crossed for a try which he converted himself. At the interval Newport were ahead by 8 points to nil.

A clever tackle by London Welsh captain Willie Llewellyn.

Courtesy of The Tatler

With the London Welsh half-backs unable to feed their three-quarters, Willie Llewellyn, Rhys Gabe and Teddy Morgan were consigned to purely defensive roles and as a consequence Newport took more control of the game in the second half. London Welsh were struggling to compete and four second half tries by Partridge, Dunn, Lloyd and Adams, the latter of which was converted by Lloyd, gave Newport a convincing victory by 22 points to nil. The game was not as one-sided as the score suggests and had the Welsh been better served at half-back the result would have been much closer.

In late August the *Evening Express* had observed that 'Fred Bush has received an appointment as an art master in London and if he is able to spare time, of which there is little doubt, he will be found playing for the London Welsh this ensuing season.' In the same edition the paper commented on Fred's brother Percy, when it stated, 'Percy Bush is understood to have no objections to playing at half if the Cardiff committee care to select him. This suggestion was made by a correspondent in the columns of the Express one day this week.' The report went on to say how Percy had, 'suffered considerable ill-health during the summer and had lost a couple of stone in weight.'

As reported in the *Evening Express* Fred Bush played in London Welsh's second game of the season against Old Alleynians. Two tries by Arthur Harding helped London Welsh to a comfortable victory by 24 points to eight. This was one of very few games Fred played for London Welsh during the season. With regard to Percy he was back playing for Cardiff by November but in his more usual position in the three-quarters and not at half-back. He continued to play wing three-quarter for Cardiff and Glamorgan for the remainder of the season and did not play regularly at outside-half until the following season.

London Welsh struggled in their next two games and in front of 8,000 spectators were heavily defeated in the away game to Devonport Albion. Despite the Albion losing one of their wings in the first minute of the game and thus playing with seven forwards for the remainder of the match, their forwards had the better of a weak Welsh eight and Devonport Albion won by 20 points to nil. Willie Llewellyn missed the next game against Leicester because he was injured in the game against Devonport Albion. His place was taken by the Irish international and Swansea wing Albert Freear. This was the first time London Welsh had played at Welford Road and a crowd of 11,000 spectators watched the home side win a scrambling game by 13 points to nil.

Willie returned for the game against Streatham and London Welsh returned to winning ways. The Welsh were superior in all phases of the game but had Willie Llewellyn and Teddy Morgan not been so superb in defence, Streatham could well have scored a couple of tries. Making one of his brilliant characteristic runs along the touch-line, Willie scored one of four first half tries. Arthur Harding converted to give London Welsh a comfortable first half lead of 14 points to nil. This was Willie's first try of the season. Another four tries in the second half by Harding, Owen, Clay and Webster put the result well beyond doubt. Hop Maddock converted the last try and although Streatham scored a late conciliation try which they converted, London Welsh had a hansom victory by 28 points to five.

In their next game London Welsh had their best result of the season when they defeated Llanelly at the Queen's club. The report in *The Sportsman* read as follows: 'Unfortunately with the wretched weather that prevailed and the fact that Tuesday is rather an off day for rugby football, the attendance was a very meagre one, barely numbering 800 spectators. Those who attended, however, were fully rewarded by witnessing a close and interesting struggle and though the Metropolitans gained a somewhat unexpected victory by 6 points to five, they fully deserved their success when one takes the actual play into consideration. The home lot, it is true, had all the worst of the last twenty minutes play and the wonder is that Llanelly did not score, but the defence was superb, Llewellyn in particular tackling magnificently time after time.' Both teams were strongly represented and although Rhys Gabe had played for London Welsh in the first game of the season, against Newport, he had now returned to Llanelly. Nevertheless, Welsh internationals Willie Llewellyn, Teddy Morgan and Wallace Watts, all played for London Welsh. The Welsh were also assisted by Jack Hillman and Birdie Partridge of Newport. Llanelly, without the assistance of Gabe, also had the aid of several players including Irish international Arthur Freear and Welsh internationals George Davies and Dick Jones all of Swansea.

It was a keen and scrambling match and with the ground wet and the ball muddy the forwards broke up early and there was plenty of running, passing, kicking and tackling. After about ten minutes Jack Hillman picked up and passed to Wallace Watts who scored in the extreme corner. Harding's kick at goal failed. Ten minutes later, A H Owen, at half-back for the Welsh, scored another try for the home side but again Harding failed with the conversion. Nonetheless, at the interval London Welsh were ahead by 6 points to nil. Llanelly pressed from the outset of the second half but fine defence kept them out. Eventually from a loose forward rush Bowen scored for the visitors and Bob Richards converted from a favourable position. From now until the end of the game Llanelly did everything they could to break down the London Welsh defence but they could not be broken and they held on to secure a famous victory by 6 points to five.

Willie's next game was for Glamorgan in their match against Devon at Cardiff Arms Park. Glamorgan were strongly represented with seven Welsh internationals in the side. In addition, Arthur Freear the Irish international and Swansea wing three-quarter also played. Bert Winfield, who would gain his first Welsh cap later in the season against Ireland, was at full-back. Future Welsh internationals Sid Bevan (Swansea), John 'Jack' Alf Brown (Cardiff) and Howell Jones (Neath) were also in the Glamorgan team. The full team was as follows: Back, H B Winfield; three-quarter backs, A E Freear, Willie Llewellyn, R T Gabe and Lewis Thomas; half-backs, R Jones and R M Owen; forwards, A Brice, D Jones, W T Osborne, 'Buller' Rees, S Bevan, W Woolf, J Brown and Howell Jones.

Devon also fielded a strong team which included five international players: P L Nicholas, J C Matters, L R Tosswill, D D Dobson and A O'Neill. Despite the terrible weather and a small crowd of about 1,000 spectators, the game, which was regarded as a Welsh international trial match, was an exciting spectacle. The *Evening Express* reported that this was, 'certainly the finest game seen on the park this season and one of the most interesting county matches ever played.' The game was won by a single try to nil with Willie Llewellyn the try scorer. With regard to the try the *Evening Express* commented, 'It was only an exceptionally smart bit of work on the part of Dick Jones, followed by one of Willie Llewellyn's most brilliant runs that gave Glamorgan the only score of the match.' Both sides played really well and both just failed to score on several occasions. On the whole the result was a fair one with Glamorgan victors by just the 3 points to nil. Bert Winfield had a wonderful game both in attack and defence and having been reserve for the Welsh team on so many occasions he was now close to winning his first international cap.

London Welsh were unfortunate in their next game against Aberavon at the Queen's Club with Willie Llewellyn, E D Evans and Teddy Morgan all on the injured list. With a weakened side London Welsh recorded their fourth defeat of the season going down by 12 points to three.

As with the previous season the Welsh Football Union arranged a preliminary trial match to test the reserve strength of Welsh rugby. The game took place at Bridgend on Wednesday 12th November. The selection of players for the trial was confined to those who were not international players but four players who took part in the trial went on to become Welsh internationals: Fred Jowett (Swansea), David John 'DJ' Thomas (Swansea), Harry Uzzell (Newport) and Jack Brown (Cardiff). The thirty players who took part were divided into two teams, the Whites and the Stripes, with the Stripes being the eventual winners by 14 points to eight. The Welsh Football Union had arranged for the final trial match to be played at Tredegar on Saturday 6th December but because of frost earlier in the week of the trial it was decided to transfer the game to Swansea. All the necessary arrangements were made and all officials and players made their way to St Helen's on the allotted day. Prior to the trial match taking place a schoolboys' match had been arranged and the straw protecting the ground was removed for that game. As the game progressed the ground got harder and harder and by the time the game was over the ground was so hard that it was declared unplayable and the trial match had to be abandoned. The sides chosen for the trial were the Whites and Stripes with the Whites composed chiefly of international players. The teams selected were as follows:

Whites: Back, John Strand-Jones; three-quarter backs, Gwyn Nicholls, R T Gabe, Willie Llewellyn and E T Morgan; half-backs, R Jones and R M Owen; forwards, G Boots, J J Hodges, A Brice, W Joseph, A F Harding, W T Osborne, Dai Jones and Harry Jones.

Stripes: Back, H B Winfield; three-quarter backs, Cliff Pritchard, Dan Rees, Fred Jowett and Billy Trew; half-backs, Jack Hillman and George Llewellyn Lloyd; forwards, E Thomas (Newport), G Travers (Pill Harriers), D J Thomas (Swansea), Sid Bevan (Swansea), James Watts (Llanelly), Jack Brown (Cardiff), G Foley (Brynmawr) and Howell Jones (Neath).

With the trial not taking place the players selected for the international match against England at St Helen's, Swansea on Saturday 10th January would largely depend upon club form and non-availability through injury.

Having missed the game against Aberavon because of injury Willie Llewellyn returned to London Welsh for their next game against London Irish at the Queen's Club. The Welsh were fairly well represented despite Teddy Morgan playing for Guy's Hospital. The Irish were without Nicholson, their best forward. The game was tame and uneventful and played almost completely between the forwards. London Welsh lost their scrum-half A H Owen in the first half and at the interval there was no score. The second half was a repeat of the first with the forward battle fairly even and the game ended in a no score drawn game. With regard to the game the *Evening Express* reported, 'Harding was by far the best forward on the field, while Llewellyn was very nippy, but was carefully watched. A pointless draw was about the best thing that could happen.'

Surprisingly Willie's next game was for Cardiff away to Oxford University. With Gwyn Nicholls and Percy Bush absent from the three-quarters and Owen and O'Neill away in the forwards, both Willie Llewellyn and Arthur Harding played for Cardiff. Also in the team was Tommy Vile of Newport. This was almost certainly the first time Tommy and Willie had played alongside each other in a rugby match but they would play together many times for both Newport and the 1904 British Isles on their tour to Australia and New Zealand. With regard to the game the weather was awful and the wind and rain completely spoilt the game. Cardiff had the advantage of the wind in the first half and scored two tries through Biggs and Thomas. Arthur Harding converted the try by Thomas to give Cardiff an eight point advantage at the interval. In the second half unconverted tries by Cartwright and Eberle brought the University right back into the game. A try by Raphael which was converted by Wordsworth gave Oxford a lead they never relinquished. Cardiff tried hard to score but the fine tackling of the Oxford backs kept them out and Oxford were victorious by 11 points to eight.

Willie returned to London Welsh for their next game away to West Hartlepool. A side weakened by the absence of Rhys Gabe and Teddy Morgan and Willie Llewellyn playing out of position was well beaten by a dropped goal and three tries to nil. London Welsh, having not won since their victory over Llanelly in late October, returned to winning ways when they played the Royal Indian Engineering College at Cooper's Hill. Wallace Watts and Hop Maddock scored the tries and Maddock kicked a conversion in the 8 points to five victory. With Willie Llewellyn, possibly at home for the Christmas period, he was not selected and didn't play for London Welsh in their next game against Upper Clapton at Lower Welsh Harp, Hendon. The visitors were no match for the Welsh and were easily beaten by two goals and a try to nothing.

With Willie already having played for London Welsh, Glamorgan and

Cardiff thus far during the season he demonstrated his willingness to play rugby whenever he could irrespective of whom he was playing for by turning out for Newport in their game against Edinburgh University at Rodney Parade on Christmas Eve. The University side arrived in Newport with an unbroken record but short of Scottish international Francis Fasson, one of their regular half-backs and a couple of their regular forwards. Nevertheless good substitutes were found and Edinburgh fielded a strong team which included Scottish internationals Alec Timms, Alfred Fell and Ernest Simson and future Scottish internationals James Macdonald, Leonard West and Hugh Fletcher.

Newport were weakened by the absence of Welsh international half-back George Llewellyn Lloyd and three-quarters Charlie Lewis and Wyatt Gould, brother of the famous Arthur Gould. David Boots, the regular full-back stood down because he had signed professional papers and then decided not to go North. Knowing the Scottish Rugby Union's attitude to breaches of the amateurism laws he decided not to play to avoid any controversy. Nevertheless Newport had Welsh internationals Tom Pearson and George Boots in their side and future Welsh internationals Cliff Pritchard, Tommy Vile and Edwin 'Beddoe' Thomas Maynard. Also in the Newport team was future South African international 'Birdie' Partridge. In addition to this already strong Newport team they were assisted by Welsh internationals Willie Llewellyn and Wallace Watts of London Welsh and Reg Skrimshire of Blackheath.

The ground was in excellent condition and with two strong teams the game was well contested. In the first half both sides made strenuous efforts to score but good defence on both sides prevented any breach of the defence. After some fine passing between the three-quarters Tom Pearson was tackled well within the opposition twenty-five. Then when the University were penalised Reg Skrimshire just missed a long shot at goal. Shortly afterwards play was at the other end of the field and Alec Timms made a couple of big bursts to get through but was stopped by the determined efforts of the Newport backs. In the course of a heavily-fought tussle, Alfred Fell received a nasty cut and had to leave the field for ten minutes. It was a ding-dong battle with play moving from end to end and it was only keen tackling that kept both lines intact. Up to the interval not a single point had been scored.

The second half continued as the first half had ended with just the same keenness shown by both sides. Jack Hillman got through on one occasion but was stopped by Stuart the University full-back, then Willie Llewellyn fielded a kick but was rushed back yards by a couple of the fast Scotsmen. Finally the deadlock was broken when Tommy Vile got round the blind-side of the scrum and made an opening for Sid Adams who crossed for a try with three or four of the opposition on his back. Reg Skrimshire failed with the conversion. After another bout of determined tackling Alfred Fell had another knock in the face and had to retire. Newport pressed again and a fine round of passing between Cliff Pritchard, Reg Skrimshire and Willie Llewellyn almost resulted in another try. Finally, a splendidly judged cross-kick by Coleman, the home full-back, enabled Tom Pearson to cross for a smart try which Reg Skrimshire again failed to convert. Despite a tremendous final onslaught by the University, Newport held out and were deserved winners by 6 points to nil.

The disappointing outcome from this game was that Willie Llewellyn injured his knee. Whether this was a re-occurrence of a previous injury or not is unclear but this was the most serious injury that Willie had received during his playing career. At one point it was considered serious enough to prevent him playing for the remainder of the season which ultimately proved not to be the case. However, it was serious enough to prevent him from playing for just over two months and following the game against Edinburgh University Willie did not play again until he played for Glamorgan against Somerset at Bridgwater on Saturday 28th February.

Willie's injury caused him to potentially miss nine London Welsh games, one Glamorgan County game and the Welsh internationals against England and Scotland. Willie missed the London Welsh game against Cardiff on the Arms Park. Interest in the game was enormous and a crowd of some 20,000 spectators watched as the home team defeated the Exiles by 14 points to nil, all the points being scored in the first half. Cecil Biggs opened the scoring with a try which Bert Winfield converted. Percy Bush then scored another try which Bert Winfield again converted. Just before the interval Percy Bush brought the scoring to an end with a fine dropped goal. Although the score suggests that London Welsh were well beaten they had played a fine game and were unlucky not to score on several occasions. 'Old Stager' of the *South Wales Daily News* remarked, 'The London Welshmen proved that their high reputation among Metropolitan teams is well deserved and no-one who witnessed their performance today could do other than approve of the grant made towards the club by the Welsh Football Union.' London Welsh also lost their next game by 15 points to five at home to Leicester.

With regard to the international between Wales and England the Welsh Football Union had intended to select the team at a meeting at the Westgate Hotel, Newport on Thursday 18th December but due to the abandonment of the trial match and injuries to Gwyn Nicholls, Willie Llewellyn and Teddy Morgan it was decided to postpone the selection of the team until after the conclusion of the match between Llanelly and Cardiff at Stradey Park on Saturday 3rd January. It would also give the Welsh selectors the opportunity to consider the relative merits of John Strand-Jones as compared to Bert Winfield. The outcome of the game was a victory for Llanelly by 10 points to five and probably as a consequence Bert Winfield once again found himself as Welsh reserve to John Strand-Jones at full-back. The in-form Tom Pearson of Newport was selected captain in place of the injured Gwyn Nicholls and there was a first and only Welsh cap on the wing for Fred Jowett of Swansea, despite scoring 42 tries for Swansea during the season. The only other debutant in the team was George 'Twyber' Travers of Pill Harriers. This was the first of twenty-five caps Travers won for Wales which included the 1905 victory over New Zealand. The only change from the team selected was George Llewellyn Lloyd taking the place of the injured Dick Jones at outside-half.

With regard to the game, Wales chalked up their fifth successive win over England with a 21 points to 5 victory. Welsh captain Tom Pearson was injured in the twenty-fifth minute of the game and Jehoida Hodges came out of the pack to take his place and scored three tries. All the Welsh points were scored in the first half. Tom Pearson opened the scoring with a try which Strand-Jones converted. Dickie Owen then scored another try which Strand-Jones again converted. Hodges then scored his three tries only one of which was converted by Strand-Jones. In the second half Denys Dobson, who would join Fred Jowett on the British Isles tour to Australia and New Zealand in 1904, replied with a try for England which Jim Taylor converted. But it was too little too late and Wales were comfortable winners.

With the continued absence of Willie Llewellyn and Teddy Morgan, London Welsh were having a torrid time on the rugby field. They lost all four games between the Welsh internationals against England and Scotland, being defeated by London Irish, Guy's Hospital, the Canadians and Plymouth. On the other hand Glamorgan did very well in the game against Cornwall at St Helen's. The Glamorgan team, which included George Davies, Billy Trew, Fred Jowett, Dick Jones, Dickie Owen (Captain), David John Thomas, Dai Davies, Sid Bevan and Will Joseph all of Swansea, defeated Cornwall by 22 points to five.

The selection committee of the Welsh Football Union met at the Queen's Hotel, Cardiff on Wednesday 28th January and selected the Welsh team to face Scotland at Inverleith, Edinburgh on Saturday 7th February, unusually however, they excluded the three-quarters. This was in order to give Gwyn Nicholls and Tom Pearson the opportunity to prove their fitness. Gwyn Nicholls had been out since playing for Cardiff against Blackheath on Saturday 13th December when he sustained a serious shoulder injury. This was the first time Nicholls had been seriously hurt during his long and illustrious rugby career. Tom Pearson had not played since being injured in the game against England. Although Tom Pearson played for Newport against Gloucester he felt that he was unable to play for Wales against Scotland and informed the selection committee accordingly. When the complete team was announced there were three changes from the side which had defeated England at St Helen's; Gwyn Nicholls replaced Dan Rees at right centre, Willie Arnold of Llanelly replacing Tom Pearson on the left wing and Billy Trew replacing injured club mate Fred Jowett on the right wing.

The only change in the Welsh team on the day of the match was Dan Rees of Swansea taking the place of Gwyn Nicholls who had withdrawn from the side because he considered he was not properly fit to take part. In terrible conditions at Inverleith, Wales were defeated by 6 points to nil. In pouring rain and a hurricane wind Alec Timms kicked a penalty and William Kyle scored an unconverted try to give Scotland victory. Despite scoring 32 tries for Llanelly during the season and scoring a further 32 tries for Swansea the following season, this was Willie Arnold's only Welsh cap.

With Willie Llewellyn and Teddy Morgan still on the injured list London Welsh at last had a victory when they defeated Harlequins by 3 points to nil at Wandsworth Common. Neither side was at full strength and the game was played in soft and slippery conditions. Five minutes from the end of the game Samuels crossed for a try which Fred Bush failed to convert but it was enough to give the Welsh victory. London Welsh drew 3 points all in their next game against Oxford University and then, in front of a crowd of about 3,000 spectators, were defeated by Devonport Albion at the Queen's Club by 6 points to nil. Play was fairly even throughout the opening period of the game but in the second half the Albion forwards carried all before them. Tries apiece for Dobson and Jago, neither of which were converted, gave Devonport Albion the spoils.

At last there was some good news for both London Welsh and Wales. Willie Llewellyn and Teddy Morgan, both of whom had been on the injured list since before the New Year, were reported to be fit again. Teddy Morgan returned in fine style after his ankle injury, scoring two tries for Guy's Hospital in their 24 points to 3 victory over St Bartholomew's Hospital on Tuesday 10th February. He then played for London Welsh in their defeat against Devonport Albion. With regard to Willie's fitness the *Evening Express* reported on Wednesday 18th February that 'Willie Llewellyn has so far recovered from the injury to his knees that he will play for his old club Llwynypia against Aberavon on Saturday. Assuming that he is thoroughly fit, the odds are in favour of his reinstatement in the Welsh team against Ireland. Aberavon, it worth nothing, have never yet won a match at Llwynypia.' As it turned out Willie did not play for Llwynypia and Aberavon had their first victory there, winning by 11 points to nil. Willie did not play for London Welsh in their away defeat at Northampton, choosing instead to play his first game after his return from serious injury for Glamorgan in their match against Somerset at Bridgwater.

Glamorgan won the game quite easily by 12 points to nil. Although neither side scored up to the interval four second-half unconverted tries by Glamorgan gave them a comfortable victory. Lewis Thomas (Aberavon) scored two tries with Dai Jones (Treherbert) and D J Lewis (Swansea) scoring one apiece. Willie Llewellyn renewed acquaintances with his old club-mate Dick Hellings of Llwynypia who played in the forwards.

The *Evening Express* commented that 'Dai Jones, Willie Llewellyn, Lewis Thomas and D Rees (Aberavon) were most prominent.' Willie came through the game unscathed and a report in the *Irish Independent* stated, 'Last season's brilliant Welsh right wing, Willie Llewellyn, seen after the match at Bridgwater, last Saturday, said that he was as "fit as a fiddle." His leg stood the Glamorgan v Somerset match without any sign of weakness.' Although originally selected to play, Teddy Morgan withdrew from the game.

With the Welsh Football Union not picking the Welsh team to face Ireland until Thursday 5th March, Willie Llewellyn and Teddy Morgan had another opportunity to prove their fitness before the team was selected. They both played for London Welsh in the game against Swansea at the Queen's Club on Monday 2nd March. Swansea were too good for the Welsh and three first half tries by George Davies, Fred Jowett and Dan Rees, the latter of which was converted by Billy Bancroft, gave Swansea an eleven point lead at the interval. In the second half Swansea continued to have the better of the play and tries by Rhys Rees, converted by Bancroft, Fred Jowett and Billy Trew, again converted by Bancroft, gave Swansea an unassailable lead of 24 points to nil. A penalty kick in the last minute of the game by Arthur Harding gave London Welsh the consolation of scoring 3 points.

When the selection committee of the Welsh Football Union met to pick the team to face Ireland at Cardiff Arms Park on Saturday 14th March, both Willie Llewellyn and Teddy Morgan were in the side. There was just one new cap in the side; Bert Winfield. After being Welsh reserve full-back on so many occasion, firstly to Billy Bancroft and then to John Strand-Jones, at last, the Cardiff captain was selected for his first international. Strand-Jones had not played since the international against Scotland and therefore there had been no opportunity to judge his present form and with Bert Winfield playing consistently well for Cardiff he won the ballot by seven votes to three. Having been reserve on so many occasions you would have thought that Bert Winfield would have stood down from Cardiff's game against Moseley at the Arms Park the week before the international, but that was not the case and Bert Winfield led his side to victory over the team that had narrowly beaten them earlier in the season. After a long absence Gwyn Nicholls returned to the

Cardiff side for the same game and bagged two tries in the 36 points to nil triumph. D Thomas scored a try while Cecil Biggs had a brace and Percy Bush scored a hat trick of tries. Bert Winfield had an outstanding game and kicked six conversions. Rhys Gabe was unavailable for the game.

With just a week to go before the international against Ireland, Teddy Morgan took the opportunity to stand down for the London Welsh game against Mountain Ash at Hendon. Hop Maddock and Reuben Carpenter scored unconverted tries for their respective sides in the first half, but just before the end of the game Carpenter ran in for his second try to give Mountain Ash victory by 6 points to three.

With Willie Llewellyn also not playing for London Welsh against Mountain Ash it was thought that he, like Teddy Morgan, had decided to stand down with the international against Ireland just a week away. However, a report of the game between Penarth and Penygraig in the *Evening Express* on Saturday 7th March told another story when it stated, 'Penygraig were distinctly fortunate in having the services of Willie Llewellyn, who assured the writer that his leg has so far withstood every strain, a statement which will highly please all.' For whatever reason, maybe to fully test his injured knee before the international, Willie had decided to play his first ever game for Penygraig. Penarth won the game by 8 points to nil and the report of the match concluded by saying, 'Willie Llewellyn was a marked man throughout and Mewton never left him much room to start an attack.' Willie came through the game unharmed and after missing the internationals against England and Scotland was ready to reclaim his place on the right wing for Wales against Ireland.

Both Bert Winfield and Gwyn Nicholls came through the game against Moseley without any injuries and both lined up to face Ireland at Cardiff Arms Park on Saturday 14th March. The team took the field as selected with Gwyn Nicholls back at the helm as captain. The Welsh team was as follows:

Wales: Back, *Bert Winfield (Cardiff); three-quarter backs, Willie Llewellyn (London Welsh), Gwyn Nicholls (Cardiff, Captain), Rhys Gabe (Cardiff), Teddy Morgan (Guy's Hospital and London Welsh); half-backs, George Llewellyn Lloyd (Newport), Dickie Owen (Swansea); forwards, Alfred Brice (Aberavon), Jehoida Hodges, George Boots (Newport),

Will Osborne (Mountain Ash), George Travers (Pill Harries), Dai Jones (Treherbert), Arthur Harding (London Welsh), Will Joseph (Swansea). (* Wales Debut)

Ireland: J Fulton (NIFC); *G Bradshaw (Belfast Collegians), C Reid (NIFC), *J C Parke (Dublin U), G P Doran (Lansdowne); L M Magee (Bective), H H Corley (Captain – Dublin U); J J Coffey (Lansdowne), P Healey (Garryowen), G Hamlet (Old Wesley), F Gardiner (NIFC), C E Allen (Derry), T A Harvey (Monkstown), A Tedford (Malone), Joseph Wallace (Wanderers). (* Ireland Debut)

Referee: P Coles (England).

Swansea had five players in the reserves with Dan Rees (centre), Fred Jowett and Billy Trew (wings), Dick Jones (half-back) and Sid Bevan (forward). The other three reserve forwards were Edwin 'Beddoe' Thomas Maynard (Newport), W 'Billy' O'Neil (Cardiff) and James Watts (Llanelly). With both Wales and Ireland having beaten England and losing to Scotland the outcome of this game could decide the Home Nations Championship should England defeat Scotland in the final international of the season at Richmond the following week.

Wales Team v Ireland 1903

Back Row: G Travers, A F Harding, A B Brice, Tom Williams (WFU),
Sir John Llewellyn Bart (President WFU), D Jones, W T Osborne, W Joseph.
Middle Row: H B Winfield, W M Llewellyn, G Boots, E G Nicholls (Captain),
G Ll Lloyd, R T Gabe. *Front Row*: R M Owen, J J Hodges and E Morgan.

The pitch was a quagmire but the Welsh three-quarters had a field day, playing together for the first time this season, they scored five of the six tries. Ten minutes into the first half Alfred Brice opened the scoring for Wales with an unconverted try. Five minutes later Willie Llewellyn scored in the corner and Bert Winfield with a great kick at goal just failed to convert. Just before the interval some splendid passing resulted in Teddy Morgan scoring in the extreme corner. Bert Winfield, from a difficult angle, failed to convert. George Boots, who had broken his collar-bone after just five minutes of the game, retired at half-time. Seven minutes into the second half some brilliant passing among the Welsh three-quarters resulted in Teddy Morgan crossing for his second try of the afternoon. With the ground literally a sea of mud, place kicking was almost impossible, and once again the kick at goal failed. Five minutes later a fine forward rush and a kick towards the Irish line resulted in another try by Willie Llewellyn. Again the kick at goal failed. Ten minutes from the end of the game Rhys Gabe got away at rattling speed and scored the final try of the game. Again the kick at goal failed. Just before the end of the game Teddy Morgan was injured and had to retire but Ireland were well beaten and the game ended with Wales victorious by 18 points to nil.

Although Bert Winfield missed the kicks he had a brilliant game and having spent so much time as reserve full-back must have been delighted with the outcome. Having recently returned from injury Gwyn Nicholls, Willie Llewellyn and Teddy Morgan all played brilliantly alongside Rhys Gabe. Willie and Teddy were rewarded with two tries apiece and Rhys Gabe one. Although Wales had achieved their objective of defeating Ireland, the following week Scotland defeated England thus winning the Home Nations Championship, the Calcutta Cup and their fourth Triple Crown.

Willie missed London Welsh's next game against Rosslyn Park because he was playing for Newport against Blackheath. This was one of only two games Willie played for Newport during the season; the first when he was badly injured against Edinburgh University. He replaced the injured Tom Pearson and played in a strong three-quarter line which included Cliff Pritchard, Wyatt Gould and Charlie Lewis. Also in the team were fellow Welsh internationals George Llewellyn Lloyd and Jehoida Hodges. Welsh international Reg Skrimshire was playing in the centre for the opposition. The weather was awful and a strong wind persisted throughout the game, nevertheless, it was the Newport three-quarters that decided the outcome of the match. Time after time Llewellyn Lloyd got his backs moving and an unconverted try by Willie Llewellyn was the only score of the first half.

Early in the second half Jack Hillman made an opening for Edwin 'Beddoe' Thomas who scored an unconverted try and then Jehoida Hodges gave a scoring pass to Jack Jenkins. Llewellyn Lloyd converted. Lloyd was having a brilliant game and after breaking through the defence it looked as if he would score himself but he handed on to Wyatt Gould who crossed beneath the posts. Lloyd kicked the conversion. Although well beaten Blackheath did not give up but then Llewellyn Lloyd again broke the defence and the ball going to Pritchard and then on to Wyatt Gould, the latter crossed for his second try of the match. Llewellyn Lloyd was again successful and Newport were comfortable winners by 21 points to nil.

Willie also missed the next London Welsh game against Catford Bridge, this time because he was playing for Kent against Durham at West Hartlepool. Although Kent had the better of matters in the first half, with Dillon, Willie Llewellyn and Reg Skrimshire playing well behind a good hard working pack, they failed to score and the interval arrived with no points on the board for either side. Late in the second half Taylor dropped a well-directed goal for Durham. Kent fought back marvellously and in the last minute of the game a splendid effort by Willie Llewellyn took play well into the home twenty-five and Pat McEvedy scored an unconverted try. Unfortunately it was not enough and Durham were victors by 4 points to three. The victory gave Durham the County Championship for the second year in succession.

London Welsh brought their 1902–03 season to a close with an Easter Tour to Gloucester and South Wales. The following players undertook the tour: H T Maddock, W Llewellyn (Captain), E Morgan, R T Gabe, F F Bush, J T Timmins, E D Evans, W J Evans, Wayne Morgan, D J Thomas, C F Rowlands, F W Huggett, W H Watts, A F Harding, D L Bowen, J F Williams, W G Hodge, A E C Morgan, J Barnfield, W Lewis and Tom James. It was a tough tour with four games in five days and far as it is possible to tell, Willie played in all four games. He definitely played in the games against Gloucester, Mountain Ash and Swansea but the records of the Llanelly game are very sparse with no real detail on the teams that played. The first game against Gloucester resulted in a comfortable win for the home side by 16 points to nil. The game against Mountain Ash had a similar outcome with home team winning by 26 points to five. Reuben Carpenter, the ex-Newport three-quarter, was the best back on the field and scored 13 points from two tries, two conversions and a penalty. Willie Llewellyn made 'the best run of the match' but unfortunately just stepped into touch when a try looked certain. However, not to be denied, Willie made amends and when the next opportunity came his way he was over for a try. With the conversion successful these were the only points of the game for London Welsh. In a well contested game against Llanelly the Welsh lost by 14 points to three. The only score for the visitors was an unconverted try by Huggett.

The final game of the tour was against Swansea at St Helen's. Swansea were without Billy Bancroft, Billy Trew and Sid Bevan, their places being taken by Peter Lockman, Fred Jowett and Arthur Jones. In addition to Fred Jowett the Swansea side also included Welsh internationals Dan Rees, George Davies, Dickie Owen, Dick Jones, Will Joseph and Fred Scrine. London Welsh were strongly represented with Welsh internationals Willie Llewellyn, Rhys Gabe and Teddy Morgan all in the side. London Welsh also had the assistance of the Welsh international forward Will Osborne and A Fryer of Mountain Ash. With neither side scoring in the first half and Swansea with the wind in their favour in the second, they soon put the game beyond doubt. George Davies opened the scoring with an unconverted try. A few minutes later Fred Jowett crossed for another unconverted try. A goal from a mark for Dick Jones and another unconverted try by Frank Gordon brought the scoring to an end and Swansea were victors by 13 points to nil.

The game against Swansea brought the season to an end for both clubs. Swansea, having been Welsh Club Champions for the previous four seasons, finished runners up to Newport. Fred Jowett was top try scorer and top points scorer for Swansea and scored more tries than any other player in Wales with forty-two. Swansea scored a staggering 619 points for, with only 68 points against. The game against Swansea brought to an end Willie's tenure as London Welsh captain. It many ways it was a disappointing season with London Welsh only winning 8 of the

29 games they played. Nevertheless, Willie had put London Welsh back on an even keel and they could look forward to much more success in the coming seasons under the leadership of fellow Christ College Old Boy, Arthur Harding. During the 1902–03 season London Welsh had played 29 games, won 8, lost 19 and drawn 2. They had scored 156 points for with 325 points against. Willie played in only 13 games and scored just 2 tries.

Although this was in many ways a disappointing season for Willie, over the three years he had captained the side he had made a major contribution to the future of the club. The Welsh Football Union had readily accepted his recommendation that any Welshman playing and living in London could only be considered for a Welsh cap as long as he joined London Welsh. This attracted many great Welsh internationals of the time to play for the club including, Wallace Watts, Rhys Gabe, Teddy Morgan, Arthur Harding, J F 'Jack' Williams, Hop Maddock and Jack Jenkins. It did, however, work against one Welsh player in particular, Reg Skrimshire. He played for Newport and was an outstanding centre three-quarter who made his debut for Wales on the same day as Willie played his first game for Wales against England in 1899. He played in all three Welsh internationals during that season but never played for Wales again. After playing for Newport he joined Blackheath and although he was playing brilliantly for his club and was one of the best Welsh centres, he was never picked by Wales again. Skrimshire was the only Welshman on the 1903 British Isles tour to South Africa and was top points and try scorer with 59 points.

Returning to Willie's contribution to London Welsh, in his 1903 book *Rugby Football*, Captain Phillip Trevor, paid special tribute to Willie when he wrote, 'The executive have had no little trouble in securing the services of men who are by birth and association, entitled, indeed called upon, to play for London Welsh. It is, of course, a matter

Willie Llewellyn's London Welsh Cap.

of common knowledge that the organisation owes a great deal to the celebrated Welsh international, W Llewellyn. One swallow, however, we know, does not make a summer, but fortunately his good example has been followed by others.' This extract appeared in Paul Beken and Stephen Jones' book *Dragon in Exile, The Centenary History of London Welsh RFC*, in the same paragraph the authors went on to recognise the contribution Willie had made to London Welsh by saying, 'Llewellyn the man and Llewellyn the player, did as much as anyone to lead the club from mediocrity to excellence. The team to which he returned in 1905 was steadily improving, as shown by the first wins over London Scottish and Oxford University.' The foundations Willie had put in place during his captaincy of the club were firmly built upon by Arthur Harding who captained London Welsh for four consecutive seasons between 1903 and 1907. The same article in the book went on to say, 'There had been several occasions in the past when the club had appeared about to break into the very top strata of club teams but inconsistency and lack of a settled team always held them back. Yet the improved results of the period from 1903 to 1905 were the breakthrough. They heralded a vivid few seasons which became a mini golden era.'

Although the season had come to an end for London Welsh, Willie's season was not yet over and he still had three games to play. Having played for London Welsh against Swansea on Easter Tuesday, the following day Willie played for the East against the West at Cardiff Arms Park. The game was arranged in order to raise funds for a new cricket pavilion for Cardiff Cricket Club. For the East there were several defections with Gwyn Nicholls, Alec Timms, Tom Pearson, Llewellyn Lloyd, Jack Hillman, George Travers and Arthur Harding all withdrawing from the side. Their places were taken by Teddy Morgan, Cecil Biggs and Cliff Pritchard in the three–quarters, Tommy Vile and M Coughlin at half-backs and Sid Adams and H Hutchings in the forwards. The West lost the services of Dan Rees and Billy Trew, both who had been injured playing for Swansea in the Easter Monday match against Rockcliff. Rees' place was taken by Hopkins of Swansea seconds and Fred Jowett replaced Billy Trew on the wing. The teams were as follows:

East: Back, H B Winfield (Captain, Cardiff); three-quarter backs, E Morgan, W Llewellyn (London Welsh), Cliff Pritchard (Newport), and

Cecil Biggs (Cardiff); half-backs T H Vile (Newport) and M Coughlin (Cardiff); forwards, G Boots, J J Hodges, S Adams and E 'Beddoe' Thomas (Newport), W O'Neil, A Spackman, H Hutchings and P S Smith (Cardiff).

West: Back, W J Bancroft (Captain, Swansea); three-quarter backs, W F Jowett and J Hopkins (Swansea), R T Gabe and W Arnold (Llanelly); half-backs R M Owen and R Jones (Swansea); forwards, A Brice and 'Buller' Rees (Aberavon), W T Osborne (Mountain Ash), Will Joseph, D Davies, D Thomas and Aubrey Smith (Swansea) and Danny Walters (Llanelly).

Date	Team Played For	Opposition	Venue	Result	W Llewellyn Tries
27/09/1902	London Welsh	Newport	Queen's Club	Lost 0-22	0
04/10/1902	London Welsh	Old Alleynians	Hendon	Won 24-8	0
11/10/1902	London Welsh	Devonport Albion	Away	Lost 0-20	0
18/10/1902	London Welsh	Leicester	Away	Lost 0-13	Did not play
25/10/1902	London Welsh	Streatham	Hendon	Won 28-5	1
28/10/1902	London Welsh	Llanelly	Queen's Club	Won 6-5	0
05/11/1902	Glamorgan	Devon	Cardiff Arms Park	Won 3-0	1
08/11/1902	London Welsh	Aberavon	Queen's Club	Lost 3-12	Did not play
22/11/1902	London Welsh	London Irish	Queen's Club	Drawn 0-0	0
24/11/1902	Cardiff	Oxford University	Oxford University	Lost 8-11	0
29/11/1902	London Welsh	West Hartlepool	Away	Lost 0-13	0
13/12/1902	London Welsh	R.I.E. College	Away	Won 8-5	0
20/12/1902	London Welsh	Upper Clapton	Hendon	Won 13-0	Did not play
24/12/1902	Newport	Edinburgh University	Rodney Parade, Newport	Won 6-0	0
27/12/1902	London Welsh	Cardiff	Cardiff Arms Park	Lost 0-14	Injured
05/01/1903	London Welsh	Leicester	Queen's Club	Lost 5-15	Injured
10/01/1903	Wales	England	St Helen's, Swansea	Won 21-5	Injured
10/01/1903	London Welsh	London Irish	Queen's Club	Lost 8-16	Injured
24/01/1903	London Welsh	Guy's Hospital	Away	Lost 3-5	Injured
26/01/1903	London Welsh	Canadians	Queen's Club	Lost 0-5	Injured
29/01/1903	Glamorgan	Cornwall	St Helen's Swansea	Won 22-5	Injured
31/01/1903	London Welsh	Plymouth	Plymouth	Lost 0-34	Injured
07/02/1903	Wales	Scotland	Inverleith, Edinburgh	Lost 0-6	Injured
07/02/1903	London Welsh	Harlequins	Away	Won 3-0	Injured
11/02/1903	London Welsh	Oxford University	Away	Drawn 3-3	Injured
21/02/1903	London Welsh	Devonport Albion	Queen's Club	Lost 0-6	Injured
28/02/1903	London Welsh	Northampton	Away	Lost 8-12	Did not play
28/02/1903	Glamorgan	Somerset	Bridgwater	Won 12-0	0
02/03/1903	London Welsh	Swansea	Queen's Club	Lost 3-24	0
07/03/1903	Penygraig	Penarth	Penarth	Lost 0-8	0
07/03/1903	London Welsh	Mountain Ash	Hendon	Lost 3-6	Did Not Play
14/03/1903	Wales	Ireland	Cardiff Arms Park	Won 18-0	2
28/03/1903	Newport	Blackheath	Rodney Parade, Newport	Won 21-0	1
28/03/1903	London Welsh	Rosslyn Park	Away	Won 13-5	Did not Play
04/04/1903	London Welsh	Catford Bridge	Away	Won 17-8	Did not play
04/04/1903	Kent	Durham	West Hartlepool	Lost 3-4	0
10/04/1903	London Welsh	Gloucester	Away	Lost 0-16	0
11/04/1903	London Welsh	Mountain Ash	Away	Lost 5-26	1
13/04/1903	London Welsh	Llanelly	Away	Lost 3-14	0
14/04/1903	London Welsh	Swansea	Away	Lost 0-13	0
15/04/1903	East	West	Cardiff Arms Park	Won 9-5	0
23/04/1903	Welsh Internationals	Rhondda United	Belle Vue Park, Penygraig	Won 9-6	0
25/04/1903	Glamorgan	Cornwall	Camborne	Won 32-3	1
	Willie Llewellyn Games Played				W Llewellyn Tries
Totals	24				7

Willie Llewellyn Rugby Games Played and Results 1902–1903 Season

The East played in Cardiff colours and the West wore red jerseys. With fifteen Welsh internationals on show the game did not disappoint and writing in the *Evening Express* 'Forward' made the following comments: 'A grand game, one of the best of the season. Seldom, if ever, have we been treated to a more finished or attractive exhibition of Rugby football and the merit of the play alone more than warrants the suggestion that the East v West ought to be a permanent institution. In none of this season's internationals have we seen a more scientific display and the high standard of play harmonised beautifully with the glorious weather and the splendid patronage of the public.' For the 15,000 spectators the game was a thriller. The West, who were expected to win, started with a bang and almost scored on a couple of occasions. Then after another round of skilful passing Rhys Gabe scored a beautiful try which Billy Bancroft converted to give the West a five point lead. From here until half-time play was exciting but even and the only thing really of note being an injury to the referee, J H Bowen, who had to retire. His place was taken by W M Douglas.

In the second half, after some initial fine play by the West backs, the East began to get the better of the argument. On several occasions the East now looked very dangerous and when Willie Llewellyn eventually broke through he gave a scoring pass to Jehoida Hodges who crossed for a wonderful try. Bert Winfield converted and the scores were even. The East continued to attack and Teddy Morgan just missed with a drop at goal. Then, with only five minutes remaining, Tommy Vile, in the West twenty-five, got the ball away to Coughlin, who dropped a fine goal to give the East a narrow victory by 9 points to five. The report of the game by 'Forward' of the *Evening Express* concluded, 'The men of the East were unquestionably the better lot all round and thoroughly deserved their victory. Their forwards played a magnificent game and with their heeling out, the backs must have felt delighted to play behind such a pack.' As a result of the game just over £450 was raised towards the construction of a new pavilion for Cardiff Cricket Club.

The following week Willie arranged an interesting game at Belle Vue Park, Penygraig between the Welsh Internationals and Rhondda United. Tom Williams of the Welsh Football Union was the referee. The proceeds of the match were given to the Mid-Rhondda Nursing Association.

Willie's team contained no less than ten Welsh internationals including Rhys Gabe, Teddy Morgan, Fred Jowett, Dickie Owen, Dick Jones, Jehoida Hodges, George Boots, Dai Jones and Will Osborne. The Rhondda side was made up of players from Penygraig, Treorky, Mountain Ash, Treherbert and Llwynypia. Representing the Rhondda were two of Willie's old Llwynypia teammates, Billy Alexander and Dick Hellings. In a closely contested game both sides scored an unconverted try apiece in the first half. Fred Jowett scored for the Welsh Internationals and Lewis Lewis, of Treorky, scored for Rhondda United. In the second half Dick Jones scored an unconverted try for Willie's team and Gwilym Walters, of Treherbert, equalised with a similar effort for the Rhondda. Dai Jones then scored another unconverted try for Willie's team to give them victory by 9 points to six. The game proved to be a great success and as a result the sum of £90 was handed over to the Mid-Rhondda Nursing Association.

At last Willie's rugby season came to an end with the game for Glamorgan against Cornwall at Camborne late in April. Willie captained the side which included eight Welsh internationals. The team was as follows: Back, T Walton; three-quarter backs, Willie Llewellyn (Captain), Teddy Morgan, Rhys Gabe and Fred Jowett; half-backs, Dick Jones and Dickie Owen; forwards, A Brice, W T Osborne, D J Thomas, D Davies, D Fryer, W O'Neil and 'Buller' Rees. The three-quarter line and half-backs were the same as that of the previous week and they played splendidly well together. In the first half Teddy Morgan opened the scoring with an unconverted try. The Cornishmen fought back and equalised when Wedge forced his way over for an unconverted try. This, however, was the end of the scoring for the home team and from now until the end of the game Glamorgan were in total control. Before the interval Fred Jowett scored two tries the first of which was converted by Alfred Brice and the second by Walton. Just before the interval Dick Jones crossed for an unconverted try which gave Glamorgan a half-time lead of 16 points to three.

Glamorgan played against the wind in the second half but continued where they left off in the first. Teddy Morgan scored his second try of the afternoon and Walton, who came into the team in place of Bert Winfield, added the extra points. Fred Jowett then scored his third try which Walton failed to convert. Within a minute the Glamorgan backs again broke away and fine passing ended in Willie Llewellyn scoring a try in the corner which Brice converted with a magnificent kick. Just before the final whistle Fred Jowett scored his fourth try of the afternoon. Although the try went unconverted Glamorgan were convincing winners by 32 points to three.

The game for Glamorgan brought Willie's season to a close. The injury he sustained playing for Newport against Edinburgh University disrupted his season considerably. Willie only played 24 games during the season and only scored 7 tries. By his high standards this was a poor return, nevertheless, he had played really well in most games he played and scored two tries for Wales in the international against Ireland. During the season Willie's appetite for the game saw him play club rugby for London Welsh, Cardiff, Newport and Penygraig, county rugby for Glamorgan and Kent and international rugby for Wales. Willie's season culminated in him captaining Glamorgan to a very comfortable win over Cornwall.

With Willie performing well on the international rugby stage, his younger brother George, was just starting his rugby career at Christ College, Brecon. George had become a regular member of the College first fifteen rugby team and played very well. The 1902 December edition of *The Breconian* said the following with regard to George: 'An excellent kick, good tackler, and safe field; has played many very fine games this season, and for a recruit shown admirable coolness. Does not always sit on a rush.' This was a promising start for George who had another two seasons at Christ College in which to develop. George was also a member of the first eleven cricket team and played regularly for the College during the summer term. With regard to his cricket the 1903 July edition of *The Breconian* made the following comments: 'Has a good eye and can score off loose bowling, but does not play with a straight bat. A promising bowler and an excellent field.' Willie was also a keen cricketer and played regularly for Mid-Rhondda during the summer months. Early in July Willie took the Mid-Rhondda Thursday cricket team up to Christ College for a match against his old college. The same edition of *The Breconian* gave this summary of the game: '*Christ College v. Mr. W. M. Llewellyn's XI.*— Played at Brecon on July 2nd. Mr. W. M. Llewellyn, O.B., brought up a very moderate side to oppose the School. Taking first innings, they were all dismissed by Dyke and Phillips for 40 runs. The School made a poor show, though the bowling was far from good, and it was only a good stand by Schenk and James which saved them from defeat.' E M James scored 12 runs while H G Schenck scored a credible 21 runs in a total of 67 all out. This was an interesting match with George and Willie playing against each other. George was out for 3 runs caught off the bowling of his brother. Willie, however, didn't do so well and was bowled out for just 2 runs. Willie also took three catches in the game one of which was that of Louis Dyke. Although Dyke was out for a duck he had bowled brilliantly and took six wickets. Louis Dyke, who was also a member of the Christ College first fifteen, went on to play for Penarth and Cardiff. He played 107 times for Cardiff, scoring thirty-three tries and captained them during the 1911–12 season. He was capped four times by Wales, playing in the centre against Ireland in 1910 and against Scotland, France and Ireland in 1911.

Willie returned to Christ College later in July to play cricket for the Old Breconians against the College. Also in the Old Breconians team were fellow Welsh rugby internationals Rev. Willie Llewellyn Thomas and Teddy Morgan. George was again playing for Christ College. The Old Breconians won the toss and batted first. They were all out for 157 runs with Willie having a much better day with the bat than on his previous visit; he was second top scorer with 30 runs. The College fared poorly and being quite unable to cope with the bowling of Teddy Morgan, they were all out for 47 runs.

The Old Breconians' race was run after the match and there was enthusiastic interest, as both Willie Llewellyn and Teddy Morgan were running from scratch. A good race ended in a win for Teddy with Willie in second place. J C M 'John' Dyke was third.

With reference to the fifteen Welsh players who defeated New Zealand in 1905, eleven were now international players. Two more were added to the international list when George Travers and Bert Winfield were capped for Wales during the 1902–03 Season. George 'Twyber' Travers gained his first cap for Wales in the international against England. Not everyone was happy with his selection and a report in the *Evening Express* suggested that Edwin 'Beddoe' Thomas Maynard would have been a better choice. However, this was not the general consensus and Travers was worthy of his selection. He had been selected for the Welsh trial match that was abandoned in December 1902 and captained Pill Harriers to their third consecutive Monmouthshire League title. He was selected to represent the East in the match against the West in April 1903 but withdrew. George Travers went on to win twenty-five caps for Wales between 1903 and 1911. He appeared in the Triple Crown side of 1905 and the Grand Slam sides of 1908, 1909 and 1911. He captained Wales against Scotland in the Grand Slam season of 1908.

Having been the Welsh reserve full-back on eleven occasions Bert Winfield at last gained his first Welsh cap in the final international of the season against Ireland at Cardiff Arms Park. Winfield was captain of Cardiff from 1901 until 1903 and for Wales in one game, against Ireland in Belfast 1908. He ranks as one of the best full-backs to ever play for Cardiff and played 244 games. Bert Winfield was capped 15 times by Wales and scored fifty points during his international career from 14 conversion, 6 penalties and 1 goal from a mark. In December 1908 fate once more took a hand in Bert Winfield's international rugby career. He dislocated his thumb in Cardiff's victory over the Barbarians on Boxing Day and was unable to play for Cardiff in their victory over the Wallabies two days later. The injury also meant that Bert Winfield, who was selected to play

George 'Twyber' Travers of Pill Harriers won twenty-five caps for Wales between 1903 and 1911.

Bert Winfield played fifteen times for Wales between 1903 and 1908.

for Wales against England at Cardiff Arms Park on Saturday 16th January 1909, had to withdraw from the team. Once again it was to be a Bancroft that was his nemesis. This time it was Swansea's Jack Bancroft, brother of the famous W J 'Billy' Bancroft who had kept Winfield out of the Welsh team for so long. With Bert Winfield unable to play against England, Jack Bancroft came into the side for his first Welsh cap. Wales won by 8 points to nil and Jack Bancroft played in nine consecutive games for Wales by which time Bert Winfield's international career was over. Jack Bancroft went on to play eighteen times for Wales between 1909 and 1914. He was a prolific kicker and kicked 38 conversions and 4 penalty goals for Wales during his international career.

The four remaining players who played against New Zealand in 1905 and had not yet been capped for Wales were Cliff Pritchard and Charlie Pritchard of Newport, J F 'Jack' Williams of London Welsh and Percy Bush of Cardiff. Cliff Pritchard was a regular first team player for Newport and had also been selected for the Welsh trial match that was abandoned in December 1902. He was a very important member of the Newport side that won the Welsh Club Championship in 1902–03 and scored 15 tries and dropped 1 goal during the season. He played in 28 of the 33 games played by Newport and was reserve centre for Wales in the internationals against England and Scotland. He was a member of the successful East team in their victory over the West in April 1903. Charlie Pritchard's career was also progressing well. He was also a member of the Newport side that won the Championship in 1902–03. He also played in 28 of the 33 games played and scored two tries. He was a very tough scrummager and excellent in defence. Both he and Cliff Pritchard would gain their first Welsh caps the following season. Jack Williams was a regular for London Welsh and also played county rugby for Middlesex during the season. Finally, Percy Bush was still regularly playing wing three-quarter for Cardiff and was a critical member of the team. He was second top try scorer with twelve tries and also dropped two goals and kicked one penalty. Percy also played for Glamorgan County in their game against Cornwall in January 1903.

With the season over, Willie had one eye on the future. In January it had been reported that he had successfully completed his pharmaceutical examinations. A report in the *Rhondda Leader* commented, 'We are glad to find that Mr Willie Llewellyn, the well-known international footballer and Mr Iestyn Jones, son of Mr D Jones, assistant overseer, have both passed the final examinations of the Pharmaceutical Society, entitling them to act as properly qualified chemists. Both of the successful students were pupils of Mr J W Richards, chemist, Llwynypia.' In reference to Willie the report went on to say, 'Mr Llewellyn, although such a worthy exponent of football and the hero of many an international triumph, has yet maintained a level head and becoming modesty and has 'stuck to his last' and come through his examinations with success and credit.' The report was an example of the high esteem that was afforded to Willie throughout his life. A further report in the *Evening Express* in September 1903 stated, 'it is now quite certain that Willie Llewellyn will be in the Newport ranks this season. He will next month be in the shop of Messrs. Phillips Chemist, Commercial Street, as had been anticipated and will be available for football purposes.' Another report in the *Evening Express* suggested that Willie would be helping his old club Llwynypia but recognised that it was more likely that he would be playing for Newport. Willie played the first four games of the 1903–04 season for Newport and a meeting of the Welsh Football Union in early November confirmed Willie's transfer from London Welsh to Newport. In Willie's absence London Welsh was in good hands with fellow Christ College Old Boy, Arthur Harding, taking over the reins as captain. London Welsh continued to improve and the improved results in the period between 1903 and 1905 were a breakthrough in the history of the club. They heralded a brilliant few years which became a mini golden-era. In 1905–06 London Welsh won 21 of the 27 games they played. This feat was not bettered until the class of 1970–71 when, under the captaincy of John Dawes, London Welsh won 28 out of the 34 matches they played.

Chapter Seven

Newport Rugby Football Club 1903–04

A LINE IN THE *Evening Express* reported that Willie Llewellyn would play his first game of the season for Llwynypia against Pill Harriers on Saturday 19th September. As it turned out Willie did not play in that match and in fact he didn't play for them at all during the season. Willie was selected to play for Glamorgan in their match against Yorkshire at Harrogate on Saturday 26th September but both he and Teddy Morgan were unable to appear. Nevertheless, Glamorgan won the game by 11 points to three. Willie's first game of the season was for Newport in their home match against Old Merchant Taylors. Newport had beforehand beaten Tredegar and London Welsh and continued their winning ways against Old Merchant Taylors with a victory by 6 points to nil. Willie helped Newport defeat Gloucester at Kingsholm and was also a member of the team that defeated Cardiff a week later. Played at Newport before some 10,000 spectators, the game was exciting from start to finish. With no score at the interval the only score of the game came late in the second half when Charlie Lewis dropped a fine goal.

Having been injured for nearly two months the previous season luck was not on Willie's side during the early part of the 1903–04 campaign. In the first ten minutes of Newport's next game, against Blackheath at the Rectory Field, Willie broke his collar-bone and had to leave the field.

Newport Rugby Football Club 1903–04

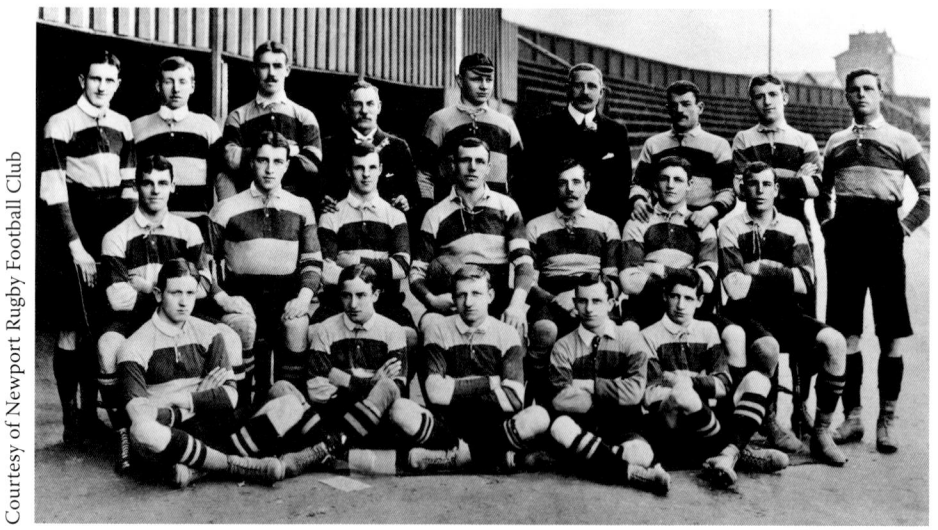

Back Row: J Evans, E Seer, S P Bland, G Thomas (Trainer), J C Jenkins,
H Packer (Hon. Sec.), G Spillane, G H Thomas, H Wetter.
Middle Row: C E Lewis, C M Pritchard, W M Llewellyn, G Boots (Captain),
J J Hodges (Vice-Captain), E Thomas, S Adams.
Front Row: R B Griffiths, T H Vile, D J Boots, F W Huggett, W Bennett.

Nonetheless, Newport took the lead when Harry Wetter crossed for a try which Charlie Lewis converted. A few minutes later Blackheath kicked a penalty and just before half-time they scored an unconverted try to put them ahead at the interval. There is no doubt that Willie's accident cost Newport the game, for having to rely on seven forwards they could not hold the Blackheath pack. Two converted tries early in the second half put the game beyond Newport and, although Charlie Lewis dropped a goal and Wyatt Gould scored a try which Charlie Lewis converted, it was not enough, Newport losing a distinctly interesting game by 16 points to fourteen.

Willie missed the next seven Newport games and was also unavailable for the Welsh international trial match played at Tredegar on Saturday 5th December. The result of a very poor game was a victory for the Possibles by 3 points to nil. The ground was hard with frost and those who had already secured their Welsh caps were 'not exerting themselves' and taking as little risk as possible. A first half unconverted try by Cecil Biggs of Cardiff was the only score of the game. Hop Maddock of London Welsh played well in his first trial match. Ten of the Welsh team that defeated New Zealand in December 1905 took part, with Bert Winfield, Gwyn Nicholls, Rhys Gabe, Dickie Owen, Jehoida Hodges, George Travers and Arthur Harding all playing for the Probables and Cliff Pritchard, Jack Williams and Charlie Pritchard playing for the Possibles.

In order to prove his fitness prior to the match against Swansea, Willie Llewellyn was selected to play for Newport Thursday's against Merthyr on 10th December. Unfortunately, the game which was to be played at Newport was cancelled because the ground was very wet and soft after heavy rain. As a result Willie didn't play against Swansea, a game which Newport won by 4 points to nil through Charlie Lewis' first half dropped goal. This was Swansea's only defeat of the season in which they were Welsh club champions for the fifth time in six seasons. Willie also missed the away victory against Leicester.

Although Willie did not travel to Leicester, he played for the first time since his injury at Blackheath when he turned out for the Christ College Old Boys when they played the Present at Brecon on Thursday 17th December. The game in the first half was very evenly contested with the College leading at the interval by 10 points to five. F Davies scored for the Old Boys after a clever corkscrew run by Willie Llewellyn, who played in the centre. Lack of training told on the Old Boys in the second half and although Willie scored a try, they were completely outclassed by the College who ended the game victorious by 39 points to ten. Willie's younger brother, George, along with J P Jones and Eric Thomas were outstanding for the College. Old Boy Hinckley Williams was the referee.

Willie returned to the Newport team for the Christmas Eve game against Pontypool. The original opponents on that day were intended to be Edinburgh University but they cried off and Pontypool filled the vacancy. Pontypool were the only undefeated team in the Monmouthshire League and the holiday crowd were treated to some excellent football. The only score of the first half was an unconverted try for Newport by Jehoida Hodges. Early in the second half Willie Llewellyn was tackled just short of the line and then Pontypool retaliated with a try which their captain, J Price, scored with about four Newport players on his back. Chick Jenkins converted to put Pontypool two points ahead. In the latter stages of the game, Willie Llewellyn, after some clever play, scored his first Newport try of the season. Charlie Lewis failed to convert but the try was enough to give Newport a narrow victory by 6 points to five. The report in the *South Wales Daily News* made the following observation: 'Willie Llewellyn was given few chances. Once he made a remarkably pretty run and all but scored, but on the whole he was not in his usual form and considering that he has not played for some months this could hardly be expected of him. There were however, times when he brought off some clever bits of play.' With Willie back in the team, Newport could look forward to the remainder of the season. Willie played in all seventeen remaining games, only four of which Newport lost: twice to Swansea and twice to Llanelly.

On Boxing Day Newport drew 3 points all with Watsonians and then on the 28th December faced the Barbarians at Rodney Parade. In front of 8,000 spectators the Barbarians were the first to score when after about fifteen minutes Bingham crossed for a try which Wayne Morgan converted. Two minutes later Charlie Lewis delighted the home crowd by dropping an excellent goal. However, this was a tough game and shortly afterwards Ronald Huggett had to withdraw with a dislocated knee-cap. His place at half-back was taken by Sid Adams from the forwards. Just before the interval there was great concern when Willie Llewellyn was injured going flat out for the Barbarians' line. He was heavily tackled and was laid out for a minute or two. Fortunately he was able to continue and suffered no lasting effects from the heavy knock. At the interval the visitors led by 5 points to four.

Newport attacked strongly in the second half and after a couple of smart rounds of passing, Willie Llewellyn crossed for an unconverted try. George Boots was the next to score and this time Charlie Lewis was successful with the conversion. Shortly afterwards Cliff Pritchard added another try which Charlie Lewis again converted. Just before the end of the game David Boots, the Newport custodian, made a fine tackle and prevented an almost certain try by Barbarian winger King-Stephens. Newport won the game by 17 points to five and played more to their true form than in any other match over the Christmas period. The forwards, although weakened for the greater part of the game by the retirement of Ronald Huggett, played wonderfully well.

On the evening following the game against the Barbarians the match committee of the Welsh Football Union met at the Queen's Hotel, Cardiff and selected the Welsh team to face England at Welford Road, Leicester on Saturday 9th January. Willie was in the team which included just three changes from the Welsh team that had played so well against Ireland the previous season. With Will Osborne having gone North to Huddersfield in September 1903 and Dai Jones still seriously ill with typhoid fever, David John Thomas of Swansea and Sam Ramsay of Treorchy were selected in the pack. Dick Jones of Swansea returned to the side in place of George Llewellyn Lloyd who played his last game for Wales in the victory over Ireland the previous season.

The away match against Llanelly heralded the resumption of fixtures which had been suspended for two years because of a dispute between the two clubs. Newport were well beaten and although neither side had scored up to the interval Llanelly ran away with the game in the second half. Newport were the first to score when Eddie Seer crossed for an unconverted try. Following some fairly even play Llanelly scored their first try when Harry Watkins galloped over and Bob Richards converted. Alby Davies was the next to score after he received the ball and put in a huge kick which he followed up brilliantly, gathered himself and scored. Bob Richards again converted from a difficult angle. Llanelly were now all over Newport and just before the end of the game Newport were penalised for off-side. The ball was placed for Bob Richards, who hit the post, but Jim Watts, following up smartly, gathered the ball and dived over for a try under the posts that Bob Richards converted. Shortly afterwards the final whistle went and Newport were well beaten by 15 points to three.

When Wales played England at Welford Road, Leicester, there was only one change from the team originally selected. Jack Evans of Blaina came into the team in place of the injured George Travers. This was Jack Evans' only cap for Wales. He spent his working life in the collieries and turned down several offers to go North. The teams were as follows:

Wales: Back, H B Winfield (Cardiff); three-quarters, W M Llewellyn (Newport), E G Nicholls (Cardiff, Captain), R T Gabe (Llanelly), E Morgan (London Welsh); half-backs, R H Jones and R M Owen (Swansea); forwards, A F Harding (London Welsh), A B Brice (Aberavon), J G Boots, J J Hodges (Newport), *D J Thomas, W Joseph (Swansea), *J W Evans (Blaina), S H Ramsay (Treorchy). (* Wales Debut)

England: Back, H T Gamlin (Devonport Albion); three-quarters, E J Vivyan (Devonport Albion), A T Brettargh (Liverpool OB), *E W Dillon (Blackheath), E W Elliott (Sunderland); half-backs, *P S Hancock (Richmond), W V Butcher (Bristol); forwards, *C J Newbold, B A Hill (Blackheath), *G H Keeton (Richmond), P F Hardwick (Percy Park.), V H Cartwright (Nottingham), *N J N H Moore (Bristol), *J G Milton (Bedford GS), F M Stout (Richmond, Captain). (* England Debut)

Referee: J Crawford Findlay (Scotland).

The early exchanges of the match were fairly even and it was a ding-dong battle with play going from end to end. Eventually the English forwards broke from the centre and getting past Bert Winfield, Edgar Elliott crossed for a try with Gwyn Nicholls on his back. The kick at goal failed and shortly afterwards Wales were penalised for about the seventh or eighth time in the game and Herbert Gamlin kicked the goal to give England a 6 point advantage at the break.

Wales Team v England 1904

Back Row: Mr G E Bowen (Touch-judge, WFU), A F Harding, J Evans, S H Ramsay, D J Thomas, W Joseph, Mr W E Rees (Sec. WFU). *Middle Row*: J J Hodges, A B Brice, J G Boots, E G Nicholls (Captain), H B Winfield, W M Llewellyn, E Morgan. *Front Row*: R M Owen, R T Gabe, R H Jones.

Wales started well in the second half and after Dick Jones cleverly broke through he got the ball away to Gwyn Nicholls. The Welsh captain passed on to Willie Llewellyn who raced over for a brilliant try which Bert Winfield converted. With Wales just one point behind they attacked at every opportunity and just when they looked like scoring again, Herbert Gamlin turned defence into attack by dribbling and kicking past Bert Winfield. Edgar Elliott again dashed up from the right wing and kicking over the line touched down for his second try of the game. With Wales now four points behind the Welsh forwards worked hard to give their half-backs plenty of the ball but try as they did Dickie Owen and Dick Jones could not break through the English defence. Eventually however, they had the ball and after brilliant passing by Dick Jones, Gwyn Nicholls, Rhys Gabe and Teddy Morgan, the Welsh wing scored in the far left corner. Bert Winfield, with a truly magnificent kick, converted to give Wales a one point lead. A mistake by Bert Winfield let England in for another try when he misfielded a kick by Elliott. Brettargh, following up, scored near the post and Frank Stout converted. All was not lost and when Will Joseph made a mark just about on the half-way line the ball was placed for Bert Winfield. The Cardiff custodian, with another brilliant kick, landed one of the finest goals ever seen at the ground.

With the scores even at 14 points all, Wales attacked more aggressively than at any other point in the game and following a brilliant round of passing between the Welsh three-quarters Teddy Morgan crossed for a try. To everyone's astonishment the referee disallowed the try and although Wales had two further chances of scoring, with Rhys Gabe missing a drop at goal and George Boots passing forward in front of the posts, there was no further scores and the game was drawn at 14 points all.

In reference to the game, Howard Evans, in his book *Welsh International Matches 1881–2011*, made the following comments: 'Wales were unhappy that a Morgan try was disallowed and Dickie Owen was so heavily penalised for feeding it crooked at the scrums that he left opposite number Walter Butcher put it in. Scotland-born Sam Ramsay returned after an eight year absence and England wing Elliott Vivyan missed five goal attempts. The Scotland referee was heavily criticised by the Welsh press.'

Willie returned to the Newport team the week after the international and scored the only try in the 3 points to nil away victory over Devonport

Albion. Llewellyn Lloyd, playing his first game of the season for Newport, gave the scoring pass to Willie Llewellyn. Devonport had much the better of the argument in the second half but still they were unable to score. The magnificent Newport defence stood firm with Elliot Vivyan being held on the Newport line on no fewer than three occasions.

Having beaten Swansea earlier in the season, Newport faced the impending Welsh club champions for the thirty-seventh time at St Helen's on Saturday 23rd January. The Swansea side, captained by Will Parker, contained eleven Welsh internationals and Sid Bevan, who was soon to be capped against Ireland. Within five minutes of the start Dick Jones scored an unconverted try and ten minutes later Billy Trew scored another which Will Joseph converted. The Newport forwards looked as if they were well beaten but they rallied marvellously and played really well up to the interval when Swansea held the lead by 8 points to nil. The score remained the same right up until the last two minutes of the game when Fred Jowett intercepted a Newport pass and sprinted the full length of the field. The kick at goal failed but Swansea were deserved winners by 11 points to nil.

Although selected to play for Glamorgan against Devon at Exeter, Willie, along with four other players originally selected, did not appear. Nevertheless, Glamorgan fielded a strong team with five out of the seven backs being Welsh internationals. With the game being played the day before the Welsh team to face Scotland at St Helen's was selected, the match was considered as a full-dress trial and five of the Glamorgan forwards were selected with this in mind. As it turned out no actual fresh talent was discovered beyond D H Davies of Neath who unquestionably proved his worth and looked a very strong candidate for international honours. Glamorgan won the game quite comfortably by 16 points to three and David Harris Davies was duly selected to represent Wales against Scotland two weeks later.

The Welsh team selected to face Scotland at St Helen's included Willie Llewellyn with Gwyn Nicholls as captain. There was considerable doubt about Gwyn Nicholls' fitness after he badly injured his right knee playing for Cardiff against Llanelly the previous Saturday. Dan Rees was put on standby if Nicholls were unavailable. There were four changes from the team that had drawn with England at Leicester, all in the forwards.

George Boots (Newport), Sam Ramsay (Treorchy), David J Thomas (Swansea) and Jack Evans (Blaina) were dropped and replaced by David H Davies (Neath), Harry Watkins (Llanelly), Edwin 'Beddoe' Thomas (Newport) and Billy O'Neil (Cardiff).

Willie was not having his best season and had struggled to find his best form since returning from injury. The Welsh press were not on his side and prior to the Welsh team being selected the *Cambrian* had a snipe at him. Referring to Willie's performance in the game against Swansea, they wrote, 'Playing opposite Trew, Willie Llewellyn looked quite a second rater and his performance was such that nothing short of favouritism will take him into the Welsh team to meet Scotland.' Nonetheless, Willie was selected to face Scotland but the criticism did not stop. An article in the *Evening Express* two days after the team was selected made the following comments: 'The player to deputise Gwyn Nicholls is Dan Rees; Pritchard comes in for Gabe and Biggs for Llewellyn. The injury to Nicholls, if it keeps him out of the field, will seriously weaken the defence. And in this particular perhaps, sufficient attention has not been given to the selection of the wing. With Nicholls in there is no doubt that Llewellyn (who, by the bye, will captain in his captain's absence) deserves again to be included. But I confess that, if Nicholls be an absentee and Rees takes his place, I should prefer to see Trew performing at the side of his club-mate against Scotland. There is a feeling and not only down West, that Willie Llewellyn is far from his best at present and that all round Trew is just now the better man.' For the first time in his international career questions were being asked about Willie's selection and only his performance in the international match against Scotland would confirm whether the selectors were right or wrong.

In the meanwhile Willie still had one more game to play before facing Scotland, for Newport in their home game against Gloucester. It was an awful game because, after heavy rain the turf was very soft and greasy. The ground was covered with mud and the ball was difficult to handle. In the first couple of minutes Gloucester opened the scoring with a dropped goal by Harrison, but just before the interval Jack Jenkins forced his way over for a try which Charlie Lewis converted to give Newport a one point lead at the break. There was no score in the second half and when no-side was called the spectators and the players were relieved the game was over.

Wales Team v Scotland 1904

Back Row: Mr D H Bowen (Touch-judge, WFU), H V Watkins, A F Harding, D H Davies, W Joseph, W O'Neil, H B Winfield. *Middle Row*: J J Hodges, C C Pritchard, W M Llewellyn (Captain), R T Gabe, E Thomas, A B Brice. *Front Row*: R M Owen, E Morgan, R H Jones.

Willie's next game was for Wales against Scotland at St Helen's, Swansea, on Saturday 6th February. Gwyn Nicholls had not recovered from the knee injury sustained in the game against Llanelly and Cliff Pritchard of Newport came into the side for his first Welsh international cap. It was originally intended that Dan Rees of Swansea should play if Gwyn Nicholls was unavailable but an injury to Rees's hand prevented him from playing and Cliff Pritchard was summoned by the Welsh Football Union. This was the only change from the team originally selected other than Willie Llewellyn taking over the captaincy.

Wales: Back, H B Winfield (Cardiff); three-quarters, W M Llewellyn (Newport, Captain), *Cliff C Pritchard (Newport), R T Gabe (Cardiff), E Morgan (London Welsh); half-backs, R H Jones and R M Owen (Swansea); forwards, A F Harding (London Welsh), A B Brice, *W O'Neil

(Cardiff), W Joseph (Swansea), J J Hodges (Newport), *D H Davies (Neath), *H V Watkins (Llanelly), *E Thomas (Newport). (* Wales Debut)

Scotland: Back, W T Forrest (Hawick); three-quarters, *G E Crabbie (Edinburgh Acads), H J Orr (London Scottish), *L M MacLeod (Cambridge U), J S McDonald (Edinburgh U); Half-backs, *A A Bissett (RIEC), E D Simson (Edinburgh U); forwards, M C Morrison (Royal HSFP, Captain), W E Kyle (Hawick), W P Scott, G O Turnbull (West of Scotland), D R Bedell-Sivright (Cambridge U), A G Cairns (Watsonians), *E J Ross (London Scottish), L H Bell (Edinburgh Acads). (* Scotland Debut)

Referee: F W Nicholls (England).

A crowd of 35,000 spectators watched Wales defeat Scotland by 21 points to three. The match was as good as over by half-time when Wales were leading by 13 points to nil. Wales opened their account when, after fifteen minutes, Bert Winfield kicked a penalty goal. A quarter of an hour later Teddy Morgan cleared the way for Rhys Gabe to score and Bert Winfield added the extra points. Just on half-time some clever work by Dickie Owen enabled him to get the ball away to Willie Llewellyn who opened up the Scottish defence and put Dick Jones in for another Welsh try. Bert Winfield again converted and Wales were well ahead at the break.

In the first five minutes of the second half Teddy Morgan put the result beyond doubt when he crossed for an unconverted try. Scotland replied with an unconverted try by H J Orr but it was too little too late. In the final stages of the game Alfred Brice scored a brilliant try for Wales and Bert Winfield added the extra points to give the Principality a comfortable victory. Wales took full advantage of their chances while Scotland often squandered theirs. Although Scotland never gave up they were overshadowed at forward and outplayed behind the scrummage. Dick Jones and Dickie Owen were outstanding and Cliff Pritchard, in his

Dinner Menu from the after match function held at the Royal Hotel, Swansea.

first international, made a good impression. This was a fine victory for Wales as Scotland went on to win their next two games against Ireland and England and take the Home Nations championship.

The following week Willie returned to Newport for their game against Neath at the Gnoll. Willie was in blistering form and scored three of the five unconverted tries recorded in the 15 points to nil victory. Charlie Lewis scored the other two tries. Jack Jenkins broke his arm in this game and did not play for the remainder of the season.

Percy Bush was playing in his new position of outside-half when Newport met Cardiff for the third time during the season. Honours were even at a win apiece going into the game, and the stalemate continued when the game ended in a 3-all draw. There was no score at half-time but early in the second half Alfred Brice broke through and put Billy O'Neil in for a try which Bert Winfield failed to convert. Five minutes from the end of the match Newport scrum-half Tommy Vile crossed for a try in the corner and with Charlie Lewis failing to convert the game ended in a draw.

Willie played his only county match of the season when Glamorgan defeated Somerset at Cardiff on Wednesday 24th February. It was expected that Gwyn Nicholls would play but he had not fully recovered from his injury and was unavailable. The side included several internationals, among them Bert Winfield, Willie Arnold, Rhys Gabe and Willie Llewellyn in the backs and David H Davies and Billy O'Neil up front. Also in the side were future Welsh internationals Percy Bush (Cardiff), Howell Jones (Neath) and Sid Bevan (Swansea). George Vickery of Aberavon was one of the Glamorgan forwards; he gained one cap for England against Ireland in 1905. Glamorgan opened the scoring when Cecil Biggs scored an unconverted try. Somerset fought back and scored two unconverted tries before the break to give them a 3 point advantage.

In the second half Joey Burchell, the Neath scrum-half, scored a try which Bert Winfield converted to give Glamorgan the lead. Just before the final whistle Howell Jones scored another try for Glamorgan and although it was not converted, Glamorgan won by 11 points to six. Although not yet capped by Wales, Percy Bush had a wonderful game and was actively involved from start to finish.

Newport won their next game against Bristol quite comfortably but at a major cost. Jehoida Hodges dislocated his thumb in the game and didn't play for a month missing the Newport games against Swansea and Cardiff and the Welsh international against Ireland. The game was a perfect exhibition of forward play and Newport defeated a very strong Bristol side by 13 points to nil, all the three tries being scored by the forwards. The first was by Charlie Pritchard when he picked up and dashed his way over for a try which Jack Evans converted. Three minutes later Cliff Pritchard doubled his way through in brilliant fashion and when confronted by the last man put Harry Wetter in for an unopposed try. The conversion failed but Newport were 8 points ahead at the interval.

With snow falling at the start of the second half, Newport increased their lead when George Boots, picking up briskly, forced his way over for a try which Jack Evans splendidly converted. With no further scores Newport were the victors. Cliff Pritchard, never less than sound and occasionally brilliant, was the best back on the field. Willie Llewellyn had a tough afternoon and although he played well, his opposite number D W Smith was one of the fastest wings playing and stopped Willie getting away on several occasions during the match.

The match committee of the Welsh Football Union met at the Queen's Hotel, Cardiff on the Thursday after the Bristol game to select the team to represent Wales against Ireland at Belfast on Saturday 12th March. There was only one change from the team that had beaten Scotland: Gwyn Nicholls returned to the team in place of Cliff Pritchard and reclaimed the captaincy from Willie Llewellyn. Cliff Pritchard was selected reserve left centre.

Newport still had one match to play before Wales' match against Ireland, facing Swansea for the fourth and final time the week before the international. Swansea had only lost one game (against Newport earlier in the season) and although Jehoida Hodges had been selected to play for Wales, he still wasn't fit and didn't face the All Whites. The other two Newport players selected for Wales, Willie Llewellyn and Edwin 'Beddoe' Thomas (real name Edwin Thomas Maynard) were in the team. Cliff Pritchard was also unavailable. For Swansea, Dick Jones withdrew because of an injured thigh but Dickie Owen and Will Joseph played. Swansea thus had a very strong fifteen which also included the Welsh reserves George Davies, Dan Rees, Billy Trew and Sid Bevan. Also in the team were previously capped David John Thomas, Willie Arnold, Fred Jowett, Fred Scrine and Will Parker.

The pitch was in an awful condition because the Newport and Swansea schoolboys had played on it in the morning when sleet had fallen continuously. Seldom had the pitch been in a worse state. The bad weather also had an adverse effect on attendance and the crowd was the smallest seen at a Newport v Swansea match for many years. Frank Gordon opened the scoring for Swansea when he ran from the twenty-five and scored a beautiful try which George Davies converted. Swansea followed this up with a magnificent try after Dickie Owen broke through the Newport defence and created an opening for Dan Rees. He gathered the ball and ran to within a yard of the line where he stumbled. Quickly regaining his feet, he grounded the ball over the line. The conversion attempt failed and with no further scores Swansea led at the interval by 8 points to nil.

In the second half a fine tackle by Willie Llewellyn on Fred Scrine resulted in both players being injured. Willie resumed but Scrine had to leave the field and Swansea were reduced to fourteen men. Even with seven forwards the Swansea men were beating the Newport eight badly and controlling practically every scrum. It was only the most determined tackling by the Newport backs that prevented Swansea from scoring on several occasions. Towards the end of the game Willie Arnold took advantage of some poor passing by the Newport backs and running brilliantly he passed to Fred Jowett who put the game beyond doubt by scoring Swansea's third try. Although George Davies failed to convert Swansea cruised to victory by 11 points to nil. Once again Willie was not at his best for although he had comparatively few chances, when he was given an opportunity he seemed to lack his former resource and cleverness.

Nevertheless, Willie was in the Welsh team selected to play against Ireland and as luck turned out, with Gwyn Nicholls again unable to play Willie was captain of the Welsh team for the second time. Cliff Pritchard returned to the team in place of the injured Gwyn Nicholls. For the first time in Welsh international rugby history three reserve forwards took the field. With Jehoida Hodges, Will Joseph and D H Davies all withdrawing because of injury, Charlie M Pritchard (Newport), Sid Bevan (Swansea) and Howell 'Harry' Jones (Neath) all came into the team to gain their first Welsh caps. Although Charlie Pritchard went on to win fourteen caps for

Wales, Sid Bevan and Howell Jones gained their solitary Welsh caps in this game. The teams took the field as follows:

Wales: Back, H B Winfield (Cardiff); three-quarters, W M Llewellyn (Newport, Captain), Cliff C Pritchard (Newport), R T Gabe (Cardiff), E Morgan (London Welsh); half-backs, R H Jones and R M Owen (Swansea); forwards, A F Harding (London Welsh), A B Brice, W O'Neil (Cardiff), *C M Pritchard (Newport), *T S Bevan (Swansea), *H Jones (Neath), H V Watkins (Llanelly), E 'Beddoe' Thomas (Newport). (* Wales Debut)

Ireland: Back, *M F Landers (Cork Const); three-quarters, *H Thrift, J C Parke (Dublin U), G A D Harvey (Wanderers), C G Robb (QCB); half-backs, L M Magee (Bective), F A Kennedy (Wanderers); forwards, C E Allen (Derry, Captain), A Tedford, *R W Edwards (Malone), *H J Knox (Dublin U), F Gardiner (NIFC), *H J Millar (Monkstown), G T Hamlet (Old Wesley), Joseph Wallace (Wanderers). (* Ireland Debut)

Referee: J Crawford Findlay (Scotland).

With Ireland having been beaten in their first two internationals, firstly against England by 19 points to nil and then against Scotland by 19 points to three, it was expected that Wales would take the honours in this match played at Balmoral, Belfast. There was certainly concern that the enforced changes in the Welsh team would weaken the side but they were still quietly optimistic that victory would come their way. Wales had the advantage of a slight wind in the first half but it was Ireland that attacked first and only just failed to score when Parke missed a penalty kick at goal. Shortly afterwards, however, Robb raced through the visitors' line and gave a scoring pass to Alf Tedford. Undeterred the Welsh backs quickly got going and Rhys Gabe made a fine run before passing to Willie Llewellyn

Willie Llewellyn captained Wales for the first time against Scotland in 1904 and then again against Ireland the same year.

who, in turn transferred to Teddy Morgan who ran in for a brilliant try. Bert Winfield failed to convert but the scores were level. Willie was again prominent with a fine sprint and the Welsh forwards playing well together made matters quite warm for the home defence. But play changed quickly and Ireland, back on the attack, scored when Wallace raced in for an unconverted try to give the home side a 6–3 lead at the interval.

Ireland were without Robb for the second half and Joseph Wallace came out of the pack to take his place in the three-quarters. Early in the second half Wales equalised when Teddy Morgan put Rhys Gabe in for an unconverted try. Encouraged by their success, Wales played brilliantly and Cliff Pritchard put his side ahead with a clever try. Again Bert Winfield missed the conversion. Shortly afterwards Teddy Morgan scored another unconverted try and Wales were six points ahead. Just when it looked like Wales had the advantage, Ireland fought back and after a dazzling forward movement involving Hamlet and Tedford, Harry Thrift scored Ireland's third unconverted try. Ireland now took the upper hand and when Bert Winfield was beaten to the ball by Tedford, another try resulted for the home side to make matters bleak for Wales. Parke converted to put Ireland two points ahead. However, Wales were not yet beaten and several good runs by the backs resulted in Willie Llewellyn dashing over for a try. Unfortunately, not for the first time during this international season, the Scottish referee, Mr Crawford Findlay, disallowed the Welsh score, leaving Ireland victorious by 14 points to twelve.

The changes in the Welsh pack proved to be decisive and they were well beaten by the Irish eight in the first half and the Irish seven in the second. The Welsh players were obviously very disappointed with the result in Belfast and a report in the *Evening Express* in early April stated that a letter from the International Board had been received by the Welsh Football Union which included a copy of a report of the game from Scottish referee Crawford Findlay. In the report Mr Findlay alleged that Alfred Brice had told him after the game that he had robbed Wales of the Triple Crown. The Welsh Football Union concluded that Alfred Brice should be censured for his conduct and write a letter of apology to Mr Findlay. Brice was said to have been completely surprised by the censure and stated that 'no language had passed between him and the referee during or after the match' but he did agree that 'there was some little chaffing' but nothing offensive. Alfred Brice refused to apologise, with the outcome that he was suspended for eight months. After eighteen consecutive caps for Wales and two Triple Crowns, Alfred Brice never played for Wales again. The former Aberavon star continued to play for Cardiff and was a member of their team that defeated South Africa by 17 points to nil in 1907.

Five of the Welsh team who were defeated by Ireland were playing when Newport faced Cardiff on the Arms Park a week after the international: Willie Llewellyn, Cliff Pritchard and Edwin 'Beddoe' Thomas for Newport and Rhys Gabe and Billy O'Neil for Cardiff. After being out of the game for several months because of injury, Gwyn Nicholls returned to captain the side. Cardiff were without Bert Winfield, Percy Bush and Alfred Brice while Newport were still without the injured Jehoida Hodges. A crowd of between 10,000 and 15,000 spectators braved the awful weather to watch the two teams battle it out in the mud. An unconverted try by Cecil Biggs was the only score of the first half. Five minutes into the second half Cliff Pritchard scored an unconverted try for Newport and with no further scores the game was drawn at 3 points all.

Willie scored his ninth try of the season when Newport defeated Blackheath at home by 35 points to twelve. The following Saturday Newport narrowly lost by 3 points to nil at home against Llanelly. Played before a crowd of 4,000 spectators, rain fell throughout the game and play was chiefly confined to the forwards. The only score of the game was a first half unconverted try by D M Davies for Llanelly. Newport tried hard to equalise and although Willie Llewellyn was pulled down a yard from the line on one occasion, they failed to score and were narrowly defeated.

Willie added to his try count when Newport comfortably defeated Leicester at home. The game was evenly contested and played throughout in a good spirit. Newport had learnt the lessons of the defeat against Llanelly and although the forwards did not overcome the Leicester pack to any great extent, the backs handled better and showed all round better judgement. Jehoida Hodges returned to the side after several weeks out with injury and made an immediate impact on the game. Contrary to the Llanelly match, Newport took their scoring chances in much better style against the Midland Counties champions. First half tries by Harry Wetter, Willie Llewellyn and Edwin 'Beddoe' Thomas gave Newport a 9 point lead at the break. Early in the second half Charlie Lewis scored a brilliant try which he converted himself. Leicester replied with an unconverted try by Matthews but this was their only score of the game. Jack Evans scored again for Newport but the conversion failed. Just before the end of the game Charlie Lewis scored his second try and by successfully kicking the conversion gave Newport victory by 22 points to three.

The following Tuesday, Newport defeated Rockcliff by 12 points to three. Rockcliff scored first when English international Thomas Simpson scored an unconverted try. An unconverted try apiece for George Boots and Willie Llewellyn gave Newport the lead at the interval. In the second half Jack Evans put Willie Llewellyn in for an unconverted try and Charlie Lewis added another to give Newport the spoils.

Towards the end of the season Willie was selected to play for the East against the West at Cardiff. The three-quarter line was the Welsh international backs, Gwyn Nicholls, Rhys Gabe, Teddy Morgan and Willie Llewellyn. Also in the side were fellow international forwards Alfred Brice, Arthur Harding, Jehoida Hodges, George Boots, Billy O'Neil, Edwin 'Beddoe' Thomas and Dai Jones. Twelve of the West's side and everyone behind the scrum were from Swansea, who were unofficial Welsh champions. The half-backs were Dickie Owen and Dick Jones, both seasoned Welsh internationals. To everyone's surprise the East won by 18 points to seven.

The East v West game was played at Cardiff Arms Park on Wednesday 6th April 1904 and the comments on the game written by 'Forward' in the *Western Mail* the next day read as follows: 'Anticipations were realised in the sense that the match was one of the greatest of the season. Feeling was never more intense in any encounter between any two teams, and the display of football in all its different phases, has seldom if ever, been excelled. Comment at any length is unnecessary. The features of the game were the great play of the East forwards when they had only six men in the field, the cleverness of Percy Bush, and the brilliant run by which Teddy Morgan scored. The Westerners were fairly and squarely beaten, and without paying regard to past little differences of opinion they will, I am certain, readily agree with what I have consistently upheld, in the face of much cheap ridicule, that Bush is a great player. Vile combined beautifully with him, and the pair could be trusted anywhere on their

East Wales Team 1904

Back Row: Mr Tom Williams (Touch Judge, East), A F Harding, F Shugar, D Jones, W O'Neil, R T Gabe, W J Bancroft (Touch Judge, West). *Middle Row*: A B Brice, W M Llewellyn, J G Boots, E G Nicholls (Captain), J J Hodges, E 'Beddoe' Thomas. *Front Row*: E Morgan, D J Boots, T H Vile, P F Bush, T D Schofield (Referee).

form in this match. In the victorious East pack the two surprises were Dai Jones and George Boots, and, taking their play with that of the others, especially Shugar, my only regret is that the East pack of today did not play against Ireland at Belfast, with Joseph in the pack instead of – well, somebody.'

The game was played in front of a capacity crowd and there was only one change from the advertised teams, the veteran Frank Gordon taking the place of Fred Jowett on the right wing for the West. With twenty-two Welsh internationals, eleven in each side, taking part, expectations of a great game were high and the players did not disappoint.

East: Back, D J Boots (Newport); three-quarter backs, E G Nicholls (Cardiff, Captain), R T Gabe (Cardiff), W M Llewellyn (Newport), and E T Morgan (London Welsh); half-backs, Percy Bush (Cardiff) and T H Vile (Newport); forwards, A Brice (Cardiff), A F Harding (London

Welsh), J J Hodges (Newport), G Boots (Newport), W O'Neil (Cardiff), E 'Beddoe' Thomas (Newport), F Shugar (Penygraig), and Dai Jones (Aberdare).

West: Back, George Davies (Swansea); three-quarter backs, Dan Rees (Swansea, Captain), W Trew, F Gordon, and W Arnold (all of Swansea); half-backs, R M Owen and D Jones (Swansea); forwards, W Joseph, F Scrine, Sid Bevan, D J Thomas and D Davies (all of Swansea), H Watkins (Llanelly), George Vickery (Aberavon) and D Fryer (Mountain Ash).

A silver whistle was presented to the referee, T D Schofield of Bridgend, as a memento of the match and the two teams were photographed prior to the kick-off. Tom Williams was the touch judge for the East while Billy Bancroft undertook similar duties for the West. The West, in white jerseys, were the first onto the field about a quarter of an hour late. The East, in blue and black, quickly followed to great cheering. The West, winning the toss, decided to play with the wind at their backs, and Boots kicked off for the East. From the start it was clear that the two packs were not as evenly matched as had been anticipated, with the greater weight of the Eastern eight standing them in good stead in the tight mauls. The first score came when from a scrum, Dickie Owen passed to Dick Jones but Teddy Morgan dashed up in his characteristic style, intercepted, and running at great pace, swerved so beautifully that he gave George Davies no chance and sprinted round to score under the posts. Boots converted easily. Almost immediately after the kick out the West attacked and Gwyn Nicholls was stretched out after being tackled by one of the white forwards. Shortly afterwards Nicholls left the field with a broken rib and took no further part in the game. Jehoida Hodges was brought out of the pack to play on the wing and Teddy Morgan joined Rhys Gabe in the centre. Just before half-time George Davies, fielding the ball in the East twenty-five, dodged Hodges and dropped a beautiful goal from near the touch-line.

With the score at 5 points to 4 in the East's favour, Joseph re-started for the West. From a scrum Tommy Vile had the ball from his forwards and passed to Percy Bush, who put in the biggest kick of the match and found touch over the West's twenty-five line. From broken play Bush, fielding the ball close to the West twenty-five line and near the touch-line, dropped a magnificent goal. The Easterners, particularly Percy Bush, were showing excellent judgement by taking advantage of the wind in kicking and finding touch. The West were penalised for offside by Dickie Owen and Percy Bush just failed with a drop at goal. Almost immediately afterwards Hodges had the ball from a round of passing on the left wing, and finding he could not break through took a shot for goal. The ball struck the cross-bar, rebounded into play, where Billy O' Neil pounced on it to score a try which was easily converted by Percy Bush. Teddy Morgan had a severe crack on the head and had to leave the field for a short time. Harding was brought out of the pack to take his place in the three-quarters. The West, now playing against thirteen men, took advantage and Fred Scrine picked up a loose ball and bursting through passed to Dan Rees who ran over unopposed behind the posts. Unfortunately George Davies failed with the conversion. With the score at 14 points to 7 and the East still down to thirteen men, Rhys Gabe, taking a pass from Bush, doubled back instead of running to the wing and steadying himself dropped a clever goal. Just before the end Teddy Morgan returned, but there was no further score and the East won a vigorous and keenly contested game by 18 points to seven.

The medal presented to the players by Sir John Llewellyn, Bart at the end of the East and West encounter.

At the conclusion of the match the President of the Welsh Rugby Union, Sir John Llewellyn, Bart presented the players with a memento of the match. The money taken at the gates was counted at the Town Hall immediately after the match and totalled £487. 16s. With the addition of the grand-stand tickets the net receipts were well over £500, which was a Welsh record for a non-international match.

Newport played their penultimate game of the season away to Devonport Services. The remarkable feature of the game was that both sides did better against the wind than they did with it. Playing with the wind at their backs Newport were unable to score in the first half but Devonport Albion managed to cross for an unconverted try. In the second half, after

Willie Llewellyn's Newport Cap.

several strong attacks by the Newport forwards and some attractive passing by their backs, Charlie Lewis, Rowland Griffiths and Willie Llewellyn combined to allow Willie to cross for his final try of the season. With no other scoring the game was drawn at 3 points all.

Willie finished the season when Newport, having played all their official games, contested a friendly match against Bridgend on Saturday 23rd April. Bridgend were leading at the interval by 6 points to five, but three second half tries by Newport, two of which were converted, gave them the victory by 18 points to fourteen. Bridgend scored two further tries in the second half, one of which was converted, but it was not enough to give them the win.

At the end of the season Willie must have had mixed feelings as he reflected on his achievements. On the positive side he had played twenty-eight games which included three Welsh internationals and one county game for Glamorgan. He had captained Wales for the first time and scored a total of thirteen tries during the season. Willie played 22 games for Newport and was second top try scorer with eleven tries. Charlie Lewis was top try scorer with fifteen tries and often during the campaign Willie and Charlie had played brilliantly on the wings. It was during this season that Willie was awarded his Newport cap. Including the friendly game against Bridgend, Newport played 31 games in 1903-04 of which they won 20, lost 7 and drew 4. Injury to key players was a major factor in this not being one of Newport's best seasons, and not since the winter of 1899–1900 had they lost the same number of games.

On the negative side Willie's season had again been dogged by serious injury. The broken collar-bone sustained playing for Newport against Blackheath kept him out of the game for nearly two months and he struggled to find his true form when he returned. Moreover, for the first

Date	Team Played For	Opposition	Venue	Result	W Llewellyn Tries
	Willie Llewellyn Newport Games Played 1903-1904 Season				
	Willie Llewellyn Other Games Played 1903-1904 Season				
	Willie Llewellyn Welsh International and Welsh Trial Games Played 1903-1904 Season				
	Willie Llewellyn Glamorgan County Games Played 1903-1904 Season				
19/09/1903	Newport	Tredegar	Home	Won 29-0	Did not play
26/09/1903	Newport	London Welsh	Home	Won 15-8	Did not play
03/10/1903	Newport	Old Merchant Taylors	Home	Won 6-0	0
10/10/1903	Newport	Gloucester	Away	Won 19-3	0
17/10/1903	Newport	Cardiff	Home	Won 4-0	0
24/10/1903	Newport	Blackheath	Away	Lost 14-16	0
31/10/1903	Newport	Neath	Home	Won 17-5	Injured
07/11/1903	Newport	Swansea	Away	Lost 5-6	Injured
14/11/1903	Newport	Bristol	Home	Won 19-0	Injured
21/11/1903	Newport	Cardiff	Away	Lost 3-9	Injured
28/11/1903	Newport	Watsonians	Away	Won 5-0	Injured
05/12/1903	Probables	Possibles	Tredegar	Poss. Won 3-0	Injured
12/12/1903	Newport	Swansea	Home	Won 4-0	Injured
17/12/1903	Christ College OBs	Christ College Present	Brecon	Lost 10-39	1
19/12/1903	Newport	Leicester	Away	Won 7-0	Did not play
24/12/1903	Newport	Pontypool	Home	Won 6-5	1
26/12/1903	Newport	Watsonians	Home	Drawn 3-3	0
28/12/1903	Newport	Barbarians	Home	Won 17-5	1
02/01/1904	Newport	Llanelly	Away	Lost 3-15	0
09/01/1904	Wales	England	Welford Rd, Leicester	Drawn 14-14	1
16/01/1904	Newport	Devonport Albion	Away	Won 3-0	1
23/01/1904	Newport	Swansea	Away	Lost 0-11	0
27/01/1904	Glamorgan	Devon	Exeter	Won 16-3	Did not play
30/01/1904	Newport	Gloucester	Home	Won 5-4	0
06/02/1904	Wales	Scotland	St Helen's, Swansea	Won 21-3	0
13/02/1904	Newport	Neath	Away	Won 15-0	3
20/02/1904	Newport	Cardiff	Home	Drawn 3-3	0
24/02/1904	Glamorgan	Somerset	Cardiff Arms Park	Won 11-6	0
27/02/1904	Newport	Bristol	Away	Won 13-0	0
05/03/1904	Newport	Swansea	Home	Lost 0-11	0
12/03/1904	Wales	Ireland	Balmoral, Belfast	Lost 12-14	0
19/03/1904	Newport	Cardiff	Away	Drawn 3-3	0
26/03/1904	Newport	Blackheath	Home	Won 35-12	1
02/04/1904	Newport	Llanelly	Home	Lost 0-3	0
04/04/1904	Newport	Leicester	Home	Won 22-3	1
05/04/1904	Newport	Rockcliff	Home	Won 12-3	2
06/04/1904	East	West	Cardiff Arms Park	Won 18-7	0
09/04/1904	Newport	Devonport Albion	Away	Drawn 3-3	1
23/04/1904	Newport	Bridgend	Away	Won 18-14	0
	Willie Llewellyn Games Played				W Llewellyn Tries
Totals	28				13

Willie Llewellyn Rugby Games Played and Results 1903–1904 Season

time in his career the press were occasionally critical and on several occasions his ability was brought into question. Nevertheless, Willie survived and the 1904–05 season would be much more rewarding. In the meanwhile Willie had a tour to Australia and New Zealand to look forward to.

Thirteen of the fifteen Welsh players who would take the field against New Zealand in 1905 were now full Welsh internationals. During this season Cliff Pritchard and Charlie Pritchard, both of Newport, had joined the exclusive international club. Cliff Pritchard was one of the regular

Cliff Pritchard gained five Welsh caps between 1904 and 1906.

Charlie Pritchard gained fourteen Welsh caps between 1904 and 1910.

centre three-quarters for Newport and scored five tries during the season. He was a deadly tackler and a shrewd kicker. He played for the Possibles in the Welsh trial at Tredegar in December 1903 and was reserve left centre for Wales in the first international of the season against England at Leicester. He was selected as standby left centre for the international against Scotland and when Gwyn Nicholls stood down because of injury Cliff Pritchard came into the side for his first Welsh cap. He retained his place for the game against Ireland and scored a try in the narrow defeat. Cliff Pritchard transferred back to Pontypool at the end of the season after playing 125 games for Newport over five seasons. He won his next Welsh cap against New Zealand in 1905 and guested for Newport in their 1905 game against the All Blacks. He went on to win another two Welsh caps against England and Scotland in 1906.

Charlie Pritchard was also a regular member of the Newport first fifteen and played in 27 of the club's 31 fixtures. He was an uncompromising scrummager and excellent in defence. He was picked as a reserve forward for the Welsh team against Ireland and when Jehoida Hodges, Will Joseph and D H Davies all withdrew from the team, Charlie Pritchard was one of the replacements and gained the first of his fourteen Welsh caps. He played 219 times for Newport during a career that lasted ten seasons.

There were now only two Welsh players who played against New Zealand in 1905 who had not been capped by Wales: John Frederick Williams of London Welsh and Percy Bush of Cardiff. John 'Scethrog' Williams, as he was sometimes known, or Jack Williams, was a regular in the London Welsh first fifteen and had played for Middlesex during the season. He had also played in the international trial match at Tredegar and was selected as a reserve forward for both the Scotland and Ireland internationals. He would not have to wait too long for that elusive Welsh cap which he dully gained against Ireland in March 1905.

Although not yet capped, Percy Bush was also playing well. He had switched from the wing to outside-half for Cardiff and was making a big impression. Percy played for Glamorgan in their victory over Somerset and was outstanding for the East when they defeated the West at Cardiff in April 1904. He had also been invited to tour Australia and New Zealand with the Anglo-Australian Rugby Football Team (1904 British Team), but although he would return as top points scorer he still had to wait until December 1905 before winning his first Welsh cap, in the game against New Zealand.

With Willie playing rugby at the highest level, younger brother George was following in his footsteps at Christ College. George was playing on the wing in his second season of first fifteen rugby and was developing into a really good player of distinct promise. The 1903 December edition of *The Breconian* said the following of George: 'A capital offensive player, getting off the mark at once: if he could learn to dodge without stopping, he would be a very difficult man to bring down. A first rate kick, and sure tackler: but inclined to wait for the pass instead of going for his man.' George was not only good at rugby; he excelled in all sports including football, hockey, cricket, fives and golf. He not only played rugby for the College but also football, hockey and cricket. With regard to George's cricketing ability, *The Breconian* made the following comment: 'A hard hitting but unorthodox bat, scoring freely on the on side. A useful change bowler, and on his day an excellent field.' In addition, George was the College singles fives champion and, together with S J Marriott collected the fives pairs house championship. He was also the College golf champion and in the annual College sports held on Easter Monday 1904, George, like Willie before him, won the College Challenge Cup with 43 marks, a full 24 marks better than his nearest competitor. With another year of study remaining he was in a good position to equal Willie's record of two consecutive Challenge Cup titles.

Chapter Eight

The Anglo-Australian Rugby Football Team 1904

A REPORT IN THE *Sporting Life* early in December 1902 gave an early indication that there was the possibility of an English rugby team tour to New Zealand. The article read as follows: 'At a meeting of the New Zealand Rugby Union, held at Wellington on October 4th, it was decided to send a letter to the various New Zealand Unions stating that the New Zealand RFU was negotiating for the visit of an English team in 1904 and asking whether, in the event of a match being arranged in their centre, they would be prepared to hand over all the proceeds to the New Zealand Rugby Football Union.'

Another newspaper report in the *Yorkshire Post and Leeds Intelligencer* in December 1903 stated that the Committee of the Rugby Football Union were taking active steps towards raising a team to travel to Australia in the spring of 1904. It was intended that the principal matches would be played in New South Wales, although at this early stage of planning it was also hoped that it would be possible to play some matches in New Zealand. It was anticipated that the team, should one be raised, would leave England in May 1904 and be away for between five and six months. Late in February 1904 a report in the *Evening Express* confirmed that arrangements were being made to determine whether several distinguished rugby players from the home unions would be prepared to undertake such a tour. The article, under the heading of 'Proposed Visit of an English Team to Australia' stated, 'Mr G W M'Arthur, as representing the New South Wales Union, has, with the permission of the Rugby Union, issued a circular to a number of well-known players with a view to ascertaining whether it will be possible to raise a team to visit the Colonies this Spring. The letter sets forth that the team would leave England not later than early May, probably the 13th, arrive at Sydney about June 16th, have ten weeks in Australia and leave there at the end of August, reaching home early in October. If New Zealand is to be visited an extra fortnight would be required. The team would travel first-class and all expenses, including an allowance for daily and out-of-pocket expenses, will be paid by the New South Wales Union, which requires a definite reply by March 10th.'

Mr G W M'Arthur, assisted by Messrs J Hammond, G H Harnett and N Spicer, on behalf of the New South Wales Union, were successful in their task and twenty-four players were selected to undertake the tour. Willie Llewellyn was one of eight Welshmen selected. The team left England on 12th May 1904 and travelled overland to Marseilles where they joined the Royal Mail Steamer 'Ormuz' for the journey to Australia. They were away for just over five months, returning in mid-October 1904. They played twenty games, including the picnic game against Rotorua Natives. They won all their fourteen games in Australia, including three Test matches and of the six games they played in New Zealand they won two, drew one and lost three, including the Test match.

Although officially known as the Anglo-Australian Rugby Football Team, they were the first British team to play test matches against Australia and New Zealand. It was only from 1910 onwards that British Isles teams first became officially representative of the four home unions. In the press they were referred to as the 'English Rugby Team' or the 'British Rugby Team' and rarely, if ever, as the Anglo-Australian Rugby Football Team. There were no fewer than 14 uncapped players in the squad, which was selected more on availability for a long journey by sea and rail rather than solely on rugby ability. Four of the uncapped players would later become full internationals. C F Stanger-Leathes gained one cap for England against Ireland in 1905; Percy Bush won eight caps for Wales between 1905 and 1910; Tommy Vile also played eight times for Wales between

1908 and 1921 and Blair Swannell, who stayed on in Australia after the tour and played for New South Wales, was capped by Australia against New Zealand in 1905. Swannell, in fact, had the unusual distinction of playing in successive test matches against the All Blacks for two different teams: for the British team on 13th August 1904, and for Australia on 2nd September 1905. He also faced New Zealand twice for New South Wales when they played New Zealand on their preliminary tour of Australia in 1905.

The player manager was New Zealander Arthur B O'Brien, a three-quarter who was studying medicine at Guy's Hospital in London. The team was captained by David Revell Bedell-Sivright (Cambridge University and Scotland), who was born in December 1880 in North Queensferry. A Cambridge Blue from 1899 to 1902 and a Scottish heavyweight boxing champion, he played rugby twenty-two times for Scotland between 1900 and 1908. Willie Llewellyn and D R Bedell-Sivright knew each other very well. They had first played against each other when Willie appeared for Cardiff against Cambridge University in November 1899. Subsequently they both played for their respective countries in the Wales v Scotland fixtures of 1900/01/02 and 1904. Known as 'Darkie', Bedell-Sivright was a Royal Navy surgeon and died of blood poisoning at Gallipoli in September 1915.

The team was composed as follows: C F Stanger-Leathes** (Northern and Northumberland, England), Willie Llewellyn*** (Llwynypia, Newport and Wales), P F McEvedy* (Guy's Hospital and Kent), A B O'Brien* (Guy's Hospital and Kent, Manager), R T Gabe*** (Cardiff, Llanelly and Wales), E Morgan*** (Guy's Hospital, London Welsh and Wales, Vice-captain), J L Fisher* (Hull/East Riding and Yorkshire), W F Jowett*** (Swansea and Wales), F C Hulme*** (Birkenhead Park and England), P F Bush** (Cardiff and Wales), T H Vile** (Newport and Wales), D R Bedell-Sivright*** (Cambridge University, Edinburgh University and Scotland, Captain), D D Dobson*** (Newton Abbot, Oxford University and England), R W Edwards*** (Malone and Ireland), C D Patterson* (Malone and Ulster), T S Bevan*** (Swansea and Wales), S N Crowther* (Lennox and Surrey), D H Trail* (Guy's Hospital and Surrey), R J Rogers* (Bath and Somerset), S Mackenzie Saunders* (Guy's Hospital and Kent), B I Swannell** (Northampton and East Midlands), A F Harding***

294 CHAPTER EIGHT

The Anglo-Australian Rugby Football Team 1904.

(London Welsh and Wales), B F Massey* (Hull/East Riding and Yorkshire), and J T Sharland* (Streatham and Surrey). * denotes uncapped player; ** denotes player uncapped at the time of the tour but capped later; *** denotes player who was a full International at the time of the tour.

After a sea journey of five weeks, the team arrived in Adelaide on Monday 13th June by means of the Royal Mail Ship 'Ormuz'. They were met by Mr C W Oakes M.L.A., Vice President of the New South Wales Rugby Union and were entertained at a luncheon provided by the Mayor of Adelaide, Alderman Sir Lewis Cohen, who gave them a hearty welcome. The following day the team travelled to Melbourne by train and were formally welcomed at the Town Hall by the Lord Mayor, Councillor Sir Malcolm D McEacharn. The Prime Minister of Australia, the Hon. John Christian Watson, was also there to welcome the team to Australia.

At length, the team arrived in Sydney on Wednesday 15th June and played their first match against New South Wales at the Sydney Cricket Ground on Saturday 18th June in front of a crowd of 35,000 spectators. After just four minutes, Percy Bush dropped a beautiful goal from a very difficult angle. Bush's face wore a meaningful smile as the whistle blew as it was rumoured in the local press that he had, apparently characteristically, wagered a sovereign that he would kick a goal in the first ten minutes of the game. This he strenuously denied and had the following letter printed in the papers after the return match with New South Wales on 25th June: *'Sir, I am sorry to have to rush into print, but will you please contradict the statement which appeared in your account of the first British match v New South Wales. As I am not in the habit of betting sovereigns on football matches and this report is likely to give people an erroneous impression of me. I shall be glad if you will insert this letter. I made no such presumptuous wager as was suggested and in fact nobody was more surprised at my dropping a goal than me. Yours, Percy Bush'*. Percy Bush, with eleven,

Willie Llewellyn's 1904 Anglo-Australian blazer badge.

Courtesy of Dr Michael Jones

scored the most tries on the tour and finished top scorer with 97 points. They won this first game quite easily by 27 points to nil. In addition to Percy's drop goal Teddy Morgan scored two tries and Willie Llewellyn, Reg Edwards and Darkie Bedell-Sivright, one try apiece. Arthur O'Brien kicked three conversions and Percy Bush one. The local press were very complimentary to the team, one match report saying: 'The British Team's display in their opening match proved beyond any shadow of doubt that as far as Australia was concerned theirs will be a march to the music of victory.' And so it proved.

In the second game, against the Combined Western Districts on Wednesday 22nd June, the British team won by 21 points to six, Teddy Morgan scoring another two tries and Charlie Patterson and Darkie

**Anglo-Australian RFT v New South Wales
Saturday 18th June 1904**

Back Row: S N Crowther, S Mck. Saunders, C F Stanger-Leathes, D H Trail, R W Edwards. *Middle Row*: B I Swannell, W Llewellyn, E Morgan, D R Bedell-Sivright (Captain), A B O'Brien, R T Gabe, A F Harding.
Front Row: T S Bevan, F C Hulme, P F Bush.

Bedell-Sivright one each. Percy Bush kicked a penalty, a conversion and a goal from a mark. In the return match against New South Wales on Saturday 25th June in front of a crowd of 30,000, the 'Antipodean visitors displayed greater individual and collective ability than the local players and won most handsomely by 29 points to six.' Percy Bush had a great game scoring eleven points from three tries and a conversion. Fred Jowett, Rhys Gabe, Denys Dobson and Sid Bevan added four further tries while Arthur O'Brien kicked two conversions and Darkie Bedell-Sivright one. In their fourth game, against the Metropolitan Union, chosen from clubs in Sydney and its suburbs, tries by Rhys Gabe, Frank Hulme, Sid Bevan, Sidney Crowther and Fred Jowett, together with two conversions by Arthur Harding gave the visitors victory by 19 points to six.

Their first meeting with Australia in front of 35,000 spectators on Saturday 2nd July resulted in a victory for the Anglo-Australian team by 17 points to nil. There were no scores in the first half and the game had been in progress for close to an hour before the first score was registered. A brilliant interception and run down field by Rhys Gabe resulted in a try for Percy Bush. Bush was also responsible for the next score when he dropped a goal from a difficult angle. Within twenty minutes of the end of play it appeared that the Australians, although beaten, would not have any more points scored against them. However, in the closing stages of the match another ten points were added. Firstly Willie Llewellyn scored a try in the corner. The try was converted by Harding. Then just before the call of full-time a British player kicked over the goal-line. It looked certain that Verge would minor for Australia because he was closest to the ball, but 'the speedy Llewellyn ran clear over him and dropped on the ball to score' his second try. Such was Willie Llewellyn's pace that he gave Verge a ten yard start in twenty and beat him to the ball. O'Brien converted and the British team won by 17 points to nil.

The match against the Northern Districts at Newcastle on 6th July was marred by a couple of unpleasant incidents. One resulted in Fred Jowett having to retire at an early stage of the game when he sustained concussion after a collision with Walsh. The other happened just after play had resumed for the second half. The referee awarded a free-kick against the British team for a scrum infringement. Denys Dobson resented this and, so it was alleged, spoke offensively to the referee, who ordered him off. Bedell-Sivright, his captain, enquired what was wrong and shortly afterwards the British team marched off the field. After twenty minutes delay, the visitors returned without Dobson and play resumed. Denys Dobson always denied using any offensive language to the referee and after the game Bedell-Sivright stated that Mr Dolan was a thoroughly incompetent referee. He said that the team could abide with his failings so long as they merely affected the play, but when the team's personal honour was questioned they felt it was time to show resentment. The British team won the match by 17 points to three.

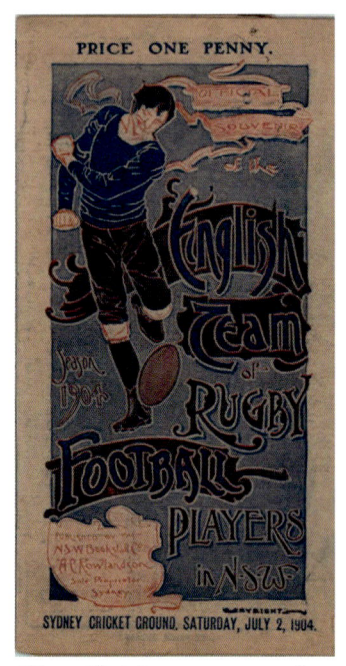

The official programme for the first test match against Australia.

The team travelled to Brisbane for their next match against Queensland, which was played at the Brisbane Exhibition Ground on Saturday 9th July. Although the British team only scored three points in the first half through a try by Darkie Bedell-Sivright, ten minutes into the second half the tourists really sprang to life. Hulme, Bush, Gabe, McEvedy, Morgan and Llewellyn engaged in several spectacular rounds of passing, and as an alternative tactic the team employed the high punt downfield which, accompanied by resolute following up by the forwards, took a lot of stopping. In a quarter of an hour spell the game underwent such a change that the odds on Queensland winning turned to the certainty of a crushing defeat. A try by Rhys Gabe converted by Arthur O'Brien and a goal from a mark by Percy Bush increased the visitors lead to twelve points. Another try by Teddy Morgan, converted by O'Brien and an unconverted try by Bush then gave the British team an unassailable 20 point lead before a splendid goal by Bedell-Sivright after a mark by Willie Llewellyn near half-way completed the British scoring. Just before the final whistle, Holmes went over from a line-out for a consolation try which Carmichael converted to leave the final score 24 points to 5.

The next game on the itinerary was against the Metropolitan Union at Brisbane where a weakened home team played well against a fairly strong British side that had rested a few key players. The visitors opened the scoring when Willie Llewellyn, following up a failed drop goal attempt by Percy Bush, crossed for a try which Percy Bush failed to convert. The home team replied with an unconverted try by Fred Nicholson. Just before the interval, after Bedell-Sivright had failed with a penalty kick at goal, Percy Bush received the ball after a scrum and dropped a spectacular goal to give the visitors a 7 points to 3 lead. In the second half, after some fine passing by the British three-quarters, Percy Bush found himself trapped in the corner. He kicked to the centre and Bedell-Sivright, swiftly following up, gathered and crossed for a try which Arthur O'Brien converted. Some slick passing by Harding, Edwards and O'Brien resulted in John Fisher shaking off a couple of opponents to score a fine try. Percy Bush added the extra points and with no further scores the visitors won by 17 points to three.

It was in this match against the Metropolitan Union that the tour captain, David Bedell-Sivright, suffered the knee injury which resulted in him being a spectator for much of the second half of the game. The injury kept him out for the next five games and although he played in the first game in New Zealand against the Canterbury and West Coast combined team he missed all the other games in New Zealand. He did, however, return for the final game of the tour against New South Wales at Sydney.

In the absence of Bedell-Sivright, Teddy Morgan took over the captaincy for the return game against Queensland. This was yet another match where injury dogged the British team. The English international Frank Hulme was injured in the first twenty minutes of the game and did not play again on tour. Tommy Vile worked the scrum after Hulme's departure and Percy Bush moved from the wing to outside-half with Arthur Harding coming out of the pack to cover the three-quarter line vacancy. Queensland opened the scoring with an unconverted try and led at the interval by 3 points to nil. Early in the second half Tommy Vile was injured, and although he too had to leave the field, he returned a short while later. The first British score came when Pat McEvedy followed up a Teddy Morgan cross-kick and crossed for a try. Percy Bush converted to give the visitors the lead. Soon afterwards exactly the same thing happened again with Pat McEvedy crossing for his second try of the game and this time Arthur Harding contributed the extras. Sid Bevan added an unconverted try before Queensland struck back with a goal from a mark by Redwood. However, it was too little too late and when Tommy Vile went round the blind side of a scrum to feed Percy Bush, the Cardiff man crossed for the final try of the game. Arthur O'Brien added the extra points and the British team won by 18 points to seven.

The next game against Toowoomba was the most closely contested game of the tour to date. In the first half the home forwards were equal to the visitors in the scrums and the loose, while at the line-out they were superior. Nevertheless, after beating several opponents, Teddy Morgan scored a magnificent try from half-way. Pat McEvedy missed the conversion. Toowoomba then replied with an unconverted try and the scores were level at the interval. In the second half it was the visitors who had the advantage. Percy Bush missed two attempts at goal from marks from exactly the same position, but shortly afterwards the British forwards broke away with the ball at their toes. Teddy Morgan joined in and dribbled the ball right down the field befored shaking off a couple of opponents to score between the posts. Stanger-Leathes added the extra points and just before the final whistle brought the scoring to an end when he dropped a wonderful goal to give the visitors victory by 12 points to three.

In the second test against Australia on 23rd July at the Brisbane Exhibition Ground the British team were again successful, winning by 3 tries, a dropped goal and a goal from a mark (17 points) to a single try (3 points). For the second time on tour Percy Bush scored 11 points in a game (a try, a drop goal and a goal from a mark). Willie Llewellyn and Arthur O'Brien scored one try each and Alex Burden scored a try for Australia. A week later, having beaten New England by 26 points to 9 on the Wednesday, the tourists defeated Australia for the third time by 16 points (4 tries and 2 conversions) to nil. Willie Llewellyn, Rhys Gabe, Teddy Morgan and Blair Swannell scored a try apiece while Percy Bush and Arthur O'Brien had one conversion each.

Having beaten an invincible path through thirteen matches in Australia, the British team travelled to New Zealand where a fatigued, injury-struck team won only two of their six games. After nearly a month on the sidelines through injury, David Bedell-Sivright returned for his only game in New Zealand when the British team beat a combined South Canterbury/Canterbury/West Coast side at Lancaster Park, Christchurch by 5 points to three. They then went on to beat the Otago and Southland combined side in Dunedin by 14 points to eight.

Then came the highlight of the visit with the game against New Zealand, which was played at Wellington on 13th August. New Zealand had made careful preparations for the game and the team was well selected and carefully trained. Captained by Billy Stead, it contained ten players who would form part of the successful All Blacks team which toured Great Britain, France and North America in 1905. Based on the results of the matches against the two South Island provincial teams the contest was expected to be a close one and if there was to be any advantage it was believed to be with the visitors. New Zealand won the toss and played with the Wellington wind and the sun behind them in the first half. Teddy Morgan captaining the British side, saw New Zealand take the lead when Billy Wallace, having missed several attempts at goal, eventually kicked a penalty goal to put his side ahead by 3 points to nil. Just before the interval there was a scrummage in the New Zealand twenty-five and after a brief burst by the British backs New Zealand were penalised for offside. Although the kick was from a difficult angle, Arthur Harding kicked a beautiful goal to bring the scores level at the break. In the second half, New Zealand were the stronger side and the British backs could not get going. Two unconverted tries by Duncan McGregor and two failed long attempts at drop goals by Arthur O'Brien and Percy Bush resulted in a victory for New Zealand by 9 points to three that sent 21,000 spectators happily on their paths home. Sadly four players in this game, Blair Swannell, David 'Darkie' Bedell-Sivright, Dave Gallaher and Eric Harper, became victims of the First World War.

Rain fell almost continually throughout the game when the British team played their match against Taranaki/Wanganui/Manawatu in front of 9,000 spectators at New Plymouth. The ground was very slippery and the game was mostly confined to forward struggles. Despite the combined team missing a penalty, the game was anybody's up until half-time with neither side able to score. For practically the whole of the second half, however, the combined team had the better of the game; both in the

The Triumphant 1904 New Zealand Team

Back Row: W S Glenn, C E Seeling, G W Nicholson, D Gallaher, B J Fanning, F A McMinn. *Middle Row*: E T Harper, T Cross, M E Wood, J W Stead (Captain), G A Tyler, W J Wallace, W Coffey (Manager). *Front Row*: R W McGregor, J P Gerrard, P Harvey, D McGregor, J Hunter.

The Anglo-Australian Team defeated by New Zealand 1904

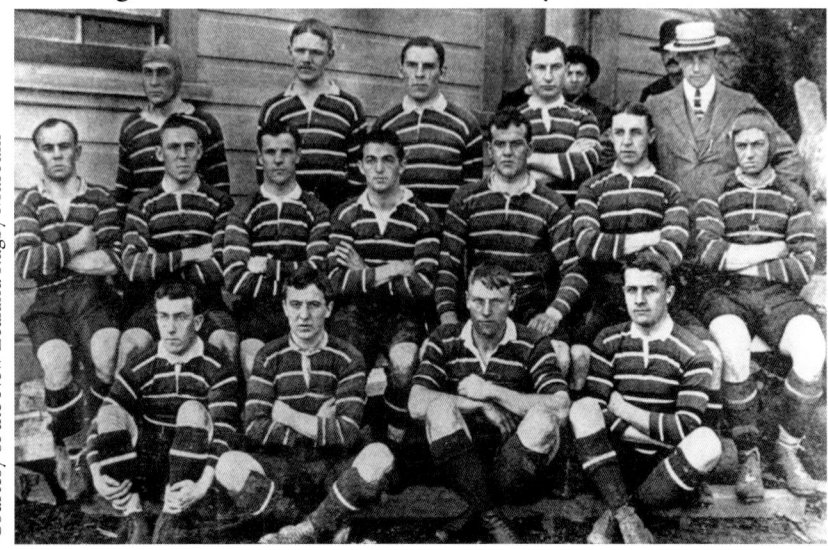

Back Row: S N Crowther, R J Rogers, D H Trail, P F McEvedy, D R Bedell-Sivright. *Middle Row*: A F Harding, R T Gabe, W Llewellyn, E Morgan (Captain), R W Edwards, T S Bevan, B I Swannell. *Front Row*: P F Bush, T H Vile, D D Dobson, A B O'Brien.

forwards and the backs, and only resolute defence by the British team prevented their opponents from scoring. The result was a pointless draw, the chief features of a tight game being the splendid kicking and sound defence of both sides.

In their next game against Auckland at Alexandra Park the British team faced six players who had played for New Zealand the previous Saturday. The early phases of the contest were fairly even and on one occasion Percy Bush and Teddy Morgan treated the spectators to a spectacular round of passing. Ronald Rogers, who injured his knee after thirteen minutes, had

Willie Llewellyn looks on as Dave Gallaher is well stopped in the game against Auckland.

to retire, and although he returned, he was little more than a spectator for the remainder of the game. The visitors almost scored when Tommy Vile, snapping the ball up from the side of the scrum, scooped the ball across to Percy Bush. Bush evaded several opponents with a clever run before passing to Rhys Gabe, who in turn transferred to Willie Llewellyn. Willie got beyond the home twenty-five and only a fine tackle by the home full-back prevented him from scoring. Shortly afterwards Arthur Harding narrowly missed a penalty kick at goal from half-way, the ball

The 1904 Auckland Team

Back Row: D Gallaher, C Seeling, A Renwick, G Nicholson, W Joyce, H Hayward. *Middle Row*: W McKenzie, W Mackrell, M E Wood, G Tyler, W Cunningham, W Harrison. *Front Row*: H Kiernan, W Murray, R McGregor.

The 1904 British Team defeated by Auckland

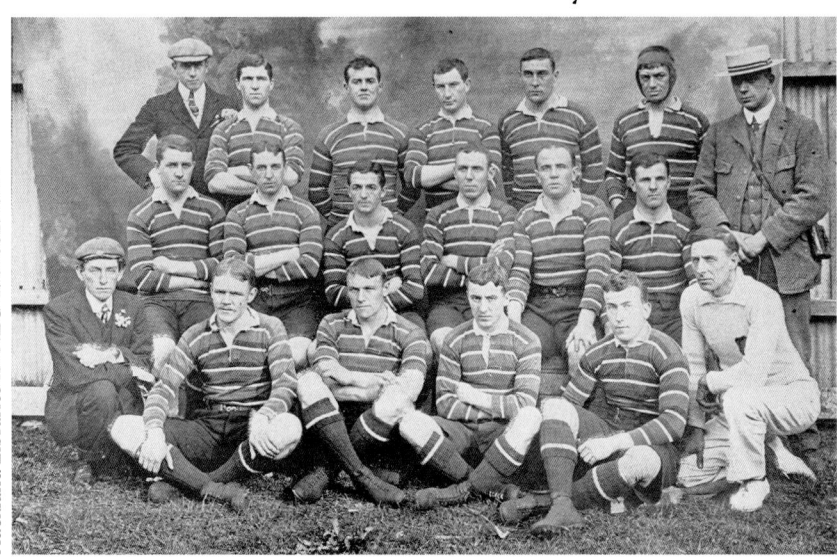

Back Row: Touch-judge, S M Saunders, R W Edwards, P F McEvedy, S N Crowther, B I Swannell, D R Bedell-Sivright.
Middle Row: A B O'Brien, T S Bevan, E Morgan (Captain), R T Gabe, A F Harding, W Llewellyn. *Front Row*: The Team's Trainer, R J Rogers, D D Dobson, T H Vile, P F Bush, P Mackie (Referee).

striking the post and rebounding into the field of play, then grazed the posts again with another splendid penalty kick at goal. Before the interval he missed a goal from a mark and Percy Bush missed a penalty, so neither side had scored when half-time was called.

The British team's failure to score with the wind at their backs gave the crowd confidence that Auckland could now win. Having the better of the loose play, some fine passing among the province's three-quarters resulted in Scobie Hay-McKenzie scoring near the corner to break the stalemate. Bill Cunningham failed to convert, but, with the British team continually under pressure, it was not long before Auckland scored again when Bill Cunningham crossed for a try which Murray converted. Dave Gallaher scored the last try of the game when he beat Arthur O'Brien to score under the posts and Murray again converted. Auckland put the British team under relentless pressure and before the end two of their backs managed to cross the visitor's goal line, but on one occasion the ball was lost and on the other they were called back for an infringement. Play ended without any further scoring, leaving Auckland deserved winners by 13 points to nil.

The British team were beaten in their final game in New Zealand by 8 points to 6 in a match against the Rotorua Natives. The game at Rotorua, which was half an hour each way, was hard from start to finish. Rain fell heavily during the first half, but the British team were leading at the

Action from the game between the Rotorua Natives and the 1904 British team.

Group of the Maori Footballers who defeated the 1904 British Team

Back Row: Pirimi i Mataiawhea (Maoris Chief, President), Honiana, Tame, Petene, Tharaira, Hare, Tamahou Te Kowhai, Kaharunga, D Steele (Referee), Kanapu, Taiapua Teane Kotuku (Vice President). *Middle Row*: Tiki, Kapu, Tihini, Nirai (Captain), Nira, Arawhata, C J Monro (Secretary). *Front Row*: Peno, Huka Amohau, Tuoro. The flag shown is the silk Union Jack presented by the Duke of York (later the Prince of Wales) to the Arawa Tribe in commemoration of his and the Duchess' visit to Rotorua.

interval as a result of two unconverted tries, one by Willie Llewellyn and one by Rhys Gabe. Percy Bush had two kicks at goal but missed them both. According to New Zealand's *Evening Star* newspaper, 'Bush had two easy shots in front of goal, but (according to his own account) he deliberately missed scoring, the idea being to give the Maoris a good game without beating them too much.'

In the second half the Maoris turned the tables. Despite the British team trying their hardest to stem the tide of the threatened defeat they could not defend against the continuous onslaught from the Maori team, and from fierce charges Tomahou Te Kowhai scored an unconverted try. A second try by the Maoris captain, Nirai, followed almost immediately and when Tuoro added the extra points the Maoris had a lead they would not surrender. The visitors strove valiantly to score again but the Maoris were not to be denied and the game ended with a home victory by 8 points to six.

The *New Zealand Herald* reported, 'The generosity of the natives of Rotorua was most marked and it is estimated that the curios and Maori treasures handed to the visitors represented a value outside their intrinsic value that is not likely to be underestimated by the recipients. The British captain received an old mere (a type of short, broad-bladed weapon in the shape of an enlarged tear drop) of great historical value, in fact, it is stated that it was so prized by the original owners that they had several times refused to part with it to guests of honour.'

Despite losing three games, the British team had had a wonderful time in New Zealand and all expressed their regret that their time there was so limited. Their captain, David Bedell-Sivright, on behalf of the team, expressed sincere thanks for the warm reception accorded to them and especially thanked the natives for the great kindness shown. Such was their popularity amongst the local residents that over a thousand of them turned up at the railway station to wish them farewell.

The British team returned to Australia where they played their final match of the tour against New South Wales at the Sydney Cricket Ground on Wednesday 31st August. They won by a converted try (5 Points) to nil. Very little public interest was taken in this final match of the tour and the attendance was comparatively meagre with only about 5,000 spectators turning up to watch the game compared with the 35,000 spectators who attended the same ground to watch the first game against New South Wales back in July. In the first half Percy Bush scored a try between the posts after he had cleverly eluded several opponents. Percy then added the extra points and with no further scores the game and the tour ended on a successful note. In total the Anglo-Australian rugby football team had played twenty matches; they won sixteen, drew one and lost three. They scored 293 points with 92 points against.

CHAPTER EIGHT

\multicolumn{5}{c	}{1904 Anglo-Australian Rugby Football Team Tour to Australia and New Zealand}
\multicolumn{5}{c	}{Australia Matches}
\multicolumn{5}{c	}{New Zealand Matches}
\multicolumn{5}{c	}{Test Matches}
Date	Opposition	Scorers	Venue	Result
18/06/1904	Game 1. New South Wales	Tries: Morgan (2), Llewellyn, Edwards, Bedell-Sivright. Drop-Goal: Bush. Conversion: O'Brien (3), Bush.	Sydney	Won 27-0
22/06/1904	Game 2. Combined Western Districts	Tries: Morgan (2), Patterson, Bedell-Sivright, Pen: Bush. Conversion: Bush. GFM: Bush.	Bathurst	Won 21-6
25/06/1904	Game 3. New South Wales	Tries: Bush (3), Jowett, Gabe, Dobson, Bevan. Conversion: O'Brien (2), Bedell-Sivright, Bush.	Sydney	Won 29-6
29/06/1904	Game 4. Metropolitan Union	Tries: Gabe, Hulme, Bevan, Crowther, Jowett. Conversion: Harding (2).	Sydney	Won 19-6
02/07/1904	Game 5. Australia	Tries: Llewellyn (2), Bush. Drop-Goal: Bush. Conversions: Harding, O'Brien.	Sydney	Won 17-0
06/07/1904	Game 6. Northern Districts	Tries: Llewellyn, Bush. GFM: Bedell-Sivright. Pen: Bush. Conversion: O'Brien (2).	Newcastle	Won 17-3
09/07/1904	Game 7. Queensland	Tries: Bedell-Sivright, Gabe, Morgan, Bush. GFM: Bush, Bedell-Sivright. Conversion: O'Brien (2).	Brisbane	Won 24-5
13/07/1904	Game 8. Metropolitan Union	Tries: Llewellyn, Bedell-Sivright. Fisher. Drop-Goal: Bush. Conversion: O'Brien, Bush.	Brisbane	Won 17-3
16/07/1904	Game 9. Queensland	Tries: McEvedy (2), Bevan, Bush. Conversion: Bush, Harding, O'Brien.	Brisbane	Won 18-7
20/07/1904	Game 10. Toowoomba	Tries: Morgan (2). Drop-Goal: Stanger-Leathes. Conversion: Stanger-Leathes.	Toowoomba	Won 12-3
23/07/1904	Game 11. Australia	Tries: Bush, O'Brien, Llewellyn. Drop-Goal: Bush. GFM: Bush.	Brisbane	Won 17-3
27/07/1904	Game 12. New England	Tries: Vile, Jowett, Bush, Gabe. Pen: Bush (2). Conversions: Bush (2), O'Brien, Harding.	Armidale	Won 26-9
30/07/1904	Game 13. Australia	Tries: Morgan, Llewellyn, Swannell, Gabe. Conversion: O'Brien, Bush.	Sydney	Won 16-0
06/08/1904	Game 14. South Canterbury/Canterbury/ West Coast Combined	Try: Bedell-Sivright. Conversion: Bush.	Christchurch	Won 5-3
10/08/1904	Game 15. Otago-Southland Combined	Tries: Bush, Dobson. Drop-Goal: Bush. Conversion: O'Brien (2).	Dunedin	Won 14-8
13/08/1904	Game 16. New Zealand	Pen: Harding.	Wellington	Lost 3-9
17/08/1904	Game 17. Taranaki, Wanganui and Manawatu, Combined	None.	New Plymouth	Drew 0-0
20/08/1904	Game 18. Auckland	None.	Auckland	Lost 0-13
22/08/1904	Game 19. Rotorua Natives	Tries: Llewellyn, Gabe.	Rotorua	Lost 6-8
31/08/1904	Game 20. New South Wales	Try: Bush. Conversion: Bush	Sydney	Won 5-0
\multicolumn{5}{c	}{Played 20, Won 16, Lost 3, Drawn 1. Points for 293. Points against 92.}

Summary of games played by the Anglo-Australian Rugby Football Team 1904

Some years later Tommy Vile wrote an article on the Australasian tour of 1904 and from it we get his personal perspective on the tour and how much the players enjoyed the experience and how happy a tour it was. 'When I look back over the past thirty years and reckon up all the gifts and gains, the wonderful Australasian tour of 1904 stands out as the finest educational experience of my life. I was raw and inexperienced, the youngest member of the party. Fortunately, there were included in the party a number of Welsh players whom I knew personally, so that I was not quite a stranger among strangers, but included also were some of the most famous players of the day, men of university education and international experience. Association with these players, combined with the opportunities of travel, was an education not only in the school of football, but in the school of life. It may be well to point out that the Anglo-Australian rugby team of 1904 was the third British team to visit Australia and New Zealand. The first team to visit Australia was captained by R L Seddon in 1888, and included one Welshman (W H Thomas of Llandovery College, Cambridge University and Wales). The next team, captained by the Rev. Matthew Mullineux, in 1899, also included one Welshman, the famous centre E Gwyn Nicholls, but the 1904 team consisted of twenty-four players of whom eight were playing under the Welsh Union.

Blair Swannell of Northampton and East Midlands was also a member of the 1899 side and was going out for the second time.

British Isles Rugby Football Team 1888

Back Row: T Banks, A E Stoddart, J P Clowes, J Lawler, Dr J Smith, A G Paul, F W McShane. *Middle Row*: J Anderton, A P Penketh, S Williams, R Burnett, W H Thomas, R L Seddon (Captain), H Eagles, T Kent, C Mathers. *Front Row*: H C Speakman, W M Burnett, Dr H Brooks, W Bumby, J T Haslam, J Nolan, A J Stuart, A J Laing.

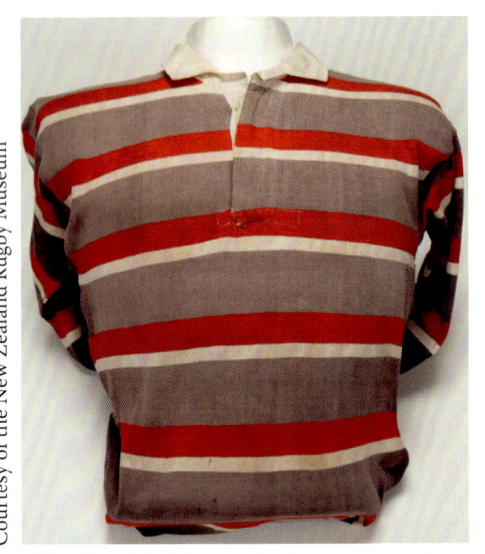

CHAPTER EIGHT

The British Isles rugby jersey worn by Willie Llewellyn in the first ever test match against New Zealand in 1904.

Courtesy of the New Zealand Rugby Museum

E 'Teddy' Morgan was appointed vice-captain for the 1904 side, A B O'Brien was manager as well as a player and D Dobson, Willie Llewellyn and R Edwards, with the vice-captain, the captain, and manager comprised the Selection Committee. Harding, Fisher, Swannell and Crowther had fought in the South African War. When the British team left England they were considered the finest combination who had ever toured the Colonies, and in my opinion they were the best lot Britain ever sent abroad.

The team left England on 12th May 1904, and travelled overland to Marseilles, where they joined the Royal Mail Steamer 'Ormuz'. It was remarkable how quickly the members of the party made friends. Although these friendships were so quickly formed, they were never broken on that five months tour, and no man was ever known to lose his temper and quarrel with another. Dobson was the favourite of all, and Percy Bush was the humourist of the party. Sharland was the biggest man in the party, and weighed about fifteen stone, I was the smallest and shortest, and we were usually called 'the long and the short of it'. Trail was the doctor of the party, and he was at the services of everyone, at any time of the night you could call him, and he would never grumble, he would always turn out like a shot, although there were six other men qualified, or qualifying, in the side. Gathered as we were from all parts of the United Kingdom, and thrown into each other's company so continually, it was most amusing for the first week or so to hear the men from the different countries talking to one another. Each had expressions the other did not understand. Often, an Irishman or North of England man would ask one Welshman what another Welshman meant by the phrase he had used. We chaffed each other, of course, but everyone was good-natured, and it was as if we all belonged to one family. F Jowett, the

Swansea three-quarter, who had short notice to sail and consequently had to order his clothes to follow by the next boat, lost all his luggage when the RMS steamer 'Australia' foundered, but everyone was so anxious to give him something that he had more clothes put in his room, boots, shirts, ties, collars and the rest, that he could have worn in five years. Our captain, Bedell-Sivright, took his duties seriously and was strict with reference to training. We started on the voyage out, and as it was in the heat of summer the work seemed very heavy. We rose at 7.30 and had half an hour's shadow exercise, then a walk round the deck, a cold bath and breakfast. Between breakfast and lunch there was a deck game such as deck cricket or quoits. In the afternoon there was skipping practise, scrummage practise, passing with sandbags, and walking. Afternoon training started quietly but became heavier as we neared Australia, and I think the first match the team played was the best they played of the tour as far as stamina was concerned, which shows what an enthusiastic team we were to have kept so fit after passing through such fearfully hot weather.

The 1904 Anglo-Australian Rugby Football Team cap belonging to Percy Bush.

Travelling on this tour was made as comfortable as possible for us, but the railway journey in Australia seemed tremendously long, and in New Zealand in those days the railways were very bad. One difficulty was that in Australia the different States had their own railways with different gauges, so that when we passed from one State to another we had to change into absolutely different trains. We were struck by the vastness of Australia. We first touched land at Fremantle, Western Australia, and we left the 'Ormuz' at Adelaide, travelled overland to Melbourne, and then went to Sydney.

In Australia we played fourteen matches, and won them all. So far as it is possible to make comparison I should say that Australian football

Action from the first game against New South Wales.

in 1904 was not quite so good as it was when the Wallabies came to Britain in 1908, and they were not quite up to the class of the last Waratahs side of 1927–28. No player stands out in memory, and my general impression is that they were a good level lot. In those days they were modelling themselves on the New Zealand game. They did not play an actual wing forward as New Zealand did when we visited them and as they afterwards did in Great Britain, but their game was rather on the lines of the Waratahs, except that they had one breakaway forward not two. This breakaway forward came down the side of the scrummage on the open side with the object of forcing a pass from the opposing inside half, while when they heeled he was a sort of shield for his own inside half. The British team were not playing a wing forward, but the inside half had some sort of protection from the two back forwards who pushed into the scrummage at an angle. The great object of my own play in those days was to try to move away from the scrummage and give a reverse pass on the run, but it was very difficult to get away from the scrummage at all, though I found a bit of extra protection from my own wing forwards which enabled me to move. In the later Australian games they started to use two men as breakaway forwards to prevent me from moving.

My attention has been drawn to a letter which I wrote from Sydney in June 1904, in which this passage occurs: 'Each man has his own particular place in the scrum, first rank, second rank and wingers. The wingers are the men who give the inside half the trouble. If you go round to stop the other half from getting the ball they detach themselves from the scrum and get in your way, and even hold you sometimes. Even when you are getting the ball on your own side you are playing three men, not one; that is the two wingers and the half'.

In making comparisons it is necessary to keep in mind the quality of the opposition, and if I say that my memory of the Australians of 1904 was that they had no combination to speak of, it must be remembered that the British team most definitely had combinations of a markedly high quality. The Australians played good straightforward football, and had men who were good individually; among the three-quarters, Redwood and Wickham, and good forwards, among whom Judd and Colton were notable. Their best half-back was the great R L 'Snowy' Baker, one of the finest all-round athletes Australia has produced, who afterwards became a boxing promoter. All these men were particularly big. They were good, but there was no real team combination, and I think it was due to the visit of the British team in 1904, combined with what the Wallabies were able to pick up on their tour in 1908, plus visits of the New Zealand teams, that Australian football became what it is now. As the humblest member of the tourists I may be permitted to say that the British team were a wonderful combination on paper and in fact. We had in Gabe, Willie Llewellyn and Teddy Morgan three of the greatest players who ever represented Wales, and as a substitute wing we had one of the greatest of Welsh scorers, Jowett, who for years held the record as an individual scorer in Wales. McEvedy and O'Brien, the other centres (both of them New Zealanders who were training as doctors at Guy's Hospital, where Teddy Morgan was at the time) were very strong runners and fitted in with the Welshmen, while these men were playing behind Percy Bush, the greatest player I have ever known as a maker of openings and a match winner. Hulme, the Cheshire and English half, was very unfortunate, for he was injured in Queensland and was able to play only a few games. We had also a wonderfully good pack of forwards among whom D R Bedell-Sivright, A F Harding, Denys Dobson, and R W Edwards were internationals, D H Trail was one of the great forwards Scotland missed, and Saunders and Crowther were both far better forwards than many men who had their caps.

In 1904 there was a tremendous interest in rugby football in the schools and universities of New South Wales and Queensland. In Western Australia, South Australia and Victoria they played Victorian, or the Australian game, which is a mixture of rugby and association. We won our first match in Australia by 27 points to nothing; the second by 21 points to 6, and the first Test match by 17 points to nil. For the first

The New South Wales team 1904.

Test match at Sydney the gate was 36,000; the second 34,000 and the third 35,000. We won the second Test match by 17 points to 3 and the third by 16 points to nil.

We left Sydney for New Zealand on 30th July 1904. In New Zealand we found we were up against a different proposition altogether. The New Zealanders were tremendously fast, they were individually clever, and their combination was perfect. Till this 1904 British team visited New Zealand people at home had no conception of the excellence of New Zealand rugby football; they had real proof of it in 1905. The quality of the football in New Zealand was not quite such a surprise to me as it might have been because of what the Australians had told me of the New Zealanders' strength. But what was a surprise to me was the style of the game they played. You can imagine my surprise the first time I got up to a scrummage and found I was opposed to a man like D Gallaher. I had no idea what he was going to do or how he was going to do it, and it took me some time to realise what he was there for and what part he took in the play. I had no possible chance of getting on to the opposing half because Gallaher simply stood there and blocked my way.

In the first two matches I played I was warned by the referee for losing my temper because of the deliberate obstruction of the New Zealand wing forwards, but the third time I played I realised that to do any good I had to stand on the opposite side of the scrummage to the wing forward when the ball was being put in. By doing that I had a chance to get at their half-back if they heeled. I also realised that there was a chance if I had to put the ball in the scrummage if I could get the referee round to my side, opposite the wing forward. But the wing forward remained a thorn in the flesh till the end of the tour, and was a thorn in the flesh when the last All Blacks were in this country. Another extraordinary thing that I could not understand was their scrummage formation of 2-3-2 with two up in the front row. This was the origination of the fight for the loose head. The British team formed up three in the front rank 3-2-3. But the New Zealand two endeavoured to get one of their front rank men outside the British forward, which meant that two of our men were in the air 'pushing against nothing'. The New Zealand aim was to gain an advantage by what I consider an unfair formation, and our struggle, of course, was to insist upon a formation whereby our middle man was between their two men and one man of ours on each side of their two. We never quite succeeded in meeting the tactics of the New Zealand forwards in this matter of formation. What gave them a secondary advantage was that in those days they would allow the first forward in the front row to hook the ball with his inside foot, and we only saw the ball two or three times in the game. We just won our first two matches, but in the Test match against New Zealand we had no hope at all. They had taken the New Zealand team away for a week's training and had figured out the only thing we had up our sleeves, the reverse pass from myself to

Dave Gallaher and Billy Stead who was captain of the 1904 New Zealand team with Dave Gallaher as vice-captain. Their roles were reversed for the 1905 tour of Britain and France.

Bush, had studied the Gabe, Llewellyn, Morgan combination from the two previous matches, and weighed them up well. They picked with one exception (B J Fanning) the side which the All Blacks would have called their best fifteen when they came to this country in 1905. Stead was captain in New Zealand, and Gallaher was vice-captain; in this country the situation was reversed. I realised even in those days the tremendous importance of the lock man in the scrummage. Tyler was the lock man in the Test match in New Zealand. A massive man, of great strength and solidity, he played against us in two games, and was absolutely the ideal man for the position. He had to keep the two front men solid, and he had four men pushing on him. The reason why the New Zealand scrum was so good in this country was because they had in Tyler and Cunningham ideal forwards to lock the scrum.

We were beaten in the Test match in New Zealand by 1 penalty goal and 2 tries to 1 penalty goal. (It is rather curious to recall that McGregor scored the two tries against Teddy Morgan, and at Cardiff, in the only match the New Zealanders lost on their British tour, the only try was scored for Wales by Teddy Morgan against McGregor).

We were thoroughly beaten. In extenuation I must say that we were at the end of a hard tour, that the travelling was very bad, and that through injuries it was with difficulty that we fielded a team at all. Bush, whom we were more or less relying upon, had one of his bad days, but the New Zealanders knew he was a danger, and their forwards were after him relentlessly. He was never at any time the greatest of defensive players. The tactics of the New Zealanders were new to us, and we could not get down to them. Sivright and some of the older players thought that these tactics were not above suspicion, I refer to the wing forward obstruction and to those two men in the front rank, but we could not do anything to counteract it. There was only one thing we taught the New Zealanders, as we taught the Australians, the value of the cross kick. (We seem to have lost the knack of it ourselves now). The New Zealanders could not understand the cross kick, and it was the use of it which enabled us to save the games in which we were not defeated in New Zealand. With reference to the Auckland game we never saw the ball, it was the only game in which I ever played in which I never got the ball once from the scrummage. The thing that struck me most in New Zealand was that rugby is indeed a national game. Everybody plays it or takes an interest in it. Even small towns and districts run their own leagues. They are bound to be good, and always will be good so far as their representative teams are concerned, so long as everybody is interested and so many people play. It struck me that the players had been well taught. When I look back I cannot help thinking that a lot of good men who had played rugby football in this country and had settled down there, to be received with open arms, had handed on all that they knew about the game, and had found there keen and persevering students.

Bill Cunningham played for Auckland in their victory over the 1904 British team and was one of the last players to be selected for the 1905 New Zealand tour of Britain and France.

When we were there we came across E F Fookes, the old English, Yorkshire and Blackheath wing three-quarter. The New Zealanders in 1904 were very keen to send a team to the Old Country, and as it largely depended upon the result of the Test match with the British team whether a team would be sent or not, they were very keen on winning. Though I was sore at the time that we were beaten, I was glad afterwards, for it would have been a calamity and a great loss to rugby football throughout the world if the All Blacks had not paid their visit and shown us what rugby football could be. Opinions differ I know, but to my mind, the All Blacks of 1905 were the best team who ever toured this country. When I was out there I was asked what I thought of the prospects of New Zealand if they paid a visit, and I said then that I thought they would beat all our county and club sides but that they would be beaten by our international sides. As it transpired, they were beaten only by Wales.

The New Zealanders taught me many things, and I was able in later life, as a player and referee, to counteract their wing forwards. One thing I learnt was not to throw the ball into the scrummage haphazardly; to always study the strength of the hooker, not to throw the ball in

A New Zealand postcard depicting the All Blacks' victory over the 1904 British team.

front of my centre man's right foot if his left foot was his strong one. The New Zealanders had even brought putting the ball into the scrummage to a fine art. It is rather pathetic to look back upon those happy days of 1904, to recall that glorious company of players, and to remember that Bedell-Sivright died at the Dardanelles; that Crowther, also, was killed in the war; that Swannell, who stayed in Australia, was killed with the Australian Expeditionary Force; that Rogers and Dobson, also were killed.' Denys Dobson, who gained six caps for England between 1902 and 1903, joined the Colonial Civil Service and was District Resident in Nyasaland and in charge of Sleeping Sickness Operations there. He died in July 1916 at Dowa, Nyasaland, from injuries inflicted by a charging rhinoceros. The *Nyasaland Times* said of him, 'He always gave his last tin of beef to a comrade, black or white.' It is no wonder that he was 'favourite of all' the 1904 British team players.

With all fixtures fulfilled and David Bedell-Sivright together with Percy Bush being honoured with the freedom of one of the Australian cities, the team headed for home. The team sailed on the Canadian-Australian line ship 'Aorangi' from Sydney on Monday 5th September bound for Vancouver via Brisbane, Suva, Laucala Bay, Honolulu and Victoria. David Bedell-Sivright, Blair Swannell, Denys Dobson and Sidney Crowther all remained behind in Australia while the other twenty tourists made their way home. They arrived in Victoria, British Columbia on Thursday 29th September and from Vancouver they travelled across Canada and the United States to New York, paying a visit to the spectacular Niagara Falls on the way. They sailed on the Cunard Liner 'Campania' from New York in early October 1904 and arrived at Queenstown (Now known as Cobh), County Cork, Ireland on Friday 14th October. They arrived at Liverpool the following morning having been away for five months, yet despite travelling a total of about 40,000 miles, they were the picture of health and in excellent spirits. They had a very warm welcome home and at Cardiff on Wednesday 19th October, Rhys Gabe, Willie Llewellyn, Percy Bush and Tommy Vile were guests at a gala evening in their honour. The following evening the members of the Newport Athletic and Football Club assembled in force at the Westgate Hotel for a smoking concert to welcome home Willie Llewellyn and Tommy Vile. Arthur Gould presided and in response to the toast to the players Willie Llewellyn said he appreciated to the full the honour of being selected as he was only a young member of the club. He concluded by saying that even at the team's best, they found the New Zealanders

The 1904 British team on a visit to Niagara Falls during their journey home.

Courtesy of St Fagans National Museum of History

too good for them. In an interview with a reporter from the *Rhondda Leader*, Willie said that Sydney was the best football ground he had ever played on and in all three matches played in New South Wales a total of over 100,000 spectators were present. He added that the team had been treated excellently both by the officials and the spectators, and wherever they went they were splendidly received. Willie concluded by saying that 'a better lot of chaps than the tourists you could never get together and everything went off without a hitch.'

Tommy Vile later wrote: 'It was remarkable how quickly the members of the party made friends. Although these friendships were so quickly formed, they were never broken on that five month tour, and no man was ever known to lose his temper and quarrel with another.' The strength of those friendships was underlined by the fact that members of the 1904 British team held annual reunions at the Charing Cross Hotel, London, usually over an international match weekend. These reunions were still taking place in 1958, fifty-four years after the tour and when there were only five remaining members of the team; Willie Llewellyn, Rhys Gabe, Max Saunders, C F Stanger-Leathes and Tommy Vile.

Members of the 1904 British team raise their glasses for a toast at one of their reunions. Willie Llewellyn is at the head of the table with Rhys Gabe to his left. Tommy Vile is on the far left front and Percy Bush far right.

1904 Anglo-Australian Rugby Football Team Tour to Australia and New Zealand – Player Statistics

Player	Position	Games Played	Scores	Tries	Points
Arthur Boniface O'Brien (Manager) Guy's Hospital & Kent.	Three-quarter	(17) All games except games Nos. 4.19 & 20.	16 Con.	1	35
*David Revell 'Darkie' Bedell-Sivright (Captain) Cambridge University & Scotland.	Forward	(9) Game Numbers: 1.2.3.5.6.7.8.14 & 20.	2 GFM. 1 Con.	5	25
*Edward 'Teddy' Morgan (Vice-Captain) Guy's Hospital, London Welsh, Kent & Wales.	Three-quarter	(13) Game Numbers; 1.2.5.6.7.9.10.11.13.14.15. 16 & 18.	None	8	24
*Arthur Flowers 'Boxer' Harding London Welsh, Cardiff & Wales.	Forward	(20) Played in all games.	5 Con. 1 Pen.	None	13
Percy Bush Cardiff & Glamorgan.	Half-back	(19) All games except game No. 4.	10 Con. 5 DG. 4 Pen. 3 GFM.	11	97
Sidney Nelson Crowther Lennox and Surrey.	Forward	(19) All games except game No. 10.	None	1	3
*Thomas Sidney 'Sid' Bevan Swansea & Wales.	Forward	(18) All games except games Nos. 2 & 8.	None	3	9
*Rhys Thomas 'Rusty' Gabe Cardiff, London Welsh & Wales.	Three-quarter	(17) All games except games Nos. 2,8 & 10.	None	6	18
*Denys Douglas Dobson Oxford University, Devon & England.	Forward	(17) All games except games Nos. 1,2 & 20.	None	2	6
Thomas Henry 'Tommy' Vile Newport & East Wales.	Half-back	(16) All games except games Nos. 1,5,6 & 7.	None	1	3
Blair Inskip Swannell Northampton & East Midlands.	Forward	(15) All games except games Nos. 10,12,17,19 & 20.	None	1	3
*Willie Llewellyn Newport & Wales.	Three-quarter	(15) All games except game Nos. 4,9,10,12 & 15.	None	8	24
Patrick Francis 'Pat' McEvedy Guy's Hospital.	Three-quarter	(15) All games except games Nos. 1,3,5,6 & 15.	None	2	6
Stuart Mackenzie Saunders Guy's Hospital, Blackheath & Kent.	Forward	(15) All games except games Nos. 3,6,8,13 & 16.	None	None	0
David Herbert Trail Guy's Hospital, London Scottish & Surrey.	Forward	(13) Game Numbers: 1.2. 3.5.9.10.11.13.15.16.17.19 & 20.	None	None	0
*Reginald Weston 'Reg' Edwards Malone, Belfast, Ulster & Ireland.	Forward	(12) Game Numbers: 1.7. 8.9.11.12.13.14.15.16.18 & 20.	None	1	3
Christopher Francis Stanger-Leathes North Yorkshire & Northumberland.	Full-back	(12) Game Numbers: 1.2. 3.4.5.8.10.12.15.17.19 & 20.	1 Con. 1 DG.	None	6
Ronald Joseph Rogers Western Super Mare & Somerset.	Forward	(7) Game Numbers: 3.6.8. 12.16.17 & 18.	None	None	0
John T Sharland Streatham & Surrey	Forward	(7) Game Numbers: 2.4.6. 8.10.17 & 20.	None	None	0
*William Frederick 'Fred' Jowett Swansea & Wales.	Three-quarter	(7) Game Numbers: 3.4.6. 12.15.19 & 20	None	3	9
*Frank Croft Hulme Birkenhead Park, Cheshire & England.	Half-back	(6) Game Numbers: 1.4.5. 6.7 & 9.	None	1	3
John L Fisher Hull & East Riding.	Three-quarter	(4) Game Numbers; 4.8. 10 & 19.	None	1	3
Charlie D Patterson Malone.	Forward	(4) Game Numbers: 2.4. 10 & 19.	None	1	3
Burnett F Massey Yorkshire	Forward	(3) Game Numbers; 10.12 & 13.	None	None	0
*International		Points Totals	125	168	293

The Anglo-Australian Rugby Football Team 1904 – Individual Player Statistics

The Anglo-Australian Rugby Football Team 1904

Back Row: C F Stanger-Leathes, D H Trail, J L Fisher, P F McEvedy, R J Rogers, C D Patterson, S M Saunders, S N Crowther, J T Sharland.
Middle Row: R W Edwards, W Llewellyn, A B O'Brien, D R Bedell-Sivright (Captain), E Morgan, R T Gabe, W F Jowett, B I Swannell.
Front Row: A F Harding, P F Bush, T H Vile, F C Hulme, T S Bevan.

Chapter Nine

Willie Captains Wales to a Fourth Triple Crown

THE 1904–05 SEASON under the captaincy of Jehoida Hodges was Newport's worst season thus far. Of the 30 games they played they won 15 and lost 15. They scored 238 points with 183 points against. Willie Llewellyn was elected as vice-captain for this season. It is remarkable that Newport's worst season was experienced when a really great player led the team. Hodges was certainly one of the finest forwards to play for Newport and Wales. One of his most remarkable experiences of a remarkable career was in the Wales match against England at Swansea in 1903, a game Willie Llewellyn missed because of injury. Wing and captain Tom Pearson was injured and had to retire and Jehoida Hodges took his place on the wing. Hodges scored three tries in the 21 points to 5 victory. Eight of Newport's fifteen defeats during the 1904–05 season were against non-Welsh sides. Blackheath beat Newport twice for the first time in their history. They were also beaten by Leicester, the Barbarians, Watsonians, Plymouth, Bristol and Devonport Albion. This was the first time they had been beaten by Devonport Albion since fixtures began in 1901. The Welsh defeats came from Swansea who beat them four times, two to Cardiff and one to Llanelly. Unfortunately for Newport, Cliff Pritchard, who had played centre for the previous five seasons, returned to his former club, Pontypool. Wyatt Gould, the youngest of the famous brothers, was still suffering from an injury sustained in the Welsh trial match the previous season and did not play during the 1904–05 campaign. However, Newport had two exceptional new recruits in Alby Davies, the smart Llanelly three-quarter, and Willie Thomas, the pick of Aberavon's backs. Rowland Griffiths played in 28 matches, George Boots, Jack Jenkins and Willie Thomas played in 26 matches. Willie Thomas was top try scorer with twelve tries, Willie Llewellyn scored ten and Harry Uzzell six.

Willie Llewellyn only played fourteen games for Newport during the 1904–05 season. He missed the first four games because he did not return from Australia and New Zealand until Saturday 15th October and, although the game against Blackheath was played on Saturday 22nd October he did not play his first game until the following week when he turned out for Newport against Neath at the Gnoll. Although selected

Newport Athletic Club, Rugby First XV, 1904–05

Back Row: H Uzzell, A Davies, S H Williams, R B Griffiths, Gus Jones,
J C Jenkins, W H Williams, Harry Packer (Hon. Sec.).
Middle Row: W J Martin, W M Llewellyn (Vice-Captain), C M Pritchard,
J J Hodges (Captain), G Boots, E Thomas, J E C Partridge.
Front Row: W Thomas, C T Jones, D J Boots, T H Vile, W Bennett.

to play for Newport in their next game against Swansea, for some reason, probably an injury, Willie didn't play. It was in this game that Tommy Vile began his legendary half-back partnership with Walter Martin. They played together 212 times as half-backs for Newport and twice for Wales between 1904 and 1921.

The Newport home game against Swansea on Saturday 5th November 1904 marked the beginning of the legendary half-back partnership between Tommy Vile and Walter Martin.

Willie also missed the game against Bristol but returned for the game against Cardiff. Willie missed the Christmas fixture against the Barbarians because he was injured in the game against Watsonians but returned for the last game of the year against London Welsh. Willie was away at London Hospital on a dentistry course between January and March 1905 during which time he returned to play for his old club London Welsh. During that period Willie missed seven Newport games, including the important fixtures against Llanelly, Swansea (twice) and Cardiff, all of which Newport lost. The loyal Newport supporters were not too pleased with the fact that Willie was away and this was brought to a head when Newport were heavily defeated by 21 points to nil in the away match against Cardiff on Saturday 18th February. An article in the *Evening Express* conveyed their mood: 'A good many Newport people do not like the way that Willie Llewellyn served the committee over the Cardiff engagement last Saturday. He has been vice-captain for the team and has said he would help the Usksiders in their more important engagements. Yet, with the London Welsh only having a soft thing on last Saturday he could not find it convenient to make the journey to Cardiff. Of course, there may be good and sufficient reason that the general public know nothing of, but as appearances go they are not to the liking of Newport people.' Willie had remained in London and played for London

Welsh against United Services on the day in question and the Newport supporters were obviously not happy about it. Nevertheless, Willie returned to the Newport side four weeks later for their return fixture against Cardiff and with Willie scoring both tries in the 6 points to three victory, I guess he would have been forgiven.

Two weeks later Willie was at it again, this time missing the home game against Llanelly because he was playing for London Welsh in their match against Catford Bridge. Finally, Willie missed the home game against London Welsh on Tuesday 25th April and the penultimate game of the season at home to Percy Park. Willie had missed a total of sixteen games in what was a poor season for Newport. He had played in less than half of Newport's total number of games and the following season, after playing just four games, Willie's Newport playing career came to an end.

As previously mentioned, Willie played his first game of the season for Newport in their game against Neath at the Gnoll. Two unconverted tries, one by Willie Thomas and the other by Willie Llewellyn, together with a dropped goal by Eddie Seer gave Newport the spoils by 10 points to nil. Although selected to play for Glamorgan against Devon at Cardiff the following Tuesday and for Newport against Swansea the following Saturday, Willie did not play in either matches. Willie also missed the away game against Bristol on Saturday 12th November.

When Willie returned to the Newport team for the home game against Cardiff on Saturday 19th November, the visitors were without their most brilliant attacking player, Percy Bush. On the same day as Willie Llewellyn was playing for Newport against Neath, Percy Bush was playing centre for Cardiff Reserves in their match against Merthyr and sustained a fractured arm. It was ironic that Percy should play in nineteen games in Australia and New Zealand without a scratch only to break his arm in a reserve team fixture. This injury prevented Percy from playing for most of the season and although he returned to play for Cardiff in December, his injured arm was not right and he did not play again until late in the season. Although it had been rumored that Bert Winfield, the Welsh international full-back, had retired, he played in this game. A report in the *Evening Express* on Tuesday 13th December following Cardiff's practice match the previous Saturday stated, 'The name of Gwyn Nicholls, of course, will be missed at once and also that of H B Winfield, who it appears, is far from being in good health. At the present time Winfield has no intention of playing football again. I am giving this fact (wrote 'Forward') on the authority of his brother (Walter Winfield), who has also given up the game.' It had also been rumored that Gwyn Nicholls had retired, but he was still in training and both he and Bert Winfield had played for Cardiff Rowing Club in a match against Old Monktonians at the end of October. A game they unfortunately lost by a goal and a try (8 points) to a try (3 points). Gwyn Nicholls did, however, have the satisfaction of scoring the try for the Rowing Club.

Within two minutes of the start of the game against Cardiff, Newport's Willie Thomas tried to catch the ball in flight but missed it and Rhys Gabe dashed up and threw himself on the ball to score directly under the cross-bar. Cecil Biggs converted easily and the visitors were five points ahead. Stanley Williams reduced Cardiff's lead to one point when he dropped a very fine goal from a mark. After a loose scramble following a line-out, the Newport forwards completely overpowered the Cardiff defence and Edwin 'Beddoe' Thomas crossed for an unconverted try to give Newport a 7 points to five interval lead. With neither side able to score in the second half Newport took the spoils.

A report in the *London Daily News* on Friday 25th November suggested that Willie was not going to play for Wales again. It stated, 'Willie Llewellyn, the Newport three-quarter, is unlikely to be again available for the Welsh team, the clever wing finding it impossible to devote the necessary time to training. In the circumstances the Welsh officials are looking around for his successor. Choice will probably fall either on W Trew of Swansea or Cecil Biggs, the Cardiff captain, both of whom are capable players.' Reports of Willie's retirement from the Welsh team were premature and Willie would go on to have one of his most successful seasons in the coveted red jersey.

Willie's next game was for the Newport Barbarians in their match against Newport Thursdays on Thursday 1st December. Several of the Newport first team played for the Barbarians, Tommy Vile and Charlie Lewis joining Willie Llewellyn in the team. Although Willie Llewellyn and Charlie Lewis scored unconverted tries for the Barbarians, they lost the game by 8 points to six. Newport Thursdays scored a goal and a penalty goal.

The preliminary Welsh trial match which should have taken place at Cardiff on Thursday 24th November did not go ahead because of a frozen ground, but the final trial scheduled to take place at Neath on Saturday 3rd December was played. Willie was selected to appear for the Probables but cried off. Tom Williams of the Welsh Football Union stated that the only reason Willie did not play was that his business obligations made it impossible for him to leave Newport and travel down to Neath. It was confirmed that Willie was as keen as ever and may be regarded as a serious candidate for further international honours. Willie was not the only player to withdraw; there was great disappointment that Dick Jones and Dickie Owen of Swansea were also absent. In addition Cliff Pritchard, Billy Trew, Dan Rees and Alfred Brice were all absentees. Nevertheless, the Probables had a convincing victory winning by 30 points to five.

There is no doubt that Willie was very busy at work and often worked late into the evening. Although he was accustomed to the rough and tumble of the rugby field, he was probably unprepared for the incident that happened late in the evening of Wednesday 7th December. At about 6.20 p.m. a sailor named Thomas Baldwin entered Willie's place of work at Messrs. Phillips and Son, Chemists, Commercial Street, Newport. Baldwin was carrying on like a 'madman', singing, jumping, dancing and rolling about all over the place. The police were called and when Police Constable Moseley arrived and asked Baldwin to leave the shop, he was butted in the head and pinned against the counter. They fell on the floor together and in the course of rolling over one another, the sailor kicked out desperately. Henry George 'Sarspa' Thomas, himself a Newport footballer, had seen what was happening from his shop across the street and came to the assistance of Willie and the policeman. Eventually the sailor was apprehended and carried to the police-station by three constables, Sarspa Thomas and Willie Llewellyn. Apparently the sailor had been paid off from his ship, the steamer 'Isle of Kent', and had been drinking spirits heavily all day. When Baldwin came before the magistrates later that week he said he could recollect nothing of the incident and was fined 40 shillings with the option of a month in prison with hard labour. The magistrates expressed their gratitude to Willie Llewellyn and Henry George Thomas for the assistance they rendered the police. Willie and Sarspa Thomas had probably seen nothing quite like it on the rugby field.

Willie played in five of Newport's next six games. In the first of these games they lost to a very strong Swansea side by nine points to three. This was the first of four games Newport would play against Swansea during the season and they lost them all. Two first half unconverted tries by Dick Jones and Dan Rees gave Swansea a 6 point advantage at the interval. It was in the first half, however, that Willie Arnold broke his ankle after a fairly innocuous tackle by Willie Llewellyn. This resulted in Swansea playing the remainder of the game with fourteen men. Nevertheless, with Fred Scrine taking Arnold's place on the wing, Swansea more than held their own. Frank Gordon scored another unconverted try for Swansea in the second half and, although Newport scored an unconverted try though Mike Buckley, they were unable to score again and despite the closeness of the margin they were, in fact, well beaten. This was an invincible season for Swansea who, under the captaincy of Frank Gordon, played 31 games, won 27 and drew four.

Newport defeated Plymouth in their next game by 20 points to six. Then, two tries by Willie Llewellyn helped Newport give Neath a real walloping by 23 points to nil. Willie was injured in the next game against Watsonians and missed the holiday game against the Barbarians which Newport lost by 10 points to six. Willie next played for Newport in their final game of 1904 against his old team, London Welsh, at Queen's Club. The Exiles included four Old Breconians in Arthur Harding (Captain), Teddy Morgan, Hop Maddock and Jack Williams. Willie Llewellyn, for some reason appearing under the pseudonym of 'Player', opened the scoring for Newport with a try that Stanley Williams failed to convert. Shortly afterwards, William H Williams, in his first game of the season for Newport, crossed for another unconverted try.

Early in the second half London Welsh lost their half-back A H Owen and Hop Maddock moved to partner Rowlands behind the scrum. One of the forwards filled the vacancy in the three-quarter line and despite the handicap at forward, the Welsh held their own in some determined exchanges. After some fairly aggressive play by the London Welsh forwards, Jack Jenkins got away for Newport and, running down the touch-line, scored a simple try wide out. Again the conversion failed. London Welsh retaliated and after some sharp following up, Stringer, the London Welsh custodian, dropped a wonderful goal from thirty-five yards. Five minutes from the end of the game Willie Thomas handed off several opponents to score yet another unconverted try and with no further scores Newport won the game by 12 points to four.

When the Welsh Football Union met in Cardiff to select the team to play against England at Cardiff on Saturday 14th January, Willie Llewellyn was in the side. Moreover, he was once again selected to lead the team. There had been some speculation that Willie would lose his place to Billy Trew of Swansea but despite the speculation Willie retained his place and the captaincy. Several English and Scottish papers had speculated that Willie would be displaced by Billy Trew. The *Gloucestershire Echo* stated, 'Trew (Swansea), who was expected to displace Llewellyn is a reserve wing' while the *Edinburgh Evening News*, in reference to the Welsh side, said, 'The team gives satisfaction locally with the exception of W Llewellyn who has been in indifferent form both this and last season, and is generally conceded to have lost much of his dash.' The Welsh papers, too, were a little critical of Willie's selection but on the whole were a little more pragmatic about his inclusion. An article by Harry Bowen in the *Evening Express* read as follows: 'The Welsh captain's injury early in the season, together with a decision on his own part to retire finally into the cares of business, gave the idea that further international honour was quite unwished for. But during the last month, and especially the last fortnight of it, according to report, he has been playing as well as ever. If that be so, then it is good news, but as for my own part and on this season's form, I think Billy Trew is the better wing, and should have been selected. The Swansea man's play has been brilliantly consistent throughout.'

The article went on to say, 'Now that the majority of the committee decided in favour of Willie Llewellyn, it is a comfort to remember that he has never "let his side down" in an international engagement. Another is that his turning out is the signal that he is as fit as careful training can make him. So that, all things considered, as Trew is not in, I am glad the position is in the safe hands of Willie Llewellyn.' Several of these comments have an element of truth. It was certainly the case that Willie Llewellyn had never let Wales down; he had played for Wales on sixteen occasions and only been on the losing side four times. He had played in two Triple Crown winning sides and scored thirteen tries, and he was not about to disappoint the Welsh supporters. However, although it is

Wales Team v England 1905

Back Row: W M Douglas (Touch-judge), G Travers, D Jones, W Joseph, H V Watkins, C M Pritchard, C Lefevre (Referee). *Middle Row*: W O'Neil, J J Hodges, D Rees, W M Llewellyn (Captain), R T Gabe, E Morgan, A F Harding. *Front Row*: R M Owen, G Davies, R H Jones.

possibly true that Willie did not play at his best in every game, it must be remembered that he had played rugby continually from the start of the 1903–04 season. Willie had played 51 games between October 1903 and January 1905, including the British team tour to Australia and New Zealand, so it is probably not surprising that he did not always play to his best form.

The team that faced England at Cardiff on Saturday 14th January was exactly as selected. Cliff Pritchard was not considered because of injury and Dan Rees of Swansea was chosen in his place. The team, with no debutants, took the field as follows:

Wales: Back, G Davies (Swansea); three-quarters, W M Llewellyn (Newport, Captain), D Rees (Swansea), R T Gabe (Cardiff), E Morgan (London Welsh); half-backs, R H Jones and R M Owen (Swansea);

forwards, W Joseph (Swansea), A F Harding (London Welsh), D Jones (Aberdare), C M Pritchard, J J Hodges (Newport), W O'Neil (Cardiff), H V Watkins (Llanelly), G Travers (Pill Harries).

The Reserves were as follows: Back, Frank Young (Cardiff); three-quarters, 1st Hop Maddock (London Welsh), 2nd Frank Gordon (Swansea), right or left centre. Cecil Biggs (Cardiff), right wing. Billy Trew (Swansea), left wing; half-backs, Dai Gent (Gloucester) for Owen. Billy Trew, first reserve for Dick Jones. R Gibbs (Penarth), second reserve for Dick Jones; forwards, J F Williams (London Welsh), R Thomas (Penygraig), T Evans (Llanelly) and W Taylor (Bridgend).

England: Back, *S H Irvin (Devonport Albion); three-quarters, *F H Palmer (Richmond), J E Raphael (OMT's), E W Dillon, S F Coopper (Blackheath); half-backs, W V Butcher (Bristol), F C Hulme (Birkenhead Park); forwards, F M Stout (Richmond, Captain), *J L Mathias (Bristol), V H Cartwright (Nottingham), B A Hill, *W T C Cave, C J Newbold, *W L Y Rogers (Blackheath), *T A Gibson (Northern). (* England Debut)

Referee: C Lefevre (Ireland).

In the region of 40,000 spectators were present when Willie Llewellyn, Rhys Gabe, Teddy Morgan and Arthur Harding renewed acquaintances with fellow 1904 tourist Frank Hulme. It was a great day for Willie but a disappointing one for Frank whose side was comprehensively beaten by 25 points to nil, the heaviest defeat since fixtures began between the two countries in 1881. Within three minutes of the start Teddy Morgan crossed for an unconverted try for Wales. George Davies failed to convert. Shortly afterwards Wales had a wonderful chance to score but a poor pass from Dan Rees to Willie Llewellyn spoiled a golden opportunity. Not to be outdone, a minute or so later, Willie Llewellyn snapped up a loose ball and ran over for a magnificent try which George Davies again failed to convert. England now began to improve and for a time their forwards were controlling the scrums and heeling out much better than the Welsh eight. Before the interval, however, Wales scored a brilliant try from their own twenty-five when Jehoida Hodges, with a clever pick up and strong run, got clear of the English three-quarters. When faced by Sam Irvin he passed to Harry Watkins, who ran like a three-quarter from the half-way line to score a brilliant try under the posts. George Davies added the extra points and Wales were ahead by eleven points at the break.

In the second half, Wales continued where they left off in the first and after a slick round of passing Teddy Morgan crossed for what looked like a brilliant try. Unfortunately the referee saw things differently and called Wales back for a forward pass. Not to be outdone, Wales attacked again and when Dickie Owen passed to Dick Jones on the blind side of the scrum the Swansea outside-half made no mistake and crossed for a try which George Davies failed to convert. Fifteen minutes later, a masterful pass from Dickie Owen from the base of the scrum put Dick Jones into space and, cutting through between the English centres, he got the ball away to Dan Rees. Running to within ten yards of the line, Dan Rees passed to Rhys Gabe who crossed for another wonderful try. The conversion again failed, but within ten minutes came one of the best tries of the game. Dan Rees made a magnificent opening by beating Raphael and at the right time passed to Rhys Gabe, who ran strongly over the English twenty-five yard line before passing to Teddy Morgan who slipped away from the full-back and scored a beautiful try under the posts. This time George Davies made no mistake and added the extra points. Ten minutes from the end of the game Arthur Harding completed the scoring when he crossed for an unconverted try. England were well and truly beaten and Willie Llewellyn was very pleased with the Welsh performance. When interviewed after the game, Willie stated, 'I am too much delighted to say much I can assure you, but it was a grand win.'

Willie only played one game between the English game and the international against Scotland at Inverleith, Edinburgh, on Saturday 4th February. He played for Glamorgan in the game against Somerset at Bath. Willie and Rhys Gabe were the only non-Swansea players in a back line that included Frank Gordon, Billy Trew and Dan Rees. Dick Jones was outside-half with Dai Gent at scrum-half. The forwards were Dai Jones, E Harding, D 'Port Tennant' Davies, R Thomas, G Mears, A F Harding, W Taylor and D Galloway. With seven Welsh internationals in their team Glamorgan won quite comfortably by 15 points to three. Tries were scored by Dan Rees, Billy Trew (2), Frank Gordon and Rhys Gabe. Arthur Harding, although getting close on several occasions, failed to convert any of the tries.

When the Match Committee of Welsh Football Union met on Wednesday 25th January they selected precisely the same team to

Wales Team v Scotland 1905

Back Row: W O'Neil, C M Pritchard, G Travers, J S Jones (Touch-judge), D Jones, W Joseph. *Middle Row*: G Davies, H V Watkins, J J Hodges, A F Harding, W M Llewellyn (Captain), E Morgan, R T Gabe, D Rees. *Front Row*: R M Owen, W J Trew.

face Scotland at Inverleith as that which had defeated England on the 14th January at Cardiff. The reserves, too, were unchanged with the exception of T Evans (Llanelly) who was replaced by Dai 'Port Tennant' Davies (Swansea). A week before the international against Scotland, Dick Jones sprained his ankle playing for Swansea against Newport at St Helen's. With no prospect of playing in the game against Scotland, Jones was happy to see his club mate Billy Trew called into the side as his replacement. This was the only change to a Welsh team which took the field as follows:

Wales: Back, G Davies (Swansea); three-quarters, W M Llewellyn (Newport, Captain), D Rees (Swansea), R T Gabe (Cardiff), E Morgan (London Welsh); half-backs, W J Trew and R M Owen (Swansea); forwards, W Joseph (Swansea), A F Harding (London Welsh), D Jones

(Aberdare), C M Pritchard, J J Hodges (Newport), W O'Neil (Cardiff), H V Watkins (Llanelly), G Travers (Pill Harries).

Scotland: Back, W T Forrest (Hawick); three-quarters, J E Crabbie (Edinburgh Acads), L M MacLeod (Cambridge U), *J L Forbes (Watsonians), J S McDonald (Edinburgh U); half-backs, *P Munro (London Scottish), E D Simson (Edinburgh U); forwards, *A W Little, W E Kyle (Hawick), W M Milne, R S Stronach (Glasgow Acads), *A Ross (Royal HSFP), H N Fletcher (Edinburgh U), W P Scott (West of Scotland, Captain), A G Cairns (Watsonians). (* Scotland Debut)

Referee: G H B Kennedy (Ireland).

Wales lost the toss and Hodges kicked off against a strong wind. After some fairly even play Scotland opened the scoring when Arthur Little picked up and forced his way over the Welsh line for an unconverted try. With Scotland taking full advantage of the wind George Davies was continually under pressure, often struggling to field the ball safely. Even so, the Welsh forwards, after a poor start, began to heel the ball more efficiently thus enabling the Welsh backs to make determined attacks on the Scottish line. After several near misses a fine round of passing between the Welsh backs resulted in Dan Rees giving Willie Llewellyn a perfect pass which enabled his captain to score a brilliant try in the corner. Although George Davies struck the ball beautifully, the wind just carried the ball away from the post and no extra points were added. Wales pressed hard from the restart and Will Joseph was all but over for a try, just being held up a few yards short of the line, and so with no further scoring the teams were level at the break.

In the second half, try as they did Wales could not add to their score. On several occasions they looked like scoring, but each time play broke down at the last moment. Teddy Morgan was pushed into touch a few yards from the line and Dan Rees missed a lovely pass from Billy Trew when he had a clear opening. A minute later the same player threw the ball forward when the Scottish defence was beaten. Then Billy Trew, after breaking away in great style, spoilt a sparkling passage of play by holding on too long when Rhys Gabe had a clear run in. Several opportunities were wasted but then, after Teddy Morgan had almost crossed, Wales had another great chance. Dickie Owen, receiving from his forwards, passed on to Dan Rees just at the right moment. Rees ran strongly and ten yards from the line gave a beautiful pass to Willie Llewellyn, who rounded Forrest and scored a great try. George Davies missed the conversion but Wales had secured a lead they would not relinquish and when the final whistle blew they were ahead by 6 points to three. In an article in the *Evening Express* Harry Bowen, in reference to Willie Llewellyn, said the following: 'Willie Llewellyn, who scored the two tries, the finishing touches of which required much doing, played strongly throughout. This should be his red-letter day.' This was the first time Wales had beaten Scotland at Inverleith, having failed on their previous three visits to the ground.

With Willie back up in London on a dentistry course at London Hospital he took the opportunity to turn out for his old club, London Welsh. The week following the international against Scotland, Willie played for London Welsh in their away game against Bedford which celebrated the opening of the new grand stand at Goldington Road. The only score of the first half was a try for London Welsh by S H Coppock which was converted by Charlie Lewis. Then in a fast and exciting second half, Willie scored a brilliant try behind the posts which Charlie Lewis converted, and with no further scores London Welsh won by 10 points to nil.

The following Wednesday Willie found himself playing for Kent in their county match against Middlesex. Willie was playing alongside fellow 1904 tourists Stuart Mackenzie Saunders and Pat McEvedy, together with Newport and London Welsh teammate J E C 'Birdie' Partridge. Also in the Kent team were English internationals S F Coopper and W T Cave, who Willie had played against a month earlier. Kent were beaten at forward and half-back and consequently their three-quarters had very few opportunities. A goal from a mark by English international Harry Alexander was the only score of the game, Kent losing by 4 points to nil.

On the day Newport were getting thumped by Cardiff, Willie was playing for London Welsh in their game against United Services at Queen's Club. This was the first of three games Willie played for the Exiles in eight days. Firstly he scored a try in the 26 points to three victory over United Services. Willie then scored the only try for London Welsh in their 16 points to three defeat away to Cambridge University before

London Welsh were comprehensively beaten by 33 points to three in their away game against Northampton. Willie had been selected to represent Glamorgan in their match against Yorkshire at Cardiff on the same day, but instead chose to turn out for London Welsh at Northampton.

London Welsh selected a very strong team for their next game to be played at Queen's Club against Bristol. There were six Welsh internationals in the side originally picked, including Bert Winfield, Willie Llewellyn, Gwyn Nicholls, Teddy Morgan, Arthur Harding and Wallace Watts. Gwyn Nicholls withdrew but the Welsh still had a strong side which also featured J F Williams, the Welsh reserve forward. With Willie Llewellyn, Teddy Morgan, Arthur Harding and John 'Scethrog' Williams in the side, Christ College, Brecon was well represented. Bristol opened the scoring when Meyer crossed for a try which Moore converted. Shortly afterwards London Welsh equalised thanks to some brilliant work by Teddy Morgan. He received near the half-way line and dodging his opponents reached the twenty-five. Running across the goal he passed to A E Evans, who crossed for a try which Bert Winfield converted. With neither side scoring in the second half the game ended in a 5 points all drawn game.

When the Match Committee of the Welsh Football Union met at the Queen's Hotel, Cardiff, on Thursday 23rd February they selected the same Welsh team that had defeated Scotland to represent Wales in their Triple Crown match against Ireland at St Helen's, Swansea on Saturday 11th March, with Willie again given the captain's armband. The selection of the reserves was deferred until March 8th, three days before the match, and when they were announced they were as follows: Full-back, J C M Dyke (Penarth); three-quarters, either wing, Cecil Biggs (Cardiff); centres, Frank Gordon (Swansea) and Gwyn Nicholls (Cardiff); half-backs, D R Gent (Gloucester) for Owen and Reggie Gibbs (Penarth) for Windham Jones; forwards, J F Williams (London Welsh), J C Jenkins and E Thomas Maynard (Newport).

Although Billy Trew was selected, there was considerable doubt about his fitness. He had been injured in the Swansea game against Leicester and it was unclear whether he would recover in time for the international against Ireland. Subsequently Billy Trew withdrew from the team and Windham Jones of Mountain Ash was chosen to take his place at half-back. There were three players in the running for the position: Windham Jones,

Percy Bush and Reggie Gibbs. Percy Bush lacked support through having been out of football for the previous two months with an injured arm. He would almost certainly have been chosen had he played for Cardiff the previous Saturday and satisfied the committee that he had fully recovered his fitness. There was no doubt that Percy Bush was a brilliant outside half, but there was no prospect of him being selected without proving his fitness so, unfortunately, he had to let the opportunity slip, and as a consequence missed the honour of representing his country for the first time. Reggie Gibbs was a serious contender, but he gave such an indifferent display when he played for Glamorgan against Yorkshire (and also for Penarth against Cardiff) that his chance slipped away. On the other hand, Windham Jones had been playing consistently throughout the season and the soundness of his defence convinced the selection committee that he should be in the team.

The Welsh team suffered another blow when two days before the match Charlie Pritchard informed Water E Rees of the Welsh Football Union that he had an ankle injury and, not being fully fit, withdrew from the team. His place was taken by John F Williams of London Welsh who, like Windham Jones, came into the side to gain his first Welsh cap.

A further change to the Welsh team to face Ireland was more controversial. It was announced the day before the match that Dan Rees of Swansea had cried off. There were very strong feelings amongst the Swansea players that their club captain, Frank Gordon, should have been in the team and rumours were rife that if Frank Gordon did not play there could be a mass withdrawal of the Swansea players from the Welsh side. The Swansea players had a reputation for making their feelings known and had a history of withdrawing from Glamorgan County games and Welsh trial matches. Walter Rees, secretary of the Welsh Football Union, confirmed that Dan Rees had informed him that he was not going to play against Ireland and consequently contacted Gwyn Nicholls to order him to, 'hold himself in readiness.' There was no nominated first or second reserve for the Welsh centre position; Gwyn Nicholls and Frank Gordon were simply listed as reserve centres. The intention of the match committee of the WFU was that the final decision as to the replacement for Dan Rees would be made at noon, at Swansea, just prior to the match. Frank Gordon was chosen with the idea that if Rhys Gabe was unable to play he would partner fellow Swansea teammate Dan Rees in the centre. If Dan Rees was unable to play Gwyn Nicholls would partner his club-mate Rhys Gabe in the centre. The logic of the selection committee could not be faulted.

At one o'clock on the day of the match it was still not known who would replace Dan Rees. Gwyn Nicholls and Frank Gordon were both ready to play and about an hour before the kick-off it was announced that Gwyn Nicholls would play. There was a general opinion that the chances of victory were considerably enhanced by the selection of Gwyn Nicholls.

Frank Gordon captained Swansea in their 'Invincible' season of 1904–05. He also captained the side in 1901–02, 1902–03 and 1905–06.

Nevertheless, there was a feeling of sympathy for Frank Gordon in that he should have been deprived at the last moment from playing for his country. The expected revolt by the Swansea players never materialised and Willie Llewellyn led his team onto the field for the traditional taking of photographs.

It was suggested that the reason Dan Rees had withdrawn was because he had pleurisy. He had however, played for Swansea in the game against Newport the week before the Ireland test, had watched the international, and then played for Swansea the Monday after the Triple Crown encounter in the game against Aberdare. It was generally believed, everywhere but Swansea, that Dan Rees had stood down in the hope that Frank Gordon would gain his Welsh cap. This was not to be but Dan Rees, the Swansea vice-captain, stuck to his story that, although not seriously ill, he was not well enough to take part in such a critical contest as the international match. He said, 'it would have been very improper of him to play for Wales feeling physically unfit.' Dan Rees continued to play county rugby for Glamorgan and was Swansea's top try scorer for the 1904–05 season with 30 tries. However, he had played his last international match for Wales and after five Welsh caps he joined fellow Swansea teammate and Welsh international Fred Jowett at Northern Union club Hull Kingston Rovers in October 1905, signing on as a professional for the reported sum of £300.

When Wales faced Ireland on Saturday 11th March it was a Triple Crown encounter of epic proportion with both teams capable of taking the coveted prize. Wales had defeated both England and Scotland and with Ireland having done the same the scene was set for a winner takes all showdown. In the previous nineteen matches between the two sides Wales had won eleven, Ireland seven with just the one drawn game in Dublin 1890. St Helen's was full to capacity with around 35,000 spectators accounting for record receipts of £2,250. The best previous gate for a

Wales Team v Ireland 1905

Back Row: A J Davies (Touch-judge), W O'Neil, D Jones, A F Harding, H V Watkins, G Travers, W Joseph, W Williams (RFU Referee).
Middle Row: J F Williams, J J Hodges, R T Gabe, W Llewellyn (Captain), E G Nicholls, E Morgan. Front Row; R M Owen, G Davies, A W Jones.
Inset: D Rees, W J Trew, R H Jones, C M Pritchard.

Welsh international match was £2,223. 10s. 8d. taken at Cardiff for the game against Ireland in 1903. The Triple Crown battle began with the following sides taking the field:

Wales: Back, G Davies (Swansea); three-quarters, W M Llewellyn (Newport, Captain), E G Nicholls, R T Gabe (Cardiff), E Morgan (London Welsh); half-backs, *A Windham Jones (Mountain Ash), R M Owen (Swansea); forwards, W Joseph (Swansea), A F Harding, *J F Williams (London Welsh), D Jones (Aberdare), J J Hodges (Newport), W O'Neil (Cardiff), H V Watkins (Llanelly), G Travers (Pill Harries). (* Wales Debut)

Ireland: Back, M F Landers (Cork Const); three-quarters, H Thrift, J C Parke (Dublin U), B Maclear (Monkstown), J E Moffatt (Old Wesley); half-backs, T H Robinson, E D Caddell (Dublin U); forwards, C E Allen (Derry, Captain), J J Coffey (Lansdowne), G T Hamlet (Old Wesley), H G Wilson, A Tedford (Malone), J H Knox (Dublin U), H J Millar (Monkstown), Joseph Wallace (Wanderers).

Referee: W Williams (RFU, England).

After some early pressure Ireland opened the scoring when Tom Robinson crossed for a try just six minutes into the game. Basil Maclear failed to convert. For quite some time matters were fairly even until Wales were awarded a penalty. George Davies, who was entrusted with the kick attempted a drop-kick at goal. The ball fell short but the Welsh forwards were on it like a flash before Landers just managed to get there first and touch down for a minor. With Wales in possession, some fine passing between Gwyn Nicholls, Rhys Gabe and Teddy Morgan almost resulted in a try, but Basil Maclear and Landers brought Morgan down short of the line. After some fierce scrummaging near the Irish line, Dickie Owen picked up and made an opening for Windham Jones. The outside-half dodged towards the crossbar, he feinted one way and then swerved passed Landers to score beneath the post. George Davies made no mistake with the conversion and Wales were ahead by 5 points to three. Five minutes from the interval a brilliant forward rush led by Harding and Hodges brushed the opposition aside until the Welsh forwards were close to the Irish line. Following a loose scrum, Teddy Morgan picked up and dashed smartly over for a try. Although the conversion was not easy George Davies succeeded with a beautiful kick to give Wales the advantage at the interval by 10 points to three.

With Wales in front they took no risks in the second half and Willie Llewellyn told his men to shut up shop. Although having much the better of the play, Ireland could not score, chiefly owing to the tenacity of the Welsh forwards, who obstinately disputed every inch of the field. Ireland had two penalty kicks at goal in the latter stages of the game, but Basil Maclear was unsuccessful on both occasions, and with the Welsh forwards serving their side superbly, they never relaxed until the final whistle blew and the Triple Crown and championship were won.

In his comments on the game 'Forward' of the *Evening Express* was very complimentary to the manner in which Willie Llewellyn had led his team, saying, 'Wales having established a lead, was expected to open up the game more than was done, but on reflection, it must be conceded that Willie Llewellyn showed the best judgement in advising his men to keep the ball close and not take any risks.' Willie, interviewed after the game, stated that it had been a terribly tight game and he had been delighted by the play of the Welsh forwards. He said, 'It was our business to keep the game close and we succeeded in that alright. Our forwards played much better in the second half than in the first and I think it is much cleverer for forwards to play well against the wind than with the wind.' In response to a remark that the Welsh three-quarters had done nothing in the second half, Willie said, 'it was of course, the result of the forwards keeping the ball tight.' He went on to say, 'The slightest mistake would have let us down at any moment. Our game was to keep the ball very tight as we got somewhere near up. Of course, we did not often get up near enough to attempt back play. On the whole, the play reflects great credit on our forwards, who played a magnificent game and acquitted themselves like demons from beginning to end.' Wales had played wonderfully well and with the sound judgement of their captain had secured their fourth Triple Crown.

From the excitement of Triple Crown glory Willie returned to club rugby for his next game, appearing for Newport against Cardiff. He scored a try in each half to give Newport victory by 6 points to three. Newport lost their next game away to Blackheath but Willie remained in London and the following week scored another try playing for London Welsh in their victory over Catford Bridge.

On Saturday 8th April, for the first time Newport succumbed to

Devonport Albion. A drop goal near to the end of the game by Summers of the Albion was the only score of the game. The following Monday the same Newport team were well beaten by Plymouth. Willie scored the only Newport try in a game they lost by 14 points to three.

Willie Llewellyn completed his 1904–05 season by playing a remarkable seven games in thirteen days. On Monday 17th April Willie took a team to Penygraig to play a match against a team representing the Rhondda clubs. The proceeds of the game were divided between the Nurses' Association and the Clydach Vale Explosion Fund. On Friday 10th March 1905 an explosion occurred at the Cambrian Collieries No.1 pit 6ft. Seam which led to the deaths of 31 men underground, and one who died later in hospital, and serious injury to 14 others. The disaster created 25 widows and resulted in 72 children losing their father. The Cambrian explosion of 1905 was a terrible tragedy, but it could have been much worse had it not been for the timing of the explosion. It occurred at 6.25 p.m., a time when the day shift had left the mine and the night shift had yet to descend. Had it not been for the fortuitous timing of the explosion the death toll could well have been between 500 and 600 men. With regard to the game there were several important changes to Willie Llewellyn's team with Rhys Gabe, Teddy Morgan, Dickie Owen, Percy Bush, George Travers and John 'Scethrog' Williams all unable to fulfil their promise to turn out. Willie's younger brother, George, took the place of Teddy Morgan on the wing. Willie's team took the field as follows:

Back, J C M Dyke (Penarth); three-quarters, W M Llewellyn (Newport, Captain), E G Nicholls (Cardiff), Jones (London Welsh), George Llewellyn (Brecon); half-backs, W Bennett (Newport), Jenkins (Ystrad); forwards, C M Pritchard, G Boots, E Thomas, J C Jenkins (Newport), A F Harding (London Welsh), Sid Bevan (Swansea), W H Williams (West of Scotland), Partridge (Kent).

George Llewellyn opened the scoring for the visitors with an unconverted try. Joe Hellings replied for Rhondda United and Simmonds gave the home team the lead when he kicked the conversion. In the second half, Simmonds scored another try for Rhondda United and added the extra points himself. Emlyn and Johnnie Lewis, the Treherbert half-backs, completely outplayed Bennett and Jenkins and as a consequence the visiting three-quarters saw little of the ball. Despite some fine play by

Willie Llewellyn late in the game and a magnificent dribble half the length of the field by Arthur Harding, there were no further scores and Willie's team were defeated by 10 points to three.

Two days later Willie played for an East Wales team against the West of England in a match promoted by Gwyn Nicholls to raise money for the Welsh National Museum at Cardiff. Played on the Cardiff Arms Park, the East Wales team included eight Welsh internationals. In addition to Gwyn Nicholls, Bert Winfield, Willie Llewellyn, Rhys Gabe, Dai Jones, Billy O'Neil, Alfred Brice and George Boots all played in the game. A penalty goal in the first half by Bert Winfield and an unconverted try by G L Jones of Cinderford brought the scores level at the interval. In the second half an unconverted try by Cecil Biggs gave the East Wales team victory by 6 points to three.

Playing his third game in five days Willie's next game was for Penarth in their victory over the Barbarians. Fellow Welsh teammate Arthur Harding was playing for the Barbarians and converted the try scored by N W Godfrey. However, Penarth took the spoils with a try by E Williams which was converted by John Dyke and an unconverted try by Willie Llewellyn.

The following day Willie scored two tries for Newport in their home victory over Northampton. Newport started a man short with Jehoida Hodges having missed his train. Northampton opened the scoring when A J Hobbs crossed for a try which Cockling failed to convert. By this time Jehoida Hodges had joined the home forwards and directly after the drop out the Newport men began to assert themselves rather more than they had done previously. Although Newport were denied in their forward rushes for a short time, Alby Davies fielded splendidly and as soon as he had taken the ball he raced off at full-speed and passed to Rowland Griffiths. With almost a clear field in front of him, Griffiths, virtually unopposed, ran over for a try wide out which was not converted. With the scores equal at the interval, Newport picked up their game in the second half when Willie Llewellyn turned the tide of events by intercepting and racing away at full-speed to round the visitors' full-back and score behind the posts. Price failed to convert but Newport had their tails in front and that is where they stayed. Further unconverted tries by Jehoida Hodges and Willie Llewellyn gave the home side victory by 12 points to three.

WILLIE CAPTAINS WALES TO A FOURTH TRIPLE CROWN

Date	Team Played For	Opposition	Venue	Result	W Llewellyn Tries
29/10/1904	Newport	Neath	Away	Won 10-0	1
19/11/1904	Newport	Cardiff	Home	Won 7-5	0
01/12/1904	Newport Barbarians	Newport Thursdays	Rodney Parade	Lost 6-8	1
10/12/1904	Newport	Swansea	Away	Lost 3-9	0
17/12/1904	Newport	Plymouth Albion	Home	Won 20-6	0
24/12/1904	Newport	Neath	Home	Won 23-0	2
26/12/1904	Newport	Watsonians	Home	Lost 3-11	0
31/12/1904	Newport	London Welsh	Away	Won 12-4	1
14/01/1905	Wales	England	Cardiff Arms Park	Won 25-0	1
26/01/1904	Glamorgan	Somerset	Bath	Won 15-3	0
04/02/1905	Wales	Scotland	Inverleith, Edinburgh	Won 6-3	2
11/02/1905	London Welsh	Bedford	Away	Won 10-0	1
15/02/1905	Kent	Middlesex	Richmond	Lost 0-4	0
18/02/1905	London Welsh	United Services	Queen's Club	Won 26-3	1
22/02/1905	London Welsh	Cambridge University	Cambridge	Lost 3-16	1
25/02/1905	London Welsh	Northampton	Away	Lost 3-33	0
04/03/1905	London Welsh	Bristol	Queen's Club	Drawn 5-5	0
11/03/1905	Wales	Ireland	Sat Helen's, Swansea	Won 10-3	0
18/03/1905	Newport	Cardiff	Home	Won 6-3	2
25/03/1905	Newport	Blackheath	Away	Lost 3-7	0
01/04/1905	London Welsh	Catford Bridge	Away	Won 20-6	1
08/04/1905	Newport	Devonport Albion	Away	Lost 0-4	0
10/04/1905	Newport	Plymouth	Away	Lost 3-14	1
17/04/1905	Willie Llewellyn's Team	Rhondda United	Penygraig	Lost 3-10	0
19/04/1905	East Wales	West of England	Cardiff Arms Park	Won 6-3	0
21/04/1905	Penarth	Barbarians	Penarth	Won 8-5	1
22/04/1905	Newport	Northampton	Home	Won 12-3	2
24/04/1905	Newport	Rockcliff	Home	Won 15-3	1
24/04/1905	Cardiff	Barbarians	Cardiff Arms Park	Lost 5-8	0
29/04/1905	Newport	Leicester	Away	Lost 4-13	0
Totals	Willie Llewellyn Games Played 30				W Llewellyn Tries 19

Willie Llewellyn Rugby Games Played and Results 1904–1905 Season

On Monday 24th April, Willie played two games on the same day. In the morning he played for Newport in the home game against Rockcliff. With one unconverted try by Harry Uzzell for Newport and a penalty goal by Adamson for Rockcliff, the scores were level at the interval. Early in the second half Willie Llewellyn smartly fielded a kick by Thomas Simpson, the English international, and taking the ball at full-speed raced clear of everybody and scored a wonderful try that went unconverted. Willie Thomas then scored another try for Newport which Rowland Griffiths converted, and a last-minute drop goal by Jack Jenkins gave Newport victory by 15 points to three. Astonishingly, the same afternoon Willie played for Cardiff against the Barbarians at Cardiff Arms Park.

Unfortunately there was no fairy-tale ending to the day as Cardiff were beaten by 8 points to five. The Barbarian team, which included Welsh international Arthur Harding, let at the interval by 3 points to nil from an unconverted try by England international Sydney Coopper. They added to their score in the second half when another England international, Arthur Brettargh, scored their second try which was converted by fellow England international Walter Rogers. Despite losing two players through injury, Cardiff still managed to score a try through future Welsh international wing Johnny Williams. Bert Winfield added the extra points but it was too little too late and Cardiff were defeated.

Willie played his seventh game in thirteen days and his last game of the 1904–05 season for Newport in their away game at Leicester. The match was very disappointing and the visitors were easily overrun by the powerful Leicester forwards. Leicester were leading at the interval by 8 points to nil and early in the second half scored another try which was converted to give them an unassailable 13 point lead. Although W Bennett scored a neat dropped goal for Newport, there were no further scores and Newport were defeated by 13 points to four.

The Leicester game brought Willie's season to an end, and by his high standards this had been a very successful one. He had played club rugby for Newport, London Welsh, Penarth and Cardiff, county rugby for Glamorgan and Kent and had captained Wales in all three internationals to claim the Home Nations Championship and a fourth Triple Crown. Despite reports in the press early in the season that Willie was not playing at his best, he had proved his doubters wrong by enjoying an outstanding season. During the 1904–05 season, Willie had played a total of 30 games and scored 19 tries. Between Saturday 3rd October 1903 and Saturday 29th April 1905 Willie had played almost constantly, featuring in 73 games and scoring 40 tries. During that period Willie played in 10 international matches and scored 8 tries. At the age of twenty-seven he had become a Welsh rugby legend, he had played for Wales on 19 occasions and 4 times in tests for the British Team in Australia and New Zealand. During his international career Willie had scored 24 tries. There was no hint of Willie retiring from international rugby and during the summer months while playing cricket for Llwynypia he could contemplate the arrival of the New Zealand rugby football team.

Early in the 1904–05 season Willie would have been very disappointed to hear of the demise of his old club Llwynypia. Willie had played for them for over six seasons during which time they had been a very successful club, winning the Glamorgan League on four occasions and achieving invincibility during the 1896–97 season. Founded in 1891, Llwynypia played all the great Welsh clubs including Neath, Cardiff, Llanelly, Bridgend, Aberavon and Newport. The club, however, of later years had been struggling to exist. The ravages of the Northern Union clubs, players switching to more popular clubs and the changing of fields being mainly responsible for its decline, until finally, in September 1904, it ceased to exist. Llwynypia had originally played at the Recreation Grounds but the field was often under water because of the river bursting it banks in severe weather. In January 1902, the club moved to the Partridge Field, which was above the level of the river, the overflowing of which would not interfere with fixtures. This report in the *Rhondda Leader* on Saturday 1st October 1904 highlighted the difficulties that were created by moving to Partridge Field: 'Since the venue of the ground was changed to the Partridge Field, which is far from being central, the team met with anything but success and the attendance at last season's games was very meagre. Also the field is in a hollow and the banks surrounding it admitted of scores of persons being able to witness the whole of play without payment. There were only a few of the old players available this year and the suggestion of amalgamation with Ystrad Stars would never be entertained by the latter. Under the circumstances, despite club secretary, Mr David Llewellyn, having arranged a good list of fixtures for the coming season, there was no other course open but to abandon the team.' The club reformed the following year, but it was unable to attract the support and quality of player that it had enjoyed in the early 1900s. After the First World War, the Rhondda Valleys saw a massive decline in the demand for coal which created an economic depression which was felt across South Wales. With little disposable income, crowds dwindled with the result that many valley clubs faced financial ruin. Llwynypia was one such club and was disbanded by the 1930s.

While Willie had made a name for himself on the international rugby scene, younger brother George was following in his footsteps at Christ College, Brecon. George was appointed captain of the first XV for the

Christ College Brecon, Rugby First XV 1904–1905

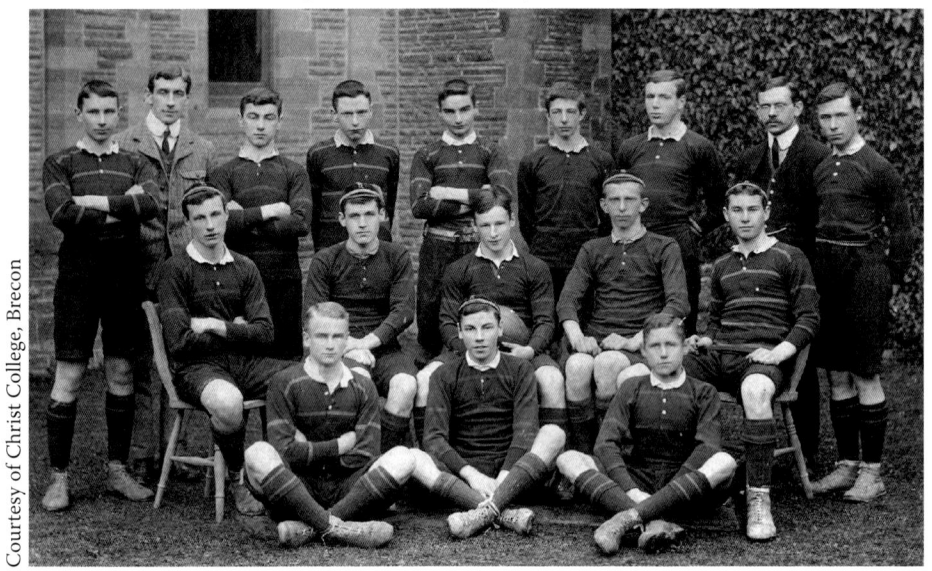

Back Row: C H Law, A E C Morgan Esq, W M Llewellyn, H Allen,
W L Gwyn Davies, T G Jones, I M Morgan, A E Donaldson Esq, W M Howells.
Middle Row: M Williams, H S Ross, G Llewellyn (Captain), F D S Harries,
T D W Williams. Front Row: J S Lovell, W E Coldicutt, E V Watkins.

1904–05 season during which time the College played twelve games with George ever-present. Although their record was not a memorable one they won more games (5) than they lost (4) and drew three. They scored 164 points for with 86 against. Without a shadow of a doubt the highlight of the season was their 9 points to 3 victory over Llandovery College, a side they had not beaten since 1898. The editorial of the 1904 December edition of *The Breconian* stated how George had 'been well-nigh overwhelmed with congratulations.' The report of the game in the same edition of *The Breconian* said, 'To G Llewellyn is the victory undoubtedly due, not only for his brilliant offence and defence, but also for the fact that by robbing their attacking line of the ball he prevented them adopting their usual tactics.' With regard to the whole season, the same edition of *The Breconian* paid tribute to George when they stated, 'The captain's share in the season's games is hinted elsewhere. It is enough to say that he trod worthily in his brother's footsteps and to point out that he scored at least one try in every match, on many occasions running quite half the length of the ground to do so. The intercepted pass, brilliant as its results often were, is still a slight cause of weakness to an otherwise strong defence, but there, until the time comes to judge him in higher company, criticism ends.' In a résumé of the first XV players *The Breconian* said of George: 'G Llewellyn (right centre three-quarter), Captain. – Combining great speed with remarkable swerving power is a most dangerous offensive three-quarter and would do better still in his proper place on the wing. Sound in defence and kicks with great judgement. An excellent captain, who had a large personal share in all the success of his side.'

There is no doubt that George was an exceptional rugby player, the fact that he was first XV captain in his penultimate year at Christ College is testimony to that. In addition to rugby, George was an outstanding athlete. Under his captaincy, the College hockey team also had a successful year. Out of the 9 matches they played, they won 5, lost 3 and drew one. Although not a startling record, the College had no weak opponents and every victory was well earned. George was also a good cricketer; he was fourth in the batting averages and fifth in the bowling averages. Also very good at fives, George won the fives cup for singles and, together with Arthur Williams, carried off the House Cup for fives pairs. In fact it was one sporting victory after another for George that year, for he also won the golf prize: playing off scratch he scored 91 points, the next best being 103.

The culmination of George's athletic prowess during the year was becoming *Victor Ludorum* for the second time by the winning of the Challenge Cup for the athletic sports, thus emulating his elder brother Willie who also achieved this honour at Christ College. In addition to winning the two fives competitions and the golf competition, George, also won the Long jump (open), Hurdle race (open) and the 100 yards (open), and with 60 marks was well ahead of W Williams the second placed man with 15½ marks.

While I am confident that Willie would have been very proud of George's achievements at Christ College, he would surely also have been distracted by the anticipated arrival of the New Zealand rugby football team in just a few months' time. Ever since the British rugby team, under the captaincy of R L Seddon, toured New Zealand in 1888, the leaders of the rugby union game in New Zealand had looked forward to the idea of returning the visit. This expectation took a major step to becoming a reality in late 1902 after a lengthy correspondence between the New Zealand Rugby Union, the Agent-General (Hon. W P Reeves) of New Zealand and Mr Rowland Hill of the Rugby Football Union (RFU). One major difficulty which needed to be overcome was the ability of the New Zealand players to comply with the strict regulations in respect of amateurism enforced by the RFU. The great majority of New Zealand players were from the working classes and it seemed impossible for them, or at least many of them, to fulfil the English requirements. Mr Rowland Hill indicated that there was no likelihood of the RFU relaxing its professionalism regulations, but that aside, it would do everything to make the visit of the New Zealanders a success. Another stumbling block was the financial return the New Zealanders would receive from each match. In connection with the proposed visit of the New Zealand rugby team to England in September 1904, the *Evening Express* published the following communication which was cabled to the New Zealand Premier by Mr W P Reeves (Agent-General for New Zealand in England): 'Inform Norris (Secretary of the New Zealand Union), Football Union, that international conference strongly recommend postpone till September 1905, visit to England, for simple reason that home arrangements made for next season. Terms proposed: Firstly – International matches: England and Wales can guarantee minimum of £500 per match; Ireland £100; Scotland, half gate, less expenses. Secondly – English and most probably, Welsh Union clubs will guarantee minimum of £50. Thirdly – English counties and clubs will give 70 per cent. gate, after defraying expenses. Full details by post 15th January (1904). Reply by 7th March, as South Africa anxious to send home team.' With all the complications overcome and the final team selections made, the New Zealand team had their farewell dinner in Wellington on Saturday 29th July 1905 and the next day the team left Wellington for Plymouth on the direct liner SS Rimutaka.

Finally after being the perennial reserve forward for Wales (on five occasions no less), John F Williams of London Welsh, who replaced the injured Charlie Pritchard, had finally come into the Welsh team to gain his first cap against Ireland. Also known as Jack Williams or John 'Scethrog' Williams, he was an outstanding forward. During the

New Zealand Farewell Toast List. Wellington July 29th 1905.

season he had played county rugby for Middlesex and turned out for the Possibles in the final trial at Neath after which he was reserve forward for both the England and Scotland internationals. The inclusion of J F Williams in the Welsh team to face Ireland brought the total number of Christ College Old Boys in the Welsh team to four.

There was now only one player who would play for Wales against New Zealand on Saturday 16th December 1905 who hadn't yet been capped by Wales, and that was Percy Bush who had starred for the British Team in Australia and New Zealand in 1904 as top points scorer with 97 points. But having returned unscathed from the tour, he broke his arm playing for Cardiff seconds against Merthyr

John Frederick Williams who gained four caps for Wales between 1905 and 1906.

and was effectively out of the game for most of the season. Although he was one of the favourites to take the place of the injured Billy Trew at outside-half for Wales against Ireland in March 1905 he lacked support through having been out of football for the previous two months with the injured arm. Had he played for Cardiff in their match against Gloucester the previous Saturday and proved to the selection committee that he was fully fit, he would almost certainly have been chosen. Percy Bush was unquestionably an outstanding outside-half, but there was no prospect of him being selected without proving his fitness, so, unfortunately, the opportunity was lost and consequently Percy had to wait until December before gaining his first Welsh cap, against the All Blacks. What a match in which to make your Welsh debut.

Chapter Ten

1905 and the Greatest Game Ever Played

IN HIS BOOK *The Book of fame* Lloyd Jones describes the New Zealanders' journey from Wellington to Plymouth. Although officially listed as 'Fiction' his book is based on meticulous research carried out in England, Wales and New Zealand. Wherever possible Lloyd Jones tried to follow in the footsteps of Dave Gallaher and visited many of the grounds where the 1905 New Zealanders played. In addition he spent many hours searching through the British Library's newspaper archive looking for suitable material from that period. In New Zealand Lloyd Jones spent many hours with Bob Luxford at the New Zealand Rugby Museum, Palmerston North where he combed through players' mementoes and Billy Wallace's album in order to add factual detail to his work. The following is a short summary of the final part of that journey from his book: In early September 1905 the New Zealand rugby football team were nearing the end of their long sea journey on-board the SS Rimutaka. 'All the players were training vigorously, with the exception of Jimmie O'Sullivan who was down with sunstroke.' Everyone was now counting the days and on September 5th they passed Cape Finisterre. They had been at sea for close to forty days and had 'developed a morbid shipboard stare, hanging off the rails, gazing down as though staring into their very own graves.' They had 'forgotten the point of newspapers and had stopped

After forty-one days at sea the 1905 All Blacks get ready to disembark.

talking as if any of that mattered either.' Finally at their lowest ebb the New Zealanders welcomed signs that the English shore was indeed near. 'She sent out signals that she was near. The seas thickened with fishing boats and marker buoys. Late in the day a large cruiser steamed by in the opposite direction and everyone ran to that side of the ship to wave, but no one waved back. That last night at sea they sat up writing of Arabs and pyramids on postcards they had bought in Tenerife ready to send home the moment they stepped ashore.'

Before dawn on Friday 8th September the team was up on deck, 'leaning against the rails, smoking their pipes and bumping into each other in the dark.' Crouched by an oil lamp Eric Harper concluded his letter: 'The English shores are in sight and the excitement is too great to continue.' In the dark 'England came to them in a series of noises, foghorns, ship's whistles and hissing. They strained to make her out. None of them spoke. Each entertained a private notion of what England should be like and finally there she was,' at last they were in Plymouth Sound. Despite forty-one days at sea, they were a very happy family and Dave Gallaher, in his capacity as skipper, proved himself thoroughly and justifiably popular. As they disembarked and the tugs cast off, the ship's company and passengers gave them a great sending off, cheering heartily. At last the 1905 New Zealand rugby football team had arrived.

The 1905 All Blacks played the first of their thirty-two games in Great Britain and Ireland against Devon at Exeter on Saturday 16th September. It was an overwhelming victory by 55 points to four. 'Forward' in the *Western Mail* under a column heading of, 'Sensational start of the New Zealanders' said: 'these New Zealanders are no picnic party' and added that a thrill had gone through the Rugby world when the news of New Zealand's sensational victory was flashed over the wires from Exeter. Devon County had never suffered such a crushing defeat as this, the huge score leaving no doubt that the Southern Colony had sent over its 'best men' to uphold and possibly augment its high reputation in the Rugby

The First Representative New Zealand Team to Play in Great Britain

Back Row: G Tyler, J O'Sullivan, W Cunningham, G W Nicholson, C Seeling, F Glasgow. *Middle Row*: S T Casey, W J Wallace, W Stead, G Dixon (Manager), D Gallaher (Captain), J Hunter, G Gillett. *Front Row*: G W Smith, F Roberts, H Thomson.

game. Reference was made to the play of the wing forward and how he prevented the Devon halves opening out the game for the men behind. No doubt the result was somewhat flattering to the visitors but they had entered upon their formidable programme in a manner which would go far towards making their tour a success. The report continued by saying that it did not necessarily follow that the New Zealanders would win their international engagements, yet judging by their form against Devon and the experience of the English team in New Zealand the previous year, it was certain that the Colonials had attained a high level of excellence at the Rugby game and would give the best of our fifteens a hard struggle. It would be another six matches before another team would score against them. It was thirteen weeks to the day before Wales would face the mighty All Blacks at Cardiff Arms Park and there would be a lot of rugby played before that thrilling encounter.

Even though a report in *The London Welshman* early in September 1905 stated, 'Willie Llewellyn will be playing for Newport until Christmas, but after that date he will be unable to do so, as he will be settling down in business at Llwynypia,' this was not the case. Willie played his last four games for Newport during September and October 1905, the drawn game against Blackheath on Saturday 21st October 1905 bringing down the curtain on a Newport career that included forty-seven appearances. After that Willie played his last two games for London Welsh before transferring to Penygraig. Including the first Newport trial match Willie played thirteen games all told before making his last appearance for Wales against New Zealand in 1905.

Willie's first game of the season was playing for Newport 'C' Team in the trial match at Newport on Saturday 16th September. There were two trial games that day with the 'A' Team playing the 'B' Team and the 'C' Team playing the 'D' Team. The 'A' and 'B' teams were mainly junior players whilst the 'C' and 'D' teams were largely senior players. The 'C' team was mainly the Newport first fifteen players from the previous season whereas the 'D' team contained players drawn from the wider district. Willie scored two tries in the thirty-one points to nil victory. Although Willie was selected to reappear in the second trial match the following Saturday, he did not play. Willie had also been selected for Bristol in their game against New Zealand, but although the local newspapers reported that he was in the team, he was unable to turn out and both he and Rhys Gabe had a watching brief from the grandstand with C Phillips taking Willie's place in the team. New Zealand scored nine tries and kicked seven conversion in a game they won by 41 points to nil. After the match, Willie Llewellyn and Rhys Gabe renewed acquaintances with the players they had met the previous year playing for the British Team in New Zealand, enjoying a long chat outside the pavilion on the County Ground.

Willie played in Newport's first game of the season at home to Lydney. Newport won quite easily by three goals (15 points) to nil. It seems that Willie was well marked during the game with the *Evening Express* reporting, 'Willie Llewellyn received repeated attention from Lewis, the flying Lydney captain, who was a smotherer.' Willie also played in Newport's next game at home to Old Merchant Taylors. Scoring nine tries, five of which were converted, Newport won quite easily by 37 points to nil. Willie scored one of the tries bringing his career total for the club to twenty-eight.

The Rhondda Leader of Saturday 23rd September reported, 'It has now been definitely decided to give the complimentary dinner to Mr Willie Llewellyn (captain of the famous Welsh Triple Crown winners, 1904–05) on Tuesday evening, the 10th October next, at the Imperial Hotel, Porth, when Mr W W Hood, of Llwynypia, will preside, supported by leading residents of the Rhondda Valley.' The event went ahead as planned and the *Evening Express* commented, 'The gathering was one worthy of the occasion, being one of the largest and most representative ever promoted in connection with sport in South Wales.' The report went on to say, 'It is a matter of history now that Wales, under the captaincy of Willie Llewellyn, won the Triple Crown last year, and it is pretty generally known that he has played brilliantly for his country on nineteen occasions.' Mr Leonard W Llewellyn proposed the toast of 'The Local Governing Bodies' and after describing the useful work they had accomplished in the district, referred to the honoured guest. Willie Llewellyn, he said, had good reason to be proud of the high esteem shown towards him that evening. He went on to say that Willie Llewellyn's unostentatious manner had made Clydach Vale people proud that he was one of them, and they all hoped that his football career would not be finished when he opened in business at Tonypandy. A report of the evening in *The Rhondda Leader* remarked, 'In proposing

CHAPTER TEN

'Our Guest,' the president, Mr W W Hood, said that no one could propose that toast with greater sincerity than he did.' Mr Hood went on to say that Willie's fair play in all his games had endeared him to a large and ever growing circle of friends in South Wales. He continued by saying that Willie was born an athlete and one of the best three-quarters that ever played on the football field and that his selection to the captaincy of the Welsh Football Team was eminently justified by the fact that Wales had won the Triple Crown. Mr Hood concluded his remarks by saying that they would have been delighted to have made a presentation that evening, but that was against the rules. However, at the appropriate time, which he hoped would be in the far distant future, they hoped to give him a present and he would be one of the first to subscribe. The toast having been drunk with great enthusiasm there followed a special rendering of 'For he's a jolly good fellow' composed by Mr Griffith Davies and sung by Mr Moses Jenkins. In response Willie made a brief and typically humble acknowledgement when he thanked everyone most sincerely for the honour bestowed upon him. He felt he did not deserve it stating that with regard to the football the previous season he had had very little to do with the winning of the Triple Crown. He said he had been very fortunate to be selected captain of a very fine side and it had been no trouble to be captain of such a great team. Willie concluded by saying that the honour rested a hundred per cent more with his colleagues, than with him as captain and he was very proud of the honour bestowed upon him that evening. Finally he thanked all his friends very sincerely for that honour.

Willie's penultimate game for Newport was in the home game against Cardiff on Saturday 14th October. Percy Bush was in brilliant form and captained his side to a 17 points to three victory. There was no score in the first half but a brilliant try by former Newport wing and future Welsh international Johnnie Williams fifteen minutes into the second half gave Cardiff the lead. Bert Winfield converted and Cardiff had a five point advantage. Fifteen minutes later a bad pass from Protheroe, the Newport centre, to Willie Llewellyn saw the ball cannon off Willie's shins. Rhys Gabe seized the opportunity and after a magnificent run and a fine dummy scored under the posts. Bert Winfield was again successful with the conversion and Cardiff were ten points ahead. Almost immediately afterwards Reggie Gibbs scored another try for Cardiff but this time

Bert Winfield failed to add the extra points. A minute later Percy Bush thrilled the spectators with a spectacular drop goal form the half-way line. Although Newport rallied and scored an unconverted try through Charlie Pritchard just before the end of the game, they were well beaten with Percy Bush the hero of the day.

Willie Llewellyn, Billy O'Neil and Bert Winfield were all injured in the Newport game against Cardiff and despite being selected to play for Glamorgan against Monmouthshire at Pontypool on Monday 16th October, they all withdrew. Concerning the absence, the *Evening Express* reported, 'Willie Llewellyn, W O'Neil and H B Winfield who were picked to play for Glamorgan were forced to decline the invitations owing to injuries received in the Cardiff v Newport match on Saturday. Llewellyn's leg is damaged, but fortunately, not seriously. O'Neil strained his neck when, but for a fine tackle by G Boots, he must have scored, and Winfield's leg was hurt when he was charged by Protheroe after he had kicked the ball.'

Percy Bush captained Cardiff in the 1905–07 and 1908–09 seasons. He gained the first of his eight Welsh caps against New Zealand in 1905.

The injury to Willie's leg was not so serious that it prevented him playing his last game for Newport the following Saturday away to Blackheath. This was the last of the forty-seven games Willie Llewellyn played for Newport. Apart from the absence of the sick Wyatt Gould, Newport had a full-strength side which included five Welsh internationals: Willie Llewellyn, Charlie Pritchard, Jehoida Hodges, George Boots and Edwin Thomas Maynard. In addition, they had four future Welsh internationals in Billy Dowell, Tommy Vile, Ernie Jenkins and Harry Uzzell. The Blackheath team contained eight English internationals: B C 'Jock' Hartley, Basil Hill, Walter Rogers, Charles Newbold,

William Cave, Reginald Hobbs, Sydney Coopper and Edward Dillon, as well as J E C 'Birdie' Partridge, a Newport forward who had been capped by South Africa in their first test against the British Lions in 1903. Future English international Harry Lee was outstanding at full-back and if it had not been for his fine play, Newport could well have won a poor game. With so many internationals on show an exciting game was in prospect. However, a crowd of 5,000 spectators watched a disappointing match at the Rectory Field. The game was mainly a battle between the forwards who were quite evenly matched. Willie Llewellyn was starved of the ball and had little opportunity to demonstrate his great scoring ability. Harry Uzzell scored an unconverted try for Newport but the best try of the afternoon was scored by Anderson after Robson created an opening which Sydney Coopper exploited to put Anderson away for a brilliant try. Blackheath failed to add the extra points and a disappointing game ended in a draw.

The Tuesday following the game against Blackheath the *Evening Express* reported that Willie Llewellyn was giving up football. The report read as follows: 'W M Llewellyn, last year's Welsh captain, has intimated verbally that he intends going into business and will consequently retire from football. On the strength of this statement he has not been picked for Newport against Llanelly on Saturday.' Even without Willie Llewellyn, Wyatt Gould and Jehoida Hodges Newport defeated Llanelly at Rodney Parade by 14 points to five. Nevertheless, Willie Llewellyn had played his last game for the club and with several newspaper reports having indicated that Willie Llewellyn was likely to retire from rugby because he was launching a business in either London or Tonypandy, it was unclear as to what, if any, his rugby playing future would be. The *Evening Express* reported on Saturday 21st October: 'Willie Llewellyn is not going to open a business in London after all, but will stay in the Rhondda.' It also stated that he would play for Newport until the business started but this rumour had no substance as he never played for Newport after the game against Blackheath.

There is no mention of Willie Llewellyn playing rugby during the two weekends following the Newport game against Blackheath but he did take a team to Christ College on Wednesday 8th November. Willie captained a strong team which included R C Thomas and Reggie Gibbs of Cardiff,

Rowland Griffiths of Newport, John Dyke of Penarth and Wayne Morgan of London Welsh and Cardiff. Although the College expected a good thrashing, they did manage to give Willie's team a tough game. Rowland Griffiths and Willie Llewellyn were particularly prominent in a first half that saw Willie's team score two goals and two tries. Willie Llewellyn, Rowland Griffiths, Ivor Morgan and one of the forwards scored tries for the visitors while Willie's younger brother George, who captained the College team, and Hazard scored tries for the home team. At the interval Willie's team were leading by 16 points to six. In the opening stages of the second half, M Williams scored another try for the College and George Llewellyn added the extra points. After this Rowland Thomas and Reggie Gibbs got tries as Willie's team piled on the points with five second half tries, two of which were converted. Despite having nine tries scored against them, the College did not give up and before the end of the match Windsor Williams broke away from a line-out and went over for a good try. George Llewellyn again added the extra points and shortly afterwards the game ended with Willie's team victorious by 35 points to sixteen.

Following the game against Christ College, Brecon Willie was up in London and played for London Welsh against London Irish at the Essex County Ground, Leyton on Saturday 11th November. An undefeated London Welsh team overwhelmed London Irish by 28 points to nil on the same day that the New Zealanders beat Richmond by 17 points to nil. London Welsh had matters all their own way in the first half and early in the game T J David crossed for a try which was converted by Arthur Harding. Three more tries were added before the interval, two by David Jenkins and one by Hop Maddock. Arthur Harding converted two of the tries giving the Welsh an 18 points lead at the break. In the second half Charlie Rowlands and Hop Maddock added a try apiece and with Arthur Harding providing the extra points London Welsh won by 28 points to nil. Hop Maddock and David Jenkins played superbly and scored frequently. Arthur Harding displayed excellent kicking form and only failed to add the extra points on one occasion.

While domestic rugby was taking place in Wales the New Zealand All Blacks were sweeping all before them on their tour of Great Britain. The victory against Richmond was their eighteenth on the trot and brought their points aggregate to 571 with just 15 points against. With internationals against Scotland, Ireland, England, Wales and France ahead and four club games to negotiate in the Principality, their arrival was enthusiastically and eagerly awaited everywhere they played.

Willie's last game for London Welsh was against Swansea at Queen's Club on Monday 13th November 1905. With both teams at full strength ten Welsh internationals took the field, Billy Bancroft, George Davies, Willie Arnold, Dickie Owen, Will Joseph, Fred Scrine, David J Thomas and Will Parker for Swansea, and Willie Llewellyn and Arthur Harding for London Welsh. Heavy rain quite spoilt the match as a spectacle. Soft turf and a wet and slippery ball made handling very difficult, and although both teams did their utmost to make the game open, more often than not passing bouts broke down. London Welsh started with just fourteen players because T J David did not arrive until quite some time after the game had started. Arthur Harding played at full-back until David arrived and then returned to his normal position in the forwards. One of the few good passing movements of the game resulted in an opening try for Swansea by Willie Arnold. George Davies failed to add the extra points. Within two minutes T Arnold, the Swansea outside half, dropped a goal to give Swansea a seven point advantage. Twenty minutes into the game Billy Bancroft had his collar-bone broken in a forward rush and retired permanently from the game. George Davies took his place at full-back and D Davies came out of the pack to the three-quarter line. Although the Welsh almost scored on a few occasions, no further points were added before the interval.

Early in the second half Phil Hopkins just missed with a drop at goal and Fred Scrine just failed to cross for a try. However, further pressure by the Swansea forwards saw David J Thomas score another unconverted try for Swansea. Finally a clever combined run by the Swansea backs ended in another unconverted try for Willie Arnold. This brought the scoring to a close and at the finish Swansea were winners by 13 points to nil. The report of the game in *The Sportsman* referred to an incident that happened towards the end of the game. 'Towards the close,' it said, 'there was a regrettable occurrence with Maddock and Scrine coming into collision. A section of the crowd considered the Swansea man at fault but the referee diplomatically made peace and the incident speedily terminated.'

The unfortunate injury to Billy Bancroft and the incident involving Hop Maddock and Fred Scrine resulted in some extremely heavy criticism of Welsh rugby in the press. However, no formal report was submitted to the Welsh Football Union and the matter ended there.

Although I am sure Willie would have liked to have concluded his rugby playing career at London Welsh with a victory, he could look back on a very successful time at the club. He had captained the side for three consecutive years and comments in the book *Dragon in Exile, The Centenary History of London Welsh RFC* by Stephen Jones and Paul Beken perfectly summed up Willie's contribution: 'Llewellyn the man, and Llewellyn the player' said the authors, 'did as much as anyone to lead the club from mediocrity to excellence.' Willie had played his first game for the club back in January 1900 when he scored two tries in the match against Twickenham, and the game against Swansea was the last of sixty games he played for the club. During that time he scored thirty-seven tries.

Having played his last games for Newport and London Welsh, Willie Llewellyn transferred to Penygraig. He had played one game for the club back in March 1903 but with his new chemist's shop opening in Dunraven Street, Tonypandy he now intended to play for them on a regular basis. Willie's first game of the season for Penygraig was in their away match against Penarth where, in wintery weather, there was no score during the first-half. The only points of the game were an unconverted try by T Ponsford following a forward rush. The report of the game in the *Evening Express* paid tribute to Willie Llewellyn when it stated: 'Willie Llewellyn proved a tower of strength to his side and the quartette should have scored on at least two other occasions.'

With the mighty unbeaten All Blacks continuing their successful tour, preparations for the international match against New Zealand were well underway. Welsh rugby was on a high; after all, the Principality had won Triple Crowns in 1900, 1902 and 1905. Nevertheless, the trail of rugby devastation left by the touring All Blacks began to sow the seeds of doubt for a Welsh success against the tourists. This doubt was evident in a letter sent early in November 1905 to the editor of the *Daily Mail*, headed 'Ought the Welsh XV to Train?' the letter read as follows:

"Sir, I have read with interest the remarks on stamina and endurance which have been penned by that 'Prince of Centres' Mr Arthur Gould and am firmly of the opinion that the confirmed success of the New Zealanders is due to their being in better condition than their opponents and not to their superior play. I suggest that the Welsh Football Union Committee consider seriously the advisability of sending twenty-five of the best players available to a seaside resort for a period of fourteen days, where they may undergo a thorough training prior to the contest with the New Zealanders. It is simply absurd to argue that the Welsh players can follow up their employment and meet the New Zealanders and beat them, because it is impossible for them to be in the peak of condition, as their opponents will be, unless they received a thorough training." J Davies, Ebbw Vale.

The Welsh Football Union didn't send the best twenty-five players off for two weeks by the sea but the side chosen to face New Zealand on Saturday 16th December had taken a lot of thought. The Welsh Football Union had had plenty of time to prepare; they had known the date of the Welsh game since 23rd June 1904. The Match Committee travelled to the match at Gloucester to observe and consider how the Welsh team might best oppose the New Zealand style of seven forwards, a wing forward, a scrum-half, two five-eighths, three three-quarters and a full-back. The major debate was centred on whether Wales would adopt the New Zealand style or keep to her set patterns of play.

Willie was selected and played in the first Welsh trial match that took place at Cardiff on Monday 20th November. As a trial the match was a great disappointment with many players not turning up to play. There was doubt whether the match would go ahead because of heavy overnight frost, and with only half the pitch covered in straw parts of the ground were very hard. The notable absentees from the originally selected teams included Gwyn Nicholls, Teddy Morgan, Jehoida Hodges and all of the Swansea players, namely Dickie Owen, Billy Trew, Will Joseph and Frank Gordon. Originally chosen as a reserve, Dai 'Mumbles' Davies of Swansea was asked to make the journey only to find on arrival that he was not required. In the first half the original Welsh formation was tried, with the result that the Possibles scored a goal and a try to one try. Rhys Gabe scored an unconverted try for the Probables and J Hopkins replied with a try that Reggie Gibbs converted for the Possibles. Before the interval Gibbs scored an unconverted try for the Possible to give them a five point lead at the break. In the second half several changes were made in the sides and the Possibles played with seven forwards and a five-eighth. The seven forwards played with great effect and impressed the Welsh committee. Dai Jones and Rhys Gabe scored unconverted tries for the Probables whilst J F Williams and W Bevan added converted tries for the Possibles, who ran out winners by 18 points to nine. So disgusted were the members of the Welsh Football Union at the conclusion of the game that they held a meeting and resolved to play another trial match at Cardiff on Saturday 2nd December, with the teams for that trial being selected after the match between Swansea and Cardiff the following Saturday. It is reported that Ted Lewis, the secretary of the Glamorgan League, said that New Zealand would beat all thirty players.

The following Saturday Willie was again playing for Penygraig in their home match against Blaenclydach. Rain fell heavily all day and the ground was in a really heavy condition. The game started in sensational fashion when one of the visitors charged the ball down and Edwards scored an unconverted try. Just before the interval the Penygraig forwards worked their way up the field and from a line-out Willie Llewellyn scored. The extra points were added and Penygraig led at the interval by 5 points to three.

The game in the second half was very evenly contested, but the state of the ground prevented any attempts at passing, and with no further scores the game ended with Penygraig the victors. On the same day the Welsh Football Union Committee met at the Royal Hotel, Swansea to select the teams for the final Welsh trial to be played at Cardiff the following Saturday. The committee decided to bring to the special attention of the players Rule 23, which stated: 'Any player selected to play in any trial or international match and failing to do so without furnishing the committee with satisfactory reasons shall be debarred from playing for his club for a period of four weeks.' The selection of the Probables reflected that they would be playing with seven forwards and eight backs whilst the Possibles would play in the usual Welsh formation.

The second trial match was much better attended than the first, although there were a few changes from the teams originally selected.

Teddy Morgan, Dickie Owen and George Travers were absent from the Probables side with Hop Maddock, Dickie David and Jehoida Hodges all moving up from the Possibles to take their places. The vacancies in the Possibles were then filled by Willie Thomas, Newport (Left wing), J Thomas, Neath (scrum-half) and J Blackmore (Abertillery) in the forwards. D Galloway (Pontypridd) replaced the injured R Thomas of Penygraig, who was absent from the Possibles. Although Gwyn Nicholls had indicated after the Triple Crown winning match against Ireland that he had retired from international rugby, he was still in training after a request to captain Wales once more. Gwyn Nicholls would eventually play his last game for Wales against South Africa in 1906. The teams for the second Welsh trial took the field as follows:

Probables: Back, H B Winfield (Cardiff); three-quarters, E G Nicholls and R T Gabe (Cardiff), W M Llewellyn (Penygraig) and Hop Maddock (London Welsh); extra back, C C Pritchard (Pontypool); half-backs, P F Bush (Cardiff), R David (Cardiff); forwards, C M Pritchard (Newport), W Joseph (Swansea), A F Harding, J F Williams (London Welsh), J J Hodges (Newport), J Brown (Cardiff), J C Jenkins (London Welsh).

Possibles: Back, J C M Dyke (Penarth); three-quarters, J P Jones (Pontypool), R C Thomas (Cardiff), D P Jones (Pontypool) and W Thomas (Newport); half-backs, J Thomas (Neath), R A Gibbs (Cardiff); forwards, G Boots (Newport), J Blackmore (Abertillery), J Powell (Cardiff), T Evans, Harry Watkins (Llanelly), D Jones (Aberdare), G Matthews (Penygraig), D Galloway (Pontypridd).

With the Probables in white and the Possibles in stripes, George Boots kicked off for the Possibles and the opening play went in favour of his side. However, after Willie Llewellyn had made a fine try-saving tackle on Willie Thomas, the Probables took advantage. Dickie David sent out a clean pass to Percy Bush who ran through the Possibles' backs as no other half could. He dodged man after man and on reaching John Dyke gave a perfectly-timed pass to Cliff Pritchard who, having no one to beat, ran over for a try which Bert Winfield converted. The Possibles' eight were beating the Probables' seven forwards but their backs were inferior. When Percy Bush got away again he passed on to Hop Maddock who scored a really good unconverted try. This was followed with another unconverted try by Rhys Gabe. Scores came thick and fast and Hop Maddock made a fine run to put Cliff Pritchard in for his second try. This time Bert Winfield added the extra points but was then injured trying to take the ball on his goal-line as several stripes forwards charged down on him. George Boots took advantage, picked up the loose ball and scored a try for the Possibles. Just before the interval Hop Maddock scored another stunning try, running from his own half and dummying John Dyke he scored a beautiful try in an easy position, but the injured Bert Winfield missed the conversion. At the interval the Probables were leading by 19 points to three.

Bert Winfield retired at half-time and John F Williams took over as full-back for the Probables in the second half, Matthews playing as an extra back for the Possibles. Evans scored an unconverted try for the Possibles and shortly afterwards Cliff Pritchard dropped a goal for the Probables. This was followed by a fine try by Jehoida Hodges that Percy Bush converted. Before the final whistle Cliff Pritchard scored the best try of the match and Percy Bush again added the extra points. Towards the end of the game Evans scored another try for the Possibles with John Dyke adding the extra points, leaving the Probables winners by 4 goals, 1 dropped goal and 3 tries (33 points) to 1 goal and 2 tries (11 points).

From the outset it was fairly obvious that the seven forward experiment was a disappointment. For one reason or another, the Probables' seven were badly beaten by the Possibles' eight in the scrums. They would, however, be playing against another seven forward formation if they adopted this formation for the match against New Zealand. The *Evening Express* ran the rule over the players, observing that John F Williams was the best forward on the field and, together with Jehoida Hodges, Arthur Harding and Will Joseph, were certainties for the Welsh team to play New Zealand. Concerning the back play, the outstanding feature was the brilliant success of Percy Bush. He contributed some wonderfully clever work and made himself a certainty for his place at outside-half. Dickie David, the Cardiff scrum-half, did remarkably well, and if needed, would be a more than adequate substitute for Dickie Owen. Hop Maddock had a number of opportunities and made full use of them. Willie Llewellyn and Rhys Gabe both ensured their selection. After Percy Bush the next best back on the Probables' side was Cliff Pritchard, he had a wonderful game scoring three tries and a dropped goal and was another certainty for the team. Having captained Wales to a fourth Triple Crown early in 1905 it would have been expected that Willie Llewellyn would have captained Wales against New Zealand. In the absence of the injured Gwyn Nicholls, Willie had taken over the captaincy for the international against Scotland in 1904 and although Gwyn Nicholls returned for the Triple Crown showdown against Ireland in 1905, Willie retained the captaincy. In an unpublished letter by Willie in 1957 he states that he stood down from the captaincy to enable Gwyn Nicholls to once again lead the Welsh team against New Zealand in the 1905 match.

After the trial the Match Committee of the Welsh Football Union selected the Welsh team to play New Zealand on Saturday 16th December. Percy Bush was the only debutant, although he had played international rugby for the British team in Australia and New Zealand. The team and reserves were as follows:

Wales: Back, H B Winfield (Cardiff); three-quarters, E G Nicholls and R T Gabe (Cardiff), W M Llewellyn (Penygraig) and E T Morgan (London Welsh); extra back, C C Pritchard (Pontypool); half-backs, P F Bush (Cardiff), R M Owen (Swansea); forwards, C M Pritchard (Newport), W Joseph (Swansea), A F Harding, J F Williams (London Welsh), J J Hodges (Newport), G Travers (Pill Harriers), D Jones (Aberdare).

Reserves: Full-back, J C M Dyke (Penarth); centres, C C Pritchard (Pontypool), H T Maddock (London Welsh); wings, H T Maddock (London Welsh) 1st reserve, Willie Thomas (Newport) 2nd reserve; scrum-half, R David (Cardiff); outside-half, R A Gibbs (Cardiff), also reserve to C C Pritchard; forwards, Harry Watkins (Llanelly), G Boots (Newport), J Powell (Cardiff).

On Thursday 7th December thirteen of the selected Welsh fifteen met in Cardiff to practise various moves under the direction of Dickie Owen. The forwards practised various pack formations. Some of the team were able to have more practise that Saturday when Teddy Morgan and Willie Llewellyn joined Gwyn Nicholls and Rhys Gabe in the three-quarters for Cardiff in their away game against Blackheath. Bert Winfield was at full-back and Arthur Harding played in the forwards. Gwyn Nicholls scored a try in the first minute of the game and Bert Winfield added the extra points. Late in the half, J Powell added another try which Bert Winfield again converted. Despite Blackheath having more than their fair share of possession in the first half, they were ten points in arrears at the interval. They did well for the first twenty minutes of the second half and against Bert Winfield's penalty goal Anderson dropped a goal for Blackheath. Then in the last quarter of an hour Blackheath succumbed and tries by Gibbs, Northmore (converted by Winfield), and Gabe, gave Cardiff a comfortable victory by 24 points to four.

For their unprecedented second practise on Tuesday 12th December, the Welsh team concentrated on drop kicking and the scrum. The second session allowed the backs to practise a set move devised by Dickie Owen and involving Cliff Pritchard as an extra outside-half. Meanwhile, the forwards concentrated on denying the All Blacks constant access to the loose-head in the scrums. The Welsh forwards planned that only five forwards would go down in the first formation of the scrum, two in the front allowing New Zealand to get the loose-head. When the scrum was set the two remaining Welsh forwards would then pack down, one outside the New Zealand loose-head and the other to complete the formation. Thus they insured that the two New Zealand hookers' heads were in the middle. The practise complete, no Welsh team was better prepared.

Christ College, Brecon was very well represented in the Welsh team selected to face New Zealand in 1905. The College never missed an

Christ College Old Boys John F Williams, Arthur Harding, Willie Llewellyn and Teddy Morgan.

opportunity to congratulate its past pupils and the 1905 December edition of *The Breconian* made the following statement: 'We congratulate the following O.B.'s on being picked to play for Wales against New Zealand: W M Llewellyn, E Morgan, A F Harding, and J F Williams. J C M Dyke and H T Maddocks are also first reserves for their respective places.'

The tourist arrived in Wales on Thursday 14th December. As they passed through Newport railway station on their way to Cardiff the platform was filled with an enthusiastic crowd. Messrs Vile and Llewellyn, members of the British team that toured New Zealand in 1904 went to the carriage window to renew old acquaintances, while Mr A J Gould, the famous old Welsh international also welcomed the team. The train arrived at Cardiff railway station at 5.50 in the evening and on their arrival they were received by the Lord Mayor, Alderman Robert Hughes, and several members of the Cardiff City Council together with Mr Walter Rees, Mr Tom Williams and Mr A J Davies of the Welsh Football Union. Outside the station the New Zealanders were greeted by the largest crowd that had welcomed them so far on the tour. The open space in front of the station was packed with a dense mass of cheering people. The streets en route to the Queen's Hotel were so thickly thronged that much of the journey had to be made at walking pace. All along the route the same enthusiasm prevailed and on arrival at the Hotel the police had to make a pathway to enable the popular New Zealand visitors to check in. George Dixon, the New Zealand manager, said that the welcome to Wales would long live in the memory of every member of the team.

On Friday morning, light exercise was indulged in on the Cardiff Club ground, and after lunch all the visitors attended a reception by the Lord Mayor in the Municipal Chambers of Cardiff Town-hall. Here the Mayor formally welcomed the team on behalf of the citizens of Cardiff. After those present had sung 'Hen Wlad fy Nhadau' the Lord Mayor frivolously observed that he had heard that the New Zealanders could sing something that was like Welsh and he therefore asked them to sing their war song. Led by Bill Cunningham, the New Zealanders sang the inspiring Maori war song the meaning of which was 'Be strong and fight to the death.' It was very impressive and the audience demanded an encore with the result that George Nicholson led the visitors in a second verse. Later the Lady Mayoress presented each member of the touring party with a very striking souvenir of their visit to Cardiff. This was a handsome medal on a chain bearing the City Arms with scroll and motto on its face. Below was the red dragon of Wales supported by two silver fern leaves, the badge of the New Zealand team. On the reverse was inscribed: 'A memento from the Lord Mayor of the City of Cardiff, Alderman Robert Hughes, JP, 1905.' The rest of the day was spent quietly looking around the city.

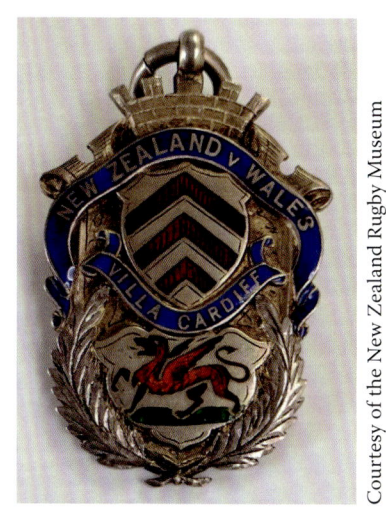

The Souvenir Medal presented to Jimmy Hunter by the Lady Mayoress of Cardiff.

On the day of the match the order of singing would be reversed with the New Zealanders performing their Maori war song and the Welsh players and spectators singing the Welsh National Anthem. An article in the *Evening Express* on Friday 15th December gives us a clue why the Welsh team sang the Welsh National Anthem at the match the following day. The article read as follows: 'Mr Tom Williams (Llwynypia), who is an ardent and patriotic Welshman, as well as a recognised authority on rugby football wishes to make a suggestion, through the medium of the *'Evening Express,'* that the Welsh players on Saturday should sing together the refrain of 'Hen Wlad fy Nhadau' immediately after the New Zealanders have given the Maori war cry. Thirty thousand out of the forty thousand spectators would join the Welshmen in chorus and such a volume of sound would, surely, be unique. All patriotic Welshmen will thoroughly approve of the suggestion and Mr Williams will doubtless, use his influence as a member of the Welsh Union to see that it is acted upon. We must play the Colonials at their own game, not only in kicking and running, passing and tackling, but in singing our own little 'war song' as well.' And so the scene was set, Wales would sing their own 'war song' in response to the New Zealand Haka.

The New Zealand All Blacks arrived in Cardiff with an impressive record. They had played twenty-seven games and won them all.

The Wales Team v New Zealand 1905

Back Row: Mr Ack Llewellyn (WFU). *Third Row*: Mr Tom Williams (WFU), J F Williams, G Travers, D Jones, W Joseph, R T Gabe, Sir John Llewellyn, Bart. *Middle Row*: C M Pritchard, J J Hodges, W Llewellyn, E G Nicholls (Captain), H B Winfield, C C Pritchard, A F Harding. Front Row: E Morgan, R M Owen, P F Bush.

They had beaten the best teams in England, Scotland and Ireland, including all three international teams, much to the surprise of those who had not expected such a run of results when the tourists began their unbeaten path through the British Isles. They began their tour by beating champion county, Devon, by 55 points to 4, and by the time they arrived in Cardiff they had scored 801 points with only 22 against. Their line had only been crossed three times, once each by Durham, Midland Counties and Scotland. Their success was attributed to their superior fitness and skilful combined play, and was heralded as a wonderful advertisement for the outdoor way of life of the Southern Colonies.

The New Zealand captain, Ireland-born Dave Gallaher (Auckland), caused controversy because of his role as a wing forward detached from the pack. He was the subject of considerable abuse in the press and on the field for the way he allegedly spun the ball into the scrum. Gwyn Nicholls, the

Welsh captain, largely dismissed this and considered that the rapid heeling of the ball by the New Zealand forwards was the result of the better 2-3-2 pack formation and not the spinning of the ball into the scrums. Also worrying for Wales was Gallaher's legitimate obstruction of the opposing halves. Both of these manoeuvres Wales would need to counter if they were to be successful.

In addition, New Zealand had outstanding forwards like Charles 'Bronco' Seeling (Auckland), a prolific try scorer who would go on to score 8 tries on tour and Frank Glasgow (Taranaki) another outstanding forward who would play in 28 of the 36 tour matches, including all five test matches. No less worrying for Wales were the players behind the pack like Jimmy Hunter (Taranaki) who would emerge as one of the superstars on this the 'Original' All Blacks tour. Hunter would appear in twenty-five tour matches including all five tests and score an astonishing forty-four tries. With the hard-running Bob Deans (Canterbury) and Billy Wallace (Wellington), who scored 28 points in the opening match against Devon, Wales would certainly have their work cut out if they were to be victorious.

Wanted – A Giant Killer.

Courtesy of the *London Opinion*

The New Zealanders had their final run out on the Arms Park on Friday 15th December. George Smith (Auckland) had broken his Collarbone after Ireland's heavyweight Basil Maclear crash-tackled him in the Munster match at Limerick and was replaced on the wing by Billy Wallace, a gifted footballer capable of playing anywhere in the backline, but usually on the wing or at full-back. For the Welsh game, George Gillett (Canterbury) played in the full-back position and Simon Mynott (Taranaki) came in for Billy Stead (Southland), who was unavailable with boils, and played alongside Jimmy Hunter. Gallaher was there to feed the scrum with Fred Roberts (Wellington) at scrum-half. Joining Billy Wallace in the three-quarters was R G 'Bob' Deans, the twenty-one year old centre, and Duncan McGregor (Wellington), whose last All Black test would be against Wales at Cardiff. Despite losing George Smith, the All Blacks had a formidable set of backs that had been a prolific points scoring machine throughout the tour.

The forwards too were formidable. Charles 'Bronco' Seeling was a striking specimen, at 6 feet tall and weighing over 13½ stone was a very big man for his time. To his robust physique Seeling added considerable pace, natural athleticism and, as a tackler, was absolutely fearless. Frank Glasgow (Taranaki) was also selected; he had played in 20 of the 27 tour matches so far and had scored 6 tries and kicked 4 conversions and a penalty goal. Steve Casey (Otago), together with George Tyler (Auckland), formed the most effective front row combination in the 2-3-2 scrum formation used by New Zealand. Alex McDonald (Otago) would be playing his seventeenth game for the All Blacks against Wales and this

The New Zealand Team v Wales 1905

Back Row: J W Stead (Vice-captain), C Seeling, R G Deans, J O'Sullivan, F Newton, A McDonald. *Middle Row*: F Roberts, F Glasgow, D McGregor, D Gallaher (Captain), G Gillett, G Tyler, W J Wallace.
Front Row: H J Mynott, J Hunter, S Casey.

would be his fourth test appearance. James 'Jimmie' O'Sullivan (Taranaki) would also be in the Cardiff line up. He was in good form on the tour and had played 16 out of the 27 matches before coming to Wales, including the tests against Scotland, Ireland and England. Finally there was Freddy Newton (Canterbury), brought in for the tests against England and Wales when injury and then a heavy cold kept Bill Cunningham (Auckland) out of the side.

Despite being mid-December the morning of Saturday 16th was bright, described as spring-like at the time. There was no hint of wind or rain to spoil proceedings. It is estimated that 47,000 people saw the game. In those pre-ticket-only days most travelled in hope of getting a ticket. Tickets were sold from pay boxes in the street and entry to the ground had to be made through tall wooden barriers. Field and enclosure tickets would be on sale when the gates opened at 12 noon for one and two shillings respectively. Grandstand ticket holders, at 3 shillings a time, and those with seats inside the ropes were to be in place by 2.00 pm ready for the 2.30 kick-off. There were two programmes sold on the day of the match, the official programme and an unofficial 'Pirate' programme. The legitimate programme sellers were fitted out with red dragon badges to prove their official status. The gates were actually opened at 11.00 am and the ground was speedily filled, people passing the weary hours of waiting by singing their national songs. It was a novel and thrilling spectacle. With the ground so full the officials found it necessary to close the gates at 1.30 pm, thus shutting out thousands of would-be spectators, many of whom had travelled considerable distances. The excitement was at fever pitch. To understand why this game stands out to those who attended,

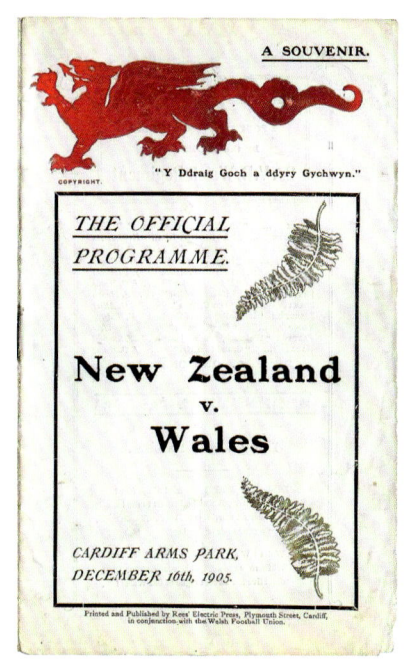

The official match programme for the game between Wales and New Zealand played on Saturday 16th December 1905.

it is necessary to recall what was at stake. The invincible record of a touring side who seemed the most brilliant rugby players who ever came from overseas against Welsh pre-eminence so jealously guarded since the late 1890's.

Once inside there was a swaying wait until the 2.30 pm kick-off. The trees lining the far perimeters were festooned with shivering boys. The new stands put up at the start of the season were so full that they moved dangerously beneath their human weight.

At ten minutes past two a thick mist blotted out the pale sunshine. It hung over the ground for the whole match, not obliterating the game but making distant incidents difficult to see. The Welsh Regiment's Second Battalion Band was engaged to play a selection of arias. It was felt that there needed to be an antidote to the New Zealand Haka, the Maori war song which Dave Gallaher's men performed before every match. In a first reference to the first All Blacks Haka on Welsh soil, the *Western Mail* reported that the earlier suggestion of Tom Williams that the Welsh players should sing 'Hen Wlad fy Nhadau' after the New Zealanders had given their Maori war cry was accepted by the Welsh Football Union. They hoped that the spectators would join the chorus and therefore ensure that the song had its biggest choir in its slow ascent to the status of Welsh National Anthem.

The opinion outside Wales was firmly in favour of New Zealand. The Welsh critics were sure it would be a 'titanic struggle,' the highpoint of a quarter of a century of football in Wales. Whichever newspaper you read on the morning of the match, the intense excitement was the same. The outcome was unpredictable, too close to call, and C C Reade, a New Zealand journalist, travelling with the All Blacks, wrote: 'the world's championship in rugby will be decided in Wales today.'

At 2.20 pm the New Zealanders appeared; the All Blacks had arrived and roars of welcome and good cheer came from the 47,000 supporters. The visitors wore black jerseys, black pants, black stockings and black boots. On each man's shoulder was a large white ticket with a large black number. The Welshmen too were numbered. Shortly after the New Zealand team took the field the Welsh team appeared led by their captain Gwyn Nicholls. The All Blacks had taken the field a minute or two ahead of schedule, giving Nicholls a few precious moments to address his men.

This is what he said:

"Gather round men,

The eyes of the rugby world are on Wales today. It is up to us to prove that the Old Country is not quite barren of a team that is capable of giving New Zealand at least a hard fight. It has been suggested by some of the English papers that they come to Wales more or less stale; but as they played two English Counties last week and won each match by thirty to forty points with half their best players resting, for today's game the staleness is not very apparent. We have already discussed tactics. So it only remains for me to appeal to you to be resolute in your tackling. You all know what New Zealand are like if they are given latitude. They throw the ball about, and their systems of intensive backing-up make them very dangerous. So there must be no hair-combing. Every man in possession must be put down, ball and all. As for the forwards, you already know what to do to get the loose head.

Come on! Let's get out there."

Gwyn Nicholls the Welsh captain who rallied his men before the game.

The Illustrated Sporting and Dramatic News

The New Zealanders stood in the centre of the field and in a silence that could almost be felt, performed their Maori war cry, the Haka.

When they had finished, once more cheers rang out. Now it was their turn to feel the full effect of the crowd's pent-up fervour as the frail melody of 'Hen Wlad fy Nhadau' rose up, first from the Welsh players themselves until it was picked up by the multitude and they all joined in, the whole vast swaying crowd, men and women alike. It was a wonderful sight and the air was electric with excitement. Dave Gallaher said afterwards that he had never been more impressed in his life than when he stood there and listened to the chorus of Welsh voices. The *Lyttleton Times*, the paper with the largest circulation in New Zealand, reported, 'The Welsh were there to sing and to cheer their champions to victory. Imagine some forty thousand people singing their National Anthem with all the fervour of which the Celtic heart is capable.' We know that it was Tom Williams of the Welsh Football Union that had suggested that the Welsh players should sing 'Hen Wlad fy Nhadau' in response to the New Zealand Haka, but who actually started singing the National Anthem is unclear. The *Western Mail* stated: 'The Welshmen followed with the chorus of 'Hen Wlad fy Nhadau' led by Willie Llewellyn.' However, the *South Wales Daily News* stated: 'The Welshmen follow the example of the New Zealanders and sing their war chant, 'Hen Wlad fy Nhadau' Teddy Morgan acting as conductor.' The *London Daily News* remarked, 'After the Colonials had rendered their blood-curdling Maori war song, the Welshmen, led by Teddy Morgan, sang 'Hen Wlad fy Nhadau,' the crowd joining in with gusto.' Although there are conflicting newspaper reports of who actually began the singing, Willie always maintained to the family that it was

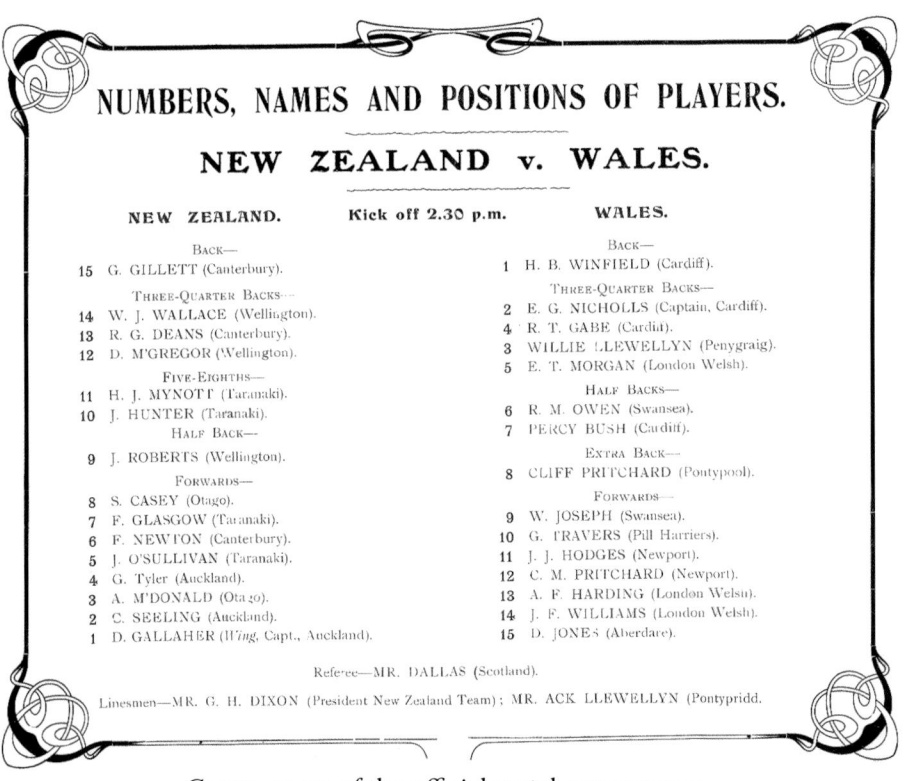

NUMBERS, NAMES AND POSITIONS OF PLAYERS.

NEW ZEALAND v. WALES.

Kick off 2.30 p.m.

NEW ZEALAND.		WALES.	
Back—		Back—	
15	G. GILLETT (Canterbury).	1	H. B. WINFIELD (Cardiff).
Three-Quarter Backs—		Three-Quarter Backs—	
14	W. J. WALLACE (Wellington).	2	E. G. NICHOLLS (Captain, Cardiff).
13	R. G. DEANS (Canterbury).	4	R. T. GABE (Cardiff).
12	D. M'GREGOR (Wellington).	3	WILLIE LLEWELLYN (Penygraig).
		5	E. T. MORGAN (London Welsh).
Five-Eighths—		Half Backs—	
11	H. J. MYNOTT (Taranaki).	6	R. M. OWEN (Swansea).
10	J. HUNTER (Taranaki).	7	PERCY BUSH (Cardiff).
Half Back—		Extra Back—	
9	J. ROBERTS (Wellington).	8	CLIFF PRITCHARD (Pontypool).
Forwards—		Forwards—	
8	S. CASEY (Otago).	9	W. JOSEPH (Swansea).
7	F. GLASGOW (Taranaki).	10	G. TRAVERS (Pill Harriers).
6	F. NEWTON (Canterbury).	11	J. J. HODGES (Newport).
5	J. O'SULLIVAN (Taranaki).	12	C. M. PRITCHARD (Newport).
4	G. Tyler (Auckland).	13	A. F. HARDING (London Welsh).
3	A. M'DONALD (Otago).	14	J. F. WILLIAMS (London Welsh).
2	C. SEELING (Auckland).	15	D. JONES (Aberdare).
1	D. GALLAHER (Wing, Capt., Auckland).		

Referee—MR. DALLAS (Scotland).

Linesmen—MR. G. H. DIXON (President New Zealand Team); MR. ACK LLEWELLYN (Pontypridd).

Centre pages of the official match programme.

he who started the choral response to the Haka, after which the Welsh spectators joined in to electrifying effect.

At 2.27 pm Hodges kicked off for Wales and for ten minutes it was thrust and counter-thrust. The pace was hot from the start with Wales intent on taking the initiative. Their placing of the third front row man at the loose head was impeding a quick New Zealand heel whilst Dickie Owen darted around his own scrum to whip the ball away or, typically, leave the ball in the back row of the Welsh scrum and accepting the burly New Zealander's tackle in return for a penalty. When the All Blacks did break to the open field it was Dickie Owen who fell on the ball. He was knocked out but was soon up and turning the psychological screw by noticeably grinning at Dave Gallaher.

After fifteen minutes the All Blacks, though tackling ferociously, had not managed a single sweeping attacking movement. Their forwards were being beaten in the set pieces and finding it hard to hold the Welsh seven in the loose. When George Gillett kicked away possession, Bert Winfield caught it and sent them back to their encampment in the New Zealand twenty-five where the All Blacks were reeling under the incessant Welsh onslaught. Dave Gallaher was repeatedly penalised for infringements feeding the scrum, off-side and obstruction. These decisions, from a referee who evidently had fixed views regarding wing forward play, had a dispiriting effect on the New Zealanders. On one occasion Owen gave rapidly to Percy Bush who feinted to go blind, wrong-footed the converging tacklers and dropped for goal. It was on target but fell short. Within a minute Wales almost scored again when J F Williams fielded a cross-kick and passed to Willie Llewellyn. It was an awkward low pass that Willie took almost behind his back, and with no one to beat he dropped the ball after taking half a dozen strides. There had been twenty-six minutes of play and Wales were attacking strongly, but each time Wales had run the ball the New Zealanders had moved in on their men, rightly fearful of the individual genius of the Welsh backs. Percy Bush in particular had already reprised his role of elusive pimpernel, able to stop dead in his tracks leaving opponents to flounder past, beaten by their own momentum. Wales, however, had other cards up their sleeve and after about twenty-seven minutes Dickie Owen chose to play their joker.

The Bystander Wednesday 20th December 1905

Willie Llewellyn and Dickie Owen look on as the Welsh forwards struggle for possession from a line-out.

Gwyn Nicholls had taken the ball as the New Zealanders tried to break out and sent it back. A few more robust exchanges led to a scrum fifteen yards in front of the right touch-line and about mid-way between the half-way line and the New Zealand twenty-five. Here was the place and now was the time. Nicholls confirmed with his line that the manoeuvre was definitely on. There would be no second chance. So far, Cliff Pritchard had been deliberately shunned in any Welsh attacks, all of which had been orthodox four three-quarter movements. The idea was to use him when the chance arose to widen the attack unexpectedly. Dickie Owen renowned for his reverse pass from a standing position, now used his skill to switch the point of attack with a blind-side feint that brought the famous score.

With Willie Llewellyn on the short side of the scrummage and Percy Bush about two yards inside Llewellyn and also to the right of the scrummage, there remained about two-thirds of the width of the field to the left of Dickie Owen. From the scrum Owen received possession from a quick heel. Owen ran a few yards to the right touch-line knowing how the blind side of the Welsh scrummage would attract an anxious New Zealand defence. Gwyn Nicholls, the right centre, according to plan followed Owen on his run to the right so as to further deceive the New Zealand defence. In a flash, Dickie Owen realised that the gap on the right had been filled. Seeing Teddy Morgan unmarked, Owen changed direction and made for the left. After a few yards he passed to Cliff Pritchard who picked the ball off his toes as it went to ground. Pritchard swerved to the left, evading one man before feeding Rhys Gabe who went as if to run inside, straightened and handed on to Teddy Morgan twenty yards out. Morgan outpaced the trailing McGregor and sped past George Gillett, caught in two minds by a barely perceptible change of pace, and crossed the line in a lung-bursting surge of acceleration. There had been almost twenty-eight minutes played. Teddy Morgan had scored far out on the left at the Westgate Street end. Hats, handkerchiefs and leeks went up into the air accompanied by cheers that sounded more like screams and roars from those who could not suppress their emotion or delight any more. There was sheer pandemonium, celebrations were loud and prolonged, and even continued well after Bert Winfield missed the difficult conversion.

Time after time Wales gained ground by means of long touch-finding kicks and in this respect there was certainly no comparison between the two sets of backs. The New Zealand kicking in the first half consisted of long lofty punts up field to enable their forwards to get under the ball and terrorise any Welshman waiting to catch it. But Bert Winfield was at his best; he consistently fielded the ball safely and either responded to touch or made marks.

The delighted Welsh fans celebrating Teddy Morgan's try.

After the Welsh score, New Zealand retaliated and as the first half petered out it was Wales who were pressed back. The All Black forwards won more and more ball, only to see it squandered by their backs. Cliff Pritchard cleverly intercepted a pass after one New Zealand attack and kicked up-field. Shortly afterwards, Dickie Owen was injured and referee

John Dallas cautioned the New Zealand players. Every time New Zealand made an effort to get the ball to the backs somebody's usually safe hands let them down, and rather than combine with colleagues who were out of form Roberts and Deans tried to utilise their individual skills of speed and strength. When the whistle blew early for the interval, no allowances having been made for at least two minutes lost for injuries, New Zealand were hotly attacking the Welsh goal line.

During the interval the crowd sang to encourage a team that was nursing a slender lead. The second half saw some of the toughest exchanges ever meted out on a rugby field. It was dauntingly hard play. In the first session the Welsh forwards had given their backs the chances they needed. Those same forwards now ensured, by play as intelligent as it was resolute, that the prize would not be lost. Often beaten in the tight, they nevertheless broke up quickly to act as auxiliary units in defence, harrying, tackling and covering like men possessed.

The Welsh pack swarmed on the ball. Will Joseph and George Travers, both tireless pursuers, would join Arthur Harding, John Williams and

Willie Llewellyn, Bert Winfield and Teddy Morgan discuss tactics at half-time.

John 'Scethrog' Williams cleaning the mud from his boots at half-time.

Jehoida Hodges in foot rushes or back up Dai Jones in the line-out and scrums where his strength was sorely needed. The star of the pack was undoubtedly Charlie Pritchard of Newport, 'always in the thick of the fight,' throwing himself at the man in possession as did all the Welsh tacklers in their efforts to disrupt New Zealand's rhythm. Behind the scrum, time and again the deadly tackling of Cliff Pritchard, the Welsh extra back, prevented the New Zealand backs from making any attacking inroads into Welsh territory.

Wales would have other chances; Percy Bush scurried around the blind side to put Teddy Morgan away only for that hero to drop the ball. Bush himself narrowly missed another drop goal and late in the second half, Gwyn Nicholls made a searing run only to see Arthur Harding fumble the ball with the posts in front of him.

Even so, on the whole the second half was chiefly in favour of New Zealand as the shape of the game was altered dramatically and it became Wales' turn to defend desperately and counter-attack sporadically. The New Zealand team, unsteadied by the crowd and the force of early play, bit the bullet that Dickie Owen had manufactured. They stopped lofting the ball up in favour of low trajectory kicks, but Winfield still gobbled them up and pushed them back as he had done all afternoon in an incredible demonstration of line kicking.

A section of the orderly crowd watches anxiously as Wales defend their line.

The Illustrated Sporting and Dramatic News

Nevertheless, New Zealand were several times on the verge of scoring and twice were actually over the line. Once, from a loose scrum following a centre kick by Duncan McGregor, it appeared that any one of the half-dozen forwards who attempted to gather the ball only had to pick it up and a score was certain. Another time, Mynott crossed from a short pass from Roberts but was held up before he could ground the ball.

With about ten minutes left, from a line-out won by Wales just inside the New Zealand half, the ball was kicked over Roberts' head. Billy Wallace, lurking on the left wing, swooped on it to set off on one of those runs across the face of his opponents for which the long-striding and deceptively fast winger was famed. Wallace crossed half-way, cut left across Nicholls and sped away up-field as Rhys Gabe converged on him. Wallace went through the Welsh back division and it looked as if nothing would stop him. Outside the Welsh twenty-five Wallace was confronted by Bert Winfield, who made this wonderful three-quarter hesitate a fraction. In that instance Wallace, throwing a pass left to Bob Deans, was tackled by Willie Llewellyn, who had raced in field from the right wing. Deans was thirty yards out and running in a line mid-way between the goal posts and the corner flag with no Welsh player in front of him. To make sure of the five points he made the fatal error of turning in towards the posts which put him, as he could see out of the corner of his eye, into the path of the fastest man on both sides, little Teddy Morgan who had hared back to cover from his left wing position. Deans straightened up about ten yards from the Welsh goal line and as he approached the line was tackled, firstly by Rhys Gabe and then by several other Welsh players.

Bob Deans believed he had grounded the ball six inches over the goal line and that he was pulled back by some of the Welsh team before the referee arrived. John Dallas, the referee, who, it is said was fully thirty yards away, came up and awarded a scrum to Wales five yards out. There were no further scores but with about three minutes to go Wales were again attacking. New Zealand were awarded a free-kick and once again Bert Winfield safely returned to touch. Shortly afterwards the final whistle went, the game was over and Wales had won a famous victory.

The crowd burst onto the field and carried Teddy Morgan and Percy Bush around the ground in triumph. It was later discovered that Dickie Owen had displaced a cartilage in his chest and was in agony for most of the game. He said that if it had been any other match he would have left the field.

'Gallant Little Wales Achieved the Great Distinction' was the headline in the Monday edition of the *Athletic News*. They reported, 'the beautiful record has been besmirched at last. Welshmen have done what others have failed to attain and the New Zealanders are now suffering from the pangs of defeat.'

The report continued, 'the victory was gained by a mere try and it is even questionable whether the issue might not have been a draw, for it is asserted that a try had been registered by Deans for the New Zealanders, but the referee decided otherwise and that one try, that Morgan scored after a moment characteristic of all that is ideal in Welsh football, was sufficient to bring misfortune to the Colonials.'

George Dixon the New Zealand manager said of the Welsh backs: "There was no doubt that Winfield at full-back, was the star of the side." He said that his kicking was the best he had seen for years. Of the others he felt Gabe was probably the best with Pritchard also doing good work and the whole back division working well together. Although he felt Percy Bush was remarkable chiefly for his quick kicking, he wasn't so complimentary about Dickie Owen. In Dixon's judgement Owen did not justify the reputation he enjoyed. He was more complimentary about the Welsh forwards whom he thought were fast, hard-working, sound and very solid in the scrums, as well as being vigorous tacklers.

Highlights of the game as seen by the *Western Mail*.

The gold medal awarded to Willie Llewellyn by the Welsh Football Union in commemoration of the first meeting between Wales and New Zealand.

Courtesy of Dr Michael Jones

It is difficult to convey any adequate idea of the delight with which the news of the Welsh team's victory was received throughout Wales. At every town throughout the Principality crowds awaited the arrival of the result at the newspaper offices, and the enthusiasm when it was at last announced that Wales had achieved a victory over the New Zealanders was unbounded.

The *South Wales Graphic* reported, 'The singing of 'Hen Wlad fy Nhadau' in reply to the Haka fired Welsh blood as nothing else could have done. Even when Wales were hard-pressed and victory seemed likely to be snatched from their grasp, the refrain 'Land of My Fathers' would persist in floating above the ground, putting new life into our men.'

The *South Wales Daily News* said of the match, 'It would be idle to deny that the New Zealanders were not formidable opponents, for there are points about their play which demand recognition. Their following up and speed all round as a side has probably never been excelled, but in opportunities and in tactics, as a strategy, they were a long way behind their Welsh opponents.' The report continued: 'There have been occasions when individual Welshmen have shown greater powers of defence than individual members of the present team did, but never has there been a Welsh side which, from forward to full-back, showed such uniform excellence as the fifteen men whose names will live as having defeated the hitherto all-conquering New Zealanders, every man of whom played with a grim determination that deserved the honour of victory.'

The *London Morning Post* reported: 'The Scotsmen at Inverleith gave the New Zealanders a gruelling in the scrummage. The Irishmen at Lansdowne Road swept down the field in irresistible rushes but the

Welshmen possessed the double nature of the Scots and Irish. They pounded away at the New Zealanders in the close scrummaging; they broke quickly, hanging for ever on the ball. They used their feet in short rushes with telling effect, always keeping the ball under command and their tackling was deadly.' The report described how Bert Winfield was invariably given the innumerable penalty kicks against the New Zealanders, and how with length and consistency he never once failed to find touch. It was said that the Welsh side played excellently to a man and that they had beaten New Zealand at their own game.

Gwyn Nicholls, the Welsh captain, stated in the *Daily Mail* how the all-conquering career of the New Zealanders had at last been checked, and how proud Wales were of having achieved what others had failed to do. At an informal news conference on the Sunday morning after the game, Gwyn Nicholls told pressmen of the black cat which had strolled into the Victoria Laundry while he and Bert Winfield sat in his office passing the time and steadying their nerves before the big game. Both players had made sure of stroking it.

In an article for the *Evening Express* in November 1910 Gwyn Nicholls reflected on the famous game when he wrote: 'In my reminiscent moods my thoughts always recur to that greatest and most exciting match; Wales v New Zealand. It will remain in my memory as long as I live and in the memories of all who took part in the game. I had retired (for the first time) and it was the proudest moment of my football career when I received a letter from Mr Tom Williams, the best and keenest of sportsmen, that it was his wish and the wish of his colleagues on the Welsh Union, that I should seriously consider returning to the fray. "Rhys Gabe, Teddy Morgan and Willie Llewellyn will be more at home and more confident if you are with them in the three-quarter line" was the flattering and irresistible way in which he couched his appeal and I succumbed. This was just a month before the match.'

The leading New Zealand journalist C C Reade reflected, 'The game was absolutely the finest I have seen in the history of rugby football. By the end of the day the play of the Welshmen became a revelation. They demoralised the New Zealand defence with their deadly and persistent onslaught on the blind side of their opponents' formation. The development of that attack, swift as a knife thrust, was a creation of genius.'

Not everyone was disposed to magnify the Welsh victory. The *London Daily Chronicle* said, 'The chief explanation of the New Zealanders' defeat is to be found in staleness which must have induced itself before they encountered a foe almost as strong as themselves.' In fact George Dixon felt after the game against Yorkshire that the team were showing signs that hard travelling and hard playing was having an effect upon them. He suspected they were getting stale. After the Welsh game, he believed – Roberts and Deans apart – that there was not a back who did not play well below his true form. However, staleness was not the only cause of their downfall. He said, 'A record such as the team possessed was a heavy load to carry and this combined with nerves and over-anxiety accentuated by intense excitement prevailing amongst the crowd all contributed to the poor passing, indifferent fielding and faulty kicking.'

Whatever the opinion, nothing could change the result and the history books show that Wales achieved a memorable victory. In the words of 'Philistine' of the *Athletic News*, 'The Welshmen played the game of their lives, they broke the ranks of the New Zealand forwards and they broke the hearts of the New Zealand backs.'

The evening of the game both teams attended the official after-match dinner at the Queen's Hotel, Cardiff where the New Zealanders were staying. The menu included: Native Oysters, Consommé á la Princess, Fillets of Sole Morney, Fried Smelts, Welsh Saddle of Mutton, Pheasants, Wild Duck and Seddon Pudding with Brandy Sauce.

New Zealand continued their tour with games against Glamorgan, Newport, Cardiff and Swansea. For the encounter with Glamorgan six of the backs who played in the historic Welsh victory over New Zealand were originally selected for the county, but Bert Winfield, Teddy Morgan, Gwyn Nicholls, Rhys Gabe, Percy Bush and

The Menu Card for the complimentary dinner held at the Queen's Hotel, Cardiff after the match.

The Glamorgan Team v New Zealand 1905

Back Row: Mr A J Davies (WFU), J F Williams (London Welsh), Dick Thomas (Mountain Ash), Dai Jones (Aberdare), Dai Westacott (Cardiff), Howell Jones (Neath), W H 'Harry' Hunt (Swansea).
Second Row: W 'Billy' Pullen (Cardiff), J C M Dyke (Penarth), Will Joseph (Swansea, Captain), R A Gibbs (Cardiff), J L Williams (Cardiff), Jack Powell (Cardiff). *Front Row*: J 'Bala' Jones (Aberavon), Phil Hopkins (Swansea), Willie Arnold (Swansea).

Dickie Owen, along with another established international, Billy Trew, all withdrew for various reasons. Three of the victorious Welsh pack did play, with Will Joseph (Captain), Dai 'Tarw' Jones and John 'Scethrog' Williams all turning out. Unconverted tries by George Smith, Alex McDonald and Billy Wallace gave the All Blacks a 9 points to nil victory.

Cliff Pritchard of Pontypool guested for Newport in their game against New Zealand. This was a very close game with Newport narrowly losing by 6 points to three. Cardiff did even better, losing by just two points. The result could have been so much better but a mistake late in the game by Percy Bush let George Nicholson in for a try which Billy Wallace converted to give the All Blacks victory by 10 points to eight.

In their final game of the Britain and Ireland leg of the tour, the New Zealanders defeated Swansea by 4 points to three. Fred Scrine scored an unconverted try after twenty-five minutes to give Swansea the lead but a fantastic left-footed drop goal by Billy Wallace in the second half gave the visitors the spoils. New Zealand then played an international match against France in Paris, an unofficial game against New York, and two games against British Columbia. In total they played 36 games, won 35, drew none and lost just one. They scored 1022 points and conceded just 72. In Britain and Ireland they played 32 games, won 31, drew none and lost just the one game against Wales. They scored 830 points and conceded 39.

Several of the Welsh team that defeated the 1905 New Zealanders played against them on more than one occasion. Will Joseph played against them three times, turning out for Wales, Glamorgan and Swansea. John 'Scethrog' Williams also appeared on three occasions against them for Middlesex, Wales and Glamorgan, while Arthur Harding featured twice, playing for Middlesex and Wales. In addition to playing for Wales against New Zealand, Cliff Pritchard, Charlie Pritchard and Jehoida Hodges were in the Newport XV against New Zealand, and Bert Winfield, Gwyn Nicholls, Rhys Gabe and Percy Bush all played for Cardiff against the All Blacks. Dickie Owen and Will Joseph were in Swansea's team against New Zealand.

With Willie Llewellyn having retired from international rugby, it also appeared that he had retired completely from the game. Although he transferred to Penygraig in November 1905, just before his final inter-

Advertisement from the 6th January 1906 edition of the *Rhondda Leader*.

national match for Wales, he only played two games for them during their Glamorgan League Cup-winning season. The advertisement from the *Rhondda Leader* on Saturday 6th January 1906 clearly shows that Willie had opened his new Chemist's shop at 135 Dunraven Street, Tonypandy. Willie was obviously concentrating on his new business and rugby was not a priority. Despite not playing regular rugby, Willie did make appearances in three friendly games between January 1906 and the end of the season.

On the afternoon of Thursday 22nd February 1906 he captained a team of Welsh internationals against V W Evans XV at Porthcawl. Unfortunately the game could not be concluded in consequence of a violent storm of wind and sleet. Before the game was abandoned Willie Llewellyn's team had scored a goal and two tries with no reply and, as the second half was not played, Willie's team won by 11 points to nil.

Considerable interest was taken in the next game Willie played when he represented Gwyn Nicholls' Welsh Fifteen in a match against V J W Jarman's West of England Fifteen at Bristol on Wednesday 28th March. The Welsh XV were well represented and included Welsh internationals Bert Winfield, Willie Llewellyn, Gwyn Nicholls, George

Willie Llewellyn Newport Games Played 1905-1906 Season						
Willie Llewellyn Other Games Played 1905-1906 Season						
Willie Llewellyn Welsh International and Welsh Trial Games Played 1905-1906 Season						
Date	Team Played For	Opposition	Venue	Result	W Llewellyn Tries
16/09/1905	Newport 'C' Team	Newport 'D' Team	Newport	Won 31-0	2
30/09/1905	Newport	Lydney	Home	Won 15-0	0
07/10/1905	Newport	Old Merchant Taylors	Home	Won 37-0	1
14/10/1905	Newport	Cardiff	Home	Lost 3-17	0
21/10/1905	Newport	Blackheath	Away	Drawn 3-3	0
08/11/1905	Willie Llewellyn's Team	Christ College, Brecon	Brecon	Won 35-16	1+
11/11/1905	London Welsh	London Irish	Layton	Won 28-0	0
13/11/1905	London Welsh	Swansea	Queen's Club	Lost 0-13	0
18/11/1905	Penygraig	Penarth	Away	Won 3-0	0
20/11/1905	Probables	Possibles	Cardiff	Lost 9-18	0
25/11/1905	Penygraig	Blaenclydach	Home	Won 5-3	1
02/12/1905	Probables	Possibles	Cardiff	Won 33-11	0
09/12/1905	Cardiff	Blackheath	Away	Won 24-4	0
16/12/1905	Wales	New Zealand	Cardiff	Won 3-0	0
22/02/1906	W M Llewellyn's XV	V W Evans' XV	Porthcawl	Won 11-0	1
28/03/1906	Gwyn Nicholls Welsh XV	V J W Jarman's XV	Bristol	Won 11-0	1
23/04/1906	Llwynypia Past	Llwynypia Present	Llwynypia	Lost 6-19	1
	Willie Llewellyn Games Played				W Llewellyn Tries
Totals	17				8+

Willie Llewellyn Games Played and Results 1905–1906 Season

Boots and Jehoida Hodges. The West of England team fielded a strong line-up that included no less than ten English internationals in Wallace Jarman, Norman Moore, John Mathias, Raphael Jago, James Peters, Cecil Milton, John 'Jumbo' Milton, John Jackett, Arthur Hudson and Harry Shewring. The game was one of the best seen in Bristol for quite some time. Harding, the Cardiff forward, opened the scoring for the Welsh XV with a try from a line-out and Bert Winfield added the extra points. Before the interval, Jehoida Hodges and Willie Llewellyn added unconverted tries to give the Welsh XV an eleven point advantage at half-time, and with no further scores in the second half the game ended in a victory for Gwyn Nicholls' Welsh Fifteen.

Willie's last game of the 1905–06 season was for a Llwynypia past fifteen against a present fifteen played at the Partridge Grounds on Monday 23rd April. The game which was for the benefit of the Llwynypia and District Cricket and Tennis Club ended in defeat for the past representatives of this once famous club. H Piper, G Pinkham, E Phillips and Morgan Evans scored tries for the present team, and Willie Llewellyn and Wayne Morgan scored unconverted tries for the senior team leaving the juniors victors by two goals, a penalty goal and two tries to two tries (19–6).

Christmas 1905 brought to an end George Llewellyn's schooldays at Christ College. His time at Brecon almost exactly mirrored Willie's international rugby career, going up to Christ College in 1899 and completing his studies in December 1905. He had also equalled his elder brother's achievement of becoming *Victor Ludorum* for two consecutive years: 1904 and 1905. George had again played cricket for the College during the summer term and, although he did not bowl to any great extent, he was second in the batting honours with an average of 14.46. George played 15 innings, made 188 runs and his best score was 64 not out. George actually surpassed Willie's rugby achievements by captaining the first XV for two successive seasons, though his final season in charge of the first fifteen was not altogether a fruitful one. Of the twelve matches they played up until December 1905, they won only three, lost eight and drew one. George missed three games because of injury but played in the other nine. Despite the poor results, *The Breconian* was very complimentary with regard to his rugby ability and stated: 'G LLEWELLYN (left wing).—A dashing runner, with great pace and plenty of resource. Hardly had the same opportunities as last season, and was handicapped by an accident. Much improved in defence, and is now almost as good in this department as in attack. A fine kick, and (as Captain) managed his side with judgment.'

The disappointing results during the season were somewhat misleading and didn't really reflect two very important facts: the powerful character of the opposing teams met during the term, and the continued misfortunes which caused the College side to barely ever take the field at full-strength. To be beaten by stronger sides was no disgrace, and this happened on one or two occasions, but to be beaten owing to the absence of four or five of their best men was their frequent misfortune at the height of the season. It said much for the pluck and determination of

Christ College Brecon, Rugby First XV 1905–1906

Back Row: A E C Morgan Esq, W F Griffith, W M Howells, W Ll Gwyn Davies, G B Llewellyn, Rev. A E Donaldson. *Third Row*: T H Phillips, C P Hazard, W M Llewellyn, E V Watkins, W H Schenk, A Williams.
Second Row: M Williams, G Llewellyn (Captain), T D W Williams.
Front Row: T H K Gregory, F R Stephens.

the XV that, in spite of their misfortunes, they made an excellent show on many occasions. They were never badly beaten or demoralised, even at their weakest moments, and just a little more good fortune might have turned at least two or three of their defeats into well-deserved victories.

However, George's time at Christ College was now over and in a final tribute to their captain *The Breconian* paid the following compliment: 'Of the captain, G Llewellyn, it may be said at once that he served his side as well in adversity as he had done before in prosperity. If less conspicuously brilliant in attack than in the previous year, he was not, we think, given equal opportunities; he is a player of no less ability in attack, and his defence was beyond a doubt very much sounder than ever before. Moreover he managed his side in a season of unusual difficulty with tact and judgment, and deserved better luck as the results of his untiring efforts for its success.'

The 1905 Wales game against New Zealand brought to an end the illustrious international rugby career of Willie Llewellyn. In his debut match for Wales against England at Swansea in 1899 Willie scored four tries. The Llwynypia wing set two records that day, four tries on debut and four tries in a match, and nearly one hundred and twenty years later they have still not been broken. Since that game only eight other Welsh players have run in four tries in an international match and equalled the record. Reggie Gibbs scored four tries for Wales against France at Cardiff in 1908 and sixty-one years later Maurice Richards scored four tries for Wales against England in 1969. Ieuan Evans matched the record when he scored four tries against Canada in the 1987 World Cup and Nigel Walker did so for Wales when they played Portugal at Lisbon in the 1995 World Cup qualifier. Four years later Gareth Thomas equalled the record when he scored four tries against Italy at Treviso. It is fitting that Wales' top try scorer, Shane Williams, should also have equalled the record which he achieved against Japan at Osaka in 2001. In the 2004 November Lloyds TSB Autumn Series at the Millennium Stadium the record was equalled twice in the space of fifteen days. Firstly Tom Shanklin scored four tries against Romania and two weeks later Colin Charvis became the first Welsh forward to score four tries in a match when he, too, equalled the record playing against Japan.

Willie played throughout Wales' second Triple Crown in 1900 before going to London to study at the Pharmaceutical College, Bloomsbury. Willie captained London Welsh for three seasons and oversaw a significant improvement in their fortunes. Many, in fact believed that without Willie Llewellyn the club would probably have gone into extinction. Willie as a man and captain was one of life's gentlemen. He was a modest man who generously gave advice and encouragement in equal measure. Willie was a top-class wing three-quarter by any standard and, although he was lucky enough to have played outside such outstanding centres as Tom Williams, Gwyn Nicholls and Rhys Gabe, he often demonstrated that he was also an accomplished individual player. The skills he learnt at Christ College under the tutorship of Welsh rugby international William Llewellyn Thomas stood him in great stead throughout his brilliant international rugby career. Willie had exceptional speed and a very safe pair of hands. His outstanding footballing skills together with his remarkable judgement made Willie Llewellyn one of the all-time greats of Welsh rugby. Not only was he skilful, he was tough. He was quite capable of beating a man with speed and cunning, but he was also capable of running straight through an opponent. Defensively he was strong and fearless, his tackling being absolutely ferocious. Willie certainly made the most of his relatively small physique; he was 5ft 7½ins tall (1.71m) and weighed 11st 2lbs (71kg).

In 1902, Willie gained his tenth cap against England and for the first time the Welsh three-quarter line comprised Willie Llewellyn, Gwyn Nicholls, Rhys Gabe and Teddy Morgan, the incomparable quartette who took care of the 1905 All Blacks. That 1902 campaign was another Triple Crown year for Wales and Willie scored two tries against Scotland and one against Ireland. Indeed, it was Willie's smart pick-up of a loose ball and his flashing sprint to the line in the Triple Crown decider against Ireland at Lansdowne Road that put Wales on the road to victory.

Although Willie missed the internationals against England and Scotland in 1903 because of injury, he returned for the international against Ireland and scored two superb tries. When Willie qualified as a pharmacist in the summer of 1903, he returned to South Wales where he played for Newport. Willie toured Australia and New Zealand with the British team in 1904 and played in fifteen of the twenty games undertaken. He appeared in all four internationals and scored a total of eight tries, including two in the first test against Australia and one each in the second and third tests.

Willie captained Wales for the first time in the international against Scotland at St Helen's in 1904 and then again for the final international of the season against Ireland at Balmoral, Belfast. 1905 was the pinnacle of Willie Llewellyn's rugby career and his last in top flight rugby. Willie captained Wales to their fourth Triple Crown and scored a try in the 25 points to nil rout of England at Cardiff and then scored both tries in the hard fought victory over Scotland at Inverleith. In the Triple Crown decider against Ireland, Willie led his team to a 10–3 win by adopting tactics that kept the game tight and denied Ireland the ball in a tight and scoreless second half. Willie played his final games for both Newport and London Welsh during the early part of the 1905-06 season before effectively retiring from first-class rugby by joining Penygraig in November 1905. Despite being regarded as a veteran with a junior club, Willie was selected to play for Wales against New Zealand where he ruthlessly marked down the great Billy Wallace. The rest they say is history. Having played in twenty-four international matches; twenty for Wales and four for the British team in Australia and New Zealand, Willie's international rugby career had come to an end. He had scored sixteen tries for Wales and four for the British Isles. Even today when so many international matches are played, only twelve Welsh players have scored more tries for Wales than Willie Llewellyn.

After eleven seasons of first-class rugby, during which time Willie Llewellyn played over 350 games, he effectively retired from rugby overnight. Willie would play less than twenty games over the next few seasons. Of course, over the coming years the focus of Willie's life would change dramatically. In addition to the responsibility of running his own business, he married in April 1907 and by 1910 he had a wife and two young children to provide for. He would, however, still manage to find time for relaxation through cricket and golf.

Chapter Eleven

Life Beyond Rugby

AT THE AGE of just twenty-eight Willie Llewellyn had essentially retired from rugby. Following his last international match for Wales against New Zealand in December 1905 he only played three games between that match and the end of the 1905–06 season. Over the next few seasons he played less than twenty games. In an interview with a representative of the *Rhondda Leader* in September 1906 Willie stated, 'that beyond an occasional game along with the League Champions, Penygraig, he did not intend to do much footballing.' Willie was true to his word and played very little rugby over the next couple of years. Willie played his first game of the 1906–07 campaign for Penygraig in their home game against Abertillery and scored a try in the 9 points to three victory. Before taking a team to play against Christ College, Brecon, Willie played for Penygraig against his old club Llwynypia. An unconverted try in the first half was the only score of a hard fought game which Penygraig won by 3 points to nil.

On Saturday 17th November 1906, Willie took a team to Brecon to play against his old College. Christ College kicked off into a very strong wind that threatened to spoil the game. Nevertheless, Willie's team soon pressed and after a few scrums one of the visiting forwards picked up in the loose and ran in for a try which Willie converted. This was all the scoring in the first half, the College defence proving impregnable. With the wind at their backs the College team played very well in the

Willie Llewellyn Games Played 1906-1919
Willie Llewellyn Games Possibly Played 1906-1919

Date	Team Played For	Opposition	Venue	Result	W Llewellyn Tries
27/10/1906	Penygraig	Abertillery	Home	Won 9-3	1
10/11/1906	Penygraig	Llwynypia	Tonypandy	Won 3-0	0
17/11/1906	Willie Llewellyn XV	Christ College, Brecon	Brecon	Lost 5-8	Con.
08/12/1906	Penygraig	Llanelly	Home	Lost 0-3	0
18/12/1906	Christ College Past	Christ College Present	Brecon	Won 19-0	Unknown
12/01/1907	Penygraig	Penarth	Home	Won 8-0	0
11/04/1907	Willie Llewellyn XV	Trealaw District XV	Tonypandy	Won 12-0	Unknown
23/11/1907	Penygraig	Lydney	Home	Won 8-0	0
30/11/1907	Penygraig	Cinderford	Tonypandy	Lost 0-5	0
26/03/1908	Willie Llewellyn XV	Llwynypia	Penygraig	Unknown	Unknown
09/04/1908	Tom Williams Int. XV	Treorky	Treorky	Lost 7-18	0
29/10/1908	Llwynypia Thursdays	Cowbridge	Llwynypia	Won 8-0	0
05/11/1908	Llwynypia Thursdays	Senghenydd	Unknown	Won 57-0	Unknown
12/11/1908	Llwynypia Thursdays	Mr B Lloyd's XV	Pontrhondda	Won 31-6	1
03/12/1908	Llwynypia Thursdays	Pontypridd Nondescripts	Pontypridd	Won 34-0	2
17/12/1908	Llwynypia Thursdays	Pencoed	Away	Won 3-0	0
16/09/1909	Willie Llewellyn XV	Penygraig	Penygraig	Lost 3-9	0
11/12/1919	Willie Llewellyn XV	Christ College, Brecon	Brecon	Won 20-13	Unknown
Totals	Willie Llewellyn Games Played 18				W Llewellyn Tries 4

Willie Llewellyn Games Played and Results 1906–1919

second half and soon added a converted try. Before the end of the game the College scored again from a line-out. The kick at goal failed and with no further scores the College team were victorious by 8 points to five.

Willie's next game was for Penygraig at home to Llanelly who were preparing for their upcoming encounter with the touring Springboks. A strong Llanelly side travelled to the Rhondda for the match which was played on Saturday 8th December 1906. This game was a tough encounter, played on a heavy ground and Llanelly found it very difficult to make any headway. The only score of the match was a first half penalty goal by D M Davies. The second half was a regular scramble and despite the Rhondda champions pressing Llanelly hard, they were unable to score. On one occasion Willie Llewellyn had a chance but he could not shake off Willie Thomas, the Llanelly wing. Finding it impossible to break through the Llanelly defence, Penygraig took a few shots at goal but both went wide. Notwithstanding a final effort by Penygraig, Llanelly held out and took the spoils by just three points to nil.

Willie returned to Christ College on Tuesday 18th December 1906 for the annual Past v Present match. The Old Boys defeated the Present by 19 points to nil with Willie reportedly playing in the pack. Both the *Western Mail* and the *Evening Express* stated, 'the Old Boys having in their pack W M Llewellyn, the international.' Although there are no details of the teams or who scored, the Old Boys managed to score five tries, two of which were converted. The Rev. A E Donaldson of the College refereed the game.

Willie was once again in the team on Saturday 12th January 1907 when Penygraig were at home on the Mid-Rhondda Athletic Ground, to Penarth. A first half try by Baker which was converted by Gordon Thomas gave Penygraig the advantage at the interval. An unconverted try by W Ivor Williams in the second half concluded the scoring giving Penygraig the win by 8 points to nil. With regard to the game the *Evening Express* made the following remarks: 'Penygraig were in fine form and were superior in all departments. Notwithstanding the bad state of the ground, their quartette handled well and indulged in some pretty passing movements. W Ivor Williams and Willie Llewellyn were prominent in the quartette, while Gordon Thomas outshone the visiting custodian, his defence being superb.'

Willie was now playing less and less rugby and although we know he selected a team for a charity match against a Trealaw District fifteen on Thursday 11th April 1907 we do not know if Willie actually played in that game. In mid-January there are reports of him successfully undergoing an operation at a private hospital in Cardiff after twice injuring his nose and there is no mention of Willie in the report of the match which appeared in the *Evening Express*. The report states, 'The game was well contested and resulted in a win for the ex-international's team by two goals (one dropped) and one try to nil (12–0). Eddie Phillips the Llwynypia half-back dropped a fine goal in the first moiety and D Davies and G Matthews (Penygraig) scored tries.'

Irrespective of whether Willie played in the charity match or not we know that the next report of Willie playing is not until November 1907 when he played his first game of the season for Penygraig against Lydney and demonstrated that there was 'plenty of football still left in him.' Although Penygraig were weakened by the absence of seven regular first team players they still managed to defeat the Forest of Dean men by 8 points to nil.

Although Willie was still playing for Penygraig it had been reported in the *Evening Express* in October 1907 that Willie had promised to play for his old club Llwynypia and had applied for a transfer from Penygraig. The report stated, 'He will play on the wing, with Monty Williams, Trealaw, as his centre. The latter is a prominent athlete in the district, being a good cricketer, and has done well for the hockey team.' Despite having applied for a transfer Willie played one last game for Penygraig in their home match against Cinderford. Even though selected to play the following week for Penygraig against Aberavon, Willie did not play and he returned to the club for whom he had first played back on Christmas Day 1895, and where his brother George was now a member of the first fifteen.

The match against Cinderford was not altogether the happy ending that Willie would have wanted in his final game for Penygraig. They were beaten by the English county cup-holders by 5 points to nil. An intercepted pass late in the game led to a try and conversion which were enough to give the visiting team victory. Willie did however have the plaudits of the press who stated that he had tackled well and, 'was the most conspicuous of the three-quarters.' The game against Cinderford was the last of only nine games Willie played for Penygraig. He played his first game for the club against Penarth in March 1903 and then, after joining the club in November 1905 he played just a further eight games between November 1905 and November 1907.

Although Willie was playing practically no rugby, his brother George was once again following in Willie's footsteps. He made his first appearance in the Llwynypia ranks when they played against Cardiff Northern on Saturday 14th September 1907 and appeared regularly for them throughout the season. George had played for University College, Cardiff in their match against Aberystwyth University in February 1907 and the 1907 December edition of *The Breconian* reported that George played for University College, Cardiff and Llwynypia. George was also an important member of the Llwynypia Thursday team and he scored in every game up until Thursday 12th November 1908. By Thursday 17th December they had played eight matches, winning six and drawing two games against Merthyr. George was originally selected to play for the Glamorgan League against Australia at Taff Vale Park, Pontypridd on Thursday 17th December 1908, but for some reason was unable to play and his place on the left wing was taken by Johnny Williams of Cardiff: Australia won by 9 points to five. Llwynypia Thursdays remained undefeated well into

January 1909, George's splendid form being rewarded with a place in the Glamorgan team that played Monmouthshire at Cardiff on Monday 4th January 1909. Unfortunately Glamorgan were defeated by 10 points to three.

Willie was selected to play alongside George in the Llwynypia team to play against Swansea Seconds on Saturday 25th January 1908 but withdrew because of a knee injury. The next report of Willie intending to play appeared in the *Evening Express* on Saturday 21st March 1908. The article stated, 'On Thursday next Willie Llewellyn will play for his side against Llwynypia. Among those who have promised to appear are Dr 'Teddy' Morgan, Gwyn Nicholls, George Llewellyn, Bob Thomas (Mountain Ash), A F Harding (London Welsh) and probably a few more star internationals.' Although well-advertised, the result of the match, which was for the benefit of the Mid-Rhondda Nursing Association, does not appear in any of the local newspapers and for some reason may not have taken place.

Another game Willie could well have played in was the Tom Williams's International XV against Treorky on Thursday 9th April 1908. There are at least two known facts about this game, the first, that they lost by 18 points to seven and the second, that Dickie Owen was one of the International XV players. With Tom Williams being Willie's uncle it is quite possible that Willie also played in this game.

During the first half of the 1908–09 season Willie Llewellyn played regularly for Llwynypia Thursdays. He is mentioned in the match reports of the games against Cowbridge, Senghenydd, Mr B Lloyd's XV and the Pontypridd Nondescripts. A report in the *Evening Express* on Saturday 19th December 1908 stated, 'Llwynypia possess the strongest team that has ever been formed in the Thursday section. Willie Llewellyn takes a keen interest, and has contributed in compiling up the creditable score of 131 points, only eleven points having been scored against them.' As the report went on to say how Llwynypia had visited Pencoed the previous Thursday and had won by a try scored by J Davies, it is quite possible that Willie Llewellyn also played in that game. The next report relating to Willie Llewellyn appeared in the *Evening Express* on Wednesday 15th September 1909 and remarked, 'Tomorrow afternoon the Penygraig Rugby supporters will witness at the Mid-Rhondda a strong team selected and brought together by Mr Willie Llewellyn to assist the Penygraig club. Amongst others, Gabe, Winfield, W Morgan and Northmore are expected from Cardiff and several of the Swansea team have promised to be present.' The report in the *Western Mail* on Friday 17th September referred to a game between Penygraig and Mr A W Llewellyn's Team with Penygraig winning by 9 points to three. Again detail is sparse but as the visiting line-up was 'virtually a Llwynypia team' it is possible that Willie Llewellyn played.

At the annual meeting of Llwynypia Rugby Football Club held at the De Winton Hotel, Tonypandy on Friday 25th June 1909 it was reported that Willie Llewellyn had been added to the list of vice-presidents. At the same meeting Willie's uncle, Tom Williams, was voted a president of the club in company with Messrs. W W Hood and L W Llewellyn. Not for a good number of years had the Llwynypia team reminded anyone of the Llwynypia team of their halcyon days of the 1890's but during the 1908–09 season they had swept almost everything before them until the last few matches of the season. Playing on their new De Winton ground Llwynypia had a reasonable season and of the 34 games played they won 18, lost 10 and drew six. Curiously, half the matches they lost were by drop goals. During the meeting it was reported that their fixture list for the forthcoming season, although an improving one, did not contain as many of the leading clubs as they would have liked but nevertheless they had home and away fixtures with Neath, Newton Abbot and Pontardawe together with fixtures with all the Glamorgan League clubs. In addition both Cardiff and Swansea had promised to visit the new ground which was reportedly 'one of the finest in the valley.' One sad note of the meeting was the reported death of Mr David 'Dai' Llewellyn who, after a short illness, passed away at the age of forty-four. For many years he had acted as the secretary of the Penygraig and Llwynypia clubs and was, the previous year, secretary of the Mid-Rhondda (Northern Union) club.

Although there is not a great deal of detail with regard to the games Willie Llewellyn played after his international career was over, it is almost certain that Willie played his first and last games on the playing fields of Christ College, Brecon. The last recorded game Willie played was on Thursday 11th December 1919, when at the age of forty-one, in fact just twenty-one days short of his forty second birthday, Willie took a team to Brecon to play against the College. This annual encounter had not been played for five years as a consequence of the First World War but with peace once again restored Christ College resumed one of its favourite festivities. The report of the game in the 1920 April edition of *The Breconian* read as follows: 'This was a most enjoyable match, played on Thursday, Dec. 11th. It was pleasant to see the famous Old Boy internationals taking the field again. 'Teddy' Morgan and his brother W L seemed almost as good as ever, the former scoring more than once by brilliant bursts. Willie Llewellyn, though less inclined for continuous effort than his colleagues, was more than once conspicuous, and showed much of his former skill and quickness off the mark. George Llewellyn and L C Davies were other Old Boys who played very soundly for what was a strong all round combination. The School fought uncommonly well against this powerful side, and though the final score was 20 points to 13 against us, our display created a very favourable impression, and showed how much the School had trained on during the term. D S O Thomas, Lougher, I Ll Evans, R T Harries and several of the forwards distinguished themselves in various ways.' The report in the *Western Mail* on Saturday 13th December 1919 confirmed the result and under the heading of 'Brilliant Play at Brecon' made the following comments: 'Brilliant play was seen at Brecon in the annual Rugby match played between Mr W M Llewellyn's team and Christ College. Three famous old Welsh internationals appeared in the visiting side, viz., W M Llewellyn, Dr E Morgan and W L Morgan, all ex-students of the college. Playing at centre, Dr Morgan showed wonderful form and he scored three tries all in his old dazzling style. Mr Llewellyn's team won by one goal and five tries to two goals and one try.' A report in *The Brecon County Times* stated, 'It was surprising how well these veterans shaped. Willie Llewellyn himself gained his first cap for Wales 20 years ago. It would be scarcely true to suggest that he retains all his old pace and skill; time spares no man. But in the first few minutes of the game he made a dash, intercepted a pass, and ran for the line with his old incomparable quickness and agility.' Willie had not taken to the field for ten long years and when the game was over so too was his long and illustrious rugby career.

During his memorable rugby career Willie played club rugby for Llwynypia, Cardiff, Swansea, London Welsh, Newport, Treherbert,

Penygraig and Penarth. He played county rugby for Glamorgan, Surrey and Kent, and international rugby for Wales and the British Lions (Anglo-Australian Rugby Football Team 1904). Including the games Willie played for Christ College, Brecon during the early part of his playing career, he played in the region of 390 games, including 20 internationals for Wales and four internationals for the British team in Australia and New Zealand. He won three Triple Crowns with Wales and captained them on five occasions, including all three games for their fourth Triple Crown in 1905. In his first international against England at Swansea he created two Welsh records: he was the first Welsh player to score four tries in an international match and he was the first Welsh international rugby player to score four tries on his debut. Although subsequently eight Welsh players have equalled the achievement of scoring four tries in an international match, nearly 120 years on, no one has bettered this feat. His record of scoring four tries on his debut has never been equalled.

Of the twenty games Willie played for Wales, including the famous victory over New Zealand in 1905, they won 15, lost 4 and drew one. Of the games Wales played when Willie was captain they won four and lost one. When Willie retired from international rugby he was Wales' leading try scorer with 16 tries. This was not bettered until Johnny Williams of Cardiff scored his seventeenth try for Wales in his penultimate game for the Principality when he captained Wales for the only time in his career in the game against France in Paris on Tuesday 28th February 1911. This record was equalled just eleven days later when Reggie Gibbs scored his seventeenth try for Wales in the international against Ireland on Saturday 11th March 1911. Although Ken Jones also equalled the record when he scored his seventeenth try for Wales in the victory over New Zealand at Cardiff Arms Park in 1953, it has subsequently been improved upon by nine Welsh players and at the present time Shane Williams is currently top Welsh try scorer with 58 tries from 87 international appearances.

Willie Llewellyn is truly a legend of Welsh rugby and during his long life he was recognised and respected by all those who played and watched the game. He is remembered today in just the same way. As recently as the Wales v England game at Twickenham on Saturday 10th February

2018 his record of four tries for Wales in an international match was acknowledged in the official match programme.

During the early years Willie had to find a balance between playing rugby and employment as a pharmaceutical trainee. He started his career as a chemist and druggist when, in 1896, at the age of eighteen, he left Christ College, Brecon and was an apprentice to Mr J W Richards, Chemist, Tonypandy. Having trained with Mr Richards for almost four years, Willie became a student at the Pharmaceutical College, Bloomsbury in January 1900. As previously mentioned, during his time in London Willie played for and captained London Welsh RFC. Although Willie passed the minor examinations and registered as a chemist and druggist on Saturday 10th January 1903, he remained in London and worked for a while for Allen and Hanburys Ltd. who were manufacturers of pharmaceutical preparations and surgical instruments. Willie continued to play for and captain London Welsh until the end of the 1902–03 season. In January 1903, when it had been reported that Willie had successfully 'passed his final examinations in chemistry,' it was anticipated that he would return to play rugby for Llwynypia. A report in the *Evening Express* on Saturday 24th January 1903 in reference to Willie Llewellyn commented, 'It is to be hoped that he will ere long be found sporting the blue and black for Llwynypia. His home is here, and if a place were found for him in his professional capacity, his return to Llwynypia

Willie Llewellyn's chemist shop advert from the *Rhondda Leader* on Saturday 2nd February 1907.

would, doubtless, infuse a deal of life into the team. It is on the tapis that it will not be very long ere he does 'don the war paint' for Llwynypia.' However, this was not the case and in September 1903 Willie, having secured employment with Messrs. Phillips, Chemists at 92 Commercial Street, Newport, played for Newport RFC.

Willie returned to London in February 1905 to undertake a course in dentistry at The London Hospital and while there took the opportunity to turn out for his old club, London Welsh. The fact that Willie had acquired dentistry skills is reflected in the adverts Willie placed in the Rhondda Leader, making such statements as 'Painless Extractions' and 'New Teeth at Moderate Prices.' The adverts also confirm that Willie had more than one premises with adverts stating that there were shops in both Tonypandy and Clydach Vale. By 1912 three businesses were listed. In addition to Tonypandy and Clydach Vale, there were also premises at Penygraig.

Willie played his last game for Wales against New Zealand in December 1905 and effectively retired from rugby. On Saturday 30th December Willie opened his new chemist shop at 135 Dunraven Street, Tonypandy and regularly advertised in the *Rhondda Leader* newspaper. In an interview with the *Retail Chemist* magazine in June 1969 Willie described how difficult it was to balance rugby and work and how retail pharmacy and sport were not obviously compatible. Willie recalled, 'Oh it wasn't all play. Hours were long, twelve o'clock on Saturday nights. You paid a substantial premium to be apprenticed in those days and got it back in mere shillings as salary. Oh no they weren't easy days and you had to learn your trade. But Llwynypia had a first class rugby team in my teens and it was customary for the coal owners, colliery officials and other important people to sponsor activities.' Willie confirmed that because of this local sponsorship there was almost an obligation to play for the local club.

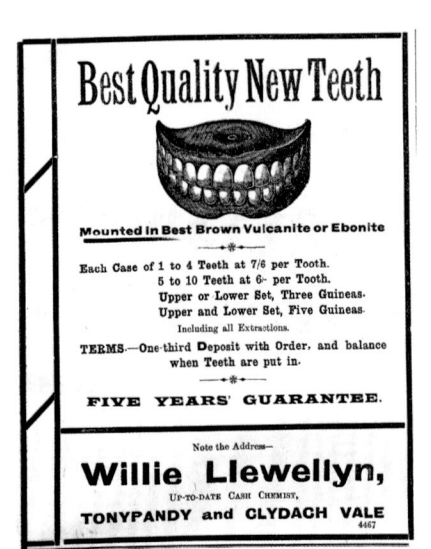

Willie Llewellyn's chemist shop advert from the *Rhondda Leader* on Saturday 14th November 1908.

Willie was always looking for innovative ways to advertise his business and in April 1912 came up with the novel ideal of a competition to guess the weight of a lump of coal placed in his chemist's shop window at Tonypandy. Willie was offering six prizes to those who could estimate the weight of the specimen: first prize of £2, second prize of £1 and four other prizes of 10 shillings each. Every purchaser at any of Willie's shops were given a coupon on which to register their attempt. There was no limit to the number of attempts, but in the event of no one getting the correct weight the prizes would be awarded to the nearest answer. The coal was to be weighed and all coupons checked by a committee of well-known local gentlemen, whose decision was final. The competition was to close on Thursday 23rd May and the weight of the lump of coal and the names of the prize-winners would be posted in Willie Llewellyn's shop windows and published in the *Rhondda Leader* on Saturday 25th May.

The lump of coal in Willie's Tonypandy shop window was a source of great attraction. A report in the *Rhondda Leader* on Saturday 25th May stated, 'Even parsons are interested in it. The other day, a group of miners were around the window, and in their midst a clergyman, with paper and pencil in hand, asked all manner of questions as to the weight of a cubic foot of coal and the average length, breadth and height of the identical lump. Having worked out the sum, he halved the answer, jotted it down on the coupon, and with a smile on his face handed it over the counter.' The winners of the competition may well have been posted in Willie Llewellyn's shop windows but it seems they were never posted in the *Rhondda Leader* as promised, and so, disappointingly, we may never know how heavy it was or who the prize-winners were.

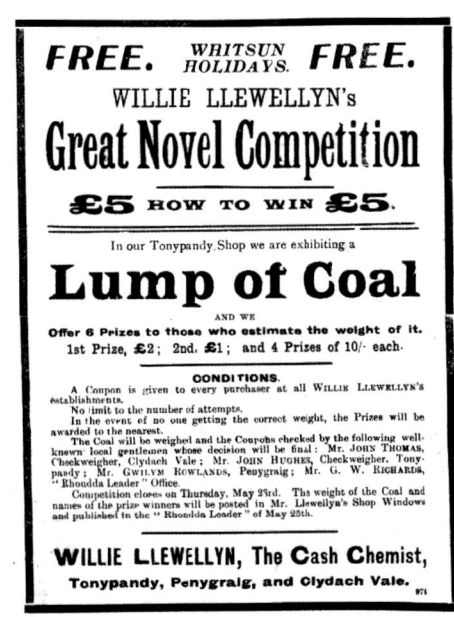

Willie Llewellyn's chemist shop advert for the 'Lump of Coal' competition from the *Rhondda Leader* on Saturday 4th May 1912.

Willie Llewellyn's photographic competition as advertised in the *Rhondda Leader* on Saturday 20th July 1912.

Later that year Willie ran a photographic competition with a camera to the value of £4 as the prize. A coupon was given to every purchaser of photographic goods to the value of 6d and the customer who returned the greatest number of coupons was the winner.

In order to sustain his Rhondda business Willie was very diverse with regard to the services he offered and what items he sold in his shops. In addition to his chemistry and dentistry skills, he offered the full range of pharmaceutical products from cough syrup to remedies for constipation, from perfumery to magic nerve pills and by Christmas 1908 he was also selling magic lanterns, cinematographs, cameras and the full range of photographic sundries, tobacco, cigars and cigarettes. For footballers he supplied knee caps, anklets, bandages, flesh gloves and embrocations; there was nothing it seems that he could not provide. In June 1906, Willie was granted an off-licence to sell wine at his Tonypandy premises. In March 1912, a similar application to sell wine at his Clydach Vale and Penygraig premises was refused. In January 1916, he made a similar application to sell wine to be drunk or consumed off the premises at his Clydach Vale shop.

Although it was initially thought that only three of the Llewellyn brothers: Johnnie, Willie and George, studied at Christ College, Brecon, further research has revealed that Ivor Llewellyn, the youngest brother, studied at Christ College from 1905 until 1908. A report in the *Rhondda*

Leader on Saturday 2nd April 1910 revealed that Ivor had recently passed his 'Preliminary Examinations for Chemists' and was apprenticed to his brother Willie at Dunraven Street, Tonypandy. Ivor passed the final examinations of the Pharmaceutical Society in early 1916 and became a qualified chemist who later practised at Gilfach Goch.

A former employee of Willie's became a war hero. At the outbreak of the First World War James Oliver Richard Evans, aged twenty-one, was a dispenser under the Tredegar medical scheme and employed by Willie Llewellyn at his chemist shop in Tonypandy. Evans joined the Royal Army Medical Corps (RAMC) in September 1914 and was promoted to sergeant the following November. He received a commission as Second-Lieutenant in the 12th Regiment, Royal Welsh Fusiliers, in March 1915. After being in a training college for only a month he passed out second on the list into the 3rd Battalion of the Royal Welsh Fusiliers and was transferred to the Machine Gun Corps in May 1915. James Evans went out to France in July 1916 and remained there for the duration of the war. It was reported in the *Western Mail* in June 1917 that Second-Lieutenant James Oliver Richard Evans had been awarded the Military Cross for the following act of bravery: 'He led his men forward in a most gallant manner and succeeded in capturing two enemy machine guns.' The article went on to say, 'He set a splendid example to his men and rendered invaluable assistance throughout.' He was promoted to Lieutenant in 1917 and to Captain the following year. It was reported in the *Rhondda Leader* in December 1918 that he had been awarded a bar to his Military Cross.

James Evans relinquished his commission on completion of service in 1920 and was granted the rank of Captain. Later that year he joined the Auxiliary Division of the Royal Irish Constabulary (ADRIC), generally known as the Auxiliaries or Auxies, who were a paramilitary unit of the Royal Irish Constabulary (RIC) during the Irish War of Independence. It was set up in July 1920 and made up of former British Army officers, most of whom came from Great Britain. Its role was to conduct counter-insurgency operations against the Irish Republican Army (IRA). In 1921 Evans' rifle went off accidentally killing a RIC constable. In January 1922 he was discharged on the demobilisation of ADRIC and in March of the same year he joined the British Gendarmerie section of the Palestine Police as a constable. In August 1925 he was still with the

Bridgend Rugby Football Club 1929–30 Season
Club Officers and Committee

Back Row: Wyndham Jones, Ned Davies, J Watyer, Jim Evans, Harry Guard, Aubrey Brown, Alfie Whitchurch, H J Speck, Taylor (the Tailor), J Scott.
Middle Row: Gwynne James, Gwilym Stradling, E Storey, Willie Llewellyn, Harry Lambert, W J Llewellyn, Bert Grinnell.
Front Row: Percy Alexander, Dai Gregory, Stanley Schofield, Arthur Hardwick, Cyril Evans, Alcwyn Jones, Billy Rees.

Palestine Gendarmerie but in June 1926 he arrived in Canada from the UK. Although his mother lived in Penygraig, his passport was issued in Palestine. In July 1931 he enlisted in the ranks in Canada and died in British Columbia in October 1960. Quite an interesting character, I am sure that not all of Willie's employees had such an interesting background.

Returning to Willie, he remained in the Rhondda until 1924 after which time his Royal Pharmaceutical Society registration chronicles that he worked at 77 Nolton Street, Bridgend which was recorded as a pharmaceutical premises. Initially Willie and Annie lived at Rhoscelyn, Cowbridge, the home of Annie's parents. Later he, Annie and the two children moved to Fairfield, Merthyrmawr Road, Bridgend where they lived until 1930. In October 1930 Willie and his family are recorded as living at 33 Ewenny Road, Bridgend. Interestingly, Willie's brother

Johnnie, together with his wife Annie and two of their three children, Gwladys and Robert, are recorded as now living at Fairfield, Merthyrmawr Road, Bridgend.

Willie lived in Bridgend for over forty years and during that time was associated with Bridgend Rugby Football Club and appeared in many club photographs. He was initially a committee member and later Chairman of the club. He was Chairman in September 1928 when the club celebrated the opening of its new ground (the former ground of Bridgend Town AFC) with a match against Newport which they won by 16 points to four. On the 4th January 1929 Bridgend played Mr Rowe Harding's XV in aid of the Bridgend Distress Fund. An interesting feature of this game was that Willie Llewellyn and Gwyn Nicholls acted as linesmen. Willie was still Chairman of the club the following season and still a member of the committee during the 1930–31 campaign. There is no information with regard to how long he served on the committee or the duration of his chairmanship.

In 1934 Willie's name was removed from the Royal Pharmaceutical Society register probably because Willie, at that time, was not practising as a chemist. A newspaper report from around that time reported that 'He resides at Bridgend, where he is an official under the Public Assistance Board.' Public assistance boards were the bodies created after the abolition of the Boards of Guardians in 1930 when workhouses were abolished. Public assistance committees inherited responsibility for the administration of poor relief in the United Kingdom.

By October 1934 Willie and Annie had moved from Ewenny Road to 36 Brynteg Avenue, Bridgend where they lived until 1967. When Willie retired after the Second World War he occupied himself with many locum appointments; his name was restored to the Royal

Willie and Annie celebrated their diamond wedding anniversary in April 1967.

Courtesy of Dr Michael Jones

Pharmaceutical Society register in 1946. At the age of 80 Willie was still working a 44 hour week in the dispensary department of a Bridgend chemist's shop. Willie's grandson, Dr Michael Jones, recalls that his grandfather at that time would walk the two mile return journey to his place of work twice a day. He walked to work each morning, returned home for lunch, returned to work and walked back home in the evening. Willie never drove and never owned a car. Returning to the article in the *Retail Chemist* Willie recalled how he had 'begun his career with Mr Richards of Llwynypia at the age of eighteen and was eighty-eight when he dispensed his last prescription.' In 1967 Willie and his wife Annie moved to 5 Heol Y Felin, Pontyclun where he died on Thursday 22nd March 1973. Willie's name was removed from the Royal Pharmaceutical Society register on his death in 1973. His passing was reported in both the *Pharmaceutical Journal* and the *Chemist and Druggist* of 31st March 1973. The *Pharmaceutical Journal* made reference to Willie's international rugby career and reported, 'He was the oldest international rugby player in the world, and was the last of the 1905 Welsh side that defeated the All Blacks.' The *Chemist and Druggist* in reporting Willie's death quoted the tribute from the *South Wales Echo* which read as follows: 'When the rioters of Tonypandy surged through the streets wrecking 63 shops on a wild night in 1910 the one store they left untouched was the chemist's shop of Willie Llewellyn. No-one wanted to raise a stone in anger to the man who scored four tries to demolish the English in his international rugby debut.' More about the Tonypandy riots later.

When Dr Edward 'Teddy' Morgan was married on Wednesday 3rd April 1907 at St Cross Church, Knutsford, Cheshire, Willie Llewellyn was his best

Mr Willie Llewellyn and Miss Annie Thomas.

man. Just four weeks later Willie married Miss Annie Thomas at St Peter's Church, Pentre. The wedding took place on Tuesday 30th April 1907 and Willie's younger brother Evan was best man. Annie was the second daughter of Mr & Mrs Dan Thomas, Pentre Cottage and granddaughter of the late Mr Edmund Thomas, Maindy Hall, Ton Pentre. Dan Thomas was previously well known in connection with the mining industry. Long before the formalities began hundreds of people could be seen hurrying along to the church and by the time the ceremony commenced the church was crowded. The service was fully choral and as the bridal party entered the church the organist, Mr David Jones, played the Bridal March from 'Lohengrin.' The Rev. D T James, vicar of Llwynypia, officiated, assisted by the Rev. D T Griffiths, curate at St Peter's. The bride was given away by her father and two of the bridesmaids were Willie's sisters, Mary Jennett and Annie. The third bridesmaid was Miss Morgan of Penarth, who was a cousin of the bride. At the close of the ceremony, Mendelssohn's Wedding March heralded the happy couple as they were covered with showers of rice as they left the porch of the church. The wedding breakfast was served at the home of Annie's parents and during the afternoon Willie and his new wife, Annie, left for London and the Isle of Wight where the honeymoon was spent.

William Glyn Llewellyn DFC.

Willie and Annie celebrated their diamond wedding anniversary in April 1967 and had been married for nearly sixty-six years when Willie died in March 1973. They had two children, a son William Glyn Llewellyn, born at 135 Dunraven Street, Tonypandy on Monday 4th January 1909 and a daughter Mary (Mollie) Llewellyn, born at 135 Dunraven Street, Tonypandy on Thursday 29th September 1910.

As a schoolboy Glyn stayed with his grandparents in Cowbridge and attended Cowbridge Grammar School. In 1935 Glyn married Marguerite

(Peggy) Williams of Bridgend. They had one daughter, Judy who was born in March 1939. Before the Second World War Glyn worked at the National Provincial Bank and previous to working in Southgate, London he was at the Bridgend branch. Glyn was a member of the Southerndown Golf Club and the Bridgend Tennis Club and distinguished himself in both sports. Early during the Second World War Glyn joined the RAF Volunteer Reserve as a Pilot Officer and later volunteered as an air gunner. As a member of 166 Squadron he was based at Kirmington, Lincolnshire. The squadron, which had originally been formed in 1918, was reformed in 1936 as a heavy-bomber squadron. In January 1943 the squadron was reformed again at Kirmington as a bomber squadron flying Wellingtons and from September 1943, Lancasters.

Glyn died on active service over France on the 15th July 1944 while a rear-gunner in an Avro Lancaster with Bomber Command. He was just 35 years old and is buried in the Lusigny-Sur-Barse, Communal Cemetery, near Troyes east of Paris. Glyn was killed on his second tour of duty bombing rail junctions on the French-German border. Having already completed one tour (30 flights), Glyn volunteered for a second, which he had almost completed when he was killed. Glyn's wife Peggy, living in the family home at The Garth, Park Street, Bridgend received official notification that her husband, Flying Officer William Glyn Llewellyn, had been posthumously awarded the Distinguished Flying Cross. The citation stated: 'As air gunner, he completed numerous operations against the enemy in the course of which he invariably displayed the utmost fortitude, courage and devotion to duty.'

On receiving news of Glyn's death, Cowbridge Grammar School paid him the following tribute: 'W Glyn Llewellyn (1924–25), Flying Officer, RAF, entered this School as a senior in 1924 and quickly made his mark owing to high ability as a Scholar and athlete. He got an excellent School Certificate with Matriculation Exemption in 1925, and after winning several events in the Athletic Sports, played for the School in Association Football and Hockey. He then left to join the National Provincial Bank, and was stationed successfully at Brecon, Birmingham, Bridgend and Southgate. Here he continued the good record of his schooldays, and at Bridgend won the Open Tennis Championship Cup in 1925, 1927 and 1928. He was a golfer of much distinction, and won the National

Provincial Bank Open Tournament of England and Wales in 1927, and was "runner up" in 1928.

He joined the RAF as a Pilot Officer early in the War, later volunteering as an air-gunner. On the last flight of his operational tour he was posted as missing, and later known to have been buried near Troyes, France. He will be remembered in School as a boy of character and personality, whose stay with us was all too short. He kept up in after-life the good record of his schooldays.'

Glyn was one of the 55,573 Bomber Command crew members killed during the Second World War. In 1946 Willie, Annie and other members of the family visited Glyn's grave in France and there is a memorial tablet to him on his grandparent's grave in the Church of the Holy Cross, Cowbridge.

Mary (Mollie) was born at 135 Dunraven Street, Tonypandy on Thursday 29th September 1910. When the family moved from Tonypandy to Bridgend Mollie attended St Margaret's School, Bridgend. She trained as a nurse and for some time worked at Putney Hospital, London. In 1932 Mollie married Dr Evan Gordon Jones, son of Customs Officer Wyndham Jones who was a Welsh Bowling international and secretary of the Welsh Bowling Association for over twenty years. Known as Gordon, Mollie's husband was a graduate of Cardiff University and The London Hospital; he was a GP at Pontyclun for over 20 years. Mollie and Gordon had three children, Michael, Geraint and Gillian (Lawrence).

Mollie was born virtually five weeks before the Tonypandy riots took place, and which resulted in a night of violence where nearly every shop window between Pandy Square and the Trealaw Bridge was smashed. David Maddox and Gwyn Evans in their book, *'The Tonypandy Riots 1910–11'* described the riots as 'a series of violent

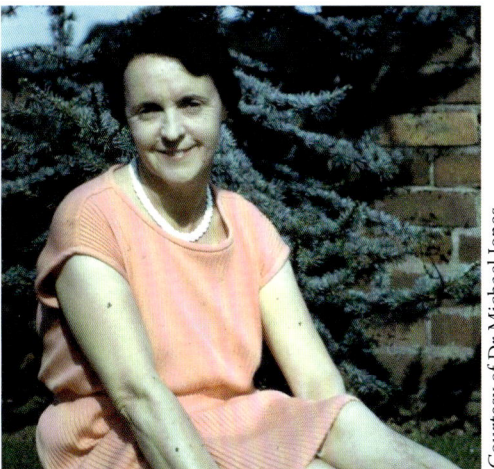

Willie and Annie's daughter Mary, known as Mollie.

Courtesy of the D Maddox and G Evans Collection

The boarded up shop windows in Dunraven Street, Tonypandy. Only two shops remained undamaged: a jewellers owned by Barney Issac which had shutters to protect its windows and the chemist shop owned by Willie Llewellyn. In the photograph Willie Llewellyn's shop can just be seen on the right with Barney Issac's shutters just visible on the far right. Willie's shop is also boarded, which may have been done for protection the day after the riots.

confrontations between coal miners and police that took place at various locations in and around the Rhondda mines of the Cambrian Combine, a cartel of mining companies formed to regulate prices and wages in South Wales.' The riots were the culmination of an industrial dispute between the workers and the mine owners which arose when the Naval Colliery Company opened a new coal seam at the Ely Pit, Penygraig. After a short test period to determine the price list to be paid for coal mined from that seam, the mine owners claimed that the miners deliberately worked more slowly than they could. The miners argued that the new seam was more difficult to work because of a stone band that ran through it and the allegation that they worked more slowly than the seam demanded was absurd because they were paid per ton of coal extracted, rather than by the number of hours they worked.

On 1st August the owners posted lockout notices to take effect from

1st September 1910 which closed the pit to all 800 workers despite the fact that the dispute only involved roughly 70 miners at the newly opened Bute seam. The issue was eventually discussed by the South Wales Miners Federation who then balloted its members about possible strike action. It was agreed that from November 1st all 12,000 men working for the mines owned by the Cambrian Combine would be brought out on strike. A conciliation Board was formed to try and reach an agreement with Liberal MP William Abraham acting on behalf of the mine workers and F L Davies for the mine owners. Despite the Board reaching an agreed price of 2s 3d per ton, the Cambrian Combine workmen rejected the agreement.

During the first week of the strike rumours (later substantiated) spread that black-leg labour was being employed at the Mid-Rhondda collieries. The miners reacted by agreeing to a policy of mass picketing to stop all men working, including the officials. On Monday 7th November vigorous picketing was effective in shutting down all of the Combine collieries except the Glamorgan Colliery, Llwynypia which was guarded by over 100 policemen including mounted police under the control of Chief Constable, Lionel Lindsay. The disturbances had begun on Monday 7th November when striking mineworkers marched on the Cambrian Colliery at Clydach Vale and attacked the stokers who were at work, and frogmarched them home. They afterwards raked out the fires under the boilers and brought the colliery machinery to a standstill. A similar sequence of events took place at all of the local collieries affected by the strike. Later that day a mass picket proceeded to the Glamorgan Colliery at Llwynypia where thousands of miners converged on the colliery entrance with the intention of gaining admission into the Power House to persuade the strike-breakers to join the strike. They were unable to gain entry and the Power House windows were bombarded with stones shattering every window and showering those inside with glass. The outcome of this violent confrontation was the Chief Constable ordering his men to draw truncheons and charge the crowd of miners. Realising that it was impossible to gain entry to the Power House, the mine workers avenged themselves by tearing down the strong timber fencing which separated the colliery yard from the main road. The debris was thrown across the tramway track with the intention of preventing a charge by the mounted police. The situation was now so serious that the Chief Constable called for the troops.

The following evening, Tuesday 8th November, strikers again surrounded the entrance of the Glamorgan Colliery. A second night of confrontation occurred with the police drawing truncheons and making several baton charges. The resulting skirmishes between the striking mine workers and the police resulted in injuries on both sides and one miner was killed. By about seven o'clock, with the mine workers again failing to gain access to the Power House, there was a welcome abatement of the rioting outside the colliery yard and many miners moved away from the colliery towards Tonypandy, gathering on Tonypandy Square.

With all policemen deployed to the local collieries and protecting the homes of mine officials, Tonypandy remained unguarded and from about eight o'clock onwards the town was entirely in the hands of the strikers. It is reported they smashed nearly all the windows of the business premises from Pandy Square to Penygraig, a distance of a quarter of a mile. *The South Wales Daily Post* reported, 'With loud shouts the strikers rushed along, hurling huge stones at the large plate glass windows and belabouring them with sticks. Terror-stricken, the shop owners rushed into their premises and left the contents of the windows to the mercy of the looters who, in many instances threw the articles into the roadway. Later in the evening the broken windows were barricaded.' Although it is reported that around sixty-three business premises were damaged that evening, including the chemist shop of Mr J W Richards, Willie Llewellyn's chemist shop was left undamaged. A report in the *Evening Express* on Wednesday 9th November stated, 'Among the few who escaped the dastardly bombardment of their windows was Mr Willie Llewellyn, the old international, who has settled down to business as a chemist at Tonypandy.' With an identical report appearing in the *Weekly Mail* on Saturday 12th November and the fact that no police were present to restrict the behaviour of the rioters, it is probably safe to say that their actions were systematic rather than indiscriminate and they chose not to damage Willie Llewellyn's shop. In addition David Maddox and Gwyn Evans in their book confirm that 'in a contemporary newspaper report which lists the shop keepers who were awarded damages, Willie Llewellyn's shop is not mentioned.'

Almost three hours after the rioting had begun the Metropolitan Police arrived in the town square by which time the disturbance had subsided of its own accord. Although things calmed down after the events of the 7th and 8th November, skirmishes and unease remained and the final confrontation in July 1911 was at the Ely Pit where the conflict had begun over ten months earlier. In August 1911 the miners were forced to accept the original price offer of 2s 3d per ton and return to work.

Sadly on Tuesday 4th February 1913 Willie lost a good friend and confidant when, at the age of 53, his uncle Tom (Williams) of Llwynypia died. The funeral took place on Friday 7th February and he was buried at Llethr Ddu cemetery, Trealaw. Willie was one of nine bearers who carried the coffin and amongst the other bearers were W D Phillips, W M Douglas, T D Scofield, Ack Llewellyn and Walter Rees, all committee members of the Welsh Football Union. Solicitor, Tom Williams had been associated with rugby for most of his life; he played for Pontypridd and Cardiff and was capped by Wales once in the game against Ireland at Lansdowne Road, Dublin on 28th January 1882. He served on the committee of Llwynypia Football Club before becoming a committee member of the Welsh Football Union and the Glamorgan League. Tom Williams was a Welsh selector, a member of the International Board from 1901 until 1908 and served as a Mid-District representative from 1899 to 1910 when he was made a life vice-president of the Welsh Football Union. He refereed the match between England and Ireland in 1904 and appears in several Welsh team photographs as a touch judge. He was survived by his widowed mother, who at one time occupied the old Llwynypia Farm, his wife Jenny and their son Tommy. The Llewellyn family were well represented at the funeral with Willie's father and brothers Johnnie, George, Evan, Ivor and Tom Thomas among the mourners.

Willie was second eldest of ten children born to Howell and Catherine Llewellyn. In addition there was a half-brother, Thomas 'Tom' Thomas, who was the only child from Catherine's first marriage to coal miner Richard Thomas. Richard died from scarlatina maligna in 1871 and three years after Richard's death Catherine married Howell Llewellyn. Although the 1881 census makes no reference to Thomas living at the family home at the Bridgend Inn, Tonypandy we know that Thomas was in regular contact with the family and was often present on special family

Willie and Johnnie in later life.

occasions such as weddings and funerals.

With regard to Willie's other siblings there is quite a lot of information available and it is probably worth a slight diversion to reflect a little on their lives. Born in 1876 Johnnie was the eldest child and the first of the four boys who studied at Christ College, Brecon. Johnnie left Christ College in 1893. An entry in the 1901 census lists Johnnie as a twenty-five year old single man working as a brewery agent and living at home with his parents at the Clydach Vale Hotel, Tonypandy. Johnnie married Annie Williams the eldest daughter of Mr and Mrs John D Williams JP, of Clydach Court, Trealaw on Wednesday 19th March 1902 at Salem Church, Porth. The bride was given away by her uncle Tom Williams (Llwynypia and WFU) and Willie was best man. Mary Jennett, Johnnie's sister, was chief bridesmaid. By the time of the 1911 census Johnnie and Annie had three children, Doris aged eight, Gwladys aged six and Robert aged three. At this time they were living at Pimmer House, Penygraig. Like Willie, Johnnie was a keen golfer and they regularly played golf together. Johnnie was secretary of the Ystrad Hunt in 1916.

Willie's younger brother Evan was born two years after Willie in 1880 and at the time of the 1911 census he was living at home with his parents at Brynawel, 100 & 101 Brithweunydd Road, Trealaw. Sadly Evan died on Tuesday 21st September 1915 aged just thirty-five. Evan, formerly a hotel keeper, had been ill for quite some time and at the time of his death was living at home with his parents at Brynawel, Trealaw. He is buried at Llethr Ddu cemetery, Trealaw. Amongst the mourners was Evan's father, Howell and his brothers Johnnie, Willie, George and Ivor. His half-brother Tom Thomas of Tonyrefail was also present at the funeral. Also present were Evan's uncles on his mother's side of the family, Mr John D Williams JP, Clydach Court and Evan Williams, Fairfield. Evan's other uncle, Tom Williams, had passed away in February 1913 but his son, Tommy Williams was there to represent his family.

The eldest of Willie's sister, Mary Jennett, was born in 1882. She married Mr Alun Lewis, the only son of the Rev. W Lewis, Methodist minister, Cwmparc. The wedding took place at St Andrew's Church, Llwynypia on Wednesday 26th May 1909. The only bridesmaid was Mary Jennett's younger sister Katie. The reception was held at Brynawel, Trealaw the family home of Mary Jennett's parents Howell and Catherine. In addition to all the brothers, sisters, sisters-in-law and brothers-in-law, Tom Thomas, Mary Jennett's half-brother was also at the wedding ceremony. There are no details of subsequent family members or when Mary Jennett and Alun died.

Albert Llewellyn was one of two children that died in infancy. Born on Wednesday 1st August 1883, Albert died at the age of just seven months on Monday 3rd March 1884 at the Bridgend Inn, Tonypandy.

Annie Llewellyn, the second eldest daughter of Howell and Catherine, was born in August 1885. At the age of five the 1891 census has Annie living at home with her parents at the Clydach Vale Hotel, Clydach Vale, Ystradyfodwg. The 1901 census records Annie at the age of sixteen studying at Uplands College, Painswick, Gloucestershire. In 1906, at the age of twenty-one, Annie married Ivor Montague Morgan. Ivor studied at Christ College, Brecon around the same time as George Llewellyn. Annie and Ivor had three daughters, Vera Mildred, Muriel and Mary. Sadly Vera Mildred, who was born in December 1910, died in March 1912 aged just 15 months. Mary was born the same year as Vera Mildred died. Muriel was born in May 1914 and died in August 1977 at the age of sixty-three. Sadly, Annie died on Friday 11th October 1918, at the age of thirty-three when her two surviving daughters were just four and six years old. Annie had undergone a serious operation and was recovering well at a Cardiff nursing home when she relapsed and died suddenly. What added to the sad circumstances was the fact that Ivor was on active service in Mesopotamia (corresponding to today's Iraq, mostly, but also parts of modern-day Iran, Syria and Turkey) where he had been for two years. Sergeant-Major Ivor Morgan was the eldest son of Mrs Morgan, Maes-Yr-Haf, Trealaw and had previously seen action at the Dardanelles, from where he was invalided home. The *Rhondda Leader* reported that the mourners included Annie's sisters Mary Jennett and Katie, her brothers Johnnie, Willie and Ivor, and her half-brother Tom Thomas. In addition Willie's wife, Annie Llewellyn and Katie's husband, Bob Naunton Morgan were also present at the funeral.

George Howell Llewellyn was born on Tuesday 25th January 1887 at the Clydach Vale Hotel. George was the third of the four Llewellyn brothers to study at Christ College, Brecon and like Willie was an accomplished sportsman. George was at Christ College from 1899 until 1905 and like Johnnie and Willie before him, he attended Morton's House. On completing his studies at Christ College it is initially unclear exactly what George's career path was. The 1906 April edition of *The Breconian* records that George had played football (rugby) for Guy's Hospital and the December 1906 edition as having passed his preliminary examinations in medicine. The same edition chronicles George as having played football (rugby) for Cardiff College and hockey for Mid-Rhondda. The 1908 April edition of *The Breconian* states that George had played football (rugby) for University College, Cardiff where he was presumably a student. The 1911 census records that George was living at home with his parents at Brynawel, 100 & 101, Brithweunydd Road, Trealaw and is listed as a mining student, Cambrian Colliery. The following year George received a presentation from the Lord Mayor of Cardiff for assisting to keep the pit ponies alive at Llwynypia during the Cambrian strike. In October 1913, George took a rugby team to play against Christ College, Brecon. His team contained three Llewellyn family members who were also Old Boys of Christ College: George and Ivor Llewellyn and Ivor Morgan his brother-in-law. Between 1914 and 1918 George was a Lieutenant in the Northumberland Fusiliers. In 1922 George married Rebecca Williams and they had one daughter, Jean who sadly died at the age of twenty-two, having contracted poliomyelitis as a youngster. George worked at the Glamorgan Haematite Mine at Llanharry, Glamorgan whilst at the same time being the landlord of the "Bear Inn" in the same village together with Rebecca. George died at Llanharry on Friday 11th May 1962 at the age of seventy-five and his wife Rebecca died in 1982 at the age of eighty-eight.

Catherine, who was born on Thursday 1st November 1888, was the second child to die at an early age. After a long bout of whooping cough she died of pneumonia on Monday 20th January 1890 at the tender age of just 14 months.

Although it was originally thought that only Johnnie, Willie and George had studied at Christ College, Brecon further research has revealed that Ivor, who was born on Thursday 2nd October 1890, also studied at Christ College, Brecon from 1905 until 1908. An article in the *Rhondda Leader* on Saturday 2nd April 1910 confirmed that Ivor was studying to become a chemist. The article states, 'The many friends of Mr Ivor Llewellyn, the youngest son of Mr and Mrs H Llewellyn, Brynawel, Trealaw, will be pleased to learn of his recent success at the Preliminary Examination for Chemists. He is apprenticed to his brother, Mr Willie Llewellyn, the famous Welsh Triple Crown hero. We confidently look forward to a prosperous career.' The fact that Ivor was studying to become a chemist is confirmed by the 1911 census which records Ivor, at the age of twenty, as a chemist's apprentice. The Royal Pharmaceutical Society Museum has confirmed that Ivor registered as a chemist in 1916. On Monday 16th June 1919 Ivor married Miss Cosslett at St Andrew's Church, Tonypandy. The bride was the niece of Mr J W Richards JP, the chemist in Tonypandy to whom Willie had been an apprenticed back in 1896. A report of the wedding in the *Rhondda Leader* on Saturday 21st June commented, 'The bride was given away by her uncle, Mr J W Richards JP, chemist, Tonypandy. After the ceremony the bridal couple left for Langland Bay, where the honeymoon is being spent. Mr and Mrs Llewellyn are well known in the Rhondda and were the recipients of some very fine and valuable presents. Mr and Mrs Llewellyn will make their abode at Gilfach Goch, where Mr Llewellyn is in business as a chemist.' There are no known subsequent details of children or when Ivor and his wife died.

Katie was the youngest child born to Howell and Catherine Llewellyn. Katie was born on Monday 26th September 1892. On Wednesday 21st June 1916 at St John's Church, Cardiff, Katie married Robert Naunton Wingfield 'Bob' Morgan, a solicitor in Tonypandy. Bob Naunton Morgan was the eldest son of Dr and Mrs David Naunton Morgan JP, Gilfach Goch. Their second eldest son Dr Harry Naunton Morgan, a house surgeon at Cardiff Infirmary, assisted by his younger brother Captain Idris Naunton Morgan, acted as best man. Katie was attended by Miss Kitty

Naunton Morgan, sister of the bridegroom. The reception was held at the Angel Hotel, Cardiff after which Katie and Bob left for Bournemouth. As was the case with Ivor and his wife, there are no subsequent details of children or when Katie and Bob died.

Willie's father, Howell, died at home on Friday 26th April 1918 at the age of 72. The report of his death in the *Western Mail* read as follows: 'The death occurred on Friday, at the age of 72, of Mr Howell Llewellyn, Brynawel, Trealaw, a member of one of the oldest families in the Rhondda. He was father of Mr Willie Llewellyn, chemist, Tonypandy, the old Welsh international footballer, Lieut. George Llewellyn, Northumberland Fusiliers, and Messrs, J H Llewellyn and Ivor Llewellyn and Mrs R Naunton Morgan, Tonypandy.' Although Mary Jennett (Mrs Alun Lewis) is not mentioned we know that she was still alive because she attended her sister Annie's funeral in October that year. Willie's mother Catherine died at the family home, Brynawel, Brithweunydd Road, Trealaw on Friday 24th July 1936 at the age of 84.

The Rhondda Golf Club (Photo by Mr Levi Ladd, Tonypandy)
Back Row: Mr T Kinsey, Mr Willie Llewellyn, Mr E R Thomas, Mr T John MA, Mr J Lewis, Mr Geo. Hoyle. *Middle Row*: Mr Llewellyn Evans, Mr D J Griffiths, Mrs Geo. Hoyle, Mrs W Llewellyn, Mrs E R Thomas, Dr Gabe Jones, Mr John Davies, Mr J Morgan.
Front Row: Mr J Davies (Gelli), Mr J H Llewellyn.

Returning to Willie's life after rugby his main sporting interest was playing golf. He learnt to play whist at Christ College, Brecon and continued playing well into his eighties. Willie was one of the founder members of the Rhondda Golf Club situated at Gelli Farm on the downs of Gilfach Goch Mountain in the centre of the Rhondda Valley above Tonypandy.

Willie was an excellent golfer with a single figure handicap of six and regularly played team golf for the club. In 1911 he won the Leonard Llewellyn Challenge Cup for the first time. Mr Leonard Llewellyn was the Manging Director of the Cambrian Combine Collieries and was President of the Rhondda Golf Club. He later became Sir Leonard Llewellyn. Willie also won the cup the following year and in 1913 lost in the final to fellow Welsh international and Llwynypia teammate Billy Alexander. In September 1912 Willie played in the Welsh Championships at Royal Porthcawl and was runner up for the Tredegar Cup competition and finished in a good position in the Ebsworth competition. In October 1914 Willie won the Crawshay Bailey Bowl handicap competition in connection

Members of the Old Welsh Rugby Internationals Golf Team photographed at Pontardawe. In the front row from left to right are Phil Hopkins, Willie Llewellyn, Edgar Morgan (Captain), Howie Jones and Dr Tom Wallace (Irish International). Rhys Gabe is second from the left in the second row.

with the Rhondda Golf Club. Although he had previously been in the final for the bowl, this was the first occasion that he had captured the title. Willie and his wife Annie often played golf together and won the mixed foursomes at Whitsun 1912.

Willie Llewellyn was secretary of Rhondda Golf Club from 1910–1912, 1914–1919 and 1921–1924. He was club captain in 1921.

Rhys Gabe, Willie Llewellyn and Tommy Vile (complete with his 1904 British team blazer), preparing for one of their many games of golf.

Courtesy of Miss Mary Vile

An extract from the balance sheet at the end of December 1924 stated, 'At the close of that year Mr Willie Llewellyn, Tonypandy resigned his seat on the Directorate due to having moved from the district. Mr Llewellyn a founder member of the Club was secretary for a number of years; the Directors deplore his resignation and desire to place on record their appreciation of his valuable services.'

Willie's brother Johnnie was also a playing member of the club. He was for many years a member of the committee and was club captain in 1924. Willie and Johnnie's wives were members of the ladies committee. George Llewellyn too was a member of the club, playing off a handicap of ten.

After Willie moved to Bridgend he became a member of Southerndown Golf Club and played regularly well into his eighties. He played at Southerndown for over thirty years and towards the end of his playing days would satisfy himself by playing just four or five of the easier holes on the golf course. In 1954 former Welsh rugby international Phil Hopkins, who was a member of Pontardawe Golf Club and also a member of the committee of the newly formed Past Welsh Rugby Internationals Golf Team, had permission to play the Pontardawe team in a friendly

Members of the Past Welsh Rugby Internationals Golf Association. In the centre of the front row is Tommy Vile with Willie Llewellyn to his left.

match which took place on Monday 13th June 1954. Willie played in this match.

At the age of seventy-nine Willie won the Major Tommy Vile Cup, a competition played between members of the Past Welsh Rugby Internationals Golf Association. The following year Willie and fellow former Welsh rugby international Jack Powell demonstrated their ability to hold their own against players of a much younger generation when they beat the 1958 touring Australians' manager Terry McLenaughan and fly half Ron Harvey in a friendly match. During that same year Willie was both chairman and captain of the Past Welsh Rugby Internationals Golf Association.

Willie was a very popular figure in Welsh rugby circles and in 1961, at the age of 83, he was elected first president of the Welsh Old Internationals Association. He was proposed by Rhys Gabe and unanimously elected at the meeting of the association which was held at Cardiff on Saturday 11th March after the Wales v Ireland match. Under the chairmanship of Judge Rowe Harding, fifty former players attended the function and it was decided to hold a similar reunion each year after the second home international match at Cardiff.

In 1963 Willie was honoured by the Rhondda Recognition Committee at a function at Llwynypia. Willie was presented with a recognition plaque by Newport, Wales and British Lions' player Bryn Meredith who recalled that Willie had played against England on six occasions and Wales had not lost one of these games. The chairman of the Recognition Committee, Mr W D Jones, said, 'Mr Llewellyn was a true son of the Rhondda and a personality who had the rare distinction of being a legend in his own right and in his own lifetime.' Others who paid tributes to Willie on the evening were fellow Welsh international Rhys Gabe, Alderman Llewellyn Haycock, chairman of Glamorgan County Council, the Mayor of the Rhondda Alderman Ioan Williams and Mr Glyn Morgan, a member of the Welsh Rugby Union's 'Big Five' selection committee.

Willie was made an honorary life-member of Pontyclun Rugby Football Club in 1967.

1967 was a significant year for Willie and Annie; not only did they celebrate their diamond wedding anniversary but they also moved from their home in Brynteg Avenue, Bridgend to 5 Heol Y Felin, Pontyclun. The same year Willie, together with Cliff Jones, became the first honorary life-members of Pontyclun Rugby Football Club and in the September they were guests of honour at a special presentation evening at the club along with fellow Welsh international Dewi Bebb and Bridgend second row Colin Standing.

In September 1967, Willie's lifelong friend and fellow Welsh international Rhys Gabe died leaving Willie as the sole surviving member of the famous Welsh fifteen who had defeated New Zealand back in 1905 and the oldest surviving Welsh rugby international. There were three members of the 1905 New Zealanders still living: Billy Wallace, George Nicholson and 'Bunny' Abbott of which only Billy Wallace played in the game against Wales. In early 1967 John Sinclair, a co-founder of the New Zealand Rugby Museum, wrote to Willie Llewellyn asking if he would mind if he brought a few New Zealand supporters to visit him when the All Blacks passed through Wales that November. The reply was duly received and stated that they would be most welcome and that Willie was very excited at the proposed visit. Subsequently, in November 1967, the New Zealand rugby team that was touring Britain, France and Canada came to Wales and, although it had been almost sixty-two years since the famous Welsh victory over New Zealand, Willie was not forgotten. The week before the international at Cardiff John Sinclair and thirty-two members of the New Zealand All Blacks Goodwill Tour duly paid a visit to the man who was still revered in the land of the long white cloud.

When the bus arrived in Pontyclun with the banner 'Haere-mai' (Maori for Greetings) Willie was at the gate of his bungalow waving in welcome. For eighty-nine year old Willie this was a delightful day. John Sinclair, a member of the touring party, said, 'Mr Llewellyn is remarkable. He is the most perceptive and agile gentleman I have ever met, and he greeted us like long-lost brothers and sisters.' John Sinclair continued by saying, 'We made up our minds to visit him when our visit to Britain was first mooted, and his hospitality and that of the charming Mrs Llewellyn was all that we expected.'

Billy Wallace played 51 times for New Zealand and was capped on eleven occasions. He played in all five games in Wales on the 1905 tour.

The British Isles jersey worn by Willie Llewellyn in the first test match in New Zealand in 1904.

Willie Llewellyn being introduced to Robert Barran, the sports editor of the French '*Miroir du Rugby*' by Cliff Jones. Willie's wife Annie can be seen in the background (March 1971).

Another member of the touring party, former New Zealand captain Peter Johnstone, made a presentation to Willie of a supporter's tie and a letter from his old adversary Billy Wallace. Willie and Billy Wallace had remained firm friends over the sixty-two years since their encounter at Cardiff and had exchanged letters and Christmas cards during all that time.

When Willie's great-grandchildren came on the scene, having been allowed out of school early, George Asher, a member of the 1917 Maori Battalion team and the brother of the New Zealand Maori Opai Asher, danced the Haka on Willie's front lawn and all those present roared their approval. It was during this visit that Willie Llewellyn told John Sinclair that his 1904 Lions jersey belonged to New Zealand and that he wanted it to go to the New Zealand Rugby Museum at Palmerston North. After his death in 1973, arrangements were made by Willie's widow Annie and his grandson Dr Michael Jones to safely transport the jersey to New Zealand. Now that jersey, one of the rarest jerseys in the rugby world sits in the Rare XV cabinet of the New Zealand Rugby Museum at Palmerston North. As far as it is possible to tell this 1904 British Lions jersey is the only surviving international jersey belonging to Willie. During his playing career he had many jerseys in his collection but the family relate the story of how Willie's wife Annie, took his jerseys and removed the badges for safe keeping whilst discarding the remaining parts. All that remains

Willie with his collection of jersey and blazer badges.

today is a montage of Willie's badges and those which once adorned the jerseys of Willie's international opponents.

In 1969 another Rhondda boy equalled Willie Llewellyn's 70 year old Welsh try scoring record when Maurice Richards, born in Ystrad, scored four tries for Wales in their 30 points to 9 victory over England at Cardiff Arms Park on Saturday 12th April. On that day he equalled the record set by Willie against England at Swansea back in 1899 and became the third Welsh player to score four tries in an international after Reggie Gibbs achieved the same distinction against France at Cardiff in 1908. Amazingly, Willie Llewellyn witnessed Maurice Richards' achievement as he watched the game on television at his Pontyclun home. The victory over England helped Wales to their eleventh Triple Crown and fifteenth outright championship. In the same game Keith Jarrett became Wales' highest scorer in post-war internationals when he scored twelve points from two penalties and three conversions.

When Billy Wallace died on Thursday 2nd March 1972, Willie Llewellyn was the sole survivor from the match between Wales and New Zealand played at Cardiff on Saturday 16th December 1905. On Thursday 30th November that year, five of the 1972 All Blacks paid a visit to Pontyclun Rugby Football Club and Willie came over to meet them. Together with about thirty of the under 14's side they listened to Willie talking about rugby. Sadly four months after that visit Willie Llewellyn

Visit of the 7th All Blacks to Pontyclun RFC in 1972
Back row: Kent Lambert, Lin Colling, Ian Hurst, George Skudder, Ian Eliason.
Front Row: Hedley Benyon, Cliff Jones, Willie Llewellyn and Keith Davies.

died. Former Wales stand-off Cliff Jones later speaking about the visit said, 'Willie Llewellyn was one of my heroes, I worshipped him like boys today worship Gareth Edwards.' He went on to say, 'He was a remarkable man. A perfect gentleman, a fine sportsman and a real ambassador for Wales.' Wales indeed had lost one of their truly great sportsmen. His grandson Dr Michael Jones, who was Willie's doctor, said he was rarely ill. Dr Jones said that when Willie gave up rugby he started smoking a pipe which he gave up in his late fifties. He then began smoking cigarettes in his early eighties. Willie rarely drank alcohol, never at home, and only on social occasions. Two days before Willie died he developed an abdominal problem and with his grandson's family having planned a visit to Paris to watch the international between France and Wales, Willie insisted that whatever happened they should go to the match.

On Thursday 22nd March 1973, at the age of 95, Willie Llewellyn passed away. All the national newspapers paid tribute to this very special man. They listed all his rugby achievements and how he would be remembered as a modest man who was an excellent captain for club and country, and how he was one of the most devastating wing players in Welsh rugby history. Tributes came from all corners of the world for the man who had played twenty times for Wales and scored sixteen tries. He was in the Welsh Triple Crown sides of 1900 and 1902 and captained them to their fourth Triple Crown in 1905. Willie also played for the British team in Australia and New Zealand in 1904. The two records he set on his debut against England at Swansea in 1899 have to this day never been broken. No other Welsh player has scored four tries on their debut and although eight Welsh players have since scored four tries in an international match, no Welsh player has bettered Willie's record.

Writing in the *Western Mail* the day after Willie's death J B G Thomas paid a special tribute to Willie when he said, 'Willie Llewellyn, Wales' oldest surviving rugby international, died at his home at Pontyclun yesterday, aged 95. His passing severs the last link with rugby football's greatest legend, the 1905 match between Wales and New Zealand. The magnificent wing, Willie Llewellyn, was the last survivor from both sides that played the match at Cardiff Arms Park on 16th December 1905.' He went on to say, 'Now the last of the illustrious giants has passed from the scene he graced so well. He will be mourned by the game and its followers, but remembered with pride along with those who shared with him in the supreme moment of Welsh rugby. Their names are household words in the land.' J B G Thomas concluded by saying, 'Willie Llewellyn was 95 on January 1st and, from my records, was the oldest surviving rugby international player in the world. He was a dapper, bright-eyed, modest and likeable man. A happy man who preferred to talk about others rather than himself.' It was a wonderful tribute for a wonderful man from one of the great, if not the greatest, rugby writer of all time.

Willie's grandson Dr Michael Jones and his family duly obeyed Willie's final wish and before the funeral travelled to France for the international against Wales. It was a difficult time but Doctor Jones remembers well that there was a minute's silence for Willie before the match. It was not a good day for Wales as they went down by 12 points to three. However, the championship was shared five ways with all teams having two wins apiece. The family returned for the funeral which took place at Glyntaff crematorium, Pontypridd.

Willie was survived by his wife Annie, their daughter Mollie, four grandchildren – Michael, Geraint, Gillian and Judy – and seven great grandchildren. Annie died in Pontyclun on Wednesday 19th March 1975 at the age of eighty-nine. Wherever rugby is played or whenever rugby is talked about, Willie will be remembered. Willie Llewellyn, together with Gwyn Nicholls, Rhys Gabe and Teddy Morgan formed one of the most formidable three-quarter lines to ever play for Wales. Individually they were brilliant but when they all played together it was with devastating effect. They only played together for Wales on seven occasions and were never on the losing side, gaining two Triple Crowns along the way. In their last appearance together they defeated the all-conquering 1905 All Blacks.

After Wales won their seventh Triple Crown and third Grand Slam in 1911 their championship titles were few and far between. Wales, Scotland and England shared the championship in 1920 and Wales won three of their four games in 1922 to win the championship outright. For the next three Home Nations Championships they achieved just one victory in each campaign. In addition Wales had lost to South Africa in 1912, the New Zealand Army in 1919 and 'The Invincible' All Blacks in 1924. After Wales had started the 1926 campaign badly by drawing with England and losing to Scotland, Robert Williams Parry, one of Wales's most notable 20th-century poets, immortalised Willie Llewellyn and the Welsh team that defeated New Zealand in 1905 when he wrote, 'Pa Le Mae'r Hen Gymry?' (Where are the old Welshmen?).

> Yw'th haul wedi machlud a'r dydd ar ei hanner?
> Hen Walia dirionaf, pa fodd y bu'th gwymp?
> Pa le mae'r Hen Gymry ddyrchafodd dy faner
> Yn nyddiau gogoniant mil nawcant a pump?
> I hir frwydyr galed ar frodir y gelyn
> O'th byllau a'th fryniau, heddyw oes neb
> A ddaw a llu eilwaith fel ddoe a Llewellyn,
> Pritchard ac Owen a Nicholls a Gabe?

Pan welwyd y doctor yn gwibio fel trydan
I dderbyn taranfloedd 'rol melltenei Gais.
Dy glodydd atseiniai hyd wledydd byd lydan
Uwch clod yr Ysgotyn, y Gwyddel a'r Sais.
Yw'th haul wedi machlud a'r dydd ar ei hanner?
Hen Walia dirionaf, pa fodd y bu'th gwymp?
Pa le mae'r Hen Gymry ddyrchafodd dy faner
Yn nyddiau gogoniant mil nawcant a phump?

* * *

Has your sun set with the day only half spent?
Dearest old Wales, how have you fallen?
Where are the old Welshmen who raised up your banner
In the glorious days of one nine o five?
To the long hard battle on the enemy's ground
From your coalmines and hills, is there today no one
Who will lead again a host like yesterday's Llewellyn,
Pritchard and Owen and Nicholls and Gabe?

When the doctor was seen darting like lightning
To receive thunderous applause for his electrifying try.
Your praise resounded throughout the countries of the wide world
Surpassing that of Scot, Irishman or Englishman.
Has your sun set with the day only half spent?
Dearest old Wales, how have you fallen?
Where are the old Welshmen who raised up your banner
In the glorious days of one nine o five?

Wales did improve however, and after defeating Ireland and France they finished third in the table after Scotland and Ireland shared the championship. Wales didn't win another championship until 1931.

Willie is remembered every year at the club where he was an honorary life-member. The Badgers' Golf Society of Pontyclun RFC play an annual golf tournament, the winner of which is presented with the Willie Llewellyn Golf Trophy. The actual cup is one of Willie's athletic cups

Courtesy of Dr Michael Jones

Willie was, in the words of J B G Thomas, 'A modest and likeable man. A happy man who preferred to talk about others rather than himself.'

from Christ College, Brecon. To this day the eldest male descendant of each generation has the name Llewellyn as one of their Christian names and the tradition of wearing a bow tie on Christmas Day in memory of Willie is still observed by all male members of Willie's family. Willie Llewellyn will truly never be forgotten.

An Appreciation

PHILIP AND I first met in 2005 when, following an article I had written for the *Rhondda Leader* about Willie, he visited us at Pontyclun when he decided to write his first book *The Greatest Game Ever Played – New Zealand v Wales 16 December 1905*. At this time our relative perfunctory knowledge of Willie's rugby career added somewhat to this most successful enterprise.

We met again in March 2010 at the inauguration of Dr Teddy Morgan's blue plaque at Abernant, near Aberdare by Dennis Gethin the President of the Welsh Rugby Union. By this time Philip,

Dr Michael Ll. Jones

having spent hundreds of hours researching and travelling many miles, was ready to publish his second book *Tommy Vile: A Giant of a Man*, a detailed story of that man's rugby and civic career. Tommy Vile and Willie Llewellyn, as previously written, were members of the Anglo-Australian Rugby Football Team in 1904 and Newport and life-long friends which I was privileged to witness.

Here was a further challenge that Philip couldn't resist and it was not long before he began gathering detailed information on Willie's rugby career aided and abetted by all the artefacts in our possession ably and diligently collected and maintained by my good wife, Mary. We were fortunate that we had had a visit from "Wales Art Gallery" a project organised by David Parry Jones and Onllwyn Brace gathering material for archives at Aberystwyth so were prepared. An autograph book from the 1904 tour, personal diary and newspaper cuttings, rugby caps and jersey badges, the original 1905 Welsh team photograph and lapel badge, pictures of golf meetings and family photographs all to hand. Visits to Christ College, Brecon sitting in the same school-room and chapel overlooking the playing fields and meeting teacher and College archivist Felicity Kilpatrick (a mine of information), walking Dunraven Street and the Rhondda Golf Club renewed fond precious memories. In his house at Bridgend there was little evidence of his achievements; tucked away in a small box-room upstairs there were just the photographs of the 1904 team and that of the victorious side against the All Blacks in 1905. There was rarely talk of what he had done. Modest, unassuming and my greatest regret is that I never took the opportunity to delve more deeply into that life especially the post-rugby days.

"Seek and ye shall find; knock and it shall be opened unto you." Never has a saying been more apt than this. The family are so grateful to Philip for the incredible energy and enthusiasm which he devoted to this project over many months spending hours accessing hundreds of documents, travelling many miles and speaking to many other rugby connoisseurs. We are especially enthralled by the detail which he unveiled of Willie's private life after his rugby days. Philip must now be one of the leading authorities on those early 20th century decades of Welsh rugby and it has been an exciting fascinating time and a privilege seeing this venture come to fruition. A great friendship has evolved. Perhaps now, as he promised, he will spend more time with the family and improve his golf handicap!

These few words don't do justice to thank Philip most sincerely. I hope readers will have had as much pleasure enjoying this tale as I have done being involved.

Dr Michael Ll. Jones

Website Bibliography

Web Page Title and Website Link Address

Auckland Libraries
  https://www.aucklandlibraries.govt.nz

British Newspaper Archive: Home
  https://www.britishnewspaperarchive.co.uk

Christ College, Brecon
  http://www.christcollegebrecon.com

General Register Office (GRO)
  https://www.gro.gov.uk

Gwent Archives
  http://www.gwentarchives.gov.uk

Lions History – The History of the British & Irish Lions
  https://www.lionsrugby.com/history

National Library of Wales
  https://www.library.wales

Neath Rugby – The Official Website of Neath RFC
  http://www.neathrugby.wales

New Zealand Rugby Museum
  http://rugbymuseum.co.nz

People's Collection Wales
  https://www.peoplescollection.wales

Rhondda Golf Club
  http://www.rhonddagolf.co.uk

Rugby Memorabilia Society – Official Site
  http://www.rugby-memorabilia.co.uk

Rugby Relics
  http://www.rugbyrelics.com/

Rugby-Pioneers
  http://www.rugby-pioneers.com

Stats & Records – Rugby Union ESPN Scrum
http://www.espnscrum.com
Swansea RFC
http://www.swansearfc.co.uk
The Official Website of Bridgend Ravens RFC
http://www.bridgendravens.co.uk
The Official Website of Cardiff RFC
http://www.cardiffrfc.com
The Official Website of Llanelli RFC
http://llanellirfc.co.uk
The Official Website of Newport RFC
http://www.blackandambers.co.uk
Welsh Newspapers Online-Home
http://newspapers.library.wales
Welsh Rugby Union
http://www.wru.co.uk
Wikipedia, the free encyclopedia
https://en.wikipedia.org/wiki/Main_Page
World Rugby Museum, Twickenham
http://www.worldrugbymuseum.com

Source Material and Further Reading

Welsh International Matches 1881–2011, Howard Evans (2011), ISBN 978 184771 3568

Who's Who of Welsh International Rugby Players, John M Jenkins, Duncan Pierce and Timothy Auty (1991), ISBN 1 872424 10 4

Rothmans Rugby Union Yearbook 1995–96, Mick Cleary and John Griffiths (1995), ISBN 0 7472 7816 4

Dragon In Exile: The Centenary History of London Welsh RFC, Paul Beken and Stephen Jones (1985), ISBN 0 86254 125 5

Fields of Praise: The Official History of the Welsh Rugby Union 1881–1981, David Smith and Gareth Williams (1980), ISBN 0 7083 0766 3

Newport Rugby Football Club 1875–1960, Jack Davis (1960)

Tommy Vile: A Giant of a Man, Philip J Grant (2010), ISBN 978 0 9567271 0 7

Images of Sport: Newport Rugby Football Club 1874–1950, Steve Lewis (1999), ISBN 0 7524 1570 0

Images of Sport: Swansea RFC 1873–1945, Bleddyn Hopkins (2002), ISBN 0 7524 2721 0

Images of Sport: Neath RFC 1871–1945, Mike Price (2002), ISBN 0 7524 2709 0

Images of Sport: Cardiff Rugby Football Club 1876–1939, Duncan Gardiner and Alan Evans (1999), ISBN 0 7524 1608 1

Images of Sport: Salford Rugby League Club, Graham Morris (2000), ISBN 0 7524 1897 1

A Century of Welsh Rugby Players 1880–1980, Wayne Thomas (1980)

A Century of the All Blacks in Britain and Ireland, Dave Fox, Ken Bogle and Mark Hoskins (2006), 0 7524 3355 5

The Greatest Game Ever Played, Philip J Grant (2005)

The Triumphant Tour of the New Zealand Footballers 1905, George H Dixon (1906)

The Book of Fame, Lloyd Jones (2008), ISBN 978-0-7195-2294-9

125 Years of The British & Irish Lions: The Official History, Clem Thomas and Greg Thomas (2013), ISBN 978 1 78057 665 7

Percy Bush: Welsh Rugby's Little Marvel, Ken Poole (2015), ISBN 978 1 78461 121 7

The Barbarians 1890–1932, Emile de Lissa (1933)

The History of Bridgend Rugby Football Club: The First 100 Years, W A D Lawrie (1979)

Rhondda Golf Club 'A Century Remembered' 1910–2010, Various (2010)

Pontardawe Golf Club 1924–1999: A History of the First Seventy-Five Years, Cenfyn Hopkin (2000)